THE
McDOUGALL PLAN

by
John A. McDougall, M.D.
and
Mary A. McDougall

NEW WIN PUBLISHING, INC.

CAUTION:
If you are ill or on medication, do not attempt this diet without the supervision of a physician experienced in the effects of dietary change.

Note: Throughout the book the nutritive values for foods were taken from one of two sources unless otherwise indicated:

Nutritive Value of American Foods in Common Units. Agriculture Handbook No. 456. Agriculture Research Service. U.S. Department of Agriculture. 1975.

J. Pennington. *Food Values of Portions Commonly Used.* 13th ed. Harper and Row. New York. 1980.

The case histories are composites of actual patients. The names are ficticious.

NEW WIN PUBLISHING, INC., P.O. Box 5159, Clinton, NJ 08809
Printing code
93 94 95   43 42 41 40

Library of Congress Cataloging in Publication Data

McDougall, John.
    The McDougall plan for super health and life-long weight loss.
    Includes bibliographical references and index.
    1. Vegetarianism.   2. Complex carbohydrate diet.
3. Sugar-free diet.   4. Reducing diets—Recipes.
5. Nutrition.   I. McDougall, Mary.   II. Title.
RM236.M38 1983   613.2'6   83-19412
ISBN 0-8329-0289-6
ISBN 0-8329-0392-2

TO OUR PARENTS

John and Betty McDougall endowed me with a restless nature that drives me to look for a better way—*JOHN*.

Marinus and Margie Luyk endowed me with a patient and domestic nature that makes creating interesting foods for our family and friends my delight—*MARY*.

A BRIEF SUMMARY OF THE McDOUGALL PLAN

The *McDougall Plan* encourages you to adopt the diet and lifestyle which best supports your natural tendencies to heal and stay healthy. This supportive environment is based around proper foods, moderate exercise, adequate sunshine, pure air and water, and surroundings comfortable to your psychological wellbeing.

The primary component, the diet, is centered around a variety of starchy plant foods such as rice, potatoes, and pastas with the addition of fresh or frozen fruits and vegetables. Animal-derived foods and plant products that are refined or otherwise processed are not health-supporting and are placed in the category called delicacies. Other plant foods that are also considered delicacies are those high in fat such as nuts, seeds, and avocados; and foods high in unprotected simple sugars; for example, honey, molasses, and maple syrup. These delicacy foods are to be reserved for special occasions and consumed only by healthy individuals. There are relative degrees of harmfulness among delicacies. No portions are recommended for the meal plan except that a starch should provide most of the calories. The quantity consumed each day is variable among individuals and governed by our highly efficient hunger drive. Foods that support your health easily make the most interesting and delicious meals you can imagine.

Additions and modifications of the basic meal plan include:

1. Supplementation of a nonanimal source of vitamin B-12 after three years on the plan or if you are pregnant or nursing.

2. Addition of foods concentrated in calories (dried fruits, nuts, seeds) to the basic diet of healthy individuals with unusually high caloric needs.

3. Elimination of foods that cause adverse reactions such as an allergy or an irritation.

4. Limitation of foods high in protein (legumes) to one cup a day for most people and further restriction in persons with certain illnesses (osteoporosis, gout, kidney stones, liver or kidney failure).

5. Fruits may have to be limited in those very sensitive to simple sugars (elevated triglycerides and hypoglycemia). In general three fruits a day is reasonable for most people.

6. One teaspoon of added salt over the surface of the foods is permitted in the daily diet of those who do not suffer from salt sensitive conditions (high blood pressure, heart or kidney disease, and edema).

7. Children are solely breastfed until the age of six months, solid foods are then supplemented, but breast milk still constitutes 50-25% of the childs diet until age two. After this age, starches, vegetables, and fruits provide for the basic nutritional needs.

PERSONS WHO ARE ILL OR ON MEDICATION WHO WISH TO CHANGE THEIR DIET SHOULD DO SO ONLY UNDER THE DIRECTION OF A PHYSICIAN FAMILIAR WITH THE EFFECTS OF DIET ON HEALTH. Otherwise you are encouraged to start today this meal plan and lifestyle that have provided excellent support for the health of most of our ancestors from the beginning of time and will do the same for you.

CONTENTS

FOREWORD

By Nathan Pritikin

Vegetarianism has been advocated for thousands of years for religious, moral, and health reasons. Followers of this dietary concept were looked upon as strange, queer, or saintly, but their dietary advice certainly was not considered practical or necessary for the population.

Recent authors and spokesmen for a vegetarian life-style have argued on moral and scientific grounds for their position. The McDougalls have proposed the first scientifically documented rationale for a vegetarian diet that I have seen.

Don't confuse this plan with lacto-ovo-vegetarians, who use eggs and dairy products, or the many other "vegetarian" plans that are not an all-plant food diet. This program is strict, and those who wish to follow it must be motivated to make a complete break with their life-long food habits.

Many benefits will accrue to those who adopt it—substantial lowering of risk factors for:

- Heart disease
- Diabetes
- Hypertension
- Breast and colon cancer

and general improvement of well-being will convince families to make this a lifetime commitment.

My dietary recommendations permit a maximum of 3 ounces of animal protein a day for the general population. For those with heart disease, diabetes and hypertension, I restrict animal protein to 3 ounces a week. In essence, my strict diet is practically a vegetarian diet, and I have personally been on it for over 25 years. As a former heart disease victim, I'm not interested in cholesterol clogging my arteries.

Why would I recommend a diet different from my normal recommendations? Not enough scientific work has been done to tell us which dietary approach is best for human health. The McDougall plan does no harm and follows all of my guidelines except for the elimination of the small amounts of animal protein. Present scientific findings have not convinced me of any harm of eating small amounts of animal protein. Both dietary plans can coexist until future scientific studies establish new recommendations.

For those who would like to follow a diet completely free of animal protein, the McDougall plan is the best that I have seen, both in practicality and scientific rationale. The plan, due to the extensive documentation, can be used by physicians and health professionals as a reference source.

This book establishes vegetarianism as a healthful way of life based on the latest scientific data and should give comfort to those considering making this dietary change.

Nathan Pritikin
Santa Barbara, California
August 24, 1983

PREFACE

Eighty years ago Russell Henry Chittenden began the preface of his book, *Physiological Economy in Nutrition,* (F.A. Stokes Co., 1904) with the following words:

There is no subject of greater physiological importance, or of greater moment for the welfare of the human race, than the subject of nutrition. How best to maintain the body in a condition of health and strength, how to establish the highest degree of efficiency, both physical and mental, with the least expenditure of energy, are questions in nutrition that every enlightened person should know something of, and yet even the expert physiologist today is in an uncertain frame of mind as to what constitutes a proper diet for different conditions of life and different degrees of activity. We hear on all sides widely divergent views regarding the needs of the body, as to the extent and character of the food requirements, contradictory statements as to the relative merits of animal and vegetable foods; indeed, there is great lack of agreement regarding many of the fundamental questions that constantly arise in any consideration of the nutrition of the human body. Especially is this true regarding the so-called dietary standards, or the food requirements of the healthy adult. Certain general standards have been more or less widely adopted, but a careful scrutiny of the conditions under which the data were collected leads to the conclusion that the standards in question have a very uncertain value, especially as we see many instances of people living, apparently in good physical condition, under a regime not at all in harmony with the existing standards.

ACKNOWLEDGMENTS

Our gratitude and thanks to:

Welman Shrader M.D., Elaine French, and Oswald Bushnell, who spent countless hours making this book more readable.

Rebecca Bartholomew and Judy Banks, who gave up weekends and evenings to type and retype the manuscripts. And to my IBM computer, which eventually stopped all that nonsense.

Welman Shrader M.D., John Scharffenberg M.D., Richard Littenberg M.D., Richard Blaisdell M.D., John Westerdahl M.P.H., R.D., Jeane Windsor M.P.H., R.D., Ray Brosseau, Associate Editor, Aloha Magazine, Steve Stephens, Ruth Heidrich and the Rev. Duane VanderBrug, who reviewed the book and gave helpful comments.

Linda and Jack Oszajca, who provided the artwork for the illustrations.

Virginia Enos for help in the library.

Our children—Heather, Patrick, and Craig—who gave us the incentive to take a closer look at the nutrition of our younger generation. Special thanks to our newest joy, Craig, who focused our attention on the importance of breast feeding. Their patience with all the hours we spent on the book is recognized and will be compensated for in the many happy years we plan to share together.

Our recent patients provided the ongoing stimulus, knowledge, and confirmation that diet and lifestyle are the keys to health and healing.

THIS IS **_NOT_**
AN
ALL OR NOTHING
HEALTH PLAN

---

the more you do,
the more you gain!

CAUTION:

If you are ill or on medication, do not attempt this diet without the supervision of a physician experienced in the effects of dietary change.

Chapter

1

Let's Face Facts

The concepts of health and nutrition today are so far removed from truth that our very lives are threatened from the day we are born.* Babies suckle from bottles containing a synthesized mixture of foreign proteins and chemicals that rob them of their natural protection against viruses and bacteria and subject them to life-threatening reactions that double their chances of crib death. These dangerous formulas are recommended by well-meaning pediatricians, obstetricians, family physicians, and nurses. These health professionals were not bought cheaply. The infant formula industry spends millions of dollars each year to promote its products through the medical profession by using high-powered advertising, sales personnel, and by giving free starter kits for new mothers. The most damaging effects of artificial feeding practices are seen in the underdeveloped countries where poor sanitation conditions prevail. Infants in these countries, deprived of the advantages of breast milk, have been given the equivalent of a death sentence. World Health Organization attempts to curb formula feeding have come into direct conflict with this powerful industry. Who will be the winner remains to be seen.

Once the bottle-fed child survives the early years of malnutrition, as most do in western societies, he or she becomes the target of the

*Statements made in this first chapter are supported by references from the scientific literature cited in chapter notes throughout the remainder of the book.

meat, dairy, egg, and processed food industries. Millions of dollars are spent on countless hours of television commercials pounding out a message with a single purpose: to sell products regardless of the health consequences.

The food industry has infiltrated the educational system as well. Learning about "good" nutrition began for most of us in elementary school. On the classroom wall hung a large and beautiful poster depicting "the Four Basic Food Groups." Since this was school, where, of course, only the truth was taught, we all opened our minds to this colorful instructional aid. If we had read the small print at the bottom of the chart, we would have learned that this poster was actually a powerful advertising tool supplied by the National Dairy Council, Kellogg's, Del Monte, Pillsbury, McDonald's, or some other industrial interest. (See Figure 1.1.) Using these food groups as guidelines, parents feed their families what they have assumed to be a balanced diet. And look at the results: obesity, constipation, acne, high blood pressure, and rotting teeth are found in epidemic proportions among our children.

The food industry is so powerful that, under the guise of giving helpful nutritional advice, it can even buy advertising space in the most widely read medical journals. The clippings in Figure 1.2 from the *Journal of the American Medical Association* are advertisements for beef, pork, and processed lunch meats, three of the richest foods consumed by people in affluent societies. These meats contain no carbohydrate or fiber and are high in fat, cholesterol, protein, and contamination. They have been implicated strongly (and in some cases proved convincingly) in playing a primary role in the cause of heart disease, cancer, and many other ailments.

Another powerful advertising campaign is carried on by the pharmaceutical industry, which spends millions of dollars each year "educating" medical doctors and the public to use their products. Prevention and cure of disease by methods as simple as diet and lifestyle certainly do not advance the profit margins of these businesses. The money invested over the past eighty years in researching the connection between diet and heart disease—the number one killer in affluent nations—pales in significance when compared to the millions that are spent getting a single drug ready for market. Dollars are not easily available for projects that do not have a short-term financial return for investors.

Figure 1.1

To date, research points clearly, consistently, and overwhelmingly to rich foods in the form of meats, dairy products, eggs, sugars, processed foods, and refined grains, and to lifestyle practices involving smoking, alcohol, caffeine, and physical inactivity as the major causes of death and disability. The money interests behind these industries aren't looking for more damaging research to expose the dangers of their products. Not surprisingly, a great deal of money is actually pumped into research projects that attempt to disclaim health hazards and, in fact, insist that their product (be it cigarettes, coffee, cream, or sugar) is good and good for you.

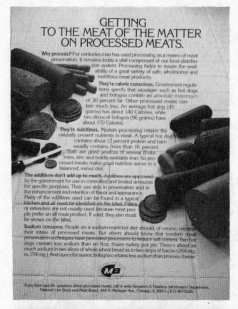

Figure 1.2

Research completed over the past eighty years not only supports
the role of diet and lifestyle in the cause and prevention of disease, but
clearly shows that most of these same diseases can be treated more

effectively by removing the causes than by using any of the drugs and surgical practices available today. Sad to say, the choice of therapy is often based on the profit margin tied to that therapy. Compare $100 worth of vegetables and a $25 pair of walking shoes to a $20,000 coronary bypass operation. The probability of positive results at one month and continuing positive results five years later are better with the $125 approach, but how many victims of heart disease know about this alternative approach?

The prevailing misconceptions about health and nutrition do not only cause illness; they promote it. They continue to exist because of one-sided, profit-oriented messages that attest to the advantages of a particular product and ignore the hazards. The benefits of a particular drug appear in large type in the advertisement. The side effects are left out or are presented in barely readable print.

Everyone knows that we need protein and that meat, dairy products, and eggs are concentrated protein sources. Few people know that recommendations to eat these excessive and harmful sources of protein are based on research dealing largely with the nutritional needs of rats. Rats at birth require ten times the amount of protein that a human baby does. How many people hear the real protein story, which reveals that the average person living in a modern society consumes enough excess protein every day to cause a mineral imbalance? Protein actually washes calcium from the body into the kidney system, leaving calcium-deficient bones and an increased risk of kidney stones. Ethical, health-oriented labeling and advertising should require a message on many of the foods accepted today as being beneficial: "Warning. This product is concentrated in protein and can be dangerous to your health. Use sparingly."

The dairy industry has one of the most successful advertising messages around. With their well-orchestrated campaign they have convinced dietitians, doctors, and parents that milk is nature's most perfect food and that poor health will be the inevitable result of a diet that fails to provide generous amounts of dairy products. The possibility of developing some vague illness imagined as "dietary calcium deficiency" haunts those not consuming milk and milk products. However, calcium deficiency of dietary origin is a myth and is virtually unknown in humans, even though most people in the world do not consume any milk after weaning. The whole truth is that dairy foods are the most harmful of the traditional four food groups. They are high in fat, protein, and environmental contaminants and deficient in fiber and carbohydrate. What carbohydrate they do have is poorly digested by most adults and results in diarrhea, gas, and stomach cramps when the average person responds to the message, "You never outgrow your need for milk." Dairy products are also the leading source of food allergy, causing a wide range of problems from headaches to bed wetting, stuffy nose, and even death.

The health food industry also answers to the principle that the dollar comes first. Polyunsaturated vegetable oils are promoted for their ability to reduce cholesterol and thus reduce the risk of heart attacks. Of all the commonly consumed foods tested, these very same oils are the strongest promoters of cancer in animals—a fact never mentioned in the advertisements for corn oil or all-natural safflower oil.

Large industries have great influence in high places. They are government subsidized when their profits go below a certain point, even if the reason for failure is that people won't buy their products because of health hazards. Witness the tobacco agriculture industries that receive financial backing from the government even though they are highly profitable and even though the Surgeon General of the United States formally warns the cigarette buyer against smoking in a statement printed on each package.

The dairy and meat industries are presently suffering from a depressed market as a direct result of increased public awareness. Officials of the U.S. government, which was founded on the principles of freedom of information, actually have suppressed printed material intended to improve health because of the material's potential harmfulness to business. Food lobbyists had little trouble convincing the Department of Agriculture to abandon publication of a relatively noncontroversial pamphlet—*Food/2*—which recommended ways to reduce fat and cholesterol in the American diet by discouraging meat, poultry, dairy, egg, fat, and oil consumption.

It is often said that literature on nutrition is controversial. This is one excuse many scientists, doctors, and dietitians give for withholding recommendations for changing your diet. In fact, to the unprejudiced mind the bulk of the literature clearly implicates rich food as the major culprit in our health problems. The Senate Select Committee Report on Nutrition and Human Needs came to a similar conclusion. This committee spent nine years reviewing medical and scientific information before publishing its report.

If the evidence from scientific studies is clear, then what is the reason for the controversy? The confusion occurs because many of the people writing and evaluating the literature follow rich diets themselves. Our primary source of health information is usually our physician. Most doctors live a fairly affluent lifestyle and eat rich foods. Steaks, cheese, butter, and white rolls are still served at Heart Association meetings, not to mention the necessary after-dinner dessert. It is not unheard of for a group of doctors and health educators to discuss the role of fat in the cause of breast cancer while eating a meal of fried chicken and french fries. It is hard for doctors and nutritionists to judge the literature objectively when their personal habits are being challenged. Most people are too defensive to handle such a situation. Thirty years ago, when many doctors smoked cigarettes, it was difficult to get proper advice from them on smoking and its relationship to lung disease. (See Figure 1.3.) Today a similar situation exists in the matter of nutrition.

Another reason why doctors seldom consider nutrition when treating patients is their lack of knowledge in the field. Medical schools have provided a shockingly inadequate education in basic nutrition for doctors. A recent investigation by a Senate subcommittee revealed that the average physician in the United States receives less than three hours of training in nutrition during four years of medical school and that less than 3 percent of the licensing exam questions are concerned with nutrition. Because of this deficiency in training, few doctors will understand or encourage any interest you may express in nutrition. Many actually feel threatened when questioned on the subject.

In spite of the obvious health benefits of a meatless diet, many people feel uneasy about becoming vegetarians. Some people have a prejudice that associates vegetarianism with hippies, Indian gurus, and others on the radical fringe of society. There is a lingering belief that vegetable eaters are socially unacceptable. But this is not the case. Many outstanding and famous people have been vegetarians. Table 1.1 gives just a partial list.

How could we expect effective nutritional advice to reach us? The clout exercised by industry through advertising, educational materials, and government subsidies has given the average person a one-sided view of well-balanced eating. Furthermore, health and nutrition professionals lack the training needed to counteract this misinformation, and many of these people whom we depend upon most for this vital information act as important vehicles for incorrect and unhealthy advice.

Let's consider what a hospital patient is given to eat. The hospital food service should provide an example of ideal nutrition for the

Figure 1.3

community, but in reality it serves its patients the very foods that, in most cases, brought them there in the first place. The sorry fact is that hospital food services actually increase the business of other departments by slowing down patients' progress. The typical hospital menu is laden with fat and cholesterol and with fiber-deficient foods. These foods, served with the stamp of approval of the hospital staff, keep patients sick and often cause the development of new diseases. Diabetics continue to need insulin, and people with high blood pressure remain hypertensive and must swallow even more pills. Surgical patients develop blood clots in their legs, partially as a result of their preoperation diets. When a person suffers a heart attack, he or she is placed in the coronary care unit, where the standard orders include a stool softener and a laxative to help compensate for the fiber-deficient diet being served. Furthermore, the patient is fed the foods that caused his or her condition to begin with. To make matters worse, the excessive fat content of the carefully planned coronary care diet tends to clot off more of the artery system that nourishes the damaged heart muscle. The cause-and-effect relationship between food and disease is so close that the food service department should be entitled to share in the profits of the hospital pharmacy.

Table 1.1 FAMOUS VEGETARIANS*

Show Business and Models

Hal Ashby	Pegeen Fitzgerald	Susan Richardson
DeDee Benrey	Doug Henning	Fred "Mister" Rogers
Christie Brinkley	Gemma Jones	Barbara Rush
Peter Brook	Judy Kahn	Renee Russo
Betty Buckley	Carol Kane	Flavia Sayner
Jeff Conway	Audrey Landers	Angela Schauss
Lindsay Crouse	Cloris Leachman	William Shatner
Pattie Reagan Davis	Patrick MacNee	Conrad Sheehan
Sandy Dennis	Pamela Sue Martin	Stella Stevens
Donna Douglas	Doug McValley	Twiggy
Samantha Eggar	Donna Mills	Dee Wallace
Pat Elliott	Belinda Montgomery	Leslie Ann Warren
Marty Feldman	Cary Nosler	Carl Weathers
Tom Fiorello	Marcia Pearson	Dennis Weaver
	Joe Regalbutto	Gwen Welles
		Gretchen Wyler

Authors and Writers

Paavo Airola
Piers Anthony
Janet Barkas
Brigid Brophy
John Christopher
E. F. Esfandiary
Stephen Gaskin
Frances Goulart
Lois Gould
Dick Gregory

LaDean Griffin
Joy Gross
Hans Holzer
Laura Huxley
Jill Johnson
Susan Smith Jones
Jane Kramer
R. D. Laing
Jim Mason
Colman McCarthy
Michael Medved

Malcolm Muggeridge
Scott and Helen
Nearing
Robert Nozick
Gary Null
Isaac Bashevis Singer
Peter Singer
Norman Walker
David Wallechinsky
Andrew Weil
Ann Wigmore

Sports

Sigfried Bauer
Horace Blackley
Jim Brewer
Roger Brown
Amby Burfoot
Peter Burwash
Andreas Cahling
Austin Carr
Dave Cash
Ernest Conners
Sheldon Deal
Tim Gallwey
Ron Gleason

Gary Fanelli
George Hackenschmidt
Connie Hawkins
Anton Innauer
Alan Jones
Jim Kaat
Killer Kowalski
Peter LaCock
Edwin Moses
Howard Mudd
Chip Oliver
Eric Ostbye

Masutatsu Oyana
Johnny Pack
Bill Pearl
Paul Powell
Stan Price
Murray Rose
Campy Russell
Dave Scott
Ralph Siegel
Ralph Sampson
Aad Steylen
Neal and Warren Walk
Bill Walton
Gogen Yamaguchi

Music

Marty Balin
David Bateau
Jeff Beck
Gerry Beckley
Stephen Jo Bladd
Phillip Bloom
Chuck Burgi
Gary Byrd
Captain and Tennille
Johnny Cash
David Cassidy
Joey Castle
Margot Chapman

The Delfonics
Donovan
Jonathan Edwards
Michael Franks
"Supe" Granda
David Green
John Hall
Pete Hamill
George Harrison
John Hartman
Lauren Hitchcock
Steve Howe
Michael Jackson

Trish Michaels
Graham Nash
Richard Perry
Michael Pinder
Artimus Pyle
Terry Riley
Johnny Rivers
Pepe Romero
Todd Rundgren
Graham Russell
Carlos Santana
Boz Scaggs
Fred Schneider

Chubby Checker
Alice Coltrane
Sir Clifford Curzon
Dave and Ray Davies

Al Jardine
Kraftwerk
Mike Love
Francisco Lupica
John McVie

Ravi Shankar
JoJo Smith
Maurice White
Paul Winter
Gary Wright

Historical

Louisa May Alcott
General William Booth
Buddha
Clement of Alexandria
Charles Darwin
Leonardo DaVinci
Albert Einstein
Ralph Waldo Emerson
St. Francis
Benjamin Franklin
Mahatma Gandhi
Horace Greeley

Mahatma
J. H. Kellogg
Dalai Lama
John Milton
Isaac Newton
Ovid
Plato
Plutarch
Alexander Pope
Pythagoras
Jean Jacques Rousseau
Albert Schweitzer

Seneca
George Bernard Shaw
Percy Bysshe Shelley
Upton Sinclair
Socrates
Rabindranath Tagore
Henry David Thoreau
Leo Tolstoy
Voltaire
H.G. Wells
John Wesley
Ellen G. White

Other Famous People

Rukmini Devi Arundale
Sai Baba
Yogi Bhajan
Gypsy Boots
Porter Briggs
Eileen Caddy
Cesar Chavez
Sri Chinmoy
Ram Das
Rennie Davis
Moraji Desai

Paul Fleiss
Uri Geller
Jack Goodall
Rabbi Schlomo Goren
Ida Honorof
Rep. Andrew Jacobs
Maharaj Ji
Da Free John
Kenneth Kaunda
Krishnamurti

Paul McGrego
Swami Muktananda
Henry Nunn
Elizabeth Clare
Prophet
Bhagavan Shree
Rajneesh
Satchidananda
Frank Serpico
Kirpal Singh

*Source: D. Benrey, "Vegetarian Celebrities," *Vegetarian Times* 62 (1982); 70 and others. (Not to be misinterpreted as followers of the McDougall Plan).

Because there is so much misinformation about the nutritional value of a diet consisting only of vegetable foods, many people are concerned about the possibility of adverse effects on their health. They worry about getting enough protein, amino acids, iron, calcium, and vitamins. However, nutritional research done over the past fifty years confirms not only the adequacy of a starch-centered diet supplemented with fresh fruits and vegetables but also its superiority.

Our entire society is set up to serve and consume rich foods provided by supermarkets, vending machines, and restaurants. The convenience of this system is attractive to busy people who do not have the time or the desire to cook. Many people have grown up with little training in the kitchen because they have set their sights on careers outside the home. Essential work once performed by the homemaker has been turned over to the food industry.

We have become accustomed to the taste of rich foods. Two of the most harmful components of our foods are salt and fat. They provide the dominant flavors for the western diet. A diet that supports health and healing avoids these substances and, therefore, the tastes of foods prepared without them are unfamiliar. The initial reaction to unfamiliar things is often dislike. Once we get used to the new flavors, these foods easily become our favorites.

Our society is oriented to illness and treatment, instead of to health and healing. To enjoy good health under such circumstances requires effort. But there are people who find the effort worthwhile. They enjoy life and want to function at the healthiest level possible. Furthermore, these people do not want their lives cut short by preventable problems such as a heart attack or cancer.

If you are among the growing number of people who believe that there is a better way, then you will find many of the answers you have been searching for in this book. Once you've read about the *McDougall Plan* you will be able to improve your health by changing the way you eat and care for yourself. Adaptation comes quickly and comfortably in a few short weeks, yet the rewards last for a lifetime.

Chapter
2
How to Look Better, Feel Better, and Stay Better

People are meant by nature to be healthy and active. However, it is obvious that most of us who live in modern and developed societies fall short of that ideal. We are tired and overweight, and we take a multitude of pills for various ailments. The calculated lifespan of a person is approximately eighty-five years, and each decade of life should be filled with activity and the continuing ability to see, hear, taste, move and think.[1] In reality, people living in western nations degenerate as they progress to premature death. If our natural condition is supposed to be good health, then why is illness so prevalent in our society?

Experts have determined that almost all diseases stem from environmental conditions.[2-9] Our most important and intimate contact with the environment is through our intake of food. (See Figure 2.1.) Each day we swallow one to five pounds of food, which eventually becomes the essential nutrients that enter our bloodstreams to form tissue. The expression "You are what you eat" is beyond dispute and emphasizes the primary importance of diet to our health.

In the introduction to a 1977 Senate report on nutrition and human needs, Dr. Mark Hegsted of the Harvard School of Public Health said:

> I wish to stress that there is a great deal of evidence and it continues to accumulate, which strongly implicates and, in some instances, proves that the major causes of death and disability in the United States are related to

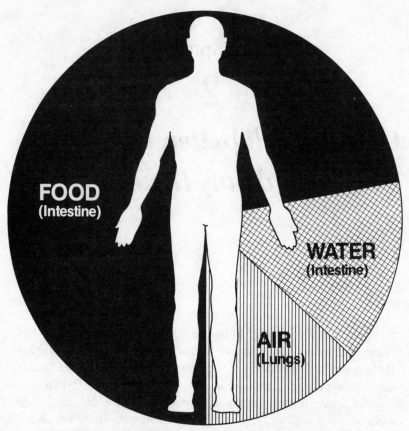

MOLECULE FOR MOLECULE FOOD IS THE STRONGEST CONTACT WITH OUR ENVIRONMENT.

Figure 2.1

the diet we eat. I include coronary artery disease which accounts for nearly half of the deaths in the United States, several of the most important forms of cancer, hypertension, diabetes, and obesity as well as other chronic diseases.[9]

In today's affluent societies, most people consume rich foods that historically were available only to aristocrats and royalty. The effects of eating these foods can be seen in our world today as clearly as in the art and literature of the past. The overfed lord was often depicted with his gout-afflicted foot propped up on a stool. (See Figure 2.2.)

What once was reserved for a few is now the only food available in our hospitals, school cafeterias, restaurants, and homes. Rich foods

Figure 2.2. The effects of rich foods and an unhealthy lifestyle was obviously seen by this artist, James Gillray (1757–1815) more than 180 years ago. The *tisick* is the name used for wasting diseases such as tuberculosis and diabetes mellitus. The *colic* refers to stomach trouble. The *gout* is a painful arthritic condition once found commonly only among the royal classes of people.

are so common that people forget that not long ago they were served as delicacies, and then only to the wealthy classes. Their use in our present culture is so extensive that these delicacies are actually recommended by supposedly qualified nutritionists as an essential part of a "well-balanced" diet.

"Rich" foods include red meat, poultry, eggs, fish, shellfish, cheeses, milk, oils, nuts, seeds, white rice, refined flour, processed foods, salt, and sugar. They were traditionally found in abundance on tables set for festive occasions. The unfortunate reality is that, in one form or another, most westerners feast at each and every meal, twenty-one times or more a week.

From a nutritional viewpoint, rich foods are those that provide poorly for our bodily needs because of either deficiencies or harmful excesses. Their inadequacies are most damaging when they involve the major components of the food, called macronutrients. The macronutrients are fat, protein, carbohydrate (complex and simple), fiber, sodium (salt), potassium, and calcium. The minor components, or micronutrients, are the vitamins and trace minerals. Although much attention is given by health food enthusiasts to the micronutrients, they contribute very little to health problems found in affluent societies.[10]

We become ill when the harmful elements of what we eat and how we live overwhelm our bodies' ability to resist these elements and keep healthy. Heredity determines to a large extent what strengths and weaknesses our bodies possess and, therefore, where our systems may first fail under a particular strain. For example, in one family poor nutrition may result in the frequent occurrence of heart disease while the strengths of another family may protect against this disease, yet their members may be more susceptible to the cancers caused by diet. The destructive and harmful element most strongly influencing the health of westerners is rich food. Polluted air and water, inadequate or excessive sunshine, physical inactivity, and mental stress are additional harmful elements working against the strength of our bodies. On the other hand, the beneficial elements of adequate sunshine, clean air, pure water, exercise, and comfortable surroundings for our psychological well-being provide necessary support for good health. Of the two primary factors—diet and heredity—that produce disease, as well as the many secondary factors involved, we must concentrate on the factors we have control over and disregard ones, such as heredity, that we cannot alter. (See Figure 2.3.)

In societies where overindulgence in rich food is common, a number of diseases predominate. The more common are listed in Table 2.1.

When we remove the factors that make us sick and provide the diet and lifestyle that support our health, we soon begin to recover. The body has an innate ability to heal itself, given the right conditions.

Throughout nature there are specific and narrow nutritional requirements for each plant and animal. For example, there is a particular diet that is best for horses and one for cats. To interchange the two diets would result in poor health for both. Westerners and their medicine have largely ignored the concept of a limited spectrum of nutrients that would allow people to look, feel, and function at their best. The foods consumed in affluent societies range from those ideal for horses (grains) to cat food (meat) and include almost any food eaten by any beast.

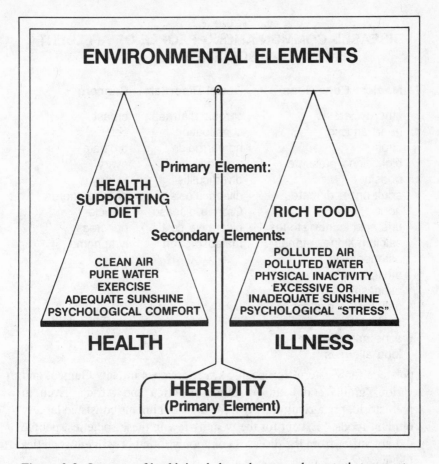

Figure 2.3. Our state of health is a balance between elements that support our bodies' strengths and harmful environmental elements. Heredity provides a background for these elements to interact upon. The ultimate outcome is either health or illness.

The diet that best supports health and healing for humans is a pure vegetable diet centered around starch foods with the addition of fresh fruits and vegetables. We will refer to this diet as a *starch-centered diet* and as a *health-supporting diet*.

Two sources of information show us that rich foods cause illness and that a starch-centered diet provides the proper nutrients for health and healing. First, the history of human diets tells of most people living successfully on a variety of starch-centered diets: rice for Asians, corn for Indians of North and Central America, bread and

Table 2.1
DISEASES COMMON AMONG PEOPLE OF AFFLUENT SOCIETIES

Medical Conditions	Bowel Disorders	Cancers
atherosclerosis	chronic diarrhea	breast
heart attacks	constipation	colon
strokes	hemorrhoids	prostate
high blood pressure	appendicitis	ovary
obesity	diverticulitis	kidney
adult-onset diabetes	diverticulosis	body of uterus
gout	Crohn's disease	testicle
uric acid kidney stones	ulcerative colitis	pancreas
calcium kidney stones	malabsorption	lymphoma
osteoporosis		
multiple sclerosis		
psoriasis		
gallbladder disease		
tooth decay		
acne and oily skin		
food allergies		

potatoes for Western Europeans, sweet potatoes in New Guinea, and various grains and beans in South America and Africa. Even in prehistoric, preagricultural eras, the diets of humans consisted largely of plant foods.[11] Except for the wealthy few in these societies, people did not suffer from the diseases commonly found in affluent societies today.

Prior to the Industrial revolution, about 100 years ago, and the subsequent large scale economic advancement of masses of people in western societies, diets were largely based on a variety of starches. For the common person, consumption of rich food was limited to a chicken added to flavor the community pot of vegetable stew several times a week or an occasional feast where a pig would be killed. During times of extreme hardship, rich food also was eaten when the family cow used to plow the fields had to be sacrificed in order to prevent starvation. This is still the case in developing countries today. The people living in these underdeveloped societies suffer mostly from illnesses caused by starvation and poor sanitation. These two basic health problems have been largely resolved by modern technology. Therefore, it would seem to be a sensible step for us to combine the advantages of the diets of less affluent societies with modern technology to achieve maximum benefits for our health.

The second source of information is provided by the abundance of medical and nutritional research carried out over the past eighty years, which consistently endorses the use of a starch-centered diet and blames rich foods for most of our ills.

If this information has been so readily available to us, why are we so unaware of it? Rich foods once were simply too expensive for the common person; they were a longed for, usually unattainable treat. However, technology has made rich food available in large quantities at a price almost anyone can afford. The industries that produce these foods promote their products for maximum profits. Their efforts have resulted in the proliferation of information that supports the "benefits" of rich foods and largely ignores the hazards. In most instances the facts on good nutrition stimulated by industry have been innocently misrepresented to us, but in some cases there has been a responsible party concealing the truth. Industry has interacted so effectively with the government, the scientific community, the medical profession, and the public that completely incorrect concepts concerning our nutritional needs are accepted with only rare dissenters. The idea that our modern diet is a major triumph for humanity stands in direct conflict with the health of those who are eating these foods. What perpetuates the problem is that most of us have become accustomed to the taste of rich foods and readily accept this misinformation, which supports our personal eating habits and avoids the threat of change.

A health-supporting diet is unfamiliar to us because we are used to rich foods and because we have been overpowered by advertising from the food and health industries. But it is important for us to realize that what we enjoy eating and what we believe is correct nutrition for our bodies is solely a result of our previous conditioning and, therefore, it can and must be changed.

Notes

[1] J. Fries, "Aging, Natural Death, and the Compression of Morbidity, *N Engl J Med 303 (1980): 130*.

[2] Report to Congress from the Office of Technology Assessment, "Assessment of technologies for determining cancer risk from the environment." June 1981.

[3] Committee on Diet, Nutrition, and Cancer, Assembly of Life Sciences, National Research Council, *Diet, Nutrition, and Cancer,* Washington, D.C.: National Academy Press. 1982.

[4] J. Higginson, "Cancer and Environment: Higginson Speaks Out," *Science* 205 (1979): 1363.

[5]D. Burkitt, "Some Diseases Characteristic of Modern Western Civilization," *Br Med J.* 1 (1973): 274.

[6]J. Stamler, "Lifestyle, Major Risk Factors, Proof, and Public Policy," *Circulation* 58 (1978): 3.

[7]U.S. Department of Health, Education, and Welfare Environmental Health Perspectives, October 1979, volume 32.

[8]D. Rustein, "Controlling the Communicable and the Man-Made Diseases," *N Engl J Med* 304 (1981): 1422.

[9]"Dietary Goals for the United States," Washington, D.C.: Government Printing Office, stock no. 052-070-03913-2.

[10]W. Connor, "Presidential Address: Too Little or Too Much, the Case for Preventive Nutrition," *Am J Clin Nutr* 32 (1979): 1975.

[11]M. Kliks, "Paleodietetics: A Review of the Role of Dietary Fiber in Preagricultural Human Diets," *Topics in Dietary Fiber Research*. Plenum Press. p. 181. 1978. New York.

Chapter

3

Even If You're Overweight, You Won't Feel Hungry on a Health-Supporting Diet

Hunger is one of our strongest drives, ensuring our personal survival as well as the survival of the human race. If you have any doubt about the intensity of this drive, try going without food for just two days and drinking only water during that time. You will quickly forget your personal problems of money, family, and job. You will have only one thought: food! (Do not try this experiment if you are ill or on medication.)

Why does eating to satisfy our hunger make us overweight? Certainly our hunger drive was not meant to cause problems with health and weight. One reasonable question that might be asked is whether, by some error in nature, our stomachs were made too big for our bodies, so that when we fill them up we take in too many calories. Such mistakes are not likely to occur in nature. The most reasonable answer is that our stomachs are not suited for the high-calorie foods commonly consumed by people in developed societies. The human stomach is best suited for a diet of starches, but many of us misunderstand the nutritional value of these low-calorie foods. Most people actually believe that starches are fattening. We often see people at dinner push aside their rice or potatoes because they are "watching their weight." However, most people around the world live primarily on the foods we are avoiding. For example, the Chinese and other Asians consume a great quantity of rice yet stay slender throughout life.

A short study of a calorie chart will help us understand why people on starch-centered diets stay so thin. A cup of cooked rice (150 grams) contains 178 calories, which means there are only about 1.2 calories per gram of rice. This is approximately one-third the number of calories found in an equivalent amount of beef (3.9 calories per gram) or cheese (4.0 calories per gram). An excellent food with which to achieve rapid weight loss is the potato, at 0.6 calories per gram or about 85 calories per potato. An average active adult male burns 3,000 calories per day. To maintain his weight he would need to eat 35 potatoes or 17 cups of rice a day. Eating all those potatoes or that much rice would be a time-consuming, but certainly not impossible task.

In developed countries, people are overweight because they eat too little starch. Instead, they consume mostly high-calorie fats and oils in the form of meat, milk, cheese, nuts, seeds, and vegetable oils. Correcting the misconception that starches are fattening would quickly and dramatically improve the appearance and health of people in western countries.

Foods are composed of five major ingredients:

1. Fats, 9 calories per gram
2. Proteins, 4 calories per gram
3. Carbohydrates, 4 calories per gram
4. Water, 0 calories per gram
5. Fiber, 0 calories per gram

The proportions of these five substances in a particular food determines the number of calories it contains. (See Figure 3.1) For example, potatoes are primarily carbohydrates (4 calories per gram), fiber (0 calories per gram), and water (0 calories per gram), with an ultimate calorie concentration of 0.6 calories per gram. Examples of calorie concentrations in various foods are given in Table 3.1.

Because most meat and dairy foods, not to mention nuts, seeds, and oils, are so concentrated in calories, it is practically impossible for us to eat them without consuming an excess of calories before our stomachs are full and our hunger is satisfied. On the other hand, starches, vegetables, and fruits quickly fill the stomach with the intake of fewer calories. Foods low in calorie concentration take longer to eat, and when people consuming different foods were compared, those on meal plans with higher calorie concentration foods were found to consume twice as many calories each day in order to satisfy their hunger.[1]

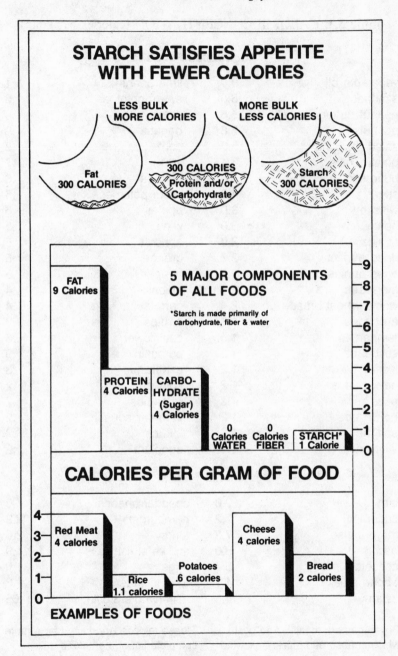

Figure 3.1. Hunger is satisfied by filling the stomach. Starches, vegetables, and fruits do this with fewer calories than meats, cheeses, and oils.

Table 3.1. CALORIE CONCENTRATION (calories per gram)

Vegetables Foods

vegetable oil	9.0	lima beans	1.1
almonds	6.0	sweet potatoes	1.0
peanut butter	5.8	yams	.9
peanuts	5.8	banana	.9
salad dressing	5.5	corn	.8
potato chips	5.4	tofu	.7
butterscotch candy	4.0	oatmeal	.6
sugar	4.0	white potatoes	.6
whiskey	3.0	apples	.6
honey	3.0	wine	.5
raisins	2.9	apricots	.5
dried apricots	2.7	orange	.5
dried apples	2.7	beer	.5
molasses	2.4	onions	.4
whole wheat bread	2.4	carrots	.4
avocados	1.7	turnips	.3
tempeh	1.5	cauliflower	.3
soybeans	1.3	pumpkin	.3
kidney beans	1.2	asparagus	.3
navy beans	1.2	spinach	.2
peas	1.2	tomatoes	.2
brown rice	1.2	summer squash	.2
spaghetti	1.1	lettuce	.2
white rice	1.1	eggplant	.2

Animal Foods

lard	9.0	cheddar cheese	4.0
butter	7.2	hamburger	2.9
mayonnaise	7.2	turkey	2.6
bacon	6.0	mackerel fish	1.9
chocolate milk	5.4	eggs	1.6
t-bone steak	4.7	tuna in water	1.3
salami	4.5	milk (whole-3.5%)	.65

Beverages are mostly "free" water which is absorbed quickly, allowing hunger to soon return.

Please refer to *Appendix I* for a more complete list of the calorie concentrations of various foods.

Most diets fail because they ask us to limit the amount of food we take in and therefore to be hungry most of the time. Satisfaction of hunger occurs primarily by filling the stomach. Those foods with a low concentration of calories will fill our stomachs without providing excess calories. Additional satisfaction comes from the slow absorption of food, and this is accomplished best by complex carbohydrate foods in which fiber is plentiful.[2]

Denying our hunger drive and restricting the intake of food takes great effort and results in misery and pain. This is commonly referred to as "dieting." And most dieters must be labeled failures, since up to 95 percent of them regain all or some of the weight they lost.[3]

Many variations of the starvation form of dieting have been tried. A very low-calorie diet (500 calories a day) has been used in combination with injections of an extract from the urine of pregnant women. These shots are supposed to make the dieter tolerate a low-calorie diet more easily and to slow the return of obesity in the postdieting period.[4] The extract, called human chorionic gonadotropin (HCG), has no more than a placebo effect when compared to injections of salt water.[5-7] "Shot clinics" are very popular even though any success they have is clearly tied to the low-calorie diet and the motivation provided by frequent clinic visits.

An attempt to improve on the poor success rates found with dieting has resulted in the development of a very unhealthy approach to dealing with the hunger drive and losing weight: low-carbohydrate, high-protein diets. The basic mechanism of this popular approach involves suppressing the hunger drive by tricking the body into making adjustments usually brought on only by disease or starvation. One of the first symptoms of illness is loss of appetite, which also occurs after several days of total deprivation of food. The loss of appetite occurs because the body shifts to using its own fat to satisfy the requirements for energy and the subsequent production of ketones from the fat metabolism. The condition is known as ketosis. Low-carbohydrate, high-protein diets change the body's energy metabolism into a state of ketosis and suppress the appetite by taking advantage of these natural processes meant to be used only during times of duress. The Atkins diet, the Stillman diet, and liquid protein diets are a few examples of regimens that burden the body in this manner. These diets have serious side effects which should discourage anyone from following them for even temporary weight loss. The Atkins and Stillman diet plans use foods very high in fat, cholesterol, and protein, and low in fiber and carbohydrate, with an emphasis on flesh and dairy foods. Current understanding of the hazards associated with these rich foods can only lead to the conclusion that the diseases caused by rich food consumption will be exaggerated by such a dietary approach.[8-9]

Suppressing your appetite by the liquid protein diet approach is the ultimate in dieting foolishness. Liquid protein diets have been condemned by the FDA because they have been the direct cause of the deaths of more than sixty people from irreversible heart arrhythmias.[10] The Cambridge Diet Plan is one of the most recent versions of a liquid protein diet. Promoters of this diet proclaim the safety of their liquid protein mixture, indicating that they have eliminated the dangers that caused the deaths with previous liquid diets.[11] This is a puzzlement, since the factors that caused those deaths have never been identified.[12-14] Recent reports have claimed serious illness associated with the use of the Cambridge Diet Plan.[15-17]

The most extreme low-calorie, carbohydrate-deficient, ketosis-producing diet is a fast. Many people have the mistaken idea that a fast is accomplished by switching the source of calories to fruit and vegetable juice. When food is consumed in the form of juice, adaptive changes seen with total calorie deprivation do not occur. A true fast with only water results in a change to fat metabolism and ketosis with a loss of appetite in just a few days.

There are several advantages to fasting under specific circumstances. Loss of appetite is a natural response to illness. This leaves the body free from the work of food preparation and digestion. The energy saved may be used for healing and recuperation. Many people force themselves to eat while they are sick, even though they are not hungry. Food eaten at this time may nourish the bacteria, viruses, cancer cells, or other agents that are making them ill, but does little to help them recover.[18-19] The desire for food usually returns two to four days after the onset of an acute illness. This is the proper time to resume eating.

Another advantage of a fast is that it is the most complete elimination diet and is one of the basic tools used by institutions, called environmental laboratories, which treat problems caused by the interaction between our environment and ourselves. In most instances, healthy people with normal appetites who routinely fast accomplish little except to learn the strength of their hunger drive. However, fasting for a few days may be an effective way of starting on a new diet. After two days without food, anything will taste delicious. You will eat unfamiliar foods with enthusiasm! But do not fast if you are on medication, and do not fast for more than three days without the supervision of someone trained in fasting. The primary drawback to fasting is that because of the implied temporary nature of this approach, any weight loss or health benefits attained during the fast will soon be lost if you return to the old way of nourishing yourself.

So, those unfortunate people who do not understand the nutritional advantages of starches are often limited to the miseries of an unsatisfied hunger drive (dieting or fasting) or chronic illness (the ketosis-producing diets) to keep their bodies trim.

Each pound of body fat represents a net gain of approximately 3,500 calories, regardless of the food source. Obesity results when more calories are consistently taken in than are expended in daily activity. One factor in successful weight loss is to reduce calorie intake, preferably by consuming a low-calorie, starch-centered diet. The other factor is an increase in activity level, which will burn more calories. A program of regular daily exercise will aid in losing excess weight and help to maintain ideal weight. Exercise also provides the added benefit of "resetting" the appetite to a level more appropriate for our energy needs.[20]

You will rarely find it necessary to limit the starches, vegetables, and fruits you eat in order to attain your desired weight. Most overweight people will lose about ten pounds per month on a starch-centered diet. This weight loss stops when a trim body weight is attained. If you are not losing weight quickly enough, you should center your diet around the lower-calorie starches such as squash, potatoes, corn, and yams. Add large helpings of fresh green and yellow vegetables, which are very low in calories. You should avoid eating large quantities of bread, which has been made more concentrated in calories through the refining of wheat berries into wheat flour with removal of a certain amount of fiber. (The amount depends on the particular brand of flour. Whole wheat flour yields 2.0 calories per gram, whereas unprocessed wheat berries release only 0.45 calorie per gram.)

You may find yourself losing more weight than you expected. If so, Table 3.2 from the Kempner Foundation may reassure you that you are not too thin. Walter Kempner M.D. developed Duke University's Rice Reduction Diet Program. The chart records what Dr. Kempner considered to be reasonable adult weight in proportion to height. He also recommended that people with diabetes or heart, kidney, or blood vessel diseases should weigh 10 to 15 percent less than the optimum figures presented in the chart.[21]

People who are very thin should center their diets around bread, and beans which are the higher-calorie starches. If you are in good health but want to gain weight, you may add foods with a very high

Table 3.2

WOMEN

Height	Weight (fully dressed) should be below (pounds):
4'11"	91
5'	94
5'1 "	97
5'2"	100
5'3"	104
5'4"	108
5'5"	112
5'6"	117
5'7"	122
5'8"	127
5'9"	132
5'10"	137
5'11"	142
6'	147

MEN

Height	Weight (fully dressed) should be below (pounds):
5'2"	110
5'3"	115
5'4"	120
5'5"	125
5'6"	130
5'7"	135
5'8"	140
5'9"	145
5'10"	150
5'11"	155
6'	160
6'1"	165
6'2"	170
6'3"	175
6'4"	180
6'5"	185

calorie concentration. These foods include dried fruits, soybean products, nuts, seeds, and small amounts of vegetable oil. For most people, the foods containing simple sugars are tolerated better than the high-fat plant foods.

Have you ever heard of people becoming ill because they breathed too much air or satisfied their thirst too often? Problems do not commonly occur from satisfying these essential drives. However, it is frequently claimed that people become overweight because they overeat. It is unlikely that the drive for food was designed any less safely and efficiently than the drives for air and water. There is no choice available when satisfying our thirst and our lungs. Only water and air will do. However, when it comes to food we have a choice of three sources of calories—fats, proteins, and carbohydrates, which are present in a tremendous variety of foods—to satisfy the hunger drive. Incorrect choices, not overeating, are what cause this "health problem" so frequently encountered in affluent societies.

The starches, vegetables, and fruits in a health-supporting diet satisfy our powerful drive for food and ensure good health. Once you have reeducated your tastes, these vegetable foods will become your favorites. This method of achieving trim body weight is easier than trying to fight hunger, and it will give you the best chance of winning in your life-long "battle of the bulge."

A health-supporting diet is simple to understand and put together. Any of a wide variety of starches make up the main or largest portion of the meal, and the vegetables and fruit are added in smaller amounts to complement the starch main course. *Starches, vegetables,* and *fruits* are overlapping terms commonly applied to foods from the plant kingdom. They are used in our every-day language, yet are poorly defined in dictionaries as well as in our thoughts. The dictionary definitions are as follows:

- *Starches*—Foods rich in natural starch.
- *Starch*—a white, tasteless, solid carbohydrate occurring in the form of minute granules in the seeds, tubers, and other parts of plants, and forming an important constituent of rice, corn, wheat, beans, potatoes, and many other vegetable foods.
- *Fruit*—The developed ovary of a seed plant with its contents and accessory parts, as a pea pod, nuts, tomato, pineapple, etc. The edible part of a plant developed from a flower, with any accessory tissues, as a peach, mulberry, banana, etc.

- *Vegetable*—Any herbaceous plant whose fruit, seeds, roots, tubers, bulbs, stems, leaves, or flower parts are used as food, as the tomato, bean, beet, potato, asparagus, cabbage, etc.[22]

The usage of these descriptive terms in this book will be somewhat different from the standard dictionary definitions.

Starches

Starches will be defined as foods that contain adequate amounts of readily available calories in the form of starch molecules. Starch molecules are made of long chains of sugars, which are the basic units of our energy supply. These chains of sugars are accompanied by just the right amounts of protein, essential fat, fiber, water, vitamins, and minerals. Starches are ideal foods around which to center your meal plan, and the starch foods should account for most of your daily calories.

Whole grains

brown rice	triticale
wheat berries	barley
bulgur (cracked)	oat
millet	corn
rye	buckwheat

Legumes

beans	*peas*
pinto	black-eyed
pink	split green
kidney	whole green
white	
black	*lentils*
lima	green
mung	red
garbanzo	brown
soy	
adzuke (azuki)	
navy	
great northern	

Flours

whole wheat pastry	oat
wheat	corn
buckwheat	rice
rye	soy
barley	garbanzo bean
triticale	lima bean

Pastas (whole wheat, spinach, buckwheat)

spaghetti	alphabet noodles
macaroni	lasagna noodles
flat noodles	

Roots

white potatoes	parsnips
sweet potatoes	taro
yams	rutabaga

Carrots, beetroot, turnips, daikon, and salsify are low in calories and will be considered under *vegetables*.

Squashes
   winter squashes
   acorn
   hubbard
   banana
   pumpkin
   spaghetti
   butternut

Summer squashes will be listed under *vegetables*. Because of their low calorie content, they usually cannot serve as the center of a meal.

Fruits

Fruits contain most of their sugars in the simple form as sucrose, glucose, or fructose and therefore taste sweet. They yield plenty of calories and are generously supplied with fiber and vitamins. Most have adequate amounts of protein, minerals, and essential fat to be considered excellent, nutritionally complete foods. Fruits form a pleasing addition to the basic starch-centered meals or can be consumed as snacks between meals. Frequently they must be restricted to one to three servings per day because of their high content of simple sugars and easily available calories.

Noncitrus

papaya	passion fruit
banana	pear
peach	pineapple
apple	plum
cherry	date
grape	watermelon
guava	cantaloupe
mango	honeydew
lichee	strawberry
nectarine	avocado
kiwi fruit	cucumber
tomato	

Citrus

tangerine	lime
orange	grapefruit
lemon	

Avocado and olives are fruits with a very high fat content. Dried fruits provide a very high concentration of calories. Initially, these are to be avoided in your diet. Tomatoes, cucumbers, avocados, and olives are actually fruits, even though many people think of them as vegetables.

Vegetables

Vegetables will be defined as plants or plant parts that are too low in calorie content to form the center of a meal. However, they do provide valuable contributions of vitamins, minerals, fiber, water, essential fat, and protein, to say nothing of the aroma, flavor, color, and variety in texture they can bring to your meal.

Summer squash
  chayote
  zucchini
  straight-neck
  crook-neck
  scalloped
  cocozelle

Flowers
  broccoli
  Brussels sprout
  artichoke
  cauliflower

Roots
  carrot
  beetroot
  turnip
  salsify
  radish
  onion

Leafy
  lettuce
  cabbage
  spinach
  chard
  kale

Pod legumes
  yellow (wax) bean
  green bean
  Chinese pea

Stalks
  asparagus
  celery
  rhubarb

Mushrooms
  button
  dried shiitake
  dried winter
  straw

Fruitlike
  eggplant
  tomato
  cucumber

Combinations of starches, vegetables, and fruits provide an unlimited variety of meals for you to enjoy. Just compare the color in the rich western diet with a starch-centered diet. Most meat, dairy products, and processed foods are white, yellow, or brown. To add color a small piece of parsley or a slice of tomato is often added to the uninteresting plate of steak and fries. Contrast this with the many shades of purple, red, orange, yellow, green, and brown provided by starches, vegetables, and fruits. Color is only one advantage of this superior meal plan, and once you become familiar with it these foods will easily become your favorites.

The primary function of food is to supply calories to provide energy for our daily activities. Complex carbohydrates found in starches, vegetables, and fruits offer the most efficient and safest source of calories for our bodies. Naturally present in these foods are also the nutritional components that support our innate healing processes and maintain our health. They contain just enough protein (amino acids), essential fat, fiber, vitamins, minerals, and other nutrients to enable us to function at our fullest. Equally important, a properly planned diet of starches, vegetables, and fruits avoids excesses of cholesterol, fat, protein, simple sugar, salt, and environmental contaminants that can burden our bodies and cause our health to fail. (See Table 3.3.)

Table 3.3. APPROXIMATION OF MACRONUTRIENTS
(percentage of calories and grams per day)

	Health-Supporting Diet	Rich Western Diet
Fat	5%	42%
Protein	10%	12%
Carbohydrate	85%	46%
Dietary fiber	60 g	10 g
Sodium	1000 mg	5000 mg
Potassium	5000 mg	2000 mg
Calcium	400 mg	800 mg
Cholesterol- (a non-nutrient)	0 mg	600 mg

Carol Van Eck—Overweight But Ready For One More Try

I've been fat since the day I was born. There have been a few times when I've been able to lose enough weight by starving myself to fit into a size 12, but I spend most of the time at the 16 to 18 rack.

My husband eats much more than I do and doesn't gain any weight. It's just not fair. I can gain weight on a 1,000-calorie diet. I call it the curse of bad metabolism.

I tried jogging recently, but I just ate more after a run. I actually gained five pounds before I quit because of sore knees and ankles. I've tried for years to perform the best exercise there is for fat people—pushing myself away from the table. But I can't keep it up. I'm always overeating and snacking between meals. My appetite is too strong, and I really feel deprived when I don't get enough to eat. When I'm on a diet it has helped to be involved in a support group like Weight Watchers, but it is still a constant battle to stick to the measured quantities I'm allowed at each meal. One of the most effective programs I tried was the shot clinic. Getting poked three times a week allowed me to focus on another source of pain besides my hunger pangs for a while. I stuck to the 500-calorie diet for two months and lost 30 pounds, but I gained it all back in three weeks.

My friend Judy recently talked me into trying the liquid protein diet she sells. After two days I was no longer hungry because the headaches and nausea had started. I got so sick after a week I couldn't continue. Just as well—I've heard those diets are dangerous.

My frustration with my weight has gone on for so long and I've failed so many times that I'm afraid to try again. Maybe I am a candidate for an operation. They could cut out part of my stomach. Heaven knows it's big enough! With half a stomach I could cut my dress size in half. Or maybe I could talk my daughter's orthodontist into wiring my teeth together.

I'm so desperate I'm about to try the craziest diet I've ever heard of. Eat all the starch you want and lose weight. Can you believe that? How gullible do they think I am? Starches are fattening, so I've avoided potatoes and rice my whole life. Can you imagine what I'd look like if I hadn't?

Comments on Carol Van Eck

Carol has tried almost every diet known to science and the paperback-book business, and she's still fat. She will remain fat as long as she fails to understand the strength of her hunger drive, and the low calories and high nutritional value of starches and other vegetables. The diets she has tried are all directed at counteracting the hunger drive.

Whole societies, past and present, have lived on starch-centered diets. Obesity is unknown among these people. What would Carol's physical condition have been if she had been born and raised under such conditions? If we were to think of the enormous problem of obesity that exists in our affluent societies as opposed to that of underdeveloped societies and their dietary practices, we might envision a day when fad diets and fat people would be something you only read about in history books.

Notes

[1]K. Duncan, "The Effects of High and Low Energy Density Diets on Satiety, Energy Intake, and Eating Time of Obese and Nonobese Subjects," *Am J Clin Nutr* 37 (1983): 763.

[2]G. Haber, "Depletion and Disruption of Dietary Fibre, Effects on Satiety, Plasma–Glucose, and Serum–Insulin," *Lancet* 2 (1977): 679.

[3]G. Bray, *Obesity in America*. U.S. Department of Health, Education, and Welfare, NIH pub 79-359, Nov. 1979, p. 12.

[4]A. Simeons, "The Action of Chorionic Gonadotropin in the Obese," *Lancet* 2 (1954): 946.

[5]R. Miller, "A Clinical Study of the Use of Human Chorionic Gonadotropin in Weight Reduction," *J Fam Pract* 4 (1977): 445.

[6]M. Stein, "Ineffectiveness of Human Chorionic Gonadotropin in Weight Reduction: A Double-Blind Study," *Am J Clin Nutr* 29 (1976): 940.

[7]K. Shetty, "Human Chorionic Gonadotropin (HCG), Treatment of Obesity," *Arch Intern Med* 137 (1977): 151.

[8]F. Rickman, "Changes in Serum Cholesterol During the Stillman Diet," *JAMA* 228 (1974): 54.

[9]"A Critique of Low-Carbohydrate Ketogenic Weight Reduction Regimens, a Review of Dr. Atkins' Diet Revolution," statement of American Medical Association Council on Foods and Nutrition, *JAMA* 224 (1973): 1415.

[10]"Liquid Protein and Sudden Cardiac Deaths—An Update," FDA Drug Bulletin, May–July 1978, p. 18.

[11]I. Baird, "Safety of Liquid-Protein Diets," *Lancet* 1 (1979): 618.

[12]Editorial, "Liquid Protein Mayhem," *JAMA* 240 (1978): 144.

[13]Editorial, "Four Questions about Protein Diets," *N Engl J Med* 298 (1978): 1025.

[14]Editorial, "Liquid-Protein Diets and Ventricular Tachycardia," *Lancet* 2 (1978): 976.

[15]"Three Trying "Improved" Crash Diet Mix Land in the Hospital," *Med World News* (Jan. 4, 1982): 61.

[16]"Near Fasting Diet: Revival Alarms Bariatric Doctors," *Med World News* (Nov. 23, 1981): 28.

[17]B. Liebman, "Losing Streak, the Latest Diet Aids Deemed Dangerous to Your Health," *Nutr Action* (Sept 1982): 10.

[18]G. Mann, "Food Intake and Resistance to Disease," *Lancet* 1 (1980): 1238.

[19]M. Murray, "Anorexia of Infection as a Mechanism of Host Defense," *Am J Clin Nutr* 32 (1979): 593.

[20]R. Woo, "Effect of Exercise on Spontaneous Calorie Intake in Obesity," *Am J Clin Nutr* 36 (1982): 470.

[21]Bulletin of the Kempner Foundation, Durham, N.C., 4 (1972): 47.

[22]*Random House Dictionary of the English Language,* unabridged ed. New York: Random House, 1969.

Chapter
4

Red Meat, Poultry, and Fish are Avoided on a Health-Supporting Diet

Developed societies commonly use animal products as their meal's main course and, as a result, suffer from diseases caused by overindulgence in rich foods.

Our evolutionary history clearly shows that humans developed primarily as herbivores (plant eaters), not as carnivores (meat eaters).[1-5] Most of our teeth are flat for grinding grains and vegetables. They are not designed to tear apart raw meat. The residual canine teeth cited by some people to justify eating meat are in no way comparable to the teeth of true carnivores. Our hands are designed for gathering, not for ripping flesh. Our saliva contains alpha-amylase, and the sole purpose of this enzyme is to digest complex carbohydrates found in plant foods. It is not found in the saliva of carnivorous animals. Our intestine is long like that of other herbivores, in order to allow for the time needed to digest the nutrients found in plants. Carnivores have short intestinal tracts that rapidly digest flesh and excrete its remnants. Carnivores also have a great capacity to eliminate the large amounts of cholesterol consumed in their diet. Our liver can only process and excrete a limited amount of cholesterol, which leaves the excess to be deposited in our tissues. Also of interest is the observation that carnivores lap up water and cool their bodies by panting. Like other herbivores, we sip our water and perspire to cool our bodies.

Attempting to live on the wrong kinds of fuel burdens our systems beyond their capacity to maintain health. A return to the foods we are designed to eat provides the body with the natural material that supports health and healing.

A health-supporting diet contains no animal products. To recommend any meat or dairy foods would compromise the basic premise that will be developed in this book, which illustrates how rich foods— heavily processed, high in cholesterol, fat, protein and contaminants and low in carbohydrate, fiber, and potassium—are detrimental to our health. We can compare this to smoking cigarettes. If someone told you that cigarettes were harmful to your health, but that it was all right to smoke a couple of them every day anyhow, you would be receiving contradictory information. You would doubt the sincerity of the message, and you might not see the importance of avoiding the product.

Even though the scientific evidence clearly shows that the consumption of animal products can be detrimental to our health, society places great emphasis on the eating of meat, eggs, and dairy products. For this reason, you may feel strong social pressures against you when you adopt a starch-centered diet. Also, in the beginning, you may miss the taste of animal foods. Do not try to compromise by merely reducing your intake of these products. Your goal is to discard your old eating habits completely and to lose the taste for harmful foods. If you continue to eat animal products, even in small amounts, you may not lose your desire for them. Restricting yourself to "only a little bit" will frustrate you, and eventually you will end up cheating by eating larger portions. This will lead you back to the eating habits that caused your health and weight problems in the first place.

Instead, you must make a decisive change by developing entirely different eating habits. This change will begin with a clear recognition of the foods that benefit your health and encourage your body's healing processes. In general, unprocessed plant products have these characteristics.

Animal foods and their byproducts are easily distinguished from plant products by the average consumer and are therefore easy to avoid. This ease of recognition makes it easy for someone to learn and remember the foods in a health-supporting diet. Most plant foods are health supporting; the foods in this category are starches, vegetables, and fruits. The exceptions to this general rule are the rich plant foods, which fall into three groups:

1. *Refined flours and grains,* such as white rice and white flour.
2. *Unprotected simple sugars,* found in sugar, honey, molasses, corn syrup, fruit juices, and fruit purees.
3. *High fat plant foods,* including coconuts, avocados, olives, nuts, seeds, soybeans, tofu, wheat germ, and vegetable oils.

Although a diet consisting of only starches, vegetables, and fruits may seem strange at first, you will soon develop a definite preference for the taste of these foods. Before long you may actually find the appearance and smell of animal foods to be offensive. Thousands of people before you have experienced this change in taste. Do not be discouraged during the initial difficult period of changeover, and do not compromise your decision to follow the basic principles. Excellent health and an increased ability to function in your daily activities will be your rewards.

When you avoid all animal products you may need to add a source of vitamin B_{12} to your diet. B_{12} is necessary for your nervous system and blood. Without adequate amounts of this vitamin in the body, anemia and degeneration of the nerves can occur. Most cases of B_{12} deficiency seen by doctors are not caused by lack of this vitamin in the diet, but rather by the inability of the intestine to absorb the B_{12} that is present in the foods consumed. This occurs when the stomach or the small intestine is removed or diseased.[6] However, very rare cases of B_{12} deficiency have been attributed to all-vegetable diets that lack concentrated animal sources of B_{12}.[7-18]

Vitamin B_{12} is produced only by microorganisms such as bacteria and algae, not by plants or animals. The original source of the B_{12} needed by all animals is the microorganisms found naturally in their mouths and intestines and mixed with their food. Animals that eat other animals take in B_{12} that is present in the flesh. Bacteria found on plants provide an additional small dietary contribution.

Our daily requirement of B_{12} is less than one-millionth of a gram.[19-20] For most people, this amount can be supplied easily by the millions of helpful microbes found in our mouths and intestinal tracts.[21] Among westerners vitamin B_{12} stores in the human body exceed the daily requirement by 1,000-fold. Since the body accumulates at least a three-to-eight-year supply of this vitamin, intake can occur sporadically without the risk of developing a deficiency. When any B_{12} is present in the diet, large quantities are absorbed efficiently. Taking vitamin C supplements and smoking may increase the need for vitamin B_{12}.[22-24]

Fewer than thirty cases of B_{12} deficiency attributed to vegetarian diets have been described in the medical literature, and most of these may actually be the result of unrecognized disease of the small intestine and stomach.[12-18,25-28] This problem is seen so rarely that when a single case is found it receives national publicity in the lay press and medical journals.

If you wonder why any deficiency might be present in a diet that seems so well suited for our nutritional needs in all other ways, one explanation is that until recently our natural living conditions allowed for a large consumption of microorganisms.[29] Since the discovery of the disease-producing capacity of germs by Louis Pasteur during the late 1800s, we have been trying to eradicate microorganisms from our environment by thoroughly washing our foods, cooking utensils, and hands. Antiseptics, antibiotics, and ultraviolet light treatments have been used in attempts to sterilize our surroundings. Unfortunately, many helpful and necessary microbes have also been removed, and this naturally occurring B_{12} source has been reduced to a level where, on a very rare occasion, a person might develop a B_{12} deficiency.

To avoid the unlikely possibility of B_{12} deficiency, we recommend the addition of a nonanimal source of B_{12} in certain situations. Fermented soybean products such as tempeh (1.5–14.8 mcg per 100 g), natto, miso (0.17 mcg per 100 g, low levels), some soyu–tamari sauces (0–10 mcg per 100 g), microorganisms such as algae (plankton-spirulina, 160 mcg per 100 g, chlorella, scenedesmus), nutritional yeast fortified with B_{12} (50 mcg per 100 g), and sea vegetables such as kombu and wakame (0–29 mcg per 100 g) can be excellent sources. The B_{12}-containing plant foods listed here may be unfamiliar to you when you are beginning to learn about healthier foods. A short time spent in a well-stocked natural food store will quickly orient you to these interesting food supplements. Don't be in a big rush; you have at least three years of consuming an all-plant diet before your body store of B_{12} is in any jeopardy. Foods high in B_{12} should be added to your diet if you have consumed plant foods exclusively for more than three years or if you're pregnant or nursing a child. Five micrograms per day is more than adequate to prevent deficiency.

Do not use vitamin pills to supply your requirements. These pills contain breakdown products of B_{12}, which have an anti-B_{12} effect and can cause B_{12} deficiency, even when adequate amounts of this vitamin are present in your diet and stored in your body.[30-31]

The danger of including animal products in your diet on a regular basis far outweighs the danger of omitting them. Your B_{12} needs are small and easily met without resorting to those harmful foods. The concern over B_{12} deficiency is the only argument against an all-vegetable diet that has significant scientific merit and deserves our concern. Understanding the facts surrounding this issue will allow you to choose a health-supporting diet and to answer those people who insist on the inclusion of animal products in your diet.

The assorted kinds of meat, poultry, fish, and shellfish that we eat are the muscles or "flesh" of animals. They are high in protein and/or fat and contain essentially no carbohydrates, fiber, or vitamin C. Flesh also tends to be higher in sodium content and lower in potassium than plant foods and is a very poor source of calcium.

Because flesh is high on the food chain, it often contains unacceptable levels of environmental contaminants. All over the world, poisonous chemicals are buried in the ground or dumped in lakes, rivers, and the sea. Pesticides and herbicides are used in growing food crops and accumulate in the soil. Growing plants absorb small amounts of these chemicals. Because they are highly attracted to and absorbed by fat, these chemicals are called fat-soluble. When animals and fish eat plants containing even low levels of contaminants, these chemicals are concentrated in the fatty tissues of their bodies. If we consume the flesh of these polluted creatures, we take in large amounts of potentially harmful substances.[32-33] (See Figure 4.1)

Animal flesh is further contaminated by the wide variety of drugs used in livestock yards. These drugs include hormones, stimulants, and antibiotics. They are used to speed animal growth and to combat the infectious diseases commonly found in such crowded conditions. When we eat meat and poultry grown under such circumstances, we consume an assortment of powerful animal drugs.[34-35] Poultry and beef "organically grown" should be less contaminated than the supermarket varieties of these products.

In 1979 a thorough government study focused on the contamination of animal products. The Government Accounting Office reported to Congress that "14 percent by dressed weight of the meat and poultry sampled by the Department of Agriculture between 1974 and 1976 contained illegal and potentially harmful residues of animal drugs, pesticides, or environmental contaminants. Many of these substances are known to cause or are suspected of causing cancer, birth defects, or other toxic effects".[35]

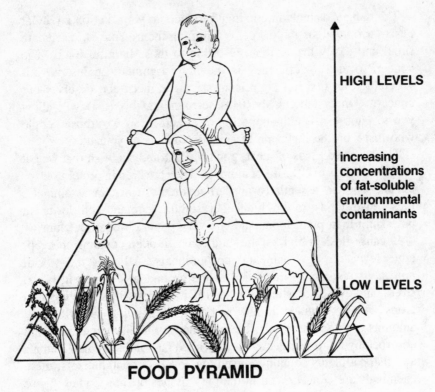

HIGH LEVELS

increasing
concentrations
of fat-soluble
environmental
contaminants

LOW LEVELS

FOOD PYRAMID

Figure 4.1

Fish and seafood in the diet can be just as harmful as the other kinds of animal flesh. Both commonly cause food allergies. In many parts of the world, fish and shellfish are so heavily contaminated that they cannot be sold legally.[32] Fish provide excessive amounts of protein, and some fish are also high in fat. The cholesterol contents of fish, meat, and poultry are about equal, and each causes a similar rise in the cholesterol level measured in the blood.[36-37] Shellfish, such as clams, crab, shrimp, and lobster, are low in fat but very high in protein and sterols similar to cholesterol. To their credit, the sterols found in shellfish are poorly absorbed into our bodies.[38] An additional risk from eating fish and shellfish comes from naturally occurring and sometimes lethal toxins found in the flesh, which can result in poisoning (paralytic shellfish poison, ciguatera, tetradotoxin, and scombroid).[39]

Because humans are animals and have biochemical systems similar to those of other animals, bacteria, parasites, and viruses that infect animals can also cause serious human disease. These harmful microorganisms are found in the animal flesh, and the infectious agents include salmonella bacteria, trichinella and other worms, toxoplasmosis parasites, hepatitis viruses, and cancer viruses.[40-44] Staphylococcus food poisoning, which accounts for 20 to 40 percent of the foodborn illnesses, is caused by toxins produced by staphylococcus aureus bacteria during their growth in foods that are mostly of animal origin.[45] Fresh plant foods, which are very different from us in their biochemical makeup, do not contain microorganisms harmful to humans unless they are contaminated with products or excretions from diseased animals or people. The infectivity of disease producing organisms found in food is decreased by thorough cooking.

When meat is cooked over high heat, chemical changes occur that can form carcinogens.[46-48] It is especially harmful to cook flesh over a charcoal fire. A one-pound steak broiled over charcoal can contain as much benzopyrene as 600 cigarettes.[47] Benzopyrene is a powerful carcinogen used since the 1940s to cause lymphomas, thymomas, stomach cancer, and leukemia in laboratory animals.[49-50] Many other carcinogens are also produced when flesh is heated by other methods and at lower temperatures.[46-48]

Approximately 4,000 healthy individuals in the United States strangle each year because of food stuck in their throats.[51] This problem is referred to as "café coronary," because the event is often confused with a person having a heart attack. Pork, beef, chicken, and other flesh foods are commonly found obstructing the person's airway because they are difficult to chew into small, easy-to-swallow pieces. The consistency of vegetable foods, especially after chewing, offers little risk for this type of accident.

The smell of the breath, sweat, urine, and stool are affected by the foods we eat.[52] Nearly everyone has recognized the odors that are produced when we eat onions, garlic, asparagus, and vitamin pills. People who consume flesh often have secretions and excretions that smell badly from the decay in the intestine.

Recently many Americans have given up eating red meat in favor of chicken and fish, in the quest for better health and more civilized eating. One very important result of this dietary trend is the effect on a person's attitudes toward food. Many people have adjusted to their new dietary changes comfortably, and they have learned that modifying eating habits is both possible and easy. The next step in changing our affluent lifestyle will come when we realize that even chicken and fish are delicacies and do not belong in a health-supporting diet.

When all animal products are removed from the diet, people again will adjust quickly to the change and will enjoy the dramatic improvement in their health.

John Cross—Successful Public Accountant

What am I going to do now? More important, how will my wife and children get along when I die? Sitting here alone in a hospital room leaves me plenty of time to worry about my future and theirs. This is my second heart attack in two years, and my doctor tells me I'll never survive another. There just isn't enough heart muscle left.

My company is finally on its feet, and we're paying our bills on time after so many years of struggling and juggling. Forty-three years old is just too young to be falling apart, even though I've seen it coming. My blood pressure and weight have been going up steadily for the past five years, and the pills I take only cause other problems.

It must be hereditary. Dad died of his first heart attack at forty-five. At least I've had some warning. But for what? I can't figure out anything I'm doing wrong. I've never smoked and I drink only at parties. After my first heart attack I started jogging, which helped me take off 10 pounds. My wife Molly takes a lot of trouble to serve well-balanced meals to the family. I know I get enough protein and calcium with the chicken, fish, and milk she makes sure to give us. We have taken the advice of the hospital dietitian and cut down on salt and switched to margarine.

If it's hereditary, what about Grandpa? He's got to be eighty-one, but he still works all day and has no trouble keeping up with his third wife, who's twenty-five years younger. He really doesn't take as good care of himself as I do. Grandpa was born and raised just north of the Mexican border. You'd never guess he's a gringo because all he eats are mounds of rice and beans with vegetables. You'd have to look pretty hard to find even a piece of chicken or fish on his plate. He looks terrific, but he must have some sort of protein or calcium deficiency. I used to worry about him a lot, and I've tried to make him drink milk, but it just makes him sick. He won't touch the hamburgers Molly tried making for him. He sure doesn't know what he's missing. If I could only be as lucky with my health as he is.

I feel cheated. I want to see my kids grow up. My wife and I had so many plans. . . .

Comments on John Cross

John is a victim of inaccurate and inadequate information and of being taught from infancy to like rich meals. He learned about the "four basic food groups," and his mother saw to it that he drank a quart of milk a day, ate at least one egg for breakfast, and had meat or fish for dinner every night. He never realized the "basic four" posters were advertisements designed to sell products, and his mother never knew the foundation she was laying would condemn him to a short lifetime of illness.[53]

Many doctors and lay persons look to heredity to blame problems on when no other explanation is acceptable to them. This is a dead-end path since we cannot alter this situation. Furthermore, the most widely accepted theory today is that a high-fat, high-cholesterol, high-salt diet is a primary element in the cause of heart disease, high blood pressure, and obesity. Environmental elements that cause disease also promote disease. If we change the things that cause our illnesses, the relentless progression to premature death will stop, and even better, there is a chance for improvement.

During World War II many people in Western Europe with established heart disease (coronary artery disease) had to switch from a rich diet high in dairy and meats to a diet of grains and vegetables. The death rate in these countries from heart disease dropped dramatically during this forced dietary change.[54] Many studies have demonstrated that a decrease in death rate from heart disease can result from a change to a low-fat, low-cholesterol diet.[55]

Even if John were lucky enough to learn of his option of a diet and lifestyle change, he would still face two most difficult tasks— changing his taste preferences for rich foods and living in a society that is convinced that meat, eggs, butter, and milk mean good nutrition and good health. He would be hard put, as a guest at friends' homes or in a restaurant, to find any sign of Grandpa's kind of diet. However, if he were to change his eating pattern, he'd find it takes only about a month to adjust comfortably to a new diet. Furthermore, if he does learn to care for himself better he will be bequeathing to his wife and children something far more valuable than wealth: a true understanding of good nutrition and the gift of good health and a long life.

Notes

[1]W. Collens, "Phylogenetic Aspects of the Cause of Human Atherosclerotic Disease," *Circulation* (supp II) 31-32 (1965): II-7.

[2]C. Prosser, *Comparative Animal Physiology,* 2nd ed. Philadelphia: W. B. Saunders, 1961, p. 116.

[3]E. Nasset, *Movements of the small intestine.* P. Bard, *Medical Physiology,* 11 ed. C. V. Mosby, 1961, St. Louis, p. 440.

[4]J. Dietschy, "Regulation of Cholesterol Metabolism, (third of three parts)" *N Engl J Med* 282 (1970): 1241.

[5]*What's Wrong with Eating Meat?* Ananda Marga Publications, 1977.

[6]V. Herbert, "The Five Possible Causes of All Nutrient Deficiency, Illustrated by Deficiencies of Vitamin B_{12} and Folic Acid," *Am J of Clin Nutr* 26 (1973): 77.

[7]J. Hines, "Megaloblastic Anemia in an Adult Vegan," *Am J of Clin Nutr* 19 (1966): 260.

[8]E. West, "The Electroencephalogram in Veganism, Vegetariansim, Vitamin B_{12} Deficiency, and in Controls," *J Neurol Neurosurg Psychiatry* 29 (1966): 391.

[9]P. Connor, "Nutritional Vitamin B_{12} Deficiency," *Med J of Aust* 2 (1963): 451.

[10]R. Ledbetter, "Severe Megaloblastic Anemia Due to Nutritional B_{12} Deficiency," *Acta Haemat* 42 (1969): 247.

[11]R. Carmel, "Nutritional Vitamin B_{12} Deficiency, Possible Contributory Role of Subtle Vitamin B_{12} Malabsorption," *Ann Intern Med* 88 (1978): 647.

[12]M. Murphy, "Vitamin B_{12} Deficiency Due to a Low-Cholesterol Diet in a Vegetarian," *Ann Intern Med* 94 (1981): 57.

[13]M. Higginbottom, "A Syndrome of Methylmalonic Aciduria, Homocystinuria, Megaloblastic Anemia, and Neurological Abnormalities in a Vitamin B_{12} Deficient Breast-Fed Infant of a Strict Vegetarian," *N Engl J Med* 299 (1978): 317.

[14]D. Shun, "Nutritional Megaloblastic Anemia in Vegan," *N Y State J of Med* 2(1972): 2893.

[15]H. Misra, "Subacute Combined Degeneration of the Spinal Cord in a Vegan," *Postgrad Med J* 47 (1971): 624.

[16]S. Winawer, "Gastric and Hematological Abnormalities in a Vegan with Nutritional B_{12} Deficiency: Effects of Oral Vitamin B_{12}," *Gastroenterology* 53 (1967): 130.

[17]M. Gleeson, "Complications of Dietary Deficiency of Vitamin B_{12} in Young Caucasians," *Postgrad Med J* 50 (1974): 462.

[18]J. Stewart, "Response of Dietary Vitamin B_{12} Deficiency to Physiological Oral Doses of Cyanocobalamin," *Lancet* 2 (1970): 542.

[19]R. Heyssel, "Vitamin B_{12} Turnover in Man," *Am J of Clin Nutr* 18 (1966): 176.

[20]S. Baker, "Evidence Regarding the Minimal Daily Requirement of Dietary Vitamin B_{12}," *Am J Clin Nutr* 34 (1981): 2423.

[21]M. Albert, "Vitamin B_{12} Synthesis by Human Small Intestinal Bacteria," *Nature* 283 (1980): 781.

[22] H. HogenKamp, Editorial, "The Interaction Between Vitamin B$_{12}$ and Vitamin C," *Am J Clin Nutr* 33 (1980): 1.

[23] J. Linnell, "Effects of Smoking on Metabolism and Excretion of Vitamin B$_{12}$," *Br. Med J* 2 (1968): 215.

[24] A. Smith, "Veganism: A Clinical Survey with Observations of Vitamin B$_{12}$ Metabolism," *Br Med J* 1 (1962): 1655.

[25] A. Immerman, "Vitamin B$_{12}$ Status of a Vegetarian Diet—A Critical Review," *Wld Rev Nutr Diet* 37 (1981): 38.

[26] R. Britt, "Megaloblastic Anemia among Indians in Britain," *Quart J Med* 40 (1971): 499.

[27] H. Grant, "Folate Deficiency and Neurological Disease," *Lancet* 2 (1965): 763.

[28] P. Godt, "Vitamin B$_{12}$ Deficiency Due to Psychotic-Induced Malnutrition," letter, *Lancet* 2 (1976): 1087.

[29] J. Halsted, "Serum Vitamin B$_{12}$ Concentration in Dietary Deficiency," *Am J Clin Nutr* 8 (1960): 374.

[30] V. Herbert, "Multivitamin/Mineral Food Supplements Containing Vitamin B$_{12}$ May Also Contain Analogues of Vitamin B$_{12}$," letter, *N Engl J Med* 307 (1982): 255.

[31] "Harmful B$_{12}$ Breakdown Products in Multivitamins?" *Med World News* (Sept. 28, 1981): 12.

[32] H. Roberts, *Food Safety*, New York: Wiley Interscience, 1981, pp. 141–180.

[33] M. Lippmann, *Chemical Contamination of the Human Environment*, Oxford: Oxford University Press, 1979, pp. 146–151.

[34] H. Mussman, "Drug and Chemical Residues in Domestic Animals," *Fed Proc* 34 (1975): 197.

[35] Comptroller General of the United States, report to Congress, Problems in Preventing the Marketing of Raw Meat and Poultry Containing Potentially Harmful Residues," Government Documents Collection, GA 1.13, HRD 79-10, April 17, 1979.

[36] B. O'Brien, "Human Plasma Lipid Responses to Red Meat, Poultry, Fish, and Eggs," *Am J Clin Nutr* 33 (1980): 2573.

[37] M. Flynn, "Dietary "Meats" and Serum Lipids," *Am J Clin Nutr* 35 (1982): 935.

[38] G. Vahouny, "Lymphatic Absorption of Shellfish Sterols and Their Effects on Cholesterol Absorption," *Am J Clin Nutr* 34 (1981): 507.

[39] H. Roberts, *Food Safety*, New York: Wiley Interscience, 1981, pp. 215–221.

[40] J. Grace, "Relationship of Viruses to Malignant Diseases," *Arch Intern Med* 105 (1960): 172/482.

[41] Committee on Salmonella, Division of Biology and Agriculture, National Research Council, "An Evaluation of the Salmonella Problem," Washington, D.C.: National Academy of Science, 1969.

[42] Centers for Disease Control, "Trichinosis Surveillance Annual Summary 1980, November 1981.

[43] D. Krogstad, "Toxoplasmosis with Comments on Risk of Infection from Cats, *Ann Intern Med* 77 (1972): 773.

[44] W. Dougherty, "Viral Hepatitis in New Jersey 1960–1961," *Am J Med* 32 (1962): 704.

[45] H. Roberts, *Food Safety*, New York: Wiley Interscience, 1981, p. 28.

[46]B. Commoner, "Formation of Mutagens in Beef and Beef Extract During Cooking," *Science* 201 (1978): 913.

[47]W. Lijinsky, "Benzo(a)pyrene and Other Polynuclear Hydrocarbons in Charcoal Broiled Meat," *Science* 145 (1964): 53.

[48]J. Gray, "Some Toxic Compounds Produced in Food by Cooking and Processing," *J of Hum Nutr* 35 (1981): 5.

[49]R. Rigdon, "Leukemia in Mice Fed Benzo(a)pyrene," *Texas Rep Biol Med* 25 (1967): 422.

[50]R. Rigdon, "Gastric Carcinomas and Pulmonary Adenomas in Mice Fed Benzo(a)pyrene," *Texas Rep Biol Med* 24 (1966): 195.

[51]H. Heimlich, "A Life-Saving Maneuver to Prevent Food-Choking," *JAMA* 234 (1975): 398.

[52]M. Smith, "The Use of Smell in Differential Diagnosis," *Lancet* 2 (1982): 1452.

[53]S. Harty, *Hucksters in the Classroom—A Review of Industry Propaganda in Schools*, Washington, D.C.: Center for the Study of Responsive Law, 1979, p. 25.

[54]A. Strom, "Mortality from Circulatory Diseases in Norway 1940–1945," *Lancet* 1 (1951): 126.

[55]J. Stamler, "Lifestyles, Major Risk Factors, Proof and Public Policy," *Circulation* 58 (1978): 3.

Chapter

5

Dairy Products and Eggs Are Avoided on a Health-Supporting Diet

Dairy Products

Dairy products have assumed a prominent position in the diets of affluent societies. The basic dairy product, whole cow's milk, is the food ideally designed for the nutritional needs of calves. This product is high in fat, protein and cholesterol and low in carbohydrates, and it contains no fiber. Products derived from whole milk include butter, cheese, cottage cheese, yogurt, buttermilk, skim milk, kefir, ice cream, whey, "imitation milk," and cow-milk based infant formulas.

Because dairy products and meat have so many similarities in their macronutrient content, dairy foods can be thought of as "liquid meat." (See Table 5.1.)

Like meats, dairy products are rich foods. The heavy consumption of these foods will result in the diseases common to affluent societies.

Dairy products are the leading cause of food allergies. They contain more than twenty-five different proteins that may induce allergic reactions in humans.[1] These reactions include the following.

- *Gastrointestinal*—canker sores (aphthous stomatitis), vomiting, colic, stomach cramps, abdominal distention, intestinal obstruction, bloody stools, colitis, malabsorption, loss of appetite, growth retardation, diarrhea, constipation, painful defecation, irritation of tongue, lips, and mouth.

49

THE McDOUGALL PLAN

Table 5.1. MACRONUTRIENTS

	Ground Chuck Beef	Cheddar Cheese	Yogurt	Whole Milk
calories as fat	68%	73%	49%	49%
calories as protein	32%	25%	19%	21%
calories as carbohydrates	0%	2%	32%	30%
fiber (grams)	0	0	0	0
cholesterol (milligrams per 100 calories)	22	27	21	22

- *Respiratory*—nasal stuffiness, runny nose, otitis media (inner ear trouble), sinusitis, asthma, pulmonary infiltrates.
- *Skin*—rashes, atopic dermatitis, eczema, seborrhea, hives.
- *Behavioral*—irritability, restlessness, hyperactivity, headache, lethargy, fatigue, allergic-tension fatigue syndrome, muscle pain, mental depression, enuresis (bed wetting, often caused when the bladder tissues become swollen and insensitive to the feeling of fullness).
- *Blood*—abnormal blood clotting, iron deficiency anemia (dairy products are the cause of at least 50 percent of childhood iron deficiency anemia and an unknown percentage of anemia found in adults; this condition results from bleeding of the small intestine caused by dairy proteins and is not responsive to iron therapy until milk and other dairy foods are eliminated), low-serum proteins, thrombocytopenia (low platelets), and eosinophilia (allergy-related blood cells).
- *Other*—anaphylactic shock and death, sudden infant death syndrome (crib or cot death).[1-8]

Several nonallergic but serious adverse reactions are also caused by dairy products. They include congestive heart failure in infants, neonatal tetany from low blood calcium levels caused by the high phosphate levels in cow's milk, tonsil enlargement, obesity, and the aggravation of ulcerative colitis.[9-16] Removal of dairy products has resulted in dramatic improvement in cases of ulcerative colitis and also in the shrinkage of enlarged tonsils and adenoids.[11-15] Dairy foods have also been implicated in the development of a cancer of the immune system called Hodgkin's disease.[17] Continuous overstimulation of the immune system by dairy proteins may eventually lead to the breakdown of the immune system into this form of cancer.

Breast-fed babies can get colic and other milk-related food allergies if the mother consumes dairy products.[18-21] Colic is a common allergic reaction infants have to the proteins found in cow's milk. When the mother eats dairy products, these proteins pass into her breast milk and eventually end up in the baby's intestine and blood. They give the baby stomach cramps, which cause persistent fussing and crying. Next to dairy proteins, eggs are the most common cause of allergic problems in breast-fed infants.[21,22] Many other types of allergic reactions caused by a variety of foods can be passed to the infant through the mother's milk.[21]

After the age of four years, most people naturally lose the ability to digest the carbohydrate known as lactose found in milk, because they no longer synthesize the digestive enzyme, lactase, which lines the small intestine. This condition, known as lactose intolerance, results in symptoms of diarrhea, gas, and stomach cramps when lactose-containing dairy products are eaten. Lactose intolerance is especially common among adult blacks and Asians, occurring in as many as 90 percent of these people.[23-25] Cheese is one dairy product that is low in lactose. Only 2 percent of the calories are lactose, and cheese causes few problems with those who have lactose intolerance.

Dairy products are high on the food chain and therefore may contain unsafe levels of environmental contaminants.[26] Even human mother's breast milk can contain dangerous amounts of these substances.[27,28] An infant, being at the top of the food chain, gets the highest levels of these environmental chemicals. The Environmental Defense Fund studied the breast milk of 1,400 women from forty-six states. This study found widespread contamination of breast milk with pesticides. The levels of contamination were twice as high in meat and dairy-consuming women as in vegetarians. Because pesticides are concentrated in animal foods, the study advised "women who expect to breast feed their babies to avoid meat, some kinds of fish, and high-fat dairy products."[28]

Antibiotics are commonly used on dairy farms to treat cows for such conditions as mastitis, an infection of the cow's udder. Contamination of milk with these drugs can be serious because many people are allergic—some severely and dangerously—to even low levels of antibiotics, such as pencillin. It is even possible for people without a known allergy to antibiotics to develop a sensitivity upon drinking contaminated cow's milk.[29-32]

Dairy products also can be contaminated with disease-causing bacteria such as salmonella, staphylococci, and E. coli, and with viruses that may cause leukemia.[33-35] Leukemia viruses are found in more than 20 percent of dairy cows. Sheep, goats, and chimpanzees fed cow's milk can become infected and develop leukemia.[35,36] There is serious concern that these viruses may be passed to humans. Staphylococcal food poisoning occurs most commonly with nonfat dry milk, cheese, and butter. People who consume "raw" dairy products run the highest risk of acquiring infectious diseases. Pasteurization reduces infectivity from microorganisms.

The dairy industry, in conjunction with the many nutritionists who believe in the healthful benefits of dairy foods, dwell on three issues to promote these products: calcium, vitamin D, and fat content.

The dairy industry attempts to sell us products based on our need for calcium, yet most people in the world have diets that contain no dairy products at all. In preindustrial Asian and African societies where milk is rarely consumed, the people have strong bones and sturdy teeth and escape diseases common to people in rich societies. The African Bantu woman provides an excellent example of good health. Her diet is free of milk and still provides 250 to 400 mg of calcium per day from vegetable sources, which is one-half the amount consumed by western women. Bantu women commonly have ten babies during their lifetimes and breast feed each of them for about ten months. But, even with this tremendous calcium drain and relatively low calcium intake, osteoporosis (thin, fragile bones) is essentially unknown among these women.[37-38] It is interesting to note, when relatives of these same people migrate to the affluent societies and adopt rich diets, osteoporosis and diseases of the teeth become common.[39]

Many people worry that a diet without dairy products will lead to disease. The amount of calcium present in the diet has little effect on the quantity of calcium that is eventually taken into the body.[40-41] The intestine absorbs from the foods consumed sufficient calcium to meet the needs of the body. On low-calcium diets, the efficiency of absorption is increased, and on high-calcium diets less absorption occurs.[42] Unprocessed vegetable foods contain sufficient calcium to meet the needs of adults and growing children. In fact, calcium deficiency caused by an insufficient amount of calcium in the diet is not known to occur in humans, even though most people in the world

don't drink milk after weaning because of custom, lactose intolerance, or unavailability.[40,41,43] Consider this the next time you hear
the dairy industry's favorite advertising pitch about the necessity of
drinking milk to meet calcium needs.

Combinations of dairy products and antacids (the Sippy diet) have
been recommended for more than seventy years to treat peptic ulcer
disease. However, studies have shown no improvement in ulcer
healing from milk products and some very serious drawbacks.[44] Acid
production by the stomach is one of the primary elements in the cause
and promotion of ulcer disease. As surprising as it may seem,
stomach acid production is actually increased when milk is fed to
ulcer and nonulcer patients.[44] British and American patients treated
for ulcer disease with dairy products developed two to six times the
number of heart attacks at the end of one year as those treated without
dairy foods.[45] The saturated fats and cholesterol present in milk were
the most important factors in causing those results. Another serious
and potentially life threatening illness, called milk–alkali syndrome,
can result from the ingestion of the high concentrations of calcium
found in dairy foods along with antacids. The result is high blood
calcium levels, an alkaline system (alkalosis), and injury to the
kidneys.[46]

High-calcium diets have also been implicated by some investigators as a cause of calcium kidney stones. People who suffer from
these stones are taken off dairy products as part of their treatment in
hopes of preventing recurrences.[47]

The dairy industry has added supplemental vitamin D to milk,
supposedly to protect people from developing rickets. Rickets is a
disorder characterized by painful and deformed bones. This disease is
common in places where there is limited exposure to sunlight.

To begin with, vitamin D is actually not a vitamin because the body
can and does under most circumstances synthesize all that it needs.
Vitamin D is really a hormone synthesized by the action of sunlight
on plant sterols found in the skin. Our body levels of vitamin D are
only slightly affected by dietary sources such as milk fortified with
vitamin D and vitamin pills.[48-52]

Because vitamin D is fat-soluble, this hormone can be stored in our
body fat for long periods of time. Therefore, intermittent exposure to
sunlight is adequate. The amount of sunlight we receive during
summer holidays is reflected all year long in our vitamin D levels.[48-52]
Our minimum requirement for sunlight is small and easily met by
most people in their daily activities.[53] Dark-skinned people such as

blacks and Asians require more exposure than light-skinned Caucasians, because the skin pigment blocks out part of the light.[54] Exposure to sunlight is unquestionably an essential part of a health-supporting lifestyle.

In response to concerns about animal fat and the relation to heart disease, the dairy industry has promoted the use of skim milk and other low-fat dairy products. However, when the fat is skimmed from the milk, the relative proportion of protein and lactose are increased. (See Table 5.2.) The proteins and lactose in milk are the ingredients that cause many of the health problems associated with dairy products, in particular food allergies and lactose intolerance. Low-fat products suffer from the same nutritional inadequacies as their whole-fat counterparts: complete lack of dietary fiber and deficiencies of vitamins and minerals. Therefore, skim milk and other low-fat dairy products are unacceptable in a health-supporting diet.

Infants who are fed whole cow's milk or skim milk as a large part of their diet can develop a nervous system susceptible to disease later on in life. The tissues of the nervous system require adequate amounts of the essential vegetable fat, linoleic acid, for proper growth.[55-56] Whole cow's milk contains only one-fifth of the amount of linoleic acid that is present in human mother's milk, and skim milk has had all of the linoleic acid removed with the fat.[10] A person with a poorly developed nervous system may run the risk of someday suffering from a degenerative disease known as multiple sclerosis later on in life. This disease most frequently appears in young adults. A person with multiple sclerosis suffers from repeated attacks that damage the brain, spinal cord, and nerves. An attack can cause blindness one time, paralysis or loss of sensation the next. Multiple sclerosis is more commonly found in areas of the world where infants and children are raised on dairy products rather than on breast milk and vegetable foods.[56,57] Based on these observations, a low animal fat dietary treatment has been developed and used at the University of Oregon by Roy Swank M.D. Over the past thirty years this diet has produced dramatic benefits for hundreds of people with multiple sclerosis.[58] Without benefit of Dr. Swank's diet, progressive deterioration, disability, and frequently death are the usual course of this disease. People who are started early in their disease on a low animal fat diet have nearly a 95 percent chance of remaining the same or improving over the next twenty years.[58]

Table 5.2. Skimming of Whole Milk to Decrease the Fat Content Increases the Relative Amount of Protein and Lactose in the Fat-Reduced Products

CHO = carbohydrate. The carbohydrate in milk is lactose.

	Whole Milk (3.5%)	Low-fat Milk (2%)	Skim Milk
*fat**	49%	31%	2%
*protein**	21%	28%	41%
*CHO**	30%	41%	57%

(*expressed as % of calories)

One more interesting bit of folklore about dairy products surrounds the health benefits of yogurt and acidophilus milk. The idea is that partial or complete replacement of the gram-negative bacterial flora of the intestine with a lactobacillus variety used in the culturing of these two dairy products results in robust health. This idea dates back to the turn of the twentieth century. However, the variety of lactobacillus used to make yogurt (*L. bulgaricus)* will not grow in the human intestine. The variety used to culture acidophilus milk *(L. acidophilus)* fails to grow in the small intestine of humans where beneficial activity would be expected to take place.[59]

Scientific evidence clearly shows that dairy products cause serious health problems for both children and adults. However, most people in our society, including groups oriented to "health foods," believe that dairy foods are good for us. This is primarily the result of a successful advertising campaign by the dairy industry. In the face of scientific fact and common logic, they have convinced most of us that calves' food is essential for good human nutrition.

Because we have been brought up believing that milk is "nature's most perfect food," most of us will have difficulty overcoming this conditioning. This will be particularly hard when emotional issues are invoked, such as the dietary needs of pregnant women and young children. In addition to the scientific and medical evidence against dairy products, we can observe the way milk is used by other animals. No other animal in its natural environment drinks milk after it is weaned. Furthermore, in nature no young animal drinks the milk of another species.

Cow's milk fails to provide adequate amounts of fiber, linoleic acid, iron, and vitamins niacin and C to meet the nutritional needs of adults and children. The few nutrients provided by dairy foods are better obtained from vegetable sources. If you add any dairy products to your health-supporting diet, they will detract from its nutritional quality.

Eggs

Egg products are commonly but incorrectly classified as dairy products. An egg is the ovum of a bird and in most circumstances is eaten in an unfertilized condition. Fertilization, however, does not appreciably change the nutritional properties of an egg. Eggs are high in protein and fat and contain very little carbohydrate and essentially no fiber or vitamin C. Of the foods commonly consumed in a rich diet, eggs contain one of the highest concentrations of cholesterol. The egg industry has provided the financial support for numerous studies designed to show that the cholesterol in eggs will neither raise the cholesterol level of the blood nor cause atherosclerosis and heart attacks.[60-64] Of the six studies in the medical literature that fail to demonstrate a significant rise in blood cholesterol level with the consumption of whole eggs, three were paid for by the American Egg Board, one by the Missouri Egg Merchandising Council, and one by the Egg Program of the California Department of Agriculture. Support for the sixth paper was not identified.[65]

The trick is in knowing how to design your experiment so you will get the results you are looking for. To get little or no increase in cholesterol levels, you first saturate your subjects with cholesterol from other sources, because studies show that once people consume more than 400 to 800 milligrams of cholesterol per day, additional cholesterol has only a minor effect on blood cholesterol levels.[66-67] Study designs can also use improper control subjects and inadequate time periods for the ingested cholesterol to show effects in the blood. Well-designed studies by investigators independent of the food industry clearly demonstrate the detrimental effects of eggs on blood cholesterol levels.[68-71] The egg industry provides a timely example of how money can buy scientific nutritional information that can be detrimental to our health.

Eggs have been promoted for their perfect pattern of essential amino acids found in the protein. However, when volunteer subjects were fed different foods to determine the ability of humans to utilize various protein mixtures, investigators found that our bodies can utilize the amino acids in a mixture of potatoes and eggs 36 percent more efficiently than those from eggs alone.[72] Others have also questioned the value of egg protein as the ideal standard for meeting the nutritional needs of humans.[73-74]

Separating the egg white from the yolk separates the protein that is concentrated in the white from the fat and cholesterol concentrated in the yolk. (See Table 5.3.)

Table 5.3.

	Whole egg	Egg white	Egg yolk
Protein	33%	85%	19%
Fat	65%	7%	80%
Carbohydrate	2%	8%	1%
Fiber	0	0	0
Cholesterol (per egg)	264 mg	0	264 mg

Egg protein is a leading cause of food allergy. Furthermore, the fatty part of eggs accumulate environmental contaminants since eggs are high on the food chain. Like other animal products, they also can contain microorganisms that cause human disease.

The nutritional makeup of an egg varies little among those from chickens, geese, turkeys, and turtles.

Many egg substitutes are made by a variety of processes that lower the fat and often the cholesterol content. However, the relative protein content increases after the processing.

Like other animal products, eggs should be considered as delicacies to be consumed only on special occasions by sturdy individuals in excellent health. Of course, anyone who is trying to recover from an illness caused by overindulgence in rich food should avoid all delicacies until full health is regained.

Mary Taylor—Former Follower of Kelsey The Cow

This is my fourth pregnancy, and what a difference good eating makes. My weight is only up 15 pounds, and I'm due next month. The other times I gained much more. I'm doing a lot better on this new meal plan. I can tell by the way I feel. I used to swell up like a balloon, but now my rings even fit. No constipation this time, and I have a lot more energy.

Just the same, I worry. Maybe I'm not getting enough protein and calcium for my baby. You know the old saying, "A tooth lost for each baby." My obstetrician tells me to drink four glasses of milk a day and to eat plenty of meat. It's very hard to ignore his advice even though I've learned that most doctors have had little, if any, training in nutrition.

I guess what convinced me was reading about the pesticides and drugs found in meat and especially the frequent contamination of cow's milk. The problem is so serious that our local mother's milk bank has had to discard about one-fifth of the mother's milk donated to them because of the high levels of pesticides. Since my baby will be at the end of the food chain, he or she will receive the highest concentration of these contaminants. I'm very concerned about the foods I eat because I know they eventually pass into my breast milk.

Don't think it was easy for me to change my diet, especially when I have to worry about my baby growing inside of me. For years "Kelsey the Cow" has been preaching to me over the TV about the benefits of drinking her milk. My complexion was supposed to improve when I drank milk as a teen, but it didn't. Milk, Kelsey claimed, was supposed to keep me trim and fit. I was overweight until my twenties.

When I found out that 50 percent of the calories of whole milk were fat and even 30 percent of the calories of low-fat milk were fat, I started to question Kelsey's honesty. When Kelsey said milk was nature's most perfect food and that you never outgrow your need for milk, I believed her, until I realized that even grown cows don't drink milk. I guess Kelsey forgot to mention that cow's milk was nature's most perfect food for baby cows. After all, there must be some benefit to cow's milk. Most calves look healthy and, come to think of it, I've never seen an overweight calf with a bad complexion.

Comments on Mary Taylor

Mary's greatest hurdle in changing her diet is her previous conditioning. Not only has she developed a taste for rich foods, but she has had years of "education" by the food industry to overcome. When it comes to emotional issues such as children, pregnant women, and unborn babies, old and familiar ideas on health are understandably more acceptable than new concepts, regardless of how much evidence supports the new idea. An objective observer could probably weigh the facts and come to a correct course of action, but how many of us can be objective and how many of us have the time to evaluate such an issue properly? Many scientific studies attest to the adequacy of a diet without animal products, including milk, to provide for excellent nutrition for adults, children, and even pregnant women.[75-81]

Our food is a very personal issue surrounded by tradition and years of eating habits. Unfortunately, most of us do not have the objectivity we need to choose the correct foods for the health of our families and ourselves. We have been successfully indoctrinated.

Notes

[1]S. Bahna, *Allergies to Milk,* New York: Grune and Stratton, 1980.

[2]P. Buisseret, "Common Manifestations of Cow's Milk Allergy in Children," *Lancet* 1 (1978): 304.

[3]S. Bahna, "Cow's Milk Allergy: Pathogenesis, Manifestations, Diagnosis, and Management," *Adv in Pediatr* 25 (1978): 1.

[4]D. Hill, "The Spectrum of Cow's Milk Allergy in Childhood," *Acta Paediatr Scand* 68 (1979): 847.

[5]E. Eastham, "Adverse Effects of Milk Formula Ingestion on the Gastrointestinal Tract—An Update," *Gastroenterology* 76 (1979): 365.

[6]J. Gerrard, "Milk Allergy: Clinical Picture and Familial Incidence," *Canad Med Ass J.* 97 (1967): 780.

[7]R. Coombs, "The Enigma of Cot Death: Is the Modified Anaphylaxis Hypothesis an Explanation for Some Cases?" *Lancet* 1 (1982): 1388.

[8]W. Parish, "Hypersensitivy to Milk and Sudden Death in Infancy," *Lancet* 2 (1960): 1106.

[9]D. Addy, "Infant Feeding: A Current View," *Br Med J* 1 (1976): 1268.

[10]Department of Health and Social Security, "Present Day Infant Feeding Practice Report," no. 9, 1974.

[11]L. Taube, *Food Allergy and the Allergic Patient,* 2nd ed. Springfield, Illinois, Charles Thomas, 1978, p. 22.

[12]T. Boat, "Hyperreactivity to Cow's Milk in Young Children with Pulmonary Hemosiderosis and Cor Pulmonale Secondary to Nasopharyngeal Obstruction," *J Pediatr* 87 (1975): 23.

[13]S. Truelove, "Ulcerative Colitis Provoked by Milk," *Br Med J* 1 (1961): 154.

[14]R. Wright, "A Controlled Therapeutic Trial of Various Diets in Ulcerative Colitis," *Br Med J* 2 (1965): 138.

[15]J. Sacca, "Acute Ischemic Colitis Due to Milk Allergy," *Ann Allergy* 29 (1971): 268.

[16]E. Acheson, "Early Weaning in the Aetiology of Ulcerative Colitis: A Study of Feeding in Infancy in Cases and Controls," *Br Med J* 2 (1961): 929.

[17]A. Cunningham, "Lymphomas and Animal Protein Consumption," *Lancet* 2 (1976): 1184.

[18]I. Jakobsson, "Cow's Milk as a Cause of Infantile Colic in Breast-Fed Infants," *Lancet* 2 (1978): 437.

[19]M. Harris, "Cow's Milk Allergy as a Cause of Infantile Colic: Immunofluorescent Studies on Jejunal Mucosa," *Aust Pediatr J* 13 (1977): 276.

[20]A. Lake, "Dietary Protein-Induced Colitis in Breast-Fed Infants," *J Pediatr* 101 (1982): 906.

[21]J. Gerrard, "Allergy in Breast-Fed Babies to Ingredients in Breast Milk," *Ann Allergy* 42 (1979): 69.

[22]H. Donnally, "The Question of the Elimination of Foreign Protein (Egg-White) in Woman's Milk," *J Immunology* 19 (1930): 15.

[23]J. Bayless, "Lactose and Milk Intolerance: Clinical Implications," *N Engl J Med* 292 (1975): 1156.

[24]"Background Information on Lactose and Milk Intolerance," *Nutrition Reviews* 30 (1972): 175.

[25]T. Gilat, "Lactase Deficiency: The World Pattern Today," *Israel J Med Sci* 15 (1979): 369.

[26]J. Smith, "Hawaiian Milk Contamination Creates Alarm, a Sour Response by State Regulators," *Science* 217 (1982): 137.

[27]J. Hergenrather, "Pollutants in Breast Milk of Vegetarians," letter *N Engl J Med* 304 (1981): 792.

[28]S. Harris, "Statement of Stephanie G. Harris before the subcommittee on Health and Scientific Research of the Senate Committee on Human Resources." June 8, 1977.

[29]H. Vickers, "Dermatological Hazards of the Presence of Penicillin in Milk." *Pro Roy Soc Med* 57 (1964): 1091.

[30]M. Zimmerman, "Chronic Penicillin Urticaria from Dairy Products, Proved by Penicillinase Cures," *Arch Dermatol* 79 (1959): 1.

[31]Report of the Joint Committee on the Use of Antibiotics in Animal Husbandry and Veterinary Medicine," London: Her Majesty's Stationery Office, 1969. p.36.

[32]K. Wicker, "Allergic Reaction to Penicillin Present in Milk," *JAMA* 208 (1969): 143.

[33]R. Fontaine, "Epidemic Salmonellosis from Cheddar Cheese: Surveillance and Prevention," *Am J of Epidemiol* 111 (1980): 247.

[34]K. Donham, "Epidemiologic relationships of the bovine population and human leukemia in Iowa," *Am J Epidemiol* 112 (1980): 80.

[35]J. Ferrer, "Milk of Dairy Cows Frequently Contains a Leukemogenic Virus," *Science* 213 (1981): 1014.

[36]Editorial, "Beware of the Cow," *Lancet* 2 (1974): 30.

[37]A. Walker, "The Influence of Numerous Pregnancies and Lactations on Bone Dimensions in South African Bantu and Caucasian Mothers," *Clin Science* 42 (1972): 189.

[38]A. Walker, "Osteoporosis and Calcium Deficiency," *Am J Clin Nutr* 16 (1965): 327.

[39]R. Smith. "Epidemiologic Studies of Osteoporosis in Women of Puerto Rico and Southeastern Michigan with Special Reference to Age, Race, National Origin, and to Other Related or Associated Findings," *Clin Orthop* 45 (1966): 31.

[40] A. Walker, "The Human Requirement for Calcium: Should Low Intakes Be Supplemented?" *Am J Clin Nutr* 25 (1972): 518.

[41] "Symposium on Human Calcium Requirements," *JAMA* 185 (1963): 588.

[42] H. Spencer, "Influence of Dietary Calcium Intake on Ca(47) Absorption in Man," *Am J Med* 46 (1969): 197.

[43] Goodhart and Shils, *Modern Nutrition in Health and Disease (Dietotherapy)*, 5th ed., Lea and Febiger, Philadelphia, 1973, p. 274.

[44] A. Ippoliti, "The Effect of Various Forms of Milk on Gastric-Acid Secretions, Studies in Patients with Duodenal Ulcer and Normal Subjects," *Ann Intern Med* 84 (1976): 286.

[45] R. Briggs, "Myocardial Infarction in Patients Treated with Sippy and Other High-Milk Diets, An Autopsy Study of Fifteen Hospitals in the U.S.A. and Great Britain," *Circulation* 21 (1960): 538.

[46] E. Orwoll, "The Milk–Alkali Syndrome: Current Concepts," *Ann Intern Med* 97 (1982): 242.

[47] F. Derrick, "Kidney Stone Disease: Evaluation and Medical Management," *Postgrad Med* 66 (1979): 115.

[48] E. Poskitt, "Diet, Sunlight, and 25-Hydroxy Vitamin D in Healthy Children and Adults," *Br Med J* 1 (1979): 221.

[49] T. Stamp, "Comparison of Oral 25-Hydroxycholecalciferol, Vitamin D, and Ultraviolet Light as Determinants of Circulating 25-Hydroxyvitamin D," *Lancet* 1 (1977): 1341.

[50] J. Pietrek, "Prevention of Vitamin D Deficiency in Asians," *Lancet* 1 (1976): 1145.

[51] D. Lawson, "Relative Contributions of Diet and Sunlight to Vitamin D State in the Elderly," *Br Med J* 2 (1979): 303.

[52] D. Fraser, "The Physiological Economy of Vitamin D," *Lancet* 1 (1983): 969.

[53] F. Loomis, "Skin Pigment Regulation of Vitamin D Biosynthesis in Man," *Science* 157 (1967): 501.

[54] M. Seelig, "Vitamin D and Cardiovascular, Renal, and Brain Damage in Infancy and Childhood," *Ann of NY Acad Sci* 147 (1969): 537.

[55] M. Crawford, "Essential Fatty Acid Requirements in Infancy," *Am J Clin Nutr* 31 (1978): 2181.

[56] B. Agranoff, "Diet and the Geographical Distribution of Multiple Sclerosis," *Lancet* 2 (1974): 1061.

[57] M. Alter, "Multiple Sclerosis and Nutrition," *Arch Neurol* 31 (1974): 267.

[58] R. Swank, "Multiple Sclerosis: Twenty Years on Low-Fat Diet," *Arch Neurol* 23 (1970): 460.

[59] R. Robins-Browne, "The Fate of Ingested Lactobacilli in the Proximal Small Intestine," *Am J Clin Nutr* 34 (1981): 514.

[60] M. Flynn, "Effect of Dietary Egg on Human Serum Cholesterol and Triglycerides," *Am J Clin Nutr* 32 (1979): 1051.

[61] T. Dawber, "Eggs, Serum Cholesterol, and Coronary Heart Disease," *Am J Clin Nutr* 36 (1982): 617.

[62] E. Flaim, "Plasma Lipid and Lipoprotein Cholesterol Concentrations in Adult Males Consuming Normal and High Cholesterol Diets under Controlled Conditions," *Am J Clin Nutr* 34 (1981): 1103.

[63] M. Porter, "Effect of Dietary Egg on Serum Cholesterol and Triglyceride of Human Males," *Am J Clin Nutr* 30 (1977), 490.

[64]J. Slater, "Plasma Cholesterol and Triglycerides in Men with Added Eggs in the Diet," *Nutr Rep Int* 14 (1976): 249.

[65]F. Kummerow, "The Influence of Egg Consumption on the Serum Cholesterol Level in Human Subjects," *Am J Clin Nutr* 30 (1977): 664.

[66]B. Liebman, "Poor Design Undercuts Cholesterol Study Results," letter/*Am J Clin Nutr* 35 (1982): 1041.

[67]W. Connor, "Reply to letter by Oster," letter *Am J Clin Nutr* 36 (1982): 1261.

[68]S. Roberts, "Does Egg Feeding (i.e. dietary cholesterol) Affect Plasma Cholesterol Levels in Humans? The results of a double-blind study," *Am J Clin Nutr* 34 (1981): 2092.

[69]B. O'Brien, "Human Plasma Lipid Response to Red Meat, Poultry, Fish and Eggs," *Am J Clin Nutr* 33 (1980): 2573.

[70]F. Mattson, "Effect of Dietary Cholesterol on Serum Cholesterol in Man," *Am J Clin Nutr* 25 (1972): 589.

[71]W. Connor, "The Interrelated Effects of Dietary Cholesterol and Fat upon Human Serum Lipid Levels," *J Clin Invest* 43 (1964): 1691.

[72]E. Kofranyi, "The Minimum Protein Requirement of Humans, Tested with Mixtures of Whole Egg Plus Potato and Maize Plus Beans," z. *Physiol Chem* 351 (1970): 1485.

[73]S. Tuttle, "Study of the Essential Amino Acid Requirements of Men over Fifty," *Metabolism* 6 (1957): 564.

[74]E. Sumner, "The Biological Value of Milk and Egg Protein in Human Subjects," *J Nutr* 16 (1938): 141.

[75]F. Ellis, "Veganism, Clinical Findings, and Investigations," *Am J Clin Nutr* 23 (1970): 249.

[76]F. Ellis "The Health of Vegans," *Pl Fds Hum Nutr* 2 (1971): 93.

[77]F. Ellis, "The Health of Vegans During Pregnancy," *Proc Nutr Soc, Abstracts of Communication,* 36 (1977): 46A.

[78]A. Kuthra, "The Nutritional, Clinical, and Economic Aspects of Vegan Diets, *"Pl Fds Hum Nutr* 2 (1970): 13.

[79]T. Sanders, "Studies of Vegans: the Fatty Acid Composition of Plasma Choline Phosphogylcerides, Erythrocytes, Adipose Tissue, and Breast Milk, and Some Indicators of Susceptibility to Ischemic Heart Disease in Vegans and Omnivore Controls." *Am J Clin Nutr* 31 (1978): 805.

[80]J. Dywer, Nutritional Studies of Vegetarian Children, *Am J Clin Nutr* 35 (1982): 204.

[81]M. Abdulla, "Nutrient Intake and Health of Vegans, Chemical Analyses of Diets Using the Duplicate Portion Sampling Technique," *Am J Clin Nutr* 34 (1981): 2464.

Chapter

6

A Health-Supporting Diet Contains No Cholesterol

Cholesterol is a fat-soluble substance synthesized by the liver, intestine, and other tissues, and converted to a variety of essential steroid hormones, bile acids, and provitamin D_3. This necessary substance also serves as a building block for cell membranes. The body produces between 500 and 1000 milligrams of cholesterol per day, which is enough to supply our needs. When we eat the diet commonly consumed by people of affluent societies, we take in an additional 500 to 1000 milligrams a day, all of which comes from animal flesh and other animal products. Approximately half of the amount consumed is absorbed into the body. Plants do not make or contain cholesterol.[1]

Cholesterol has a chemical structure that is very resistant to breakdown; however, some of the excess cholesterol we ingest can be eliminated from the body. Much is excreted through the liver, stored for a while in the gallbladder, and then passed through the intestines and out in the stool. Problems arise because the quantity that can be removed in this manner is limited. The remaining cholesterol is deposited in the tissues where it remains intact in the body for years. These deposits irritate the tissues into which they settle and cause inflammation. In the arteries this inflammation eventually results in the formation of fibrous scar tissue and the abnormal growth of smooth muscle cells which make up the artery wall. Fat accumulates among these cells, and the result is a swelling on the inside of the artery wall called a plaque. (See Figure 6.1.) In a healthy person the lumen or opening in the artery has very little plaque, and the blood can flow through it easily. When the walls of an artery are lined with extensive amounts of plaque, the condition is called "hardening of the arteries," or atherosclerosis, and this plaque eventually can plug the artery completely.[1]

When the fatty contents of plaque suddenly rupture into the artery, forming a clot (thrombosis) that completely stops the flow of blood, a life-threatening event takes place.[2] If this occurs in an artery that nourishes the heart, part of the heart will be deprived of blood, and the heart muscle in that area will die. This sequence of events is

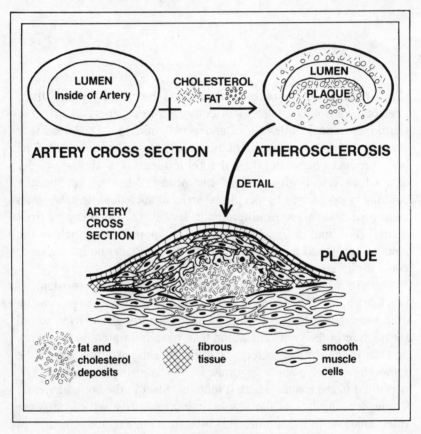

Figure 6.1. Cholesterol and fat accumulate in the wall of an artery and act as two of the components in the formation of a plaque.

known as a heart attack. (See Figure 6.2.) Heart attacks cause the deaths of half of all people living in societies where rich foods predominate.

The level of cholesterol in your blood is known as your serum cholesterol, and it can be measured by a simple, inexpensive test. The results are expressed in units of milligrams per 100 milliliters (mg/dl), or milligram percent (mg%). The average cholesterol of people who follow dietary practices of affluent societies is 210 mg%. The average male in these societies has a greater than 50 percent chance of dying from heart disease. Under these circumstances no consolation should be gained from being average. "Average" is all too frequently referred to as "normal" because of the reference population. Most laboratories will report cholesterol as being normal with values all the way up to 330 mg%. It is important for you to know your own cholesterol level, because it indicates your chances of developing heart disease and several other diseases commonly found in an affluent society.[3-4] A person with a cholesterol level of 260 mg% is five times more likely to die from a heart attack than one with a level

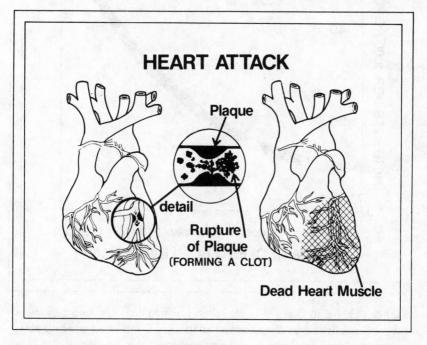

Figure 6.2

of 200 mg%.[1,4] (See Figure 6.3) Heart disease is very rare in societies where people limit the use of rich foods and maintain their cholesterol below 180 mg% for a lifetime.[1] If we can identify the factors that affect the serum cholesterol level, we can take steps to lower it.

The consumption of foods that are high in cholesterol, animal fat, and animal protein and low in fiber will raise the serum cholesterol level. Foods in this category are meats, poultry, fish, shellfish, eggs, and dairy products. On the other hand, if we eat foods that have no cholesterol, are low in fat, and are high in vegetable protein and fiber, our serum cholesterol level will fall.[5-11] Such foods would be starches,

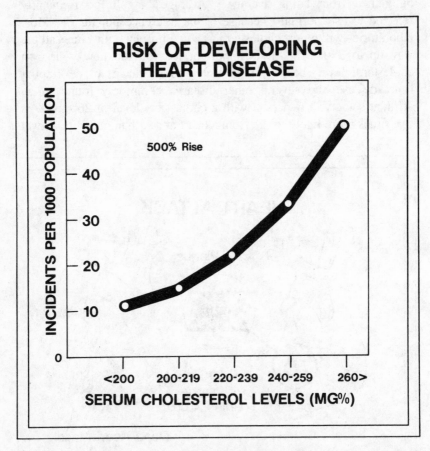

Figure 6.3. Small changes in cholesterol maintained over long periods of time reflect our chance of developing heart disease and many other illnesses common to people living in affluent societies. An average of 210% is certainly not an ideal.[1,4] Incidence is over an 8 year period.

vegetables, and fruits. Simple sugars cause a slight rise in cholesterol levels when they replace starch in a diet.[12] When plant foods are consumed along with cholesterol-containing animal products, a considerable portion of the cholesterol is blocked from intestinal absorption by the plant sterols, and a lesser rise in blood cholesterol results.[13] Fortunately, a health-supporting diet contains the optimal amounts and types of all of these nutrients, which will keep our serum cholesterol and our total body stores of cholesterol at the lowest and healthiest level possible.[14](See Figure 6.4.)

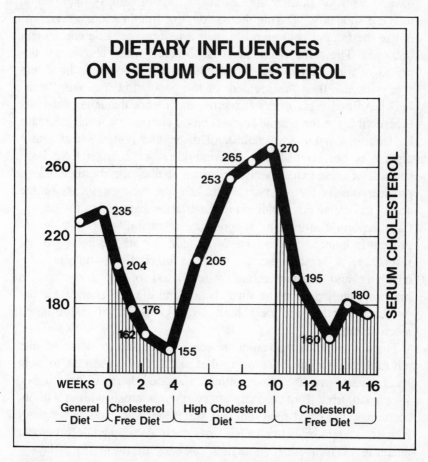

Figure 6.4. Changing from a rich diet, moderate to high in cholesterol, to a health-supporting, cholesterol-free diet typically produces a 30 mg% to 100 mg% fall in serum cholesterol levels in three weeks. Levels are stabilized for a particular pattern of eating in about three weeks.

Studies have shown that atherosclerosis in humans can be reversed by maintaining a lowered blood cholesterol level over a period of time. Subjects of one study at the University of California ranged in age from twenty-nine to sixty-five, and those who showed reversal of atherosclerosis over a period of approximately two years had dropped their cholesterol levels by an average of 65 mg%.[15] Other evidence that supports the theory that this condition is reversible is found among people who have been forced to live on less rich and even sparse diets. People who die from wasting diseases, such as cancer, have less plaque in their arteries at the time of autopsy than people who die suddenly.[16] During the last days of life these cancer victims utilize the fat and cholesterol in their arteries to provide energy and nutrients. The same phenomena is observed when people are deprived of food during war. At autopsy they are found to have less artery disease than the segment of the population that was "well-fed".[16] Animal experiments also provide evidence that atherosclerosis is reversible. In the animal studies, blood cholesterol levels decrease by feeding low-fat, low-cholesterol diets, and regression of artery disease is observed. Many different kinds of animals have been subjects of these experiments. Primates, such as the rhesus monkey, provide some of the most consistent and convincing evidence on the ability to reverse this condition in the arteries that nourish the heart.[17] Case reports continue to support the reversibility of this deadly process in humans.[18-20] To take the attitude that atherosclerosis is not reversible, at least to some extent, is in conflict with the ever-changing and healing nature of all areas of the body and is inappropriately pessimistic since dietary and lifestyle change will not do harm and may well lead to regression of established atherosclerosis.[21]

From a practical viewpoint, research is starting to show definite advantages of approaches using diet and lifestyle changes to treat heart disease over the most commonly applied therapies used today. People suffering from coronary artery atherosclerosis with or without accompanying chest pain (angina) survive longer, have fewer heart attacks, and have better relief from their chest pain—91 percent decrease in frequency of angina episodes in twenty-four days—through diet and lifestyle changes than with drugs and coronary artery bypass surgery.[20,22-30] This should not be too surprising when one considers that experts reviewing the record of bypass surgery over the last fifteen years have had to conclude that in most cases the operation has not been shown to save lives.[30-32] Still more convincing, a dietary and lifestyle approach to coronary artery disease is a better way because it avoids the tremendous pain and expense of surgery, not to mention the 15 percent (or greater) risk of brain damage following coronary artery bypass surgery.[33,34] The brain damage may be the result of emboli, clots, toxic gases, and disruption of blood cells caused by the heart-lung machine used during this extensive surgical procedure. There is absolutely no doubt that bypass surgery is big business and can lead to great riches for those promoting and performing the procedure. This is now estimated to be a $3.3 billion a year industry and some surgeons in private practice who specialize in this operation earn more than one million dollars per year.[35]

Blood cholesterol directly reflects the richness of the foods we eat, and the level can be used as a guide in changing your diet and lifestyle. Before you change your diet, you should have your cholesterol measured by your doctor. Then repeat the test every three weeks to gauge your progress, with a level of 160 mg% as your goal.[36] A reading lower than 160 mg% is even better.

Recently, reports of an association between low blood cholesterol and high rates of colon cancer have caused concern and confusion for people interested in better health through low-cholesterol diets. The bulk of scientific evidence fails to support this relationship, and even the primary investigators involved in these studies have no adequate explanation for their findings.[37]

Almost all scientific research is in direct conflict with the idea that low cholesterol intakes could be harmful to health, and, furthermore, this research implicates cholesterol in the cause of the most serious diseases found in affluent societies. Cholesterol in the diet is actually believed to act as a cocarcinogen in the development of colon cancer.[38] International data show that in countries with the highest rates of heart disease, there are also the highest rates of colon cancer. This direct correlation suggests a shared cause, and excessive cholesterol intake and elevated blood cholesterol levels are established risk factors for heart disease.

In studies done on animals to determine the effects of diet on the development of colon cancer, the greatest number of colon cancers and the greatest incidence of spread (metastasis) occur in animals on diets containing the most cholesterol.[38] Whereas diets without cholesterol have been found to retard the growth of cancer in animals and to prolong their survival.[39]

Why, then, has a relationship been found between low blood cholesterol and colon cancer? Investigators have proposed that the low blood cholesterol may be the result of an undetected cancer already present, which would suppress the person's appetite and thereby the intake of cholesterol-containing foods. Even more likely, people who develop colon cancer may metabolize cholesterol differently from healthy people. Patients with colon cancer have higher levels of cholesterol in their stools when compared to healthy subjects, and studies have suggested a reciprocal relationship between the blood and stool levels of cholesterol in persons with colon cancer.[38] Thus, one person may deposit the diet-derived cholesterol in his or her arteries while someone else leaves or excretes the cholesterol in the bowel to act as a cocarcinogen that causes colon cancer. Obviously, the only safe answer is not to consume cholesterol-containing foods in the first place.

Another explanation incriminates the recent switch to polyunsaturated vegetable oils in our diet.[40] Since 1942, researchers have found that fats, especially polyunsaturated fats, promote the development of cancer in animals.[41-43] It is also well recognized that polyunsaturated fats have a cholesterol-lowering action that drives cholesterol out of the body and into the colon.[44-46] Rats on diets of cholesterol and polyunsaturated oil have less atherosclerosis but more colon cancer than rats fed cholesterol and saturated fats.[47] (Although rat studies don't always directly apply to human health, they do provide important information, particularly in investigations of harmful effects of substances on living tissues. For example, it is well established that elements that cause cancer in animals cause cancer in humans. Using animals to determine nutrient requirements for humans has less relevance. Comparison of nutrient needs is highly dependent upon growth rates and individual habitats, which vary greatly among species and even within individual species.)

A large study in 1969 at Wadsworth Veteran's Hospital, designed to determine the benefit of a highly polyunsaturated fat diet for the prevention of heart disease, found less heart disease but more cancer in the experimental group eating the polyunsaturated oils.[48] Therefore, we should not be discouraged in our efforts to keep our cholesterol intake low by the as yet unexplained relationship of low blood cholesterol and cancer of the colon found in a few studies. A workshop sponsored by the National Institute of Health in 1981 failed to find a causal relationship between low cholesterol and colon cancer

and unanimously supported recommendations to lower dietary cholesterol intake in order to prevent heart attacks and premature
atherosclerosis.[37]

Recently, it has become popular to measure one portion of the total
serum cholesterol, which is called high-density lipoprotein (HDL)
cholesterol. There is evidence that among people of affluent societies, where almost everyone consumes rich foods, those with high
HDL levels have a lower incidence of heart disease than those with
low HDL levels.[49,50] Obesity, diabetes, and smoking are associated
with lower levels of this type of cholesterol.[51-54] Exercise, alcohol
consumption, and diets high in fiber and polyunsaturated oil and low
in calories raise levels of HDL.[55-58] Also, increasing the amount of
cholesterol in the diet will raise HDL levels because HDL cholesterol
is actually a product of cholesterol metabolism.[49,59,60] However,
international data that include people on a spectrum of rich to starch-
centered diets fail to show a beneficial effect of HDL cholesterol.
Data from populations with a wide range of eating habits actually
show that those with the lowest levels of HDL cholesterol also have
the lowest levels of total cholesterol and the lowest rates of heart
disease.[60,61] Of great concern is the possibility that a person with a
high total serum cholesterol may receive a false reassurance from a
report of an elevated HDL level and, because of this, will fail to
change his or her diet. Since total serum cholesterol is such an
accurate reflection of diet and health, this test alone is best for most
people.[62]

Excess cholesterol, along with the other harmful aspects of a rich
diet, can cause more problems. If a large amount of cholesterol is
present in the gallbladder fluids, gallstones can form.[63-66] In western
cultures cholesterol is the principal ingredient of more than 90 percent
of gallstones. Pain, which is often the main symptom found with
gallbladder disease, is quickly relieved in most instances by the time-
honored treatment of a low-fat diet.[67] Thus, surgery usually can be
avoided since the primary reason for performing most gallbladder
surgery—the pain—is removed.[68,69] A dietary approach is the best
initial choice for most who suffer with this problem because, even
after surgery, less than 50 percent of patients with pain symptoms
find complete relief.[70] Gallstones left in the gallbladder rarely cause
trouble, and a decision to delay surgery results in fewer complications

and a reduced risk of death compared to those who choose immediate surgery.[68,69] Gallstones occasionally disappear, but this should not be expected from a change in diet.

Cholesterol can accumulate in the skin and tendons to form small, flat, yellow plaques and lumps called xanthoma.[71,72] When plaques are found on the eyelids they produce a common condition of cosmetic importance known as xanthelasma. (See Figure 6.5.)

To simplify your learning about a starch-centered diet, remember that all animal products contain cholesterol. No cholesterol is found in plants. Plant products, with the exception of coconut and chocolate, and a few vegetable-derived oils, will tend to lower your body stores of cholesterol and your risk of cholesterol-related diseases.

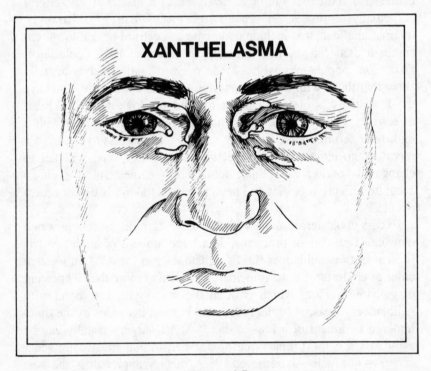

XANTHELASMA

Figure 6.5

Notes

[1]W. Connor, "The Key Role of Nutritional Factors in the Prevention of Coronary Heart Disease," *Prev Med* 1 (1972):49.

[2]P. Oliva, "Pathophysiology of Acute Myocardial Infarction, 1981," *Ann Intern Med* 94 (1981):236.

[3]R. Shekelle, "Diet, Serum Cholesterol, and Death from Coronary Heart Disease The Western Electric Study," *N Engl J Med* 304 (1981):65.

[4]W. Kannel, "Cholesterol in the Prediction of Atherosclerotic Disease," *Ann Intern Med* 90 (1979):85.

[5]F. Mattson, "Effect of Dietary Cholesterol on Serum Cholesterol in Man," *Am J Clin Nutr* 25 (1972):589.

[6]J. Anderson, "Independence of the Effects of Cholesterol and Degree of Saturation of the Fat in the Diet on Serum Cholesterol in Man," *Am J Clin Nutr* 29 (1976):1184.

[7]A. Keys, "Serum Cholesterol Response to Changes in Dietary Lipids," *Am J Clin Nutr* 19 (1966):175.

[8]K. Carroll, "Hypocholesterolemic Effect of Substituting Soybean Protein for Animal Protein in the Diet of Healthy Young Women," *Am J Clin Nutr* 31 (1978):1312.

[9]C. Sirtori, "Clinical Experiments with the Soybean Protein, Diet in the Treatment of Hypercholesterolemia," *Am J Clin Nutr* 32 (1979):1645.

[10]A. Keys, "Fiber and Pectin in the Diet and Serum Cholesterol Concentration in Man," *Proc Soc Exper Biol and Med* 106 (1961):555.

[11]D. Kritchevsky, "Dietary Fiber and Other Dietary Factors in Hypercholesterema," *Am J Clin Nutr* 30 (1977):979.

[12]F. Grande, "Dietary Carbohydrates and Serum Cholesterol," *Am J Clin Nutr* 20 (1967):176.

[13]F. Mattson, "Optimizing the Effect of Plant Sterols on Cholesterol Absorption in Man," *Am J Clin Nutr* 35 (1982):697.

[14]G. Fraser, "The Effects of Various Vegetable Supplements on Serum Cholesterol," *Am J Clin Nutr* 34 (1981):1272.

[15]R. Barndt, "Regression and Progression of Early Femoral Atherosclerosis in Treated Hyperlipoproteinemic Patients," *Ann Intern Med* 86 (1977):139.

[16]R. Wissler, "Studies of Regression of Advanced Atherosclerosis in Experimental Animals and Man," (Atherosclerosis) *Ann NY Acad Sci* 275 (1976):363.

[17]M. Armstrong, "Regression of Coronary Atheromatosis in Rhesus Monkeys," *Circulation Res* 27 (1970):59.

[18]L. Basta, "Regression of Atherosclerotic Lesions of the Renal Arteries and Spontaneous Cure of Systemic Hypertension Through Control of Hyperlipidemia," *Am J Med* 61 (1976):420.

[19]M. Sanmarco, "Arteriosclerosis: Its Progression and Regression," *Primary Cardiology* (July/Aug. 1978):51.

[20]N. Pritikin, Research Projects, Santa Monica, Calif.: Pritikin Research Foundation. 1981.

[21]Editorial, "Regression of Atherosclerosis?" *Lancet* 2 (1976):614.

[22]P. Kuo, "Lipemia in Patients with Coronary Heart Disease, Treatment with Low-Fat Diet," *J Am Diet Assoc* 33 (1957):22.

[23]P. Kuo, "Angina Pectoris Induced by Fat Ingestion in Patients with Coronary Artery Disease," *JAMA* 158 (1955):1008.

[24]P. Kuo, "The Effect of Lipemia upon Coronary and Peripheral Arterial Circulation in Patients with Essential Hyperlipemia," *Am J Med* 26 (1959):68.

[25]F. Ellis, "Angina and Vegan Diet," *Am Heart J* 93 (1977):803.

[26]D. Ornish, "Effects of Stress Management Training and Dietary Change in Treating Ischemic Heart Disease," *JAMA* 249 (1983):54.

[27] A. Williams, "Increased Blood Cell Agglutination Following Ingestion of Fat, a Factor Contributing to Cardiac Ischemia, Coronary Insufficiency, and Anginal Pain," *Angiology* 8 (1957):29.

[28] P. Podrid, "Prognosis of Medically Treated Patients with Coronary-Artery Disease with Profound ST-Segment Depression During Exercise Testing," *N Engl J Med* 305 (1981):1111.

[29] I. Hjermann, "Effect of Diet and Smoking Intervention on the Incidence of Coronary Heart Disease, Report from the Oslo Study Group of a Randomized Trial in Healthy Men," *Lancet* 2 (1981):1303.

[30] H. McIntosh, "The First Decade of Aortocoronary Bypass Grafting, 1967-1977, a Review," *Circulation* 57 (1978):405.

[31] G. Kolata, "Consensus on Bypass Surgery," *Science* 211 (1981):42.

[32] Editorial, "Coronary Artery Bypass Surgery—Indications and Limitations," *Lancet* 2 (1980):511.

[33] Editorial, "Brain Damage after Open-Heart Surgery," *Lancet* 1 (1982):1161.

[34] T. Aberg, "Release of Adenylate Kinase into Cerebrospinal Fluid during Open-Heart Surgery and Its Relation to Postoperative Intellectual Function," *Lancet* 1 (1982):1139.

[35] A. Trafford, "America's $39 billion heart business." *US News Report* March 15, 1982, p. 53.

[36] J. Elliot, "An "Ideal" Serum Cholesterol Level?" *JAMA* 241 (1979):1979.

[37] Editorial, "Cholesterol and Noncardiovascular Mortality," *JAMA* 246 (1981):731.

[38] P. Cruse, "Dietary Cholesterol Is Cocarcinogen for Human Colon Cancer," *Lancet* 1 (1979):752.

[39] M. Littman, "Effect of Cholesterol-Free, Fat-Free Diet and Hypocholesterolemic Agents on Growth of Transplantable Animal Tumors," *Cancer Chemotherapy Reports* 50 (1966):25.

[40] R. Jones, Editorial, "Cholesterol, Coronary Disease, and Cancer," *JAMA* 245 (1981):2060.

[41] P. Hill, "Diet and Endocrine-Related Cancer," *Cancer* 39 (1977):1820.

[42] Y. Nishizuka, "Biological Influence of Fat Intake on Mammary Cancer and Mammary Tissue: Experimental Correlates," *Prev Med* 7 (1978):218.

[43] K. Carroll, "Experimental Evidence of Dietary Factors and Hormone-Dependent Cancers," *Cancer Res* 35 (1975):3374.

[44] P. Nestel, "Lowering of Plasma Cholesterol and Enhanced Sterol Excretion with the Consumption of Polyunsaturated Ruminant Fats," *N Engl J Med* 288 (1973):379.

[45] H. Sodhi, "Plasma, Bile, and Fecal Sterols in Relation to Diet," *Metabolism* 16 (1967):334.

[46] S. Grundy, "The Effects of Unsaturated Dietary Fats on Absorption, Excretion, Synthesis, and Distribution of Cholesterol in Man," *J Clin Invest* 49 (1970):1135.

[47] S. Broitman, "Polyunsaturated Fat, Cholesterol, and Large Bowel Tumorigenesis," *Cancer* 40 (1977):2455.

[48] M. Pearce, "Incidence of Cancer in Men on a Diet High in Polyunsaturated Fat," *Lancet* 1 (1971):464.

[49] A. Tall, "Current Concepts: Plasma High Density Lipoproteins," *N Engl J Med* 299 (1978):1232.

[50] P. Williams, "High Density Lipoprotein and Coronary Risk Factors in Normal Men," *Lancet* 1 (1979):72.

[51] T. Gordon, "Diabetes, Blood Lipids, and the Role of Obesity in Coronary Heart Disease Risk for Women," *Ann Intern Med* 87 (1977):393.

[52] H. Chase, "Juvenile Diabetes Mellitus and Serum Lipids and Lipoprotein Levels," *Am J Dis Child* 130 (1976):1113.

[53] S. Hulley, "Plasma High-Density Lipoprotein Cholesterol Level, Influence of Risk Factor Intervention," *JAMA* 238 (1977):2269.

[54] R. Garrison, "Cigarette Smoking and HDL Cholesterol," *Atherosclerosis* 30 (1978):17.

[55] W. Castelli, "Alcohol and Blood Lipids, the Cooperative Lipoprotein Phenotyping Study," *Lancet* 2 (1977):153.

[56] P. Wood, "Plasma Lipoprotein Distributions in Male and Female Runners," *Ann NY Acad Sci* 301 (1977):748.

[57] M. Flanagan, "The Effects of Diet on High Density Lipoprotein Cholesterol," *J Hum Nutr* 34 (1980):43.

[58] I. Hjermann, "The Effect of Dietary Changes on High Density Lipoprotein Cholesterol—The Oslo Study," *Am J Med* 66 (1979):105.

[59] P. Mistry, "Cholesterol Feeding Revisited," *Circulation (abstracts)* 54 (supp 11) (1976):11-178.

[60] J. Knuiman, "HDL—Cholesterol in Men from Thirteen Countries," *Lancet* 2 (1981):367.

[61] E. Smith, "HDL—Should We Be "Chasing" It Now?" *J Hum Nutr* 34 (1980):59.

[62] W. Kannel, "Is the Serum Total Cholesterol an Anachronism?" *Lancet* 2 (1979):950.

[63] H. Sarles, "Diet and Cholesterol Gallstones," *Digestion* 17 (1978):121.

[64] L. DenBesten, "The Effect of Dietary Cholesterol on the Composition of Human Bile," *Surgery* 73 (1973):266.

[65] J. Doty, "Interaction of Chenodeoxycholic Acid and Dietary Cholesterol in the Treatment of Cholesterol Gallstones," *Am J Surgery* 143 (1982):48.

[66] T. Mabee, "The Mechanism of Increased Gallstone Formation in Obese Human Subjects," *Surgery* 79 (1976):460.

[67] R. Goodhart, *Modern Nutrition in Health and Disease*, 6th ed., Lea and Febiger, Philadelphia, 1980, p. 974.

[68] W. Grache, "The Natural History of Silent Gallstones—The Innocent Gallstone Is Not a Myth," *N Engl J Med* 307 (1982):798.

[69] J. Hoey, "Cholelithiasis: A Comparison of Surgical and Nonsurgical Management Strategies Basied on Available Evidence," *Clin Invest Med* 2 (1979):75.

[70] A. Johnston, "Cholecystectomy and Gallstones Dyspepsia: A Clinical and Physiological Study of a Symptom Complex," *Ann Roy Coll Surg Eng* 56 (1975):69.

[71] R. Fleischmajer, "Normolipemic Tendon and Tuberous Xanthomas," *J Am Acad of Dermatol* 5 (1981):290.

[72] J. Love, "Xanthomas and Lipoproteins," *Cutis* 21 (1978):801.

Chapter

7

Most Fats Are Excluded From a Health-Supporting Diet

The fat that we eat provides us with a form of energy that can be stored in large amounts and for long periods in the body and with some of the raw materials for building tissues in our body.

Dietary fats are often divided into four general groups based on their physical and chemical properties:

1. *Saturated fats* are found primarily in animal foods such as beef, pork, and dairy products. Coconut and chocolate are the only common plant products that are very high in saturated fat. Certain oils derived from plants are also high in saturated fats. They include cocoa butter, palm oil, vegetable shortening, and margarine. The saturated fats are most often solid at room temperature.

2. *Monounsaturated fats* are found in olives and olive oil and used in a liquid form.

3. *Polyunsaturated fats* are found in high concentrations in vegetables, fish, and poultry. These fats tend to be more fluid at room temperature.

4. *Hydrogenated fats and oils* are manufactured by chemically adding hydrogen to vegetable oils to make a more saturated type of fat and a more solid product.

Fats are composed of glycerol and long chains of carbon-containing molecules called fatty acids. Our bodies are capable of synthesizing most of the fatty acids we need. The only one that must be provided from the diet is a polyunsaturated fatty acid called lino*leic* acid.[1-3] In addition, lino*lenic* acid and arachidonic acid are often listed as essential fatty acids. Although lino*lenic* acid cannot be made by animals, whether or not it is actually essential is in question. Any requirement for lino*lenic* acid is likely to be substantially less than that for lino*leic* acid, and because of the abundance of lino*lenic* acid in foods of both vegetable and animal origin a dietary deficiency is unlikely.[4-5] Arachidonic acid is made in the body from lino*leic* acid. The minimum daily requirement for lino*leic* acid is small and easily met by a starch-centered diet.[1-3] Fat is found in all vegetables, and approximately half of this vegetable fat is in the form of lino*leic* acid. Animal foods, with the exception of fish and poultry, are low in lino*leic* acid and can fail to satisfy our requirements for this essential nutrient.[3] (See Table 7.1.)

Vitamins A, D, E, and K are known as fat-soluble vitamins because of their chemical property of mixing and dissolving with fat. You may have heard that a small amount of dietary fat is required for their absorption into the body. All of the fat needed for this process is present in vegetable foods.[6] A deficiency of the fat-soluble vitamins caused by the low-fat property of a starch-centered diet has yet to be reported in humans.[6]

Of all the macronutrients in a rich diet, excess fat causes the greatest burden on the body. Eventually the body fails to compensate for this burden and disease results.

After we eat a meal high in any type of fat, our blood cells can actually stick together in clumps that plug the blood vessels.[7-9] Figure 7.1 illustrates this process.

As the flow of blood gradually slows, clumps of cells block blood vessels, thereby tissues and organs receive a decreased amount of essential nutrients and oxygen. An additional process disrupting normal blood flow occurs after consuming the saturated variety of fats. Blood-clotting elements, called platelets, form irreversible aggregates that block small blood vessels and cause spasms that constrict these vessels.[10-12]

The blockage by blood cells and platelets along with the spasms of the blood vessels can severely reduce blood flow in specific areas of the body and cause:

1. Chest pain (angina) or a heart attack, especially if one has heart arteries narrowed by atherosclerosis.[12-18]

Table 7.1 Linoleic Acid in Selected Foods*

Vegetable food	Percentage of total fat
Almond	20
Avocado	13
Barley	50
Cacao butter	2
Cashews	7
Chick pea (garbanzos)	36
Chocolate	2
Coconut	trace
Corn kernel	51
Corn meal, white	45
Margarine	9
Millet	35
Mustard seed	16
Oats, rolled	41
Olive	8
Peanut butter	25
Peanuts	29
Pumpkin seed	41
Rice	35
Rye	62
Safflower oil	72
Sorgum	44
Soybeans	52
Sunflower oil	63
Watermelon seed	59
Wheat flour, white	42

Animal food	Percentage of total fat
Beef	2
Butter	3
Chicken	20
Eggs (chicken)	7
Lamb	3
Lard	10
Milk (cow)	3
Salmon	26
Tuna	25
Turkey	21

*Source: "Fatty Acids in Food Fats," Home Economics Research Report No. 7, U.S. Department of Agriculture.

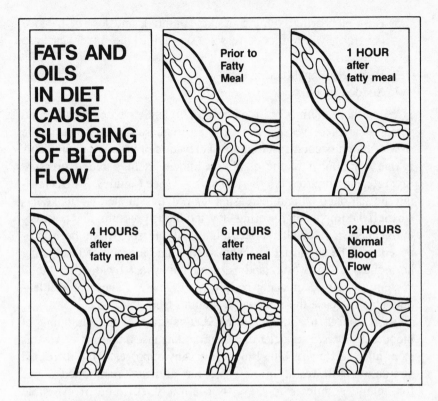

Figure 7.1. Blood cells within a blood vessel flow freely and bounce off one another prior to a meal high in fat. Approximately one hour after a fatty meal, the cells begin to stick together upon contact and form small clumps. As this clump formation progresses, the flow of blood slows (sludging). Six hours after the meal the clumping becomes so severe that blood flow actually stops in some vessels. Several hours later the clumps break up and the blood flow returns to the tissue. Many people consume high-fat meals three and more times a day, causing continuous sludging of their blood, which in turn results in a poor supply of oxygen and other essential nutrients to their tissues all day long.

2. Decreased ability to walk if one has narrowed arteries in the legs.[17,18] This condition is known as intermittent claudication.
3. A stroke if the arteries to the brain are diseased with atherosclerosis. Or a recurring condition of temporary blockage of a vessel to the brain tissue known as transient ischemic attacks (TIA).[12,18]
4. Fatigue, decreased endurance, and decreased work performance.[16,19]

5. Loss of hearing, ringing in ears (tinnitis), and loss of balance (vertigo) when blood vessels supplying the inner ear are involved.[20]

6. Reduced lung function.[21]

7. Sudden death.[22]

When these clumps of blood cells and platelets block small blood vessels and these vessels constrict, an increase in resistance to the flow of blood occurs, resulting in an elevation of blood pressure. This is one component of the condition known as high blood pressure (hypertension or arterial hypertension).[23-27] (See Figure 7.2.) Decreasing the saturated fat and increasing the polyunsaturated fat intake has a beneficial impact on lowering elevated blood pressure, and a variety of mechanisms for this effect on blood pressure have been proposed.[27,28] The suggested mechanisms include a group of fascinating hormones called prostaglandins, which may act by dilating blood vessels, thereby decreasing peripheral resistance. These prostaglandins also increase the removal of sodium from the body.[28]

Soon after a health-supporting diet is started, the clumping of blood cells ceases, platelet aggregation decreases, spasms of vessels stop, and the flow of blood to vital organs improves. This increased circulation will result in relief of the ailments mentioned above for many people who have not already suffered irreversible damage.[13-20,25,27]

All fats, including cold-pressed vegetable oils, promote the growth of cancers in animals.[29-31] (See Figure 7.3.) Current scientific evidence also supports the concept that fats enhance the development of certain cancers in people.[32-37] For example, studies show that the more fat that is consumed by the people of a particular country, the greater is the incidence of breast cancer among the women of that country.[31,38,39] This is illustrated by Figure 7.4.

Cancers of the colon, kidneys, ovaries, testicles, prostate, body of the uterus and lymphomas are also more common in populations which consume rich diets that are high in fat.[40-46] (See Figure 7.5.) A variety of mechanisms for the carcinogenic effects of fats have been proposed. Many theories have focused on the production of hormones and carcinogenic agents from components of foods eaten and also from natural substances present in our bodies. For example, the suggested mechanism for the development of colon cancer involves

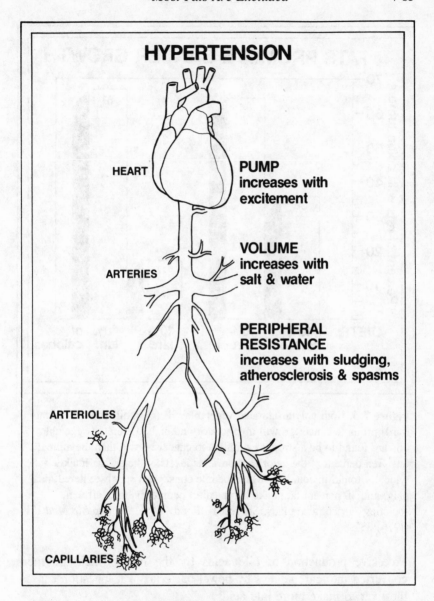

Figure 7.2. Elevation of blood pressure (hypertension) is a result of an increase in heart (pump) activity caused by excitement and exercise, an increase in blood volume from salt consumption, and/or an increase in resistance to flow caused by sludging of blood, atherosclerosis, and spasms at the level of small arteries (arterioles) and capillaries.

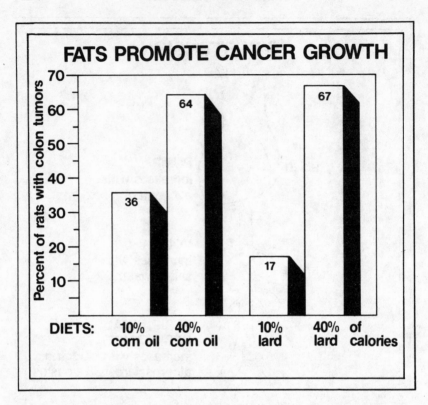

Figure 7.3. Both polyunsaturated vegetable oils (corn oil) and animal fats (lard) promote cancer growth in laboratory animals. Often the vegetable oils are found to be a stronger stimulus to cancer growth than the animal fats. Ten percent of the calories represents levels of dietary fat intake typically found in countries where people consume a starch-centered meal plan, and 40 percent fat intake is typical of people living in affluent societies on rich meal plans. Source: B. Reddy, *Proc Soc Exp Bio Med* 151 (1976):237.

excessive production of bile acids by the liver, which are then converted into carcinogens by bowel bacteria.[47] Fat ingestion causes the liver to make more bile acids.

Many of the cancers mentioned above are also found more commonly among members of the same family. The primary reason for this association is not totally genetic transmission but more importantly because the methods we use for cooking and the foods we enjoy eating are learned from our parents. An example of this is seen in breast cancer. A woman who has a mother or sister with breast cancer can run as high as a 50 percent chance of eventually

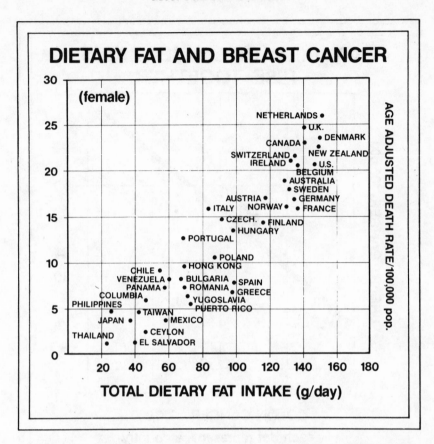

Figure 7.4. Dietary fat consumption correlates most strongly with the risk of dying from breast cancer in various countries. Source: K. Carroll, *Cancer Res* 35 (1975):3374.

developing breast cancer or another of the serious diet-related cancers.[48-50]

There is at present sufficient evidence to recommend a dietary change to victims of diet-related cancers. Animal studies performed since 1942 show that high-fat and high-calorie diets promote the growth of cancer.[29-31,51] And to reiterate, the growth of established tumors is retarded by a low-fat, no-cholesterol diet, and the animals live longer.[51] In the case of breast cancer, women with cancer who live in countries where diets low in fat are consumed survive longer than those from a country with a higher fat intake.[52-54] Also, women who are obese and have high, "normal," blood cholesterol levels die more than twice as fast as thin women with low blood cholesterol levels.[55-56]

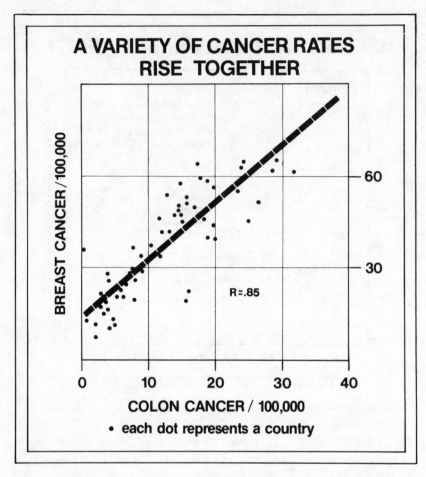

Figure 7.5. Because a rich diet is the causative factor shared by many types of cancer, people living in countries with high rates of one cancer usually have high rates of other cancers. Source: A. Lowenfels, *Cancer* 39 (1977):1809.

Both obesity and cholesterol are direct results of the richness of one's diet. Factors that cause cancer also promote its growth, and logic dictates that a person with a diet-related cancer must stop adding fuel to the fire. This is analogous to a person with lung cancer, who should obviously quit smoking; and people who do stop smoking before or at the time of diagnosis of some types of cancer of the lung survive longer than those who continue to smoke.[57] Failure to extend the same good sense to victims of other cancers and to recommend that someone with a diet-related cancer change his or her diet, is as serious an omission of sound medical advice as a failure to advise someone with lung cancer to quit smoking.

Fats also impair the function of the blood cells involved in the immune system.[58] These cells are called lymphocytes, phagocytes, and granulocytes. Their role is to inactivate and destroy bacteria, viruses, cancer cells, and other harmful elements that are present in our bodies. The impairment of the immune defense system may be one reason why obesity, which is usually the direct result of rich foods that are high in fat, is associated with an increased incidence of infection.[58]

Eating a high-fat diet also can contribute to the development of adult-onset diabetes and possibly hypoglycemia.[59-62] The pancreas operates in a manner analogous to that of a thermostat. It secretes insulin in response to sugar in the blood. A person with the adult form of diabetes produces as much and often more insulin than a normal person.[63] One of the reasons for this is that a high level of fat in the bloodstream after a meal actually blocks the action of the insulin, allowing the blood sugar level to rise too high.[64-66] Reduction of fat in the diet allows the insulin to function efficiently and can "cure" this form of diabetes. Investigators at the University of Kentucky Medical School and other centers have found that approximately 75 percent of adult-onset diabetics on insulin therapy and 75 to 90 percent of those on diabetic pills can be freed of their need for medication in a few short weeks after changing to a low-fat, high-carbohydrate, high-fiber diet.[61,62,67]

Childhood-onset diabetes is a different disease from the adult variety and is probably caused by destruction of the pancreas by a viral illness. Insulin is absent or insufficient in this disease. This type of diabetes is not caused or cured by diet. However, a health-supporting diet will benefit these people by reducing their insulin requirements by about 30 percent and by stabilizing their blood sugar levels (in medical terms, they become less "brittle"). One of the most important reasons for a person with either type of diabetes to consume a health-supporting diet is to reduce the likely possibility of complications of diabetes, such as premature atherosclerosis, heart attacks, kidney failure, and blindness, which afflict most diabetics within seventeen years of the onset of the disease.[68] Better control of insulin-dependent diabetics through closer insulin regulation and a low-fat, high-complex-carbohydrate diet has been found to be associated with a reduction in progression of diabetic tissue damage, especially in preservation of kidney and nerve function.[69] Even improvement in eye changes caused by diabetes has been seen folllowing the use of low-fat, starch-centered diets.[70-71] So, diabetics who have already suffered from serious complications of their disease should not give up hope but should change their eating habits.

The amount and type of fat in our diet also can affect our hormones, in particular the levels of prolactin, estrogen, and testosterone, which are involved in reproductive and sexual functions.[29,72-74] Hormonal changes occur in part because diets high in animal fat encourage the growth of hormone-producing bacteria (*clostridia* varieties) in the large intestine.[75] Obesity, which is usually the direct result of a high-fat diet, also affects the hormone levels of the body.[76-77] In women on diets high in animal fats, the following changes are common:

1. Menarche, the onset of maturity in young women, occurs early. Girls on low-fat diets start their menstrual periods at about sixteen years of age. Those on rich diets often begin at age twelve or earlier.[78-79] (See Figure 7.6.)
2. Menopause, the end of reproductive life, occurs approximately four years later on rich diets (fifty years versus forty-six years).[80]
3. Menstrual periods are further apart, longer, heavier, and more painful when fat intake is high.[29]
4. Hormones that may participate in intermediary steps in the cause of breast cancer are produced.[75]

High-fat diets also cause hormonal changes and early maturation in men, but the effects are not quite as obvious. It is interesting to speculate about the effects on our society caused by the precocious development of sexual drives and reproductive functions in our children.

Saturated fat raises blood cholesterol levels, which in turn increase the chance of dying of a heart attack.[81] Approximately 1,000 milligrams of saturated fat has the same effect on the blood cholesterol level as 25 milligrams of dietary cholesterol.[82] Saturated fat also promotes increased blood clotting, which contributes to the development of heart attacks, strokes, gangrene, pulmonary embolism, thrombosed hemorrhoids, and blood clots in the veins of the legs.[11,83-87]

You may have heard that polyunsaturated vegetable oils are better for your health. However, the consumption of this form of fat also can be a serious health hazard. When polyunsaturated fat is consumed, it

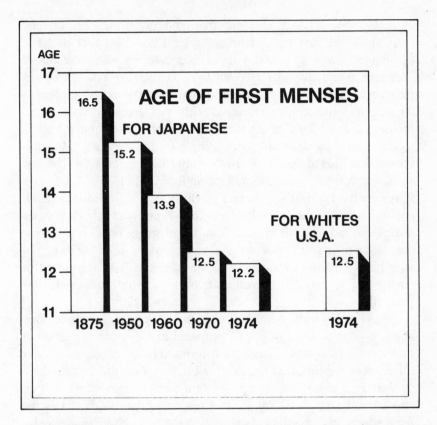

Figure 7.6. Young girls in Japan are now maturing into women three years earlier than their ancestors because of a change from a traditional starch-centered diet of rice and vegetables to a richer fat-centered diet following World War II. Similar changes in maturation have taken place over the last century in most affluent western societies. Source: Y. Kagawa, *Prev Med* 7 (1978):205.

acts like a cholesterol-lowering drug. This action drives large amounts of stored cholesterol from the body tissues, through the liver and gallbladder, and into the bowel.[88] The additional cholesterol in the gallbladder contributes to the formation of gallstones.[89-90] In the bowel the excreted cholesterol may be involved in the cause of cancer of the colon and other types of cancers.[91] Polyunsaturated fat also causes "thinning" of the blood, which can result in a serious bleeding tendency.[92-93] Polyunsaturated oils eaten in excess are dangerous. Use only the recommended starch-centered diet to lower your cholesterol and prevent disease.

Studies on diet and acne are sparse to say the least, but they certainly leave the many dermatologists who claim that diet has nothing to do with acne without adequate scientific backing.[94] Teenagers worldwide will be happy to know that their observations of the effect of certain foods on their complexions have strong support in the medical literature.[95] Drying agents and frequent washing to remove oil from the skin are the mainstays of the "pimple therapy" recommended by dermatologists. People on low-fat diets have non-greasy skin, free of excess oil. Both animal and vegetable fats can end up on the skin from handling and eating foods high in fat.[96-99] Bacteria thrive on the fats in the skin and produce the kind of inflammation commonly known as a pimple. The excess oil in your hair also comes directly or indirectly from your food. You might recall the recommendation of your veterinarian to add a tablespoon of lard or an egg to your pet's food in order to make its coat shine. If you are tired of having a shiny coat, try the opposite of the veterinarian's advice for yourself.

Fat in the diet is the number one enemy of overweight people. One gram of fat contains 9 calories, compared to 4 calories in a gram of protein or carbohydrate. Thus, the calories in fat are two and a quarter times more concentrated than the calories in a simple carbohydrate such as pure sugar. An average western diet provides 42 percent fat and 24 percent refined sugar.[32,100] Even more than sugar, fat is the main source of concentrated calories in the diets of affluent people, often served in "empty calorie" products providing little or no vitamins, minerals, protein, or fiber.

Many environmental contaminants, including pesticides, herbicides, preservatives, drugs, and waste chemical products, are soluble in fat and therefore are concentrated in the fatty tissues of animals and plants. You can easily consume dangerous amounts of these contaminants if you're on a high-fat diet.[101-102]

When butter became scarce during World War II, a synthetic substitute called margarine replaced it in many homes. The manufacturing process uses vegetable oils, which are liquid at room temperature, and adds hydrogen with the aid of a catalyst to make a solid product. In chemical terms, what occurs is that the polyunsaturated carbon-carbon linkages in the vegetable oils are saturated with hydrogen to make saturated fats. The chemical process creates a group of fats called trans-fats which are not commonly found in nature.[103] These fats are incorporated into our body fat and other tissues. These unnatural trans-fats are felt to be especially hazardous to health. Trans-fats cause an exceptionally high rise in cholesterol and triglycerides when fed to people.[104] Deaths from heart disease and cancer have been reported to be highest among consumers of this type of fat.[105-106]

Vegetable foods are generally low in total fat content. The exceptions are vegetable oils, nuts, seeds, avocados, olives, co-conuts, wheat germ, soybeans, and most of the byproducts derived from these high-fat plant foods. A health-supporting diet contains very little fat and therefore limits the intake of the high-fat plant foods. Ideally, 5 percent or less of our total calories should come from fat. Often, 8 to 10% of the calories from a starch-centered diet are provided by fat. A low fat level is especially important for people who are ill and are trying to regain their health. However, the plant fat intake for growing children, for thin, very active, healthy adults, or for pregnant or lactating (nursing) women can be increased somewhat without adverse effect. These people may include an extra 10 percent of their calories as fat from high-fat plant foods, bringing their fat intake to 15 percent of the total number of calories. This extra amount of fat provides easily accessible calories for these people with a greater need for energy. (See Table 7.2.)

Table 7.2. FAT:

Remember the few vegetable foods which are high in fat. These should be avoided if you are trying to regain your health or lose weight.

Percentage of Calories in Selected Foods

Low-fat vegetable foods

white potatoes	1	brown rice	5
yams	2	chestnuts	7
sweet potatoes	3	whole wheat bread	8
lentils	3	corn	8
spaghetti	3	broccoli	9
navy beans	4	apple	9
orange	4	oatmeal	16

High-fat vegetable foods

tempeh	25	almonds	82
wheat germ	27	avocados	88
soybeans	40	coconut	92
tofu	53	olives	98
sunflower seeds	76	vegetable oil	100
peanut butter	77		

Animal foods

skim milk	2	chocolate candy (milk)	56
buttermilk	3	mackerel fish	60
codfish	5	tuna in oil	64
tuna in water	6	egg	65
shrimp	8	cheddar cheese	73
chicken (light skinned)	18	frankfurters	80
milk low-fat	31	t-bone steak	82
ice cream	49	bacon	94
milk (whole-3.5%)	49	butter	100

Please refer to *Appendix I* for a more complete list of the percentages of fat in various vegetable foods.

Notes

[1] R. Holman, "The Essential Fatty Acid Requirement of Infants and the Assessment of Their Dietary Intake of Linoleate by Serum Fatty Acid Analysis," *Am J Clin Nutr* 14 (1964):70.

[2] A. Hansen, III "Clinical Manifestations of Lenoleic Acid Deficiency. Essential Fatty Acids in Infant Nutrition," *J of Nutr* 66 (1958):565.

[3] M. Crawford, "Essential Fatty Acid Requirements in Infancy," *Am J Clin Nutr* 31 (1978):2181.

[4] R. Moore, "Conflicting Roles of Polyunsaturated Fatty Acids," (letter) *Lancet* 1 (1980):654.

[5] Z. Freidman, "Essential Fatty Acids Revisited," *Am J Dis Child* 134 (1980):397.

[6] A. Vergroesen, *The Role of Fats in Human Nutrition*, New York: Academic Press, (1975): pp. 19-20.

[7] C. Cullen, "Intravascular Aggregation and Adhesiveness of the Blood Elements Associated with Alimentary Lipemia and Injections of Large Molecular Substances," *Circulation* 9 (1954):335.

[8] M. Friedman, "Serum Lipids and Conjunctival Circulation After Fat Ingestion in Men Exhibiting Type-A Behavior Pattern," *Circulation* 29 (1964):874.

[9] M. Friedman, "Effect of Unsaturated Fats Upon Lipemia and Conjunctival Circulation," *JAMA* 193 (1965):110.

[10] M. Hamberg, "Thromboxanes: A New Group of Biologically Active Compounds Derived from Prostaglandin Endoperoxides," *Proc Nat Acad Sci USA* 72 (1975):2994.

[11] J. O'Brien, "Acute Platelet Changes after Large Meals of Saturated and Unsaturated Fats," *Lancet* 1 (1976):878.

[12] P. Oliva, "Pathophysiology of Acute Myocardial Infarction, 1981," *Ann Intern Med* 94 (1981):236.

[13] P. Kuo, "Angina Pectoris Induced by Fat Ingestion in Patients with Coronary Artery Disease," *JAMA* 158 (1955):1008.

[14] F. Ellis, "Angina and Vegan Diet," *Am Heart J* 93 (1977):803.

[15] A. Williams, "Increased Blood Cell Agglutination Following Ingestion of Fat, a Factor Contributing to Cardiac Ischemia, Coronary Insufficiency, and Anginal Pain," *Angiology* 8 (1957):29.

[16] D. Ornish, "Effects of Stress Management Training and Dietary Changes in Treating Ischemia Heart Disease," *JAMA* 249 (1983):54.

[17] N. Pritikin, "Diet and Exercise as a Total Therapeutic Regimen for Rehabilitation of Patients with Severe Peripheral Vascular Disease," 52nd Annual Session of the American Congress on Rehabilitation Medicine, Atlanta, 1975.

[18] P. Kuo, "The Effect of Lipemia Upon Coronary Circulation and Peripheral Arterial Circulation in Patients with Essential Hyperlipemia," *Am J Med* 26 (1959):68.

[19] J. Bernard, "Effects of an Intensive, Short-Term Exercise and Nutrition Program on Patients with Coronary Heart Disease," *J Card Rehab* 1 (1981):99.

[20] J. Spencer, "Hyperlipoproteinemias in the Etiology of Inner Ear Disease," *Laryngoscope* 85 (1973):639.

[21] D. Hazlett, "Dietary Fats Appear to Reduce Lung Function," *JAMA* 223 (1973):15.

[22] H. Pirkle, "Pulmonary Platelet Aggregates Associated with Sudden Death in Man," *Science* 185 (1974):1062.

[23] E. Frohlich, "Re-examination of the Hemodynamics of Hypertension," *Am J Med Sci* 257 (1969):9.

[24] S. Malhotra, "Dietary Factors Causing Hypertension in India," *Am J Clin Nutr* 23 (1970):1353.

[25] P. Puska, "Controlled, Randomized Trial of the Effect of Dietary Fat on Blood Pressure," *Lancet* 1 (1983):1.

[26] P. Burstyn, "Fat Induced Hypertension in Rabbits, Effect of Dietary Fiber on Blood Pressure and Blood Lipid Concentration," *Cardiovascular Res* 14 (1980):185.

[27] J. Iacono, "Reduction of Blood Pressure Associated with Dietary Polyunsaturated Fat," *Hypertension* 4 (supp III) (1982):111-34.

[28] I. Rouse, "Blood-Pressure-Lowering Effect of a Vegetarian Diet: Controlled Trial in Normotensive Subjects," *Lancet* 1 (1983):5.

[29] P. Hill, "Diet and Endocrine-Related Cancer," *Cancer* 39 (1977):1820.

[30] Y. Nishizuka, "Biological Influence of Fat Intake on Mammary Cancer and Mammary Tissue: Experimental Correlates," *Prev Med* 7 (1978):218.

[31] K. Carroll, "Experimental Evidence of Dietary Factors and Hormone-Dependent Cancers," *Cancer Res* 35 (1975):3374.

[32] "Dietary Goals for the United States," Washington, D.C.: Government Printing Office, stock no. 052-070-03913-2, 1977.

[33] A. Upton, "Report Before the Senate Subcommittee on Agriculture, Nutrition, and Forestry," Bethesda, Md.: National Institute of Health, Oct. 2, 1979.

[34] T. Hirayama, "Epidemiology of Breast Cancer with Special Reference to the Role of Diet," *Prev Med* 7 (1978):173.

[35] E. Wynder, "Dietary Fat and Colon Cancer," *J Nat Ca Inst* 54 (1975):7.

[36] J. Berg, "Can Nutrition Explain the Pattern of International Epidemiology of Hormone-Dependent Cancers?" *Cancer Res* 35 (1975):3345.

[37] Committee on Diet, Nutrition, and Cancer, Assembly of Life Sciences, National Research Council, *Diet, Nutrition, and Cancer,* Washington, D.C.: National Academy Press, 1982.

[38] A. Lea, "Dietary Factors Associated With Death Rates from Certain Neoplasms in Man," *Lancet* 2 (1966):332.

[39] M. Howell, "The Association Between Colon-Rectal Cancer and Breast Cancer," *J Chron Dis* 29 (1976):243.

[40] E. Wynder, "The Dietary Environment and Cancer," *J Am Diet Assoc* 71 (1977):385.

[41] E. Wynder, "Contribution of the Environment to Cancer Incidence: An Epidemiologic Exercise," *J Nat Ca Inst* 58 (1977):825.

[42] J. Weisburger, "Nutrition and Cancer—On the Mechanisms Bearing on Causes of Cancer of the Colon, Breast, Prostate, and Stomach," *Bull New York Acad Med* 56 (1980):673.

[43] E. Wynder, "Epidemiology of Adenocarcinoma of the Kidney," *J Nat Ca Inst* 53 (1974):1619.

[44] L. Schuman, "Epidemiology of Prostate Cancer in Blacks," *Prev Med* 9 (1980):630.

[45] P. Hill, "Environmental Factors and Breast and Prostate Cancer," *Cancer Res* 41 (1981):3817.

[46] A. Cunningham, "Lymphomas and Animal-Protein Consumption," *Lancet* 2 (1976):1184.

[47] B. Reddy, "Metabolic Epidemiology of Colon Cancer: Fecal Bile Acids and Neutral Sterols in Colon Cancer Patients and Patients with Adenomatous Polyps," *Cancer* 39 (1977):2533.

[48] S. Albert, "Familial Cancer in the General Population," *Cancer* 40 (1977):1674.

[49] D. Anderson, "A Genetic Study of Human Breast Cancer," *J Nat Ca Inst* 48 (1972):1029.

[50] H. Lynch, "Management of Familial Breast Cancer," *Arch Surg* 113 (1978):1061.

[51] M. Littman, "Effect of Cholesterol-Free, Fat-Free Diet and Hypocholesteremic Agents on Growth of Transplantable Animal Tumors," *Cancer Chemotherapy Rept* 50 (1966):25.

[52] E. Wynder, "A Comparison of Survival Rates Between American and Japanese Patients with Breast Cancer," *Surg Gynecol Obstet* 117 (1963):196.

[53] A. Morrison, "Some International Differences in Treatment and Survival in Breast Cancer," *Int J Cancer* 18 (1976):269.

[54] T. Nemoto, "Differences in Breast Cancer Between Japan and the United States," *J Natl Cancer Inst* 58 (1977):193.

[55] P. Tartter, "Cholesterol and Obesity as Prognostic Factors in Breast Cancer," *Cancer* 47 (1981):2222.

[56] W. Donegan, "The Association of Body Weight with Recurrent Cancer of the Breast," *Cancer* 41 (1978):1590.

[57] A. Johnston-Early, "Smoking Abstinence and Small Cell Lung Cancer Survival-an association," *JAMA* 224 (1980):2175.

[58] J. Palmblad, "Lymphomas and Dietary Fat," *Lancet* 1 (1977):142.

[59] H. Hinsworth, "The Physiological Activation of Insulin," *Clin Sci* 1 (1933):1.

[60] S. Sweeney, "Dietary Factors That Influence the Dextrose Tolerance Test," *Arch Intern Med* 40 (1927):818.

[61] I. Singh, "Low-Fat Diet and Therapeutic Doses of Insulin in Diabetes Mellitus," *Lancet* 1 (1955):422.

[62] J. Anderson, "Update on HCF Diet Results." HCF Newsletter 4: June 1982, Lexington, Ky.

[63] S. Berson, "Plasma Insulin in Health and Disease," *Am J Med* 31 (1961):874.

[64] P. Davidson, "Insulin Resistance in Hyperglyceridemia," *Metabolism* 14 (1965):1059.

[65] J. Farquhar, "Glucose, Insulin, and Triglyceride Responses on High and Low Carbohydrate Diets in Man," *J Clin Invest* 45 (1966):1648.

[66] J. Olefsky, "Reappraisal of the Role of Insulin in Hypertriglyceridemia," *Am J Med* 57 (1974):551.

[67] J. Barnard, "Response of Non-Insulin-Dependent Diabetic Patients to an Intensive Program of Diet and Exercise," *Diabetes Care* 5 (1982):370.

[68] "Report of the National Commission on Diabetes to the Congress of the United States," vol. 111, part 2, DHEW pub. no. (NIH) 76-1022, 1975.

[69] R. Holman, "Prevention of Deterioration of Renal and Sensory-Nerve Function by More Intensive Management of Insulin-Dependent Diabetic Patients," *Lancet* 1 (1983):204.

[70] W. Kempner, "Effect of Rice Diet on Diabetes Mellitus Associated with Vascular Disease," *Postgrad Med* 24 (1958):359.

[71] W. Van Eck, "The Effect of a Low Fat Diet on the Serum Lipids in Diabetes and Its Significance in Diabetic Retinopathy," *Am J Med* 27 (1959):196.

[72] P. Hill, "Plasma Hormones and Lipids in Men at Different Risk for Coronary Heart Disease," *Am J Clin Nutr* 33 (1980):1010.

[73] B. Goldin, "Estrogen Excretion Patterns and Plasma Levels in Vegetarian and Omnivorous Women," *N Engl J Med* 307 (1982):1542.

[74] P. Hill, "Diet and Prolactin Release," *Lancet* 2 (1976):806.

[75] M. Hill, "Gut Bacteria and Aetiology of Cancer of the Breast," *Lancet* 2 (1971):472.

[76] M. Kirschner, "The Role of Hormones in the Etiology of Human Breast Cancer," *Cancer* 39 (1977):2716.

[77] Editorial, "Obesity: The Cancer Connection," *Lancet* 1 (1982):1223.

[78] Y. Kagawa, "Impact of Westernization on the Nutrition of Japanese: Changes in Physique, Cancer, Longevity, and Centenarians," *Prev Med* 7 (1978):205.

[79] G. Beaton, "Practical Population Indicators of Health and Nutrition," WHO Monograph 62(1976):500.

[80] D. Frommer, "Changing Age of the Menopause," *Br Med J* 2 (1964):349.

[81] J. Anderson, "Independence of the Effects of Cholesterol and Degree of Saturation of the Fat in the Diet on Serum Cholesterol in Man," *Am J Clin Nutr* 29 (1976):1184.

[82] A. Keys, "Serum Cholesterol Response to Changes in Dietary Lipids," *Am J Clin Nutr* 19 (1966):175.

[83] J. Mustard, "Effect of Different Dietary Fats on Blood Coagulation, Platelet Economy, and Blood Lipids," *Br Med J* 2 (1962):1651.

[84] A. Keys, "Effects of Different Fats on Blood Coagulation," *Circulation* 15 (1957):274.

[85] H. Greig, "Inhibition of Fibrinolysis by Alimentary Lipemia," *Lancet* 2 (1956):16.

[86] G. Hornstra, "Influence of Dietary Fat on Platelet Function in Men," *Lancet* 1 (1973):1155.

[87]J. O'Brien, "Fat Ingestion, Blood Coagulation, and Atherosclerosis," *Am J Med Sci* 234 (1957):373.

[88]P. Nestel, "Lowering of Plasma Cholesterol and Enhanced Sterol Excretion with the Consumption of Polyunsaturated Ruminant Fats," *N Engl J Med* 288 (1973):379.

[89]L. Bennion, "Risk Factors for the Development of Cholelithiasis in Man, (second of two parts)" *N Engl J Med* 299 (1978):1221.

[90]R. Studervant, "Increased Prevalence of Cholelithiasis in Men Ingesting a Serum-Cholesterol-Lowering Diet," *N Engl J Med* 288 (1973):24.

[91]S. Broitman, "Polyunsaturated Fat, Cholesterol, and Large Bowel Tumorigenesis," *Cancer* 40 (1977):2455.

[92]J. Dyerberg, "Haemostatic Function and Platelet Polyunsaturated Fatty Acids in Eskimos," *Lancet* 2 (1979):433.

[93]J. O'Brien, "Effect of a Diet of Polyunsaturated Fats on Some Platelet-Function Tests," *Lancet* 2 (1976):995.

[94]J. Fulton, "Effect of Chocolate on Acne Vulgaris," *JAMA* 210 (1969):2071.

[95]J. Rasmussen, "Review—Diet and Acne," *Int J Dermatol* 16 (1977):488.

[96]G. Hoehn, "Acne and Diet," *Cutis* 2 (1966):389.

[97]D. Wilkinson, "Psoriasis and Dietary Fat: The Fatty Acid Composition of Surface and Scale (Ether-Soluble) Lipids," *J Invest Dermatol* 47 (1966):185.

[98]P. Pochi, "Sebaceous Gland Response in Man to Prolonged Total Calorie Deprivation," *J Invest Dermatol* 55 (1970):303.

[99]P. Kuo, "Lipemia in Patients with Coronary Artery Disease," *J Am Diet Assoc* 33 (1957):22.

[100]R. Marston, "Nutrient content of the National Food Supply." *National Food Review U.S.D.A.* Dec 1978 p.28-33.

[101]H. Roberts, *Food Safety,* New York: Wiley Interscience, 1981, pp. 141-180.

[102]M. Lippmann, *Chemical Contamination of the Human Environment,* Oxford: Oxford University Press, 1979, pp. 146-151.

[103]L. Thomas, "Hydrogenated Oils and Fats: The Presence of Chemically-Modified Fatty Acids in Human Adipose Tissue," *Am J Clin Nutr* 34 (1981):877.

[104]J. Anderson, "Hydrogenated Fats in the Diet and Lipids in the Serum of Man," *J Nutr* 75 (1961):388.

[105]L. Thomas, "Mortality from Arteriosclerotic Disease and Consumption of Hydrogenated Oils and Fats," *Br J Prev Soc Med* 29 (1975):82.

[106]M. Enig, "Dietary Fat and Cancer Trends—A Critique," *Fed Proc* 37 (1978):2215.

Chapter
8

Protein and a Health-Supporting Diet

Proteins provide important materials to build and maintain our hormones, enzymes, muscles, and many other body tissues. Accurate estimates of human adult protein needs determined by careful studies show that as little as 2.5 percent of our daily calorie intake can be safely provided in the form of protein.[1-4] This amount is equivalent to a little less than 20 grams—two-thirds of an ounce—for an adult man. The World Health Organization (WHO) has established a higher minimum daily requirement for protein to be approximately 5 percent of the daily calorie intake, but many populations have lived in excellent health on less than this amount.[5-10] (Protein requirements for pregnancy set by the WHO are 6 percent, and for lactation 6.7 percent of the daily calorie intake.)

An average working man consumes 3,000 calories a day, so 5 percent of the total would be 150 calories from protein. Since each gram of protein is equal to 4 calories, this would represent 37 grams of protein. An average woman consuming 2,300 calories a day needs 29 grams of protein. These minimum requirements provide for a large margin of safety that easily covers people who theoretically could have greater protein needs. This quantity of protein is almost impossible to avoid if enough food is consumed to meet daily calorie needs. For example, 3,000 calories of rice alone would provide 60 grams of highly usable protein, or the same amount of white potatoes would provide 80 grams of protein.

The building blocks of protein are called amino acids. Varied combinations among twenty amino acids form the proteins found in all kinds of living creatures. All sources of unprocessed foods, including meat, dairy, fish, shellfish, plants, and microorganisms, contain all twenty of these amino acids. However, the amount of each amino acid that is present varies in different foods. Plants make all of them from carbon, nitrogen, sulfur, and water. Animals, including humans, can synthesize some of the needed amino acids, but others must be obtained from their food. The amino acids that cannot be synthesized and which must be provided by the diet are known as essential amino acids.

Many people believe that animal foods contain protein that is superior in quality to the protein found in plants. This is a misconception dating back to 1914, when Osborn and Mendel studied the protein requirements of laboratory rats.[11] They found that rats grew better on animal sources of protein than on vegetable sources. Investigators at that time suspected that the vegetable foods had insufficient amounts of some of the amino acids essential for the normal growth of rats. Because of these and other animal-based experiments, flesh, eggs, and dairy foods were classified as superior or "Class A" protein sources. Vegetable proteins were designated inferior or "Class B" proteins.

Studies in the mid-1940s found that ten amino acids were essential for a rat's diet.[12] If the level of any one amino acid was low, the rats could not efficiently utilize the protein and failed to grow normally. Animal products, such as meat, poultry, milk, and eggs, were found to contain these ten essential amino acids in just the right proportions for rats.

Based on these early rat experiments the amino acid pattern found in animal products was declared to be the standard by which to compare the amino acid pattern of vegetable foods. According to this concept, wheat and rice were declared deficient in lysine, and corn was deficient in tryptophan. It has since been shown that the initial premise that animal products supplied the most ideal protein pattern for humans, as it did for rats, was incorrect. Therefore, the idea that vegetable foods were deficient in certain amino acids for our needs was inappropriately based on a standard diet ideal for rats. At that early time no one knew the actual protein or amino acid requirements for humans.

In 1952 William Rose completed a long series of experiments to determine the amino acid requirements of human males. He fed his subjects a synthetic mixture of corn (maize) starch, sucrose, butter fat, vitamins, and highly purified amino acids, and then gradually eliminated one amino acid at a time.[13]

The study used a chemical measurement called nitrogen balance to determine whether the subjects were getting enough usable protein from the mixture. When an essential amino acid was given in insufficient amounts for approximately two days, all subjects complained of similar symptoms: a clear increase in nervous irritability, extreme fatigue, and a profound failure of appetite. The subjects were unable to continue the amino-acid-deficient diets for more than a few days at a time. From his experiments Dr. Rose found that only eight of the ten amino acids essential to rats were also essential to people. Arginine and histidine, the two other amino acids that were found essential in the rat's diet, were not essential to human adults. (However, histidine is essential in the diets of young children, and arginine is made slowly by infants. Plants are excellent sources of both of these amino acids and easily satisfy these amino acid needs of growing young children.)

Through his studies, Rose determined a minimum level of intake for each of the essential amino acids. He found small amounts of variation in individual needs among his subjects, but these differences did not seem to correlate with their weight or metabolic rate. Because of these unexplained differences among people, he included a large margin of safety in his final conclusion on minimum amino acid requirements. For each amino acid he took the highest recorded level of need in any single subject as his minimum requirement, and then doubled that amount for a recommended requirement described as "a definitely safe intake." It is important to realize that even his higher requirement is easily met by a health-supporting diet centered around any single starch.[14-15] In all but very young children, as long as energy needs are satisfied by unprocessed starches, protein needs are automatically satisfied in almost every situation because of the basic and complete design of the food.[15-17] Infants less than two years of age have difficulty consuming enough vegetable foods to meet their calorie needs because of the immaturity of their digestive systems and the bulky nature of some starches.[18-20] Although white potatoes can supply 100 percent of the protein for infants, grains often fall short of this nutritional need.[21] Therefore, as commonly practiced before modernization of societies, infants should obtain at least 25 to 50 percent of their diet from breast milk (or the best milk substitute available).[22]

The results of Rose's study are summarized in Figure 8.1, under "minimum requirements." From the chart, it is clear that even single vegetable foods contain more than enough of all amino acids essential for humans.

Many investigators have measured the capacity of plant foods to satisfy protein needs. Their findings show that children and adults thrive on diets based on single or combined starches, and grow healthy and strong.[4,5,25-43] Furthermore, many investigators have found no improvement by mixing plant foods or supplementing them with amino acid mixtures to make the combined amino acid pattern look more like that of flesh, milk, or eggs.[35-44] In fact, supplementing a food with an amino acid in order to conform to a contrived reference standard can create amino acid imbalances. For example, young children fed diets based on wheat or corn and supplemented with the amino acids tryptophan and methionine in order to conform to the standard requirements set by the Food and Agriculture Organization of the United Nations (FAO) developed negative responses in terms of nitrogen balance (the body's utilization of protein).[27]

People have actually lived for long periods of time in excellent health by satisfying their entire nutritional needs with potatoes and water alone.[33] And it is interesting that even though the amino acid patterns of potatoes and eggs are entirely different, their ability to satisfy the protein needs of people is the same.[44]

Many books popular among vegetarians today place great emphasis on combining vegetable foods to create an amino acid pattern that resembles that found in animal foods.[45] This emphasis is unnecessary and implies that it is difficult to obtain complete sources for synthesizing proteins from vegetables without detailed nutritional knowledge. Surprisingly, some followers of this concept actually believe that plant foods completely lack certain essential amino acids.[46] Because of this complicated and incorrect idea, people are frightened away from vegetable-based diets. Apparently authors of these popular cookbooks did not completely review the literature on human protein requirements and the amino acid content of plants. If they had done so, they would have understood that the combination of amino acids in proper proportions takes place long before our foods reach the dinner table. Nature has designed vegetable foods to be

ESSENTIAL AMINO ACIDS OF SELECTED FOODS

AMINO ACIDS (grams per day)	Rose's Minimum Requirem.	Rose's Recom. Requirem.	Corn	Brown rice	Oatmeal flakes	Wheat flour	White beans	Potatoes	Sweet Potatoes	Taro	Asparagus	Broccoli	Tomatoes	Pumpkin	Beef club steak	Egg	Milk
Tryptophan	.25	.50	.66	.71	1.4	1.4	1.8	.8	.8	1.0	3.9	3.8	1.4	1.5	3.1	3.8	2.3
Phenylalanine*	.28	.56	6.13	3.1	5.8	5.9	10.9	3.6	2.5	3.0	10.2	12.2	4.3	3.0	11.2	13.9	7.7
Leucine	1.10	2.20	12.0	5.5	8.1	8.0	17.0	4.1	2.6	5.2	14.6	16.5	6.1	6.0	22.4	21.0	15.9
Isoleucine	.7	1.4	4.1	3.0	5.6	5.2	11.3	3.6	2.2	3.0	11.9	12.8	4.4	4.3	14.3	15.7	10.3
Lysine	.8	1.6	4.1	2.5	4.0	3.2	14.7	4.4	2.1	3.4	15.5	14.8	6.3	5.5	23.9	15.3	12.5
Valine	.8	1.6	6.8	4.5	6.4	5.5	12.1	4.4	3.4	3.5	16.0	17.3	4.2	4.3	15.1	17.7	11.7
Methionine*	.11	.22	2.1	1.1	1.6	1.8	2.0	1.0	.8	.6	5.0	5.1	1.1	1.0	6.8	7.4	3.9
Threonine	.5	1.0	4.5	2.5	3.6	3.5	8.5	3.4	2.1	2.7	9.9	12.5	4.9	2.7	12.1	12.0	7.4
Total protein	20	37 (WHO)	109	64	108	120	198	82	45	58	330	338	150	115	276	238	160

Figure 8.1. A comparison of Rose's recommended requirements for essential amino acids for men consuming approximately 3,000 calories a day is made with single foods based on 3,000 calories consumed. Even simple starches, such as rice, satisfy Rose's recommended requirements, which are twice his minimum requirements. From these observations it is evident that it would be virtually impossible to design a diet deficient in protein or essential amino acids even if the sole source of calories were potatoes or rice. Requirements for phenylalanine and methionine are adjusted for replacement by the unessential amino acids, tyrosine and cystine. About 70 to 75 percent of the requirement for phenylalanine can be met by tyrosine and 80 to 90 percent of the requirement for methionine can be met by cystine. [23,24]

complete. If people living before the age of modern dietetics had had to worry about achieving the correct protein combinations in their diets, our species would not have survived for these millions of years. Humans have related to the world of food with primarily one drive— hunger—and in response to this one basic drive our needs for calories, proteins, amino acids, essential fat, fiber, vitamins, and minerals have been satisfied. A word of caution, however: one who follows the advice for protein combining can unintentionally design a diet containing an excessive and therefore harmful amount of protein by including too many high-protein legumes.

As the many amino acid studies have shown, the foods that provide correct nutrition for rats are not necessarily the same for humans. The diet of a rat is considerably different from that of a human. Based on weight, the adult rat requires three and a half times as much protein as a human, and the individual amino acids required are considerably different.[47] Because a rat grows rapidly into adult size as compared with a person, the rat's requirements for protein are much higher. This difference in need is especially clear when the breast milk of the two species is compared. The protein of rat breast milk is ten times more concentrated than that of milk intended for human babies.[48] (See Figure 8.2.)

The pictures one often sees of "protein-deficient" children in areas of famine in Asia or Africa are actually pictures of starvation, which is more accurately described as calorie deficiency.[16,49,50] When these children come under medical supervision, they are nourished back to health with their local diets of corn, wheat, rice, and/or beans.[15,17,18,49-52] Children recovering from starvation grow up to eighteen times faster than usual and require a higher protein content to provide for their catch-up in development. This exaggerated protein need can be met by a variety of starchy foods, including white potatoes.[21,53]

Eating excessive amounts of proteins can seriously damage our health. When our diet contains more proteins than we need, the excess is broken down in the liver and excreted through the kidneys as urea. This protein breakdown product is called BUN, or blood urea nitrogen. Urea has a diuretic action, which causes the kidneys to work harder and excrete more water. Along with the water, minerals are lost in the urine, and one of the most important minerals lost in this manner is calcium.[54-58]

On the average, Americans take in a little more than 100 grams of protein and 800 milligrams of calcium daily. In general, studies have

COMPARISON OF THE MILKS OF DIFFERENT SPECIES

	Mean values for protein content per cent.	Time required to double birth weight (days)
HUMAN	1·2	180
MARE	2·4	60
COW	3·3	47
GOAT	4·1	19
DOG	7·1	8
CAT	9·5	7
RAT	11·8	4·5

Figure 8.2. The amount of protein in the milk of an animal varies depending upon the rate of growth of the young of that species. Since rats and cows grow much faster than the human infant, the protein contents of the milk are much higher. (Values for protein are expressed as grams per 100 milliliters, not as percentage of calories.)[48]

shown that young men consuming diets containing more than 95 grams of protein daily developed a negative calcium balance, even with very high calcium intakes.[55,56] However, in one long-term study, investigators measured calcium balance in adults and found that when subjects consumed as little as 75 grams of protein a day, even with daily intakes as high as 1400 milligrams of calcium, more calcium was lost in the urine than was absorbed into the body from the diet (a negative calcium balance).[58] This would mean that most westerners have a net loss of calcium from their bodies every day. The deficit must be made up from the body stores of calcium, which are primarily the bones. The end result of this continuous process is calcium-deficient bones that break with the slightest provocation, such as a sneeze that can crack a rib or a normal step that can break a hip. This condition is called osteoporosis, and in affluent societies it occurs in about 25 percent of women over the age of sixty-five. By the time of diagnosis, 50 to 75 percent of the original bone material has been lost from the skeleton.[59] Observations of various populations worldwide show that the higher the protein intake, the more common is osteoporosis.[60] Bantus living in Africa on low-protein vegetable diets, consuming 47 grams of protein and 400 milligrams of calcium, are essentially free of osteoporosis.[61] Genetic relatives of the Bantu, a population of blacks investigated in the United States, consume a rich diet with plenty of meat and dairy foods, yet have osteoporosis nearly as commonly as do whites.[62] An excellent example of the effects of excess protein is seen in native Eskimos who consume a diet very high in protein—250 to 400 grams a day from fish, walrus, and whale, along with a high calcium intake of more than 2,000 milligrams from fishbones. Yet these very physically active people have one of the highest rates of osteoporosis in the world.[63]

The effect of protein on calcium metabolism suggests a benefit from a low-protein diet in the treatment of osteoporosis, because lowering the protein content of the diet is the most effective means of restoring a positive calcium balance. So it would follow that one of the measures of preventing this condition should also include a low-protein diet. Other factors are also involved in this condition, including physical activity and hormone status.[64]

The calcium lost on high-protein diets ends up in the urine and results in high levels of calcium in the kidney system. This contributes to the formation of painful calcium kidney stones.[65-68] Calcium stones are the most common type found in persons in affluent societies. So, a health-supporting diet that emphasizes low-protein foods would also help prevent the formation of calcium kidney stones in most people and would be of particular benefit to those who suffer from recurring stones.[65-69] (See Figure 8.3.)

For certain individuals, limiting the intake of protein can be essential not only for improving health but for staying alive. Protein consumed in excess of our needs causes destruction of kidney tissue and progressive deterioration of kidney function.[71,72] By the eighth decade of life, people in affluent societies commonly lose 75 percent of their kidney function.[71]   In someone with normal kidneys this loss rarely becomes significant because of the tremendous extra capacity

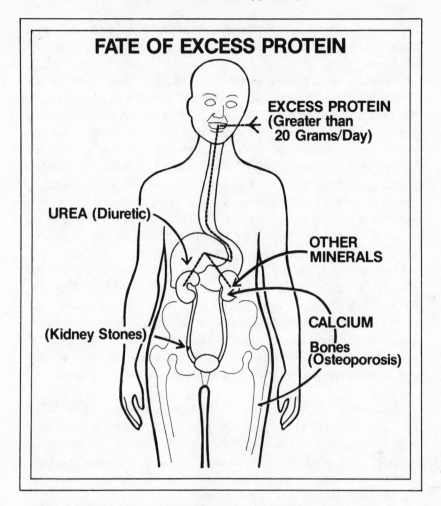

Figure 8.3. The body's capacity to store protein is minimal, at most. Protein consumed in excess of the amount needed for growth and tissue replacement is excreted. The liver and kidneys enlarge from the added work load of protein metabolism.[70] Osteoporosis and kidney stones are common consequences of prolonged consumption of high-protein foods.

the healthy kidney possesses. However, when a person suffers from an additional disease of the kidney, such as diabetes, surgical loss, or injury from toxic substances, the damage caused by the protein becomes critical. People with partial loss or damage to their kidneys, when placed on a protein-restricted diet, are able to preserve much of their remaining kidney function.[71,72] Those unfortunate patients left on high-protein diets show progressive deterioration of their kidneys to a point where all too soon most will end up needing help from kidney machines.

Protein is broken down in the liver, and the waste products are excreted through the kidneys. Failure of either of these organs to function normally will result in a buildup of protein breakdown products. Accumulation of these products will make a person extremely ill. On a low-protein diet, people with kidney or liver failure improve dramatically.[73-76] There are other dietary restrictions placed on kidney and liver patients. For example, it is extremely important for the sodium, potassium, and phosphates in the diet to be kept low with most kidney disease. Dietary and medical management of people with these and other serious ailments requires the strict supervision of someone trained in this type of care.

High-protein foods are generally high in purines, which are the primary building blocks of our genetic code material, DNA and RNA. Purines break down to form uric acid (not urea). The collection of uric acid in the joints leads to gout, a painful and deforming type of arthritis. Uric acid concentrated in the kidney system also leads to formation of uric acid kidney stones in susceptible people. Kidney stones are prevented and gout is easily cured with a low-protein, low-purine diet.[77-79]

Most animal products are inherently high in protein content. When the fat is removed from a food, the percentage of calories present as protein proportionately increases. For example, when the fat is removed from whole milk to produce skim milk, the relative protein content doubles. Therefore, removing the fat from a food is not without adverse nutritional consequences.

Vegetable products are usually lower in protein content than are animal products. The most important exceptions are the legumes, which include beans, peas, and lentils. These foods can be consumed easily in amounts large enough to yield a diet containing excessive protein. If you are in good health, legumes should be used in no more than one meal per day. The amount should not exceed one cup of cooked legumes per meal. Other high-protein vegetable foods, such as asparagus, lettuce, spinach, yeast, and mushrooms, usually are consumed in such small amounts that they don't have to be consciously limited by healthy people. Those who are placed on severe protein-restricted diets should avoid all high-protein vegetable foods. (See Table 8.1.)

Table 8.1. PROTEIN

The important points to remember are that except for a diet based on low calorie fruits, unprocessed plant foods easily meet protein needs for adults and children, and that excess intake of protein is the real potential for trouble. Protein-depleted starches and simple sugars are sometimes added to the diet of people with kidney and liver disease in order to lower the protein content of the diet even further.

Percent of Calories in Selected Foods

Low-protein vegetable foods

apple	1	mangos	4
dates	3	coconuts	5
pineapple	3		

Medium-protein vegetable foods

chestnuts	6	almonds	12
sweet potatoes	6	corn	12
oranges	8	spaghetti	14
rice	8	oatmeal	15
yams	8	onions	16
honeydew melons	10	whole wheat bread	16
white potatoes	11		

High-protein vegetable foods

celery	21	asparagus	38
artichokes	22	mushrooms	38
navy beans	26	tofu	44
peas	28	spinach	49
lentils	29	tempeh	49
soybeans	34	yeast	57
lettuce	34		

Animal foods

human breast milk	5	milk (skim)	41
milk (whole-cow-3.5%)	21	turkey	41
cheddar cheese	25	chicken (light-skinned)	76
yogurt	28	cottage cheese	79
milk (low-fat-cow-2%)	28	shrimp	84
hamburger	34	tuna in water	88
mackerel fish	37		

Please refer to *Appendix I* for a more complete list of the percentage of protein in various foods.

Misunderstandings about calcium and protein by lay persons and professional nutritionists have led to the inclusion of excessive amounts of flesh, dairy foods, and eggs in the western diet. Fortunately, the scientific studies performed during the last half-century clearly demonstrate that a starch-centered diet, with the addition of fruits and vegetables, supplies an excellent protein source and is thereby one of the foundations for excellent nutrition.

Notes

[1]W. Rose, "The Amino Acid Requirements of Adult Man, XVI, the Role of the Nitrogen Intake," *J Biol Chem* 217 (1955):997.

[2]D. Hegsted, "Minimum Protein Requirements of Adults," *Am J Clin Nutr* 21 (1968):352.

[3]W. Hoffman, "Nitrogen Requirement of Normal Men on a Diet of Protein Hydrolysate Enriched with the Limiting Essential Amino Acids," *J Nutr* 44 (1951):123.

[4]V. Dole, "Dietary Treatment of Hypertension, Clinical and Metabolic Studies of Patients on the Rice-Fruit Diet," *J Clin Invest* 29 (1950):1189.

[5]W. Kempner, "Treatment of Hypertensive Vascular Disease with Rice Diet," *Am J Med* 4 (1948):545.

[6]R. Luyken, "Nutrition Studies in New Guinea," *Am J Clin Nutr* 14 (1964):13.

[7]D. Milam, "Nutritional Survey of an Entire Rural Community in North Carolina," *Southern Med J* 37 (1944):597.

[8]V. Syndenstricker, "Nutrition Under Rationing in England," *J Am Diet Assoc* 20 (1944):4.

[9]W. Dann, "The Appraisal of Nutritional Status (Nutriture) in Humans with Especial Reference to Vitamin Deficiency Disease," *Physiol Rev* 25 (1945):326.

[10]F. Stare, "Nutrition," *Ann Rev Biochem* 14 (1945):431.

[11]T. Osborn, "Amino Acids in Nutrition and Growth," *J Biol Chem* 17 (1914):325.

[12]W. Rose, "Comparative Growth of Diets Containing Ten and Nineteen Amino Acids, with Further Observation Upon the Role of Glutamic and Aspartic Acid," *J Biol Chem* 176 (1948):753.

[13]W. Rose, "The Amino Acid Requirements of Adult Man," *Nutrition Abstracts and Reviews* 27 (1957):631.

[14]M. Hardinge, "Nutritional Studies of Vegetarians. V Proteins and Essential Amino Acids," *J Am Diet Assoc* 48 (1966):25.

[15]D. McLaren, "The Great Protein Fiasco," *Lancet* 2 (1974):93.

[16]C. Gopalan, "Effect of Calorie Supplementation on Growth of Undernourished Children," *Am J Clin Nutr* 26 (1973):563.

[17]M. Golden, "Protein Deficiency, Energy Deficiency, and the Oedema of Malnutrition," *Lancet* 1 (1982):1261.

[18]G. Lopez de Romana, "Prolonged Consumption of Potato-Based Diets by Infants and Small Children," *J Nutr* 111 (1981):1430.

[19]G. Graham, "Prolonged Consumption by Infants of Wheat-Based Diets with and without Casein or Lysine Supplementation," *J Nutr* 111 (1981):1917.

[20]W. MacLean, "Digestibility and Utilization of the Energy and Protein of Wheat by Infants," *J Nutr* 109 (1979):1290.

[21]G. Lopez de Romana, "Utilization of the Protein and Energy of the White Potato by Human Infants," *J Nutr* 110 (1980):1849.

[22]J. Gordon, "Weanling Diarrhea." *Am J Med Sci* 245 (1963):129.

[23]W. Rose, "The Amino Acid Requirements of Man. XIV The Sparing Effect of Tyrosine on Phenylalanine Requirement," *J Biol Chem* 217 (1955):95.

[24]W. Rose, "The Amino Acid Requirements of Man XIII The Sparing Effect of Cystine on Methionine Requirement," *J Biol Chem* 216 (1955):763.

[25]M. Abdulla, "Nutrient Intake and Health Status of Vegans; Chemical Analyses of Diets Using the Duplicate Portion Sampling Technique," *Am J Clin Nutr* 34 (1981):2464.

[26]S. Bolourich, "Wheat Flour as a Source of Protein for Adult Subjects," *Am J Clin Nutr* 21 (1968):827.

[27]M. Irwin, "A Conspectus of Research on Protein Requirements of Man," *J Nutr* 101 (1971):385.

[28]D. Hegsted, "Protein Requirements of Adults," *J Lab and Clin Med* 31 (1946):261.

[29]G. Arroyave, "Nutritive Values of Dietary Proteins: For Whom?" *Proc 9th Int Congr Nutrition, Mexico* 1 (1972):43.

[30]A. Truswell, "The Nutritive Value of Maize Protein for Man," *Am J Clin Nutr* 10 (1962):142.

[31]J. Dwyer, "Nutritional Status of Vegetarian Children," *Am J Clin Nutr* 35 (1982):204.

[32]G. Lopez de Romana, "Fasting and Postprandial Plasma Free Amino Acids of Infants and Children Consuming Exclusive Potato Protein," *J Nutr* 111 (1981):1766.

[33]S. Kon, "The Value of Whole Potatoes in Human Nutrition," *Biochemical J* 22 (1928):258.

[34]D. Hegsted, "Lysine and Methionine Supplementation of All-Vegetable Diets for Human Adults," *J Nutr* 56 (1955):555.

[35]C. Kies, "Determination of First Limiting Nitrogenous Factor in Corn Protein for Nitrogen Retention in Human Adults," *J Nutr* 86 (1965):350.

[36]V. Reddy, "Lysine Supplementation of Wheat and Nitrogen Retention in Children," *Am J Clin Nutr* 24 (1971):1264.

[37]J. Knapp, "Growth and Nitrogen Balance in Infants Fed Cereal Proteins," *Am J Clin Nutr* 26 (1973):586.

[38]A. Harper, "Some Implications of Amino Acid Supplementation," *Am J Clin Nutr* 9 (1961):553.

[39]C. Lee, "Nitrogen Retention of Young Men Fed Rice with or without Supplementary Chicken," *Am J Clin Nutr* 24 (1971):318.

[40]H. Clark, "Nitrogen Balances of Adult Human Subjects Fed Combinations of Wheat, Beans, Corn, Milk, and Rice," *Am J Clin Nutr* 26 (1973):702.

[41]C. Edwards, "Utilization of Wheat by Adult Man: Nitrogen Metabolism, Plasma Amino Acids and Lipids," *Am J Clin Nutr* 24 (1971):181.

[42]J. Howe, "Nitrogen Retention of Adults Fed Six Grams of Nitrogen From Combinations of Rice, Milk, and Wheat," *Am J Clin Nutr* 25 (1972):559.

[43]R. Abernathy, "Lack of Response to Amino Acid Supplements by Preadolescent Girls," *Am J Clin Nutr* 25 (1972):980.

[44]E. Kofranyi, "The Minimum Protein Requirements of Humans, Tested with Mixtures of Whole Egg Plus Potatoes and Maize Plus Beans," *Z Physiol Chem* 351 (1970):1485.

[45]F. Lappe, *Diet for a Small Planet,* New York: Ballantine Books, 1976. R. Laurel, *Laurel's Kitchen,* Berkeley, Calif.: Nilgiri Press, 1977. M. Ford, *The Deaf Smith Cookbook,* New York: Collier Books, 1973. E. Cottrell, *The Oats, Peas, Beans and Barley Cookbook,* Santa Barbara, Caalif.: Woodbridge Press, 1977.

[46]D. Peyton, "Complete Protein, Matching Pieces of the Puzzle," *Sunday Star-Bulletin and Advertiser,* Honolulu Gannett News Service (Oct. 25, 1981): C-16.

[47]M. Bricker, "The Protein Requirement of the Adult Rat in Terms of the Protein Contained in Egg, Milk, and Soy Flour," *J Nutr* 34 (1947):491.

[48]G. Bell, *Textbook of Physiology and Biochemistry,* 4th ed., Williams and Wilkins, Baltimore, 1959, pp. 167-170.

[49]E. Holt, *Protein and Amino Acid Requirements in Early Life,* New York: University Press, 1960, p. 12.

[50]D. Mclaren, "A Fresh Look at Protein–Calorie Malnutrition," *Lancet* 2 (1966):485.

[51]A. Harper, "Adaptive Changes to Low Nutrient Intake, Metabolic Adaption to Adequate and Inadequate Amino Acid Supply," *Proc 9th Int Congr Nutr, Mexico* 1 (1972):1.

[52]K. Dahlberg, "Medical Care of Cambodian Refugees," *JAMA* 243 (1980):1062.

[53]P. Pellett, "Nutritional Evaluation of Protein Foods," Food and Nutrition Bulletin, supplement 4, United Nations University Press, 1980, pp. 1–6.

[54]S. Margen, "Studies in Calcium Metabolism, the Calciuretic Effect of Dietary Protein," *Am J Clin Nutr* 27 (1974):584.

[55]C. Anand, "Effect of Protein Intake on Calcium Balance of Young Men Given 500 mg Calcium Daily," *J Nutr* 104 (1974):695.

[56]R. Walker, "Calcium Retention in the Adult Human Male as Affected by Protein Intake," *J Nutr* 102 (1972):1297.

[57]J. Cummings, "The Effect of Meat Protein and Dietary Fiber on Colonic Function and Metabolism, Changes in Bowel Habit, Bile Acid Excretion, and Calcium Absorption," *Am J Clin Nutr* 32 (1979):2086.

[58]L. Allen, "Protein-Induced Hypercalcuria: A Long-Term Study," *Am J Clin Nutr* 32 (1979):741.

[59]V. Barzel, *Osteoporosis,* Grune and Stratton, New York, 1970, pp. 1–37.

[60]J. Chalmers, "Geographic Variations of Senile Osteoporosis," *J Bone and Joint Surgery* 52B (1970):667.

[61]A. Walker, "Osteoporosis and Calcium Deficiency," *Am J Clin Nutr* 16 (1965):327.

[62]R. Smith, "Epidemiologic Studies of Osteoporosis in Women of Puerto Rico and Southeastern Michigan with Special Reference to Age, Race, National Origin, and to Other Related and Associated Findings," *Clin Orthop* 45 (1966):31.

[63]R. Mazess, "Bone Mineral Content of North Alaskan Eskimos," *Am J Clin Nutr* 27 (1974):916.

[64]J. Aloia, "Prevention of Involutional Bone Loss by Exercise," *Ann Intern Med* 89 (1978):356.

[65]"Urinary Calcium and Dietary Protein," *Nutr Rev* 38 (1980):9.

[66]W. Robertson, "Should Recurrent Calcium Oxalate Stone Formers Become Vegetarians?" *Br J Urol* 51 (1979):427.

[67]"Diet and Urinary Calculi," *Nutr Rev* 38 (1980):74.

[68]H. Andersson, "Fat-Reduced Diet in the Treatment of Hyperoxaluria in Patients with Ileopathy," *Gut* 15 (1974):360.

[69]P. Shah, "Dietary Calcium and Idiopathic Hypercalcuria," *Lancet* 1 (1981):786.

[70]E. Holt, *Protein and Amino Acid Requirements in Early Life,* New York: New York University Press, 1960, p. 9.

[71]B. Brenner, "Dietary Protein Intake and the Progressive Nature of Kidney Disease: The Role of Hemodynamically Mediated Glomerular Injury in the Pathogenesis of Progressive Glomerular Sclerosis in Aging, Renal Ablation, and Intrinsic Renal Disease," *N Engl J Med* 307 (1982):652.

[72]M. Walser, "Nutritional Support in Renal Failure: Future Directions," *Lancet* 1 (1983):340.

[73]W. Kempner, "Compensation of Renal Metabolic Dysfunction," *N Carolina Med J* 6 (1945):61, 107.

[74]J. Kopple, "Controlled Comparison of 20 g and 40 g Protein Diets in the Treatment of Chronic Uremia," *Am J Clin Nutr* 21 (1968):553.

[75]N. Greenberger, "Effect of Vegetable and Animal Protein Diets on Chronic Hepatic Encephalopathy," *Digestive Diseases* 22 (1977):945.

[76]M. Walser, "Does Dietary Therapy Have a Role in the Predialysis Patient?" *Am J Clin Nutr* 33 (1980):1629.

[77]F. Coe, "Eating Too Much Meat Called Major Cause of Renal Stones," *Intern Med News* 12 (1979):1.

[78]E. Bien, "The Relation of Dietary Nitrogen Consumption to the Rate of Uric Acid Synthesis in Normal and Gouty Men," *J Clin Invest* 32 (1953):778.

[79]N. Zollner, "Diet and Gout," *Proc 9th Int Congr Nutr, Mexico* 1 (1972):267.

Chapter

9

A Health-Supporting Diet Is Plentiful In Complex Carbohydrates But Limits Unprotected Simple Sugars

Simple Sugars

Carbohydrates have been the primary source of calories for humans throughout history: breads in Europe, corn for American Indians, rice in Asia, grains and beans in African and South American countries, sweet potatoes in New Guinea. Even today, in places where people have not been heavily influenced by wealth and industry, starch-centered meal plans predominate.

Carbohydrates are essential for our health. They provide the most efficient and most readily available source of energy for our bodies. The brain and other nervous system tissues can utilize only carbohydrates for energy. If none are available, then the body manufactures these essential molecules from protein. Carbohydrates also perform the vital function of detoxifying harmful substances that are manufactured by or taken into our bodies. Carbohydrates are stored in the liver and muscles in the form of long chains of glucose called glycogen. Endurance athletes rely heavily on these stores of energy, which often make the difference between winning and losing the event.[1-3]

Because of the popular misunderstanding that starches are fattening, many fad diets and weight-loss gimmicks have been devised to deprive the body of this essential nutrient. Such popular low-carbohydrate, high-protein diets as the Atkins, Stillman, and liquid protein diets place a serious burden on the body and are harmful to health.[4-5] Another recently introduced approach uses pills called "starch blockers," which are supposed to deprive the body of essential carbohydrates after they are eaten and make weight loss easy. These pills utilize a substance derived from beans, which prevents the absorption of carbohydrates into the body by blocking the activity of the starch-splitting enzyme alpha amylase. However, starch blockers have been found to be completely ineffective in blocking starch absorption.[6-7] This is probably because the pancreas and salivary glands secrete many more times the amount of amylase after meals than is needed to digest the amount of starch eaten. What people living on rich diets really need are cholesterol, fat, and protein blockers!

Carbohydrates are found naturally in foods in two forms: simple and complex. Simple carbohydrates, also called simple sugars, are sweet-tasting substances. They include glucose, fructose, sucrose, maltose, and lactose and are said to be simple because they consist of only one or a very few of the basic sugar molecules attached together. Some foods containing high concentrations of these simple sugars are white refined sugar, brown sugar, honey, corn syrup, molasses, maple syrup, milk, and fruit juices. These forms of simple sugar must be further classified as unprotected simple sugars, because they are not found associated with natural fiber. Each of the simple sugars has a different rate of absorption into the body and causes a different eventual rise in blood sugar. For instance, lactose (found in milk) and fructose (found in fruits and corn syrup) cause less of a rise than glucose or maltose.[8]

Fresh fruit and dried fruit also contain primarily simple sugars, but these foods are generously supplied with fiber, vitamins, and minerals. The fiber helps protect the body from some of the deleterious effects of the simple sugars by slowing down their rate of absorption. Fruit purees, such as applesauce, have had much of their fiber content damaged by the blending process.[9] Thus, a considerable amount of the protective properties from fiber is lost after the disruption caused by a mechanical blender. This results in a greater fall in blood sugar and a greater rise and fall in insulin levels after eating these foods.[9,10] (See Figure 9.1.)

Complex carbohydrates are formed when individual molecules of simple sugars are attached together to form long chains. When we eat these complex carbohydrates, the long chains are broken down into

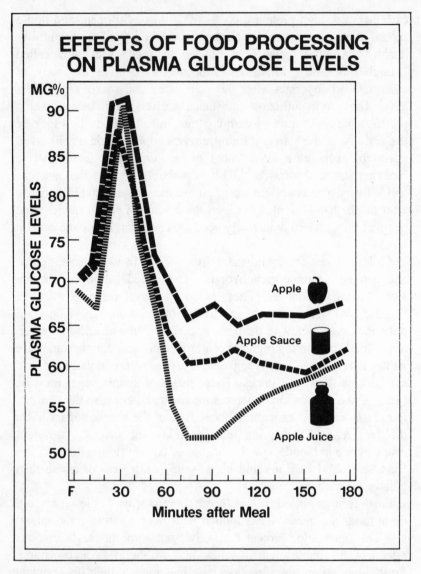

Figure 9.1. The processing of food alters the body's responses after eating. Blood sugar levels fall to lower levels when an apple is blended into applesauce and further processed into apple juice. Source: G Haber, *Lancet* 2 (1977):679.

the component simple sugars by enzymes such as alpha amylase in the mouth and intestines, and then these simple sugars are absorbed through the bowel wall. Thus, complex carbohydrates yield sugars that are released into the bloodstream over a period of many hours and provide a steady supply of energy to the body until the next meal.

Starches and vegetables contain carbohydrates primarily in the complex form. (See Figure 9.2.)

Until recently it was believed that simple sugars were more rapidly absorbed and caused a greater rise in blood sugar than complex carbohydrates. However, studies now demonstrate that this is not always the case.[8,11,12] Some complex carbohydrates are actually digested and absorbed faster than some simple sugars. Different kinds of complex carbohydrates also result in different responses in blood sugar. For example, white potatoes are more rapidly digested with a slightly higher rise in blood sugar than rice, corn, or sweet potatoes.[8] These recent observations may be of some benefit to people who are very sensitive to changes in blood sugar levels, such as diabetics or those suffering from hypoglycemia and elevated triglycerides. Unfortunately, some people have misinterpreted these findings to mean that

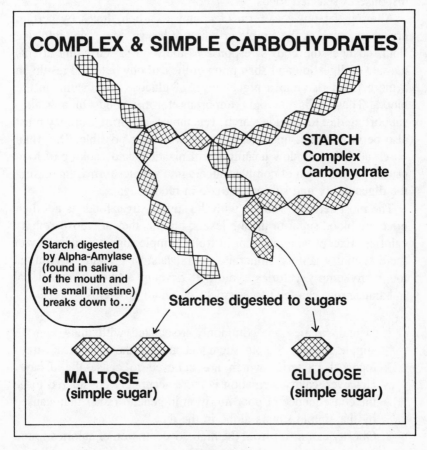

Figure 9.2

"potatoes are like candy as far as a diabetic is concerned."[13] Such sensational misstatements reflect a basic lack of understanding and appreciation for the nutritional advantages of unprocessed starches, vegetables, and fruits. Their plentiful supply of fibers, proteins, essential fat, vitamins, and minerals offer tremendous food value over the hazardous components of "empty calories," saturated fats, and contaminants found in most candies. Furthermore, simple sugars as a source of calories aren't all that bad for diabetics. People with mild diabetes fed diets containing 85% of the calories as simple sugar showed improvement in fasting blood sugars and glucose tolerance tests when compared with a diet containing 45% simple sugar.[14] This data suggests that carbohydrates including simple sugars increase the sensitivity of body tissues to insulin.[14]

The list of carbohydrates in Table 9.1 compares the blood glucose response to selected foods.

Altering the physical form of complex carbohydrates by certain processes, such as the simple grinding of brown rice grains into rice flour, changes the body's response to the food.[15-16] Grinding affects the rate of digestion and absorption of the carbohydrate and results in a more rapid rise and a higher level of glucose and insulin in the blood. Thus, it is not only important for the foods in a health-supporting diet to include starch, vegetables, and fruit, but they must also be in a whole, unprocessed form whenever possible. One final observation is that slow heating (dextrinization) and cooking of food causes a breakdown of complex sugars into simpler forms, increasing the digestibility and subsequent rise in blood sugar.

The most serious problem with the simple sugar foods is not their effect on blood sugar or insulin levels, but that they are mostly empty calories. Except when present in fruits, simple sugars contain few of the essential vitamins, minerals, fibers, fats, or proteins. If you eat too many empty calories, you will develop a serious nutritional imbalance that can lead to a variety of health problems:

1. Dental cavities are commonly associated with diets high in simple sugars. Simple sugar encourages the growth of streptococcal bacteria, which are believed to cause the decay.[17] However, cavity formation is more accurately considered to be the consequence of poor nutrition in general rather than caused by the simple sugars alone in the diet.[18-19]
2. Obesity can result from the high concentration of calories found in unprotected simple sugars (4 calories per gram).

Table 9.1. Blood Glucose Response of Selected Foods (Expressed as percentage of body's response to the simple sugar glucose.)

Glucose	100
Parsnip	97
Carrots	92
Honey	87
Broad beans	79
Whole wheat bread	72
White rice	72
Millet	71
White potato	70
White bread	69
Brown rice	66
Beet	64
Raisin	64
Banana	62
White sugar	59
Sweet corn	59
Yam	51
Buckwheat	51
White spaghetti	50
Oatmeal	49
Sweet potato	48
Pea	47
Orange juice	46
Whole wheat spaghetti	42
Orange	40
Apple	39
Garbanzo bean	36
Kidney bean	29
Lentil	29
Fructose	20

Source: D. Jenkins. Diabetologia 23 (1982):477

3. Consumption of simple sugars leads to an elevation of serum triglycerides (blood fats) in some people.[20] High triglyceride levels may aggravate diabetes, hypoglycemia, heart disease, and problems associated with poor circulation.[21-25] Even whole fruits can have an adverse effect on triglyceride levels because of their content of simple sugars. The complex carbohydrates found in starches and vegetables tend to lower triglycerides.[26-27] Alcohol, caffeine, refined cereal and grains, and polyunsaturated and saturated fats will also raise triglyceride levels.[20,28-30]

4. Cholesterol levels and blood pressure are increased slightly by replacing complex carbohydrates with simple sugars.[31,32]
5. The nutritional imbalance caused by a large amount of empty calories in the diet can lay the foundation for many serious illnesses. Eventually one's level of resistance weakens, and the defenses may be overcome by bacterial or viral infections. You also lose the ability to counteract other threats from the environment, such as pollution and physical injury.[33]

Sweetness is one of the four primary flavors recognized by the tongue (saltiness, bitterness, and sourness are the other three). We even begin our lives with a sweet-tasting food, breast milk, which is high in the simple sugar, lactose. It appears that our basic makeup causes us to seek sugar. If you have a desire to cheat on your diet and consume rich foods, your body will tolerate unprotected simple sugars better than oils, fats, or animal products. Add the sweetener to the surface of your food at the table instead of during cooking so that you get the maximum flavor from the minimum simple sugar. Provided you are in good health, a small amount of sweetness can be pleasing to your palate without seriously harming your body. Better yet, eating fresh whole fruits will satisfy your desire for sweet foods and will also provide an important part of a health-supporting diet.

Fiber

Dietary fibers are nondigestible forms of complex carbohydrates. In fiber the chains of sugars are connected by linkages that are resistant to breakdown by the enzymes made by the digestive system. Fiber has been called roughage, bulk, residue, and simply bran. This natural plant product remains in the intestine after the fat, protein, digestible carbohydrate, water, vitamin, and mineral components of the food have been digested and absorbed. Some breakdown of dietary fibers caused by bacteria occurs in the large intestine.

All animal products, including meat, poultry, dairy products, eggs, fish, and shellfish, contain no fiber. All unprocessed plant foods are high in dietary fiber. At the end of the nineteenth century, modern roller mills began to produce large quantities of white flour, rather than the traditional whole wheat flour, by removing the bran and the germ from wheat kernels.[34] Because most of the fiber in wheat is found in the bran covering, the mills were producing flour that was deficient in fiber. A similar process converted whole brown rice into white rice. At about the same time the diet of westerners was changing in other ways, all of which involved a greater emphasis on highly processed, rich, fiber-deficient foods.[34-36] Our modern diet, centered around animal foods and refined grains, often provides less than 10 grams of dietary fiber per day. A starch-centered diet can contain 60 grams or more.[34,37]

There are many kinds of fiber, and they have several important functions in the body.[34] Immediately after consumption of a meal, fiber plays an important role in the health of the stomach. Stomach and duodenal ulcer disease is found commonly in people who eat low-fiber diets.[38] Fiber also plays an important role in healing ulcer disease and preventing recurrences.[38,39] Less than half of the people suffering from ulcer disease have relapses on a high-fiber diet when compared to a low-fiber diet.[39] It should also be noted that fat consumption has been determined to be an important element in the cause of ulcer disease, and low-fat diets have been very valuable in ulcer treatment.[40]

Fiber forms the bulk of the stool. When fiber-deficient foods are the major part of a diet, little is left in the intestine to form the stool except for the bacteria that live in the colon. The result is a few hard marbles of fecal material that can be passed out of the body only by harmful straining. This condition, all too common, is known as constipation. Straining at the stool increases the pressure of blood in the veins, which can cause serious damage to these blood vessels, especially the ones in the legs and rectum.[41-42] This repeated dilation of the veins plays a large part in the formation of varicose veins and hemorrhoids.[41-43] The anal muscles are permanently pushed out into the anal opening after years of constipation and straining, thereby also contributing to the formation of hemorrhoids.[44]

This same straining activity can push the stomach up into the chest cavity from its normal location in the abdomen. This results in an enlarged opening in the diaphragm called a hiatal hernia.[45,46] (See Figure 9.3). Chest pains, indigestion, and belching are common symptoms found in people with this condition.

Blockage of the opening to the appendix by slow-moving, fiber-deficient stool may lead to appendicitis.[47,48] This disease accounts for the most common emergency surgery performed in many western nations.

After approximately forty years on a fiber-deficient diet, many people develop diverticular disease of the large intestine (diverticulosis).[41,49] (See Figure 9.4.) The high pressures in the colon,

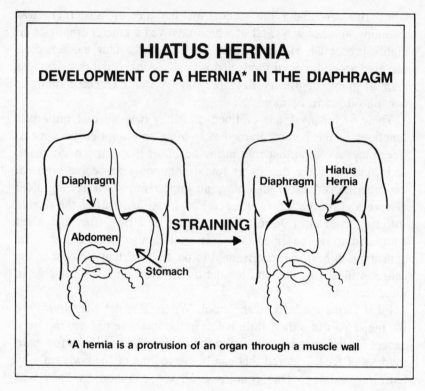

Figure 9.3

resulting from the movement of small hard stools, can eventually blow out pouches, called diverticuli, in the colon walls. Although people with this disease may have no symptoms, many suffer from recurrent pain, especially in the lower left area of the abdomen. These pouches can bleed and may also become infected like the appendix (a condition called diverticulitis). Diverticuli are found in about 35 percent of people over the age of sixty in affluent societies.[50] This condition is virtually non-existent in preindustrialized societies where starch-based meal plans are consumed.

A starch-centered diet quickly relieves constipation and the symptoms of hiatal hernia and diverticulosis for most people.[35,51] Furthermore, the chances of developing appendicitis are virtually eliminated.[35,47,48]

Irritable colon syndrome, also known as irritable bowel syndrome or spastic colon, is the most common gastrointestinal disease seen in the clinical practice of physicians who care for people consuming rich

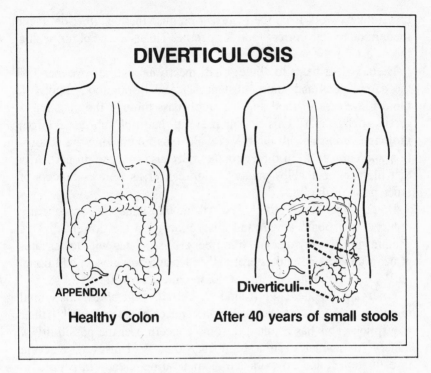

DIVERTICULOSIS

APPENDIX

Healthy Colon

Diverticuli--

After 40 years of small stools

Figure 9.4

diets. This disorder is often characterized by lower abdominal pain relieved by defecation, alternating constipation and diarrhea, mucous discharge, and the passage of small-caliber stools. The cause has traditionally been attributed to psychoneurosis found especially among middle-aged women. Remnants of the wrong food in the colon are the actual cause of this disorder in most people, and a woman or man can be "miraculously" and quickly relieved of this "emotional disorder" by switching to a high-fiber, starch-centered diet.[52-54] Medical schools teach a theory that the mind can cause illness in the body and refer to this kind of sickness as psychosomatic illness. While true in some cases, this concept gets overused and can be a means of blaming the patient for his or her problems, especially when the physician does not know the actual cause and does not care to admit to this failing. An excellent example of this phenomenon is seen in irritable bowel syndrome. Even though it may seem obvious to first consider food in an intestinal disorder, food as a cause has been overlooked for years, and the person's emotional state has been blamed. One reason for this oversight is that many health care practitioners work from the incorrect premise that our fiber-deficient modern diet is the correct food for people. This is a case of not seeing the forest for the trees.

Dietary fiber helps to dilute, bind, inactivate, and remove many of the carcinogens and toxic substances found in our food supply. A rapid movement of food and the stool mass through the intestine is produced by fiber. This action prevents harmful substances from prolonged contact with the bowel wall, thus minimizing the absorption and damage from direct contact. Because of these properties, a diet high in fiber helps prevent colon cancer as well as cancers of other parts of the body.[55-57]

Dietary fiber also binds cholesterol and bile acids and consequently reduces their contact with and absorption from the bowel.[58,59] This explains in part why diets high in fiber are associated with lower rates of heart attacks and cholesterol gallstones and provides an additional mechanism for reduced rates of colon cancer as well.[35,60]

Fiber and oxalic acid (found in certain vegetables) also bind minerals such as zinc, copper, iron, and calcium and inhibit their absorption. This has resulted in some concern over the possibility of mineral deficiencies on a high-fiber diet.[61,62] However, a recent investigation found no evidence of mineral deficiency in people on long-term, high-fiber, vegetarian diets.[63] The scientific literature is somewhat lacking in actual cases of mineral deficiency resulting from consumption of high-fiber diets to support this apparently unwarranted concern.

As mentioned previously, the rapid absorption of carbohydrates from the intestinal tract into the body is retarded by dietary fiber.[9,10] For this reason, dietary fiber is important in the prevention and control of diabetes and hypoglycemia.[9,64,65] Even persons with a distressing condition called dumping syndrome can be relieved of their symptoms of severe hypoglycemia and diarrhea by the use of a diet high in fiber.[66-68] This disorder is created when the stomach has been surgically removed for a variety of problems ranging from cancer to ulcers. The food no longer has its storage sack and rushes into the small intestine, where distressing symptoms are produced by rapid absorption. Fiber slows the absorption of the nutrients and thereby retards the hypoglycemia and diarrhea.

High-fiber foods play a similar role in preventing low blood sugar reactions in those people who suffer from a disorder known as reactive or functional hypoglycemia.[9] This condition, characterized by a rapid fall in blood sugar after eating, is found in apparently healthy people with no history of previous surgery or disease of the stomach or intestines.

Other diseases commonly found in people of affluent societies and attributed to the fiber-deficient aspect of the diet include blood clots in the veins, blood clots in the lungs (pulmonary embolism), ulcerative colitis, and Crohn's disease (an inflammatory disease of the bowel).[35,42,69-74] High-fiber diets have been reported to be of definite benefit to those with Crohn's disease.[74] People undergoing surgery suffer a high risk from blood clots in the legs, which can travel to the lungs and cause death. A high-fiber diet has been reported to reduce this surgical complication.[75] Furthermore, patients who undergo surgery frequently suffer from poor activity of the bowels after the operation (postoperative ileus). The return to normal bowel function can be greatly hastened when a high-fiber diet is fed before surgery.[76,77]

There is even evidence that attributes the lower blood pressures found in people on vegetable diets to the fiber in their food.[78-81] However, the relationship of excess sodium and fat in the diet to high blood pressure is stronger. By their natural design, health-supporting foods are low in sodium and fat and high in fiber. Rich foods generally have the opposite composition. It is difficult to know which property of the food should receive the credit for the benefits. This is why it is more important to look at the foods as a whole rather than at individual nutrients. Otherwise we run the risk of becoming too involved in senseless arguments over details that are probably unimportant for us in choosing the correct foods to eat.

Fiber aids in weight control by providing bulk. High-fiber foods fill the stomach and satisfy hunger with the intake of fewer calories. It also should be mentioned that the removal of fiber in the refining of a food usually increases the relative concentration of calories in the refined product.[82,83]

Fiber provides no calories since it is not digested or absorbed into the body. This may be the reason why food manufacturers and nutritionists failed for many years to recognize the importance of this ingredient in our diets. However, recent increased public awareness that dietary fibers are indeed essential to our health has made westerners "fiber-conscious." Unfortunately, now many people are reacting inappropriately. They continue to eat rich foods that are harmful to health, merely supplementing that diet with processed bran. Even worse, some food manufacturers are now adding processed wood fiber to the flour used in making white bread.

Processed fibers contain only a few of the many kinds of fiber occurring naturally in vegetable foods, and they satisfy very few of our bodies' needs for fiber. Furthermore, large amounts of processed fiber, even natural miller's bran, when added to the diet can cause excess stool bulk, gas, and abdominal cramps.[84]

Over the past twenty years the emphasis on fiber in our diet has gone from one extreme to the other. The function of fiber is very complex and is still poorly understood. In a health-supporting diet, unprocessed vegetable foods naturally supply the correct amounts and types of fiber that we were intended to eat. (See Table 9.2.)

Table 9.2. HIGH-FIBER FOODS*
Each serving of the following foods has approximately 2 grams of dietary fiber.

Starches

Whole wheat bread, 1 slice	Oatmeal, dry, 3 Tbsp.
Rye bread, 1 slice	Wheat Bran, 1 tsp.
Cracked wheat bread, 1 slice	
Shredded Wheat, ½ biscuit	Puffed Wheat, 1⅓ cups
	Corn on the cob, 2 inch long
Grape-Nuts, 3 Tbsp.	Potato, 2″ diameter
All Bran, 1 Tbsp.	Baked beans, 2 Tbsp.
Corn flakes, ⅔ cup	

Vegetables

Broccoli, ½ stalk	Lettuce, raw, 2 cups
Brussels sprouts, 4	Green beans, ½ cup
Carrots, ⅓ cup	Tomato, raw, 1 medium
Celery, 1 cup	

Fruits

Apple , 1 small	Orange, 1 small
Banana, 1 small	Peach, 1 medium
Strawberries, ½ cup	Pear, ½ small
Cherries, 10 large	Plums, 2 small

Source: Nutrition and the M.D. 3 (1981):3.

Donna Henrietta Levine—Diabetic in Charge of Her Life

It wasn't the far–off, almost unreal possibility of kidney failure, or an early heart attack, or even the threat of blindness that made me change my diet. Taking two shots of insulin a day at one time didn't seem as big a deal to me as having to give up my hamburgers. What finally made me realize what an inconvenience it was to be in poor health was the diarrhea I had. There isn't a place in town where I don't know where the ladies' room is located. I work as a salesperson, and I'm in the car a lot. It wasn't unusual for me to stop twenty times a day. The way my stomach growled during business meetings was really embarrassing. I've had diabetes for ten years and bowel trouble for five, and I never put two and two together and realized that food was part of the trouble.

Of course, it now seems all too logical: what I put into my stomach has a lot to do with how my intestines work. I suppose one of the reasons I didn't get the message was that my friends, who eat the same kind of food as I did, complained about constipation, not diarrhea.

Last winter when I had the flu, my diabetes got out of control. I arrived in the emergency room with my family doctor out of town. Her replacement was a physician who had a reputation for using natural methods and health foods. My remark when he said I was to be admitted was, "OK, but I'm not a rabbit and I don't want to be put on one of your vegetarian diets." After my discharge he gave me a challenge I couldn't refuse: eat a diet of starch, vegetable, and fruit for only one week, and the diarrhea would disappear. To my surprise it only took three days. Other benefits included a 50 percent reduction in my insulin doses, plus I felt a lot better. I hate to admit this, but another side benefit of what I know now is that whenever I feel a need to punish myself, I go out for a nice big steak or a couple of pork chops, and it's diarrhea and stomach cramps for the next two days, guaranteed.

Comments on Donna Henrietta Levine

Donna has bowel problems related to her diabetes in combination with the wrong food. Diabetes has damaged the nerves that supply the intestine, resulting in motility problems and poor absorption of food. High-fat, low-fiber foods overburden her intestines, and the result is diarrhea. Switching to low-fat, high-fiber foods will stop her diarrhea for two specific reasons: the fiber absorbs extra fluids, and the low-fat nature of the diet reduces bile acids made by the liver which irritate the intestinal lining.

Many cases of chronic diarrhea are dramatically benefited by health-supporting foods. Specific cases include diarrhea secondary to disease of the last part of the small bowel (the ileum) such as seen in Crohn's disease and surgical loss of this part of the intestine, and diarrhea occurring after loss of the gallbladder. Other cases of chronic diarrhea respond to the elimination of gluten from the diet. High levels of gluten are present in wheat, barley, and rye and aggravate a specific condition known as celiac disease, also called nontropical sprue.

Donna now has control over her own health. She knows what foods make her well and what foods make her sick. Human nature has a self-destructive side, and this is expressed most plainly when we do harmful things to ourselves, fully aware of the consequences. For most of us, correct information gives us at least the opportunity to take charge of our daily lives.

Notes

[1]C. Consolazio, "Dietary Carboyhydrates and Work Capacity," *Am J Clin Nutr* 25 (1972):85.

[2]"Fuel of Muscular Work," *Medical Physiology,* 14th ed., C.V. Mosby Publishing Co. Mountcastle, St. Louis, 1980, p. 1400.

[3]"Diet, Exercise, and Endurance," *Nutr Rev* 30 (1972):86.

[4]H. Sours, "Sudden Death Associated with Very Low Calorie Weight Reduction Regimens," *Am J Clin Nutr* 34 (1981):453.

[5]"A Critique of Low-Carbohydrate Ketogenic Weight Reduction Regimens, a Review of Dr. Atkins' Diet Revolution, Statement of the American Medical Association Council on Foods and Nutrition," *JAMA* 224 (1973):1415.

[6]G. Bo-Linn, "Starch Blockers—Their Effect on Calorie Absorption from a High-Starch Meal," *N Engl J Med* 307 (1982):1413.

[7]J. Garrow, "Starch Blockers Are Ineffective in Man," *Lancet* 1 (1983):60.

[8]D. Jenkins, "The Diabetic Diet, Dietary Carbohydrate and Differences in Digestibility," *Diabetologia* 23 (1982):477.

[9]G. Haber, "Depletion and Disruption of Dietary Fibre, Effects on Satiety, Plasma-Glucose, and Serum-Insulin," *Lancet* 2 (1977):679.

[10]R. Bolton, "The Role of Dietary Fiber in Satiety, Glucose, and Insulin: Studies with Fruit and Fruit Juice," *Am J Clin Nutr* 34 (1981):211.

[11]J. Bantle, "Postprandial Glucose and Insulin Responses to Meals Containing Different Carbohydrates in Normal and Diabetic Subjects," *N Engl J Med* 309 (1983):7.

[12] G. Reaven, "Effects of Differences in Amount and Kind of Dietary Carbohydrate on Plasma Glucose and Insulin Responses in Man," *Am J Clin Nutr* 32 (1979):2568.

[13] G. Kolata, "Dietary Dogma Disproved," *Science* 220 (1983):487.

[14] J. Brunzell, "Improved glucose tolerance with high carbohydrate feeding in mild diabetes." *N Engl J Med* 284 (1971):521.

[15] K. O'dea, "Physical Factors Influencing Postprandial Glucose and Insulin Responses to Starch," *Am J Clin Nutr* 33 (1980):760.

[16] G. Collier, "Effect of Physical Form of Carbohydratae on the Postprandial Glucose, Insulin, and Gastric Inhibitory Polypeptide Responses in Type 2 Diabetes," *Am J Clin Nutr* 36 (1982):10.

[17] B. Bibby, "The Cariogenicity of Snack Food and Confections," *JADA* 90 (1975):121.

[18] A. Walker, "Dental Caries and Sugar Intake," *Lancet* 2 (1975):765.

[19] R. Harris, "Biology of the Children of Hopewood House, Bowral, Australia, Observations on Dental Caries Experience Extending Over Five Years (1957-61)," *J Dent Res* 42 (1963):1387.

[20] A. Antones, "The Influence of Diet on Serum Triglycerides in South African White and Bantu Prisoners," *Lancet* 1 (1961):3.

[21] H. Hinsworth, "The Physiological Activation of Insulin," *Clin Science* 1 (1933):1.

[22] P. Davidson, "Insulin Resistance in Hypertriglyceridemia," *Metabolism* 14 (1965):1059.

[23] M. Friedman, "Serum Lipids and Conjunctival Circulation After Fat Ingestion in Men Exhibiting Type A Behavior Patterns," *Circulation* 29 (1964):874.

[24] A. Williams, "Increased Blood Cell Agglutination Following Ingestion of Fat, a Factor Contributing to Cardiac Ischemia, Coronary Insufficiency, and Anginal Pain," *Angiology* 8 (1957):29.

[25] P. Kuo, "The Effect of Lipemia upon Coronary Circulation and Peripheral Artery Circulation in Patients with Essential Hyperlipemia," *Am J of Med* 26 (1959):68.

[26] J. Anderson, "Plant Fiber, Carbohydrate and Lipid Metabolism," *Am J Clin Nutr* 32 (1979):346.

[27] N. Kaufmann, "Changes in Serum Lipid Levels of Hyperlipemic Patients Following the Feeding of Starch, Sucrose, and Glucose," *Am J Clin Nutr* 18 (1966):261.

[28] K. Pinter, "Effect of Ingestion of Various Mono- and Triglycerides on Serum Triglyceride Concentration," *Am J Clin Nutr* 18 (1966):165.

[29] W. Castelli, "Alcohol and Blood Lipids," "The cooperative lipoprotein phenotyping study," *Lancet* 2 (1977):153.

[30] J. Little, "Coffee and Serum Lipids in Coronary Heart Disease, *Lancet* 1 (1966):732.

[31] F. Grande, "Dietary Carbohydrates and Serum Cholesterol," *Am J Clin Nutr* 20 (1967):176.

[32] R. Hodges, "Carbohydrates and Blood Pressure," *Ann Intern Med* 98 (1983):838.

[33] Supplement 35, *Am J Clin Nutr* (1978).

[34] H. Trowell, "Definition of Dietary Fiber and Hypotheses That It Is a Protective Factor in Certain Diseases," *Am J Clin Nutr* 29 (1976):417.

[35] D. Burkitt, "Some Diseases Characteristic of Modern Western Civilization," *Br Med J* 1 (1973):274.

[36] W. Gortner, "Nutrition in the United States 1900 to 1974," *Cancer Res* 35 (1975):3246.

[37] J. Anderson, *"Plant Fiber in Foods,"* Lexington: HCF Diabetes Research Foundation, 1981.

[38] S. Malhotra, "A Comparison of Unrefined Wheat and Rice Diet in the Management of Duodenal Ulcer," *Postgrad Med J* 54 (1978):6.

[39] A. Rydning, "Prophylactic Effect of Dietary Fibre in Duodenal Ulcer Disease," *Lancet* 2 (1982):736.

[40] P. Childs, "Peptic Ulcer, Pylorplasty and Dietary Fat—A New Concept," *Ann Roy Coll Surg England* 59 (1977):143.

[41] D. Burkitt, "Dietary Fiber and Disease," *JAMA* 229 (1974):1068.

[42] D. Burkitt, "Varicose Veins, Deep Vein Thrombosis, and Hemorrhoids: Epidemiology and Suggested Aetiology," *Br Med J* 2 (1972):556.

[43] G. Prasad, "Studies on Etiopathogenesis of Hemorrhoids," *Am J Proctology* (June 1976):33.

[44] W. Thompson, "The Nature of Hemorrhoids," *Br J Surg* 62 (1975):542.

[45] D. Burkitt, "Hiatus Hernia: Is It Preventable?" *Am J Clin Nutr* 34 (1981):428.

[46] J. Capron, "Evidence for an Association Between Cholelithiasis and Hiatus Hernia," *Lancet* 2 (1978):329.

[47] A. Walker, "Appendicitis, Fiber Intake, and Bowel Behavior in Ethnic Groups in South Africa," *Postgrad Med J* 49 (1973):243.

[48] C. Westlake, "Appendectomy and Dietary Fiber," *J Human Nutr* 34 (1980):267.

[49] J. Gear, "Symptomless Diverticular Disease and Intake of Dietary Fibre," *Lancet* 1 (1979):511.

[50] Editorial, "Keep Taking Your Bran," *Lancet* 1 (1979):1175.

[51] N. Painter, "The High-Fiber Diet in the Treatment of Diverticular Disease of the Colon," *Postgrad Med J* 50 (1974):629.

[52] J. Piepmeyer, "Use of Unprocessed Bran in Treatment of Irritable Bowel Syndrome," *Am J Clin Nutr* 27 (1974):106.

[53] A. Manning, "Wheat Fibre and Irritable Bowel Syndrome," *Lancet* 2 (1977):417.

[54] Editorial, "Management of the Irritable Bowel," *Lancet* 2 (1978):557.

[55] B. Reddy, "Metabolic Epidemiology of Large Bowel Cancer," *Cancer* 42 (1978):2832.

[56] M. Hill, "Colon Cancer: A Disease of Fiber Depletion or of Dietary Excess," *Digestion* 11 (1974):289.

[57] A. Walker, "Colon Cancer and Diet with Special Reference to Intakes of Fat and Fiber," *Am J Clin Nutr* 29 (1976):1417.

[58] J. Kelsay, "A Review of Research on Effects of Fiber Intake in Man," *Am J Clin Nutr* 31 (1978):142.

[59] I. Ullrich, "Alterations of Fecal Steroid Composition Induced by Changes in Dietary Fiber Composition," *Am J Clin Nutr* 34 (1981):2054.

[60] H. Trowell, "Ischemic Heart Disease and Dietary Fiber," *Am J Clin Nutr* 25 (1972):926.

[61] J. Cummings, "Nutritional Implications of Dietary Fiber," *Am J Clin Nutr* 31 (1978):S21.

[62] J. Kelsay, "Mineral balances of human subjects consuming spinach in a low-fiber diet and in a diet containing fruits and vegetables," *Am J Clin Nutr* 38 (1983):12.

[63] B. Anderson, "The Iron and Zinc Status of Long-Term Vegetarian Women," *Am J Clin Nutr* 34 (1981):1042.

[64] J. Anderson, "High-Carbohydrate, High-Fiber Diets for Insulin-Treated Men with Diabetes Mellitus," *Am J Clin Nutr* 32 (1979):2312.

[65] P. Miranda, "High-Fiber Diets in the Treatment of Diabetes Mellitus," *Ann Intern Med* 88 (1978):482.

[66] A. Leeds, "Pectin in the Dumping Syndrome: Reduction of Symptoms and Plasma Volume Changes," *Lancet* 1 (1981):1075.

[67] S. Leichter, "Alimentary Hypoglycemia: A New Appraisal," *Am J Clin Nutr* 32 (1979):2104.

[68] D. Jenkins, "Effect of Dietary Fiber on Complications of Gastric Surgery: Prevention of Postprandial Hypoglycemia by Pectin," *Gastroenterology* 73 (1977):215.

[69] T. Gilat, "Epidemiology of Crohn's Disease and Ulcerative Colitis: Etiologic Implications," *Israel J Med Sci* 15 (1979):305.

[70] H. Trowell, "Food and Dietary Fiber," *Nutr Rev* 35 (1977):6.

[71] A. Walter, "Epidemiology of Noninfective Intestinal Diseases in Various Ethnic Groups in South Africa," *Israel J Med Sci* 15 (1979):309.

[72] G. Spiller, "Recent Advances in Dietary Fiber and Colonrectal Diseases," *Am J Clin Nutr* 34 (1981):1145.

[73] J. Richardson, "Varicose Veins in Tropical Africa," *Lancet* 1 (1977):791.

[74] K. Heaton, "Treatment of Crohn's Disease with an Unrefined-Carbohydrate, Fibre-Rich Diet," *Br Med J* 2 (1979):764.

[75] M. Frohn, "Left-Leg Varicose Veins and Deep-Vein Thrombosis," *Lancet* 2 (1976):1019.

[76] O. Sculati, "Preoperative Fibre and Postoperative Ileus," *Lancet* 1 (1980):1252.

[77] J. Manshande, "Fibre and Postoperative Ileus," *Lancet* 2 (1980):476.

[78] A. Wright, "Dietary Fibre and Blood Pressure," *Br Med J* 2 (1979):1541.

[79] J. Kelsay, "Effect of Fiber from Fruits and Vegetables on Metabolic Responses of Human Subjects," *Am J Clin Nutr* 31 (1978):1149.

[80] P. Dodson, "Dietary Fiber, Sodium, and Blood Pressure," *Proc Nutr Soc, Abst Communications* 40 (1981):42A.

[81] J. Anderson, "Plant Fiber and Blood Pressure," *Ann Intern Med* 98 (1983):842.

[82] D. Grimes, "Satiety Values of Whole Meal and White Bread," *Lancet* 2 (1978):106.

[83] K. Heaton, "Food Fiber as an Obstacle to Energy Intake," *Lancet* 2 (1973):1418.

[84] D. Marthinsen, "Excretion of Breath and Flatus Gases by Humans Consuming High-Fiber Diets," *J Nutr* 112 (1982):1133.

Chapter

10

Help Prevent Cancer with a Health-Supporting Diet

A diet consisting of excessive amounts of calories, fats, oils, cholesterol, and environmental contaminants, and which is deficient in fiber, has been implicated very strongly in the development of many cancers. A basic diet of starches, vegetables, and fruits contains the least amount of these harmful dietary elements and at the same time provides appropriate amounts of beneficial fiber.

An additional benefit of a starch-centered diet is that it contains generous amounts of substances with "anticancer" properties. Thus far, the following additional components of vegetable foods have been associated with a reduction in the risk of developing cancer.

Vitamin A

Low levels of vitamin A in the diet and body tissues are associated with cancer of the lung, mouth, esophagus, urinary bladder, and uterine cervix.[1-7] Betacarotene, the vitamin A precursor found in plant food, is more closely associated with a lower cancer incidence than the retinol form of vitamin A found in animal fats.[8-9] Vitamin A may act by preventing the binding of carcinogens to cells.[10] Most fruits and vegetables are high in content of vitamin A, but many dried beans and grains are low in both vitamin A and vitamin C. Green and yellow vegetables and fruits, added to complement a starch-centered meal, supply these essential vitamins. The following foods are especially good sources of betacarotene:

carrots	cantaloupes
sweet potatoes	apricots
beet greens	broccoli
spinach	asparagus

Vitamin C

In the stomach vitamin C, blocks the production of powerful cancer-causing chemicals, called nitrosamines, from the nitrates present naturally in food or from nitrites added to processed meats.[11] Most fruits and vegetables contain vitamin C, and the following foods contain high levels of it:

green peppers	Brussels sprouts
broccoli	oranges
cabbage	grapefruits
cauliflower	cantaloupes

Vitamin E

Vitamin E, like vitamin C, inhibits the formation of carcinogenic nitrosamines.[11] So many plant foods are high in vitamin E that it is virtually impossible not to get enough from a starch-centered meal plan. Green leafy vegetables and whole grains are outstanding sources.

Aryl Hydroxylases

Certain plants, especially those of the cruciferous family, contain substances that increase the activity of intestinal enzymes, called aryl hydroxylases, which block the action of carcinogens present in foods.[12-13] Plants high in aryl hydroxylase activity include:

Brussels sprouts	mustard
cabbage	kohlrabi
cauliflower	turnips
broccoli	parsnips
spinach	lettuce

Minerals

Mineral deficiencies and excesses are both associated with higher rates of certain cancers.[7] Iron deficiency is believed to be involved in the cause of some cases of cancer of the mouth and pharynx. Zinc excess or deficiency will encourage tumor growth in experimental animals. Molybdenum deficiency may result in esophogeal cancer.

Iodine excess and deficiency may result in thyroid cancer. Selenium deficiency has also been associated with higher rates of certain cancers in some populations of people. The mechanisms of action are far from being understood. Minerals become incorporated into the food chain by being absorbed from the soil by growing plants. Since both too much and too little can result in problems, the best approach to ensure proper intake would be to rely on a wide variety of unprocessed plant foods.

The foods listed here as having "anti-cancer" activity show that there are many arguments for the primary importance of vegetable foods in a health-supporting diet. A starch-centered diet, complemented with vegetables and fruits, provides a multitude of overlapping mechanisms for preventing cancer and keeping us healthy.

Many people who have become aware of the benefits of vitamins present in foods act inappropriately and take these components in the processed form as pills. Processing and refining results in new and often undesirable properties for individual components because they are more concentrated and are no longer associated with the minerals, vitamins, fiber, fats, carbohydrates, and proteins that surrounded them when present in the natural food.

Vitamin pills can have adverse effects, especially when taken in large doses. There are direct toxic effects caused by overdoses, most often seen with vitamins A and D.[14-16] Also, there are effects seen when a large dose of one vitamin or mineral inhibits the absorption and utilization of another one. If we take excessive amounts of supplements, we actually can create deficiencies by upsetting the natural balance in our foods. For example, the vitamin C in vitamin pills has been reported to destroy vitamin B_{12} and to lower B_{12} levels in the blood of persons taking large doses of vitamin C.[17-19] Interactions and imbalances are possible with mineral supplements including magnesium, molybdenum, manganese, chromium, calcium, zinc, iron, copper, and cadmium.[20] Zinc, for example, has an antagonistic action against copper and, therefore, zinc supplements could potentially create a copper deficiency in someone with marginal copper levels.[21] Zinc fed to animals raises total serum cholesterol and lowers HDL cholesterol.[22] In humans HDL cholesterol levels are lowered.[22] This effect may promote atherosclerosis. Another important drawback of supplements is the packaging. Vitamins A, D, E, and lecithin are often packaged in concentrated oil, which should be avoided for reasons previously described.

The most serious hazard of vitamin pills comes from the false sense of security people get from taking a multivitamin-mineral preparation or even a megadose quantity, in an effort to compensate for eating the wrong foods. Many mothers have said about their children, "At least they're getting all their vitamins even if they eat junk foods all day at school." Instead, mothers' attention should be focused on making sure that the children are getting foods that support their health.

People often are concerned about the quality of foods produced by present-day agriculture and food technology. They worry that a mineral deficiency might occur because the farm and garden soils have been overused and depleted of their minerals. Similar concern is expressed over the loss of vitamins during prolonged storage and cooking. There are several reasons for not placing too much emphasis on these issues. First of all, a plant has to make vitamins and accumulate minerals for its own growth processes, so for a plant to be healthy enough to grow, be harvested, and arrive at the grocery, these essential nutrients must be present. Concern should be further alleviated by the fact that most of us consume a large variety of foods from many different geographic locations with soils of varied mineral composition. A slight deficiency in one food, if it exists, will be made up for by a food grown in another location. Modern freezing and storage methods have given an advantage to the final vitamin content of many frozen products over those shipped across great distances. Lastly, vitamins and minerals are not present at levels in vegetable foods that are only marginal. There is an overabundance of these nutrients, allowing wide margins of safety to cover those situations when the food may not be eaten in the most ideal conditions or for the person who may have a greater need. A wide variety of foods consumed as fresh as possible will offer the greatest amount and widest assortment of these essential micronutrients for even the most concerned person.

Eleven of the thirteen vitamins presently known are synthesized by plants and found in abundance in a diet of unrefined starches, vegetables, and fruits. The only two vitamins not made by plants are vitamin B_{12}, which is synthesized by microorganisms, and vitamin D, which is actually a hormone synthesized in the skin with the help of sunlight.

Spend your money on health-supporting foods rather than on pills of any type to keep yourself healthy. (See Table 10.1.)

Table 10.1. MICRONUTRIENTS
VITAMINS

Vitamins	What it Does	Outstanding Vegetable Sources	Made in the Body	Stored in the body	Cooking destroys some of vitamin	Effects of Deficiency	Toxicity from overdose of Animal or Synthetic sources**
Beta carotene (A)	Helps maintain skin, eyes, urinary tract, and the lining of the nervous, respiratory, and digestive systems. For healthy bones and teeth.	Carrots, pumpkin, squash, sweet potatoes, apricots, beet greens, spinach, broccoli [Beta carotene concentration parallels the chlorophyll (green pigment) concentration of green vegetables].	no	yes (liver)	no	Night blindness, xerophthalmia (dry eye), dry rough skin, loss of appetite, fatigue, soft bones and teeth (less than 1,200 mg of Beta carotene per day).	Retinol in excess can cause nausea, vomiting, fatigue, headaches, loss of hair, brittle nails, exophthalmus, frail bones, bone pain (greater than 25,000 units per day). Beta carotene in excess causes a nontoxic condition of yellow skin called carotenemia.
Thiamine (B_1)	Needed for carbohydrate metabolism. Important for heart and nervous system function.	Yeast, peas, beans, whole wheat, corn, oats, brown rice (very widespread in nature).	no	no	yes	Loss of appetite, headache, dizziness, fatigue, beriberi—heart failure, nervous system changes (less than 0.23 mg per day).	Nontoxic

Vitamins	What it Does	Outstanding Vegetable Sources	Made in the Body	Stored in the body	Cooking destroys some of vitamin	Effects of Deficiency	Toxicity from overdose of Animal or Synthetic sources**
Riboflavin (B₂)	Important for growth. Functions in enzyme systems for the oxidation of amino acids. Involved in cellular respiration.	Yeast, yellow and green leafy vegetables, broccoli, beans, peas, oats, and green beans.	intestinal* synthesis	no	no	Cracks in the sides of the mouth, fatigue, sore tongue, scaly skin, growth retardation, hair loss, seborrheic dermatitis. (less than 0.8 mg/day).	Nontoxic
Niacin (B₃)	Essential for cell metabolism and absorption of carbohydrates. Involved in cellular respiration.	Yeast, whole grains, most vegetables and fruits.	intestinal* synthesis	very little	no	Pellagra, (early) weakness, loss of appetite and indigestion; (late) dermatitis, diarrhea, dementia (less than 7.5 mg/day).	Relatively nontoxic. Flushing of the skin, itching (greater than 100 mg/day).
Pantothenic Acid	Essential for cell metabolism. Functions in the release of energy from carbohydrates, fats, and proteins.	Yeast, whole grains, widespread in vegetables and fruits.	intestinal* synthesis	very little	yes	Extremely rare, nausea, insomnia.	Nontoxic

Vitamins	What it Does	Outstanding Vegetable Sources	Made in the Body	Stored in the body	Cooking destroys some of vitamin	Effects of Deficiency	Toxicity from overdose of Animal or Synthetic sources**
Pyridoxine (B$_6$)	Important in protein metabolism, synthesis of hemoglobin, serotonin, and aminobutyric acid. Needed for healthy gums, teeth, blood vessels, nervous system, and red blood cells.	Yeast, whole grains, bananas, cauliflower, potatoes, beans, most vegetables and fruits.	intestinal* synthesis	no	no	Convulsive disorders in infants on liquid milk formula. No clearcut symptoms in adults (less than 2 mg/day).	Nontoxic Supresses milk production in nursing mothers at commonly encountered doses[23]
Biotin	Functions in the synthesis of fatty acids and carbohydrate and protein metabolism. Important for health of the skin and circulatory system.	Yeast, whole grains, rice bran, cauliflower, peas. Fresh vegetables, (widespread occurrence).	intenstinal* synthesis	no	no	Very unlikely to occur. Seen only in diets high in raw eggs, dermatitis, muscular pain.	Nontoxic
Folic Acid	Functions in the growth and reproduction of all body cells, especially blood cell production.	Nearly all natural foods. Green leafy vegetables, yeast, fresh fruits.	intestinal* synthesis	little	yes	Blood disorder (macrocytic anemias) poor growth, tongue inflammation,	Nontoxic

Vitamins	What it Does	Outstanding Vegetable Sources	Made in the Body	Stored in the body	Cooking destroys some of vitamin	Effects of Deficiency	Toxicity from overdose of Animal or Synthetic sources**
Folic Acid (Cont.)						gastrointestinal tract disturbances (less than 50–200 mg/day.)	
B_{12}	Functions in the growth and reproduction of all body cells. Most apparent need is for blood cells and a healthy nervous system.	Yeast grown on a B_{12} medium, spirulina, fermented products such as miso, tempeh and soy sauce.	intestinal* synthesis	yes	no	Blood disorders (macrocytic anemia), degeneration of the nervous system. (less than 1 mcg/day).	Nontoxic
Ascorbic Acid (C)	Needed to maintain the integrity of the capillary blood vessels and to aid in the formation of normal teeth and bones. Regulates the formation of substances found between the cells.	Citrus fruits, tomatoes, strawberries, pineapple, cabbage, spinach, other green leafy vegetables, potatoes.	no	no	yes	Scurvy, subcutaneous hemorrhages, swollen bleeding gums, loosened teeth, weakened bones, anemia. Dry skin, lethargy, weakness (less than 6.5 mg/day).	Diarrhea, skin rash, burning on urination.

Vitamins	What it Does	Outstanding Vegetable Sources	Made in the Body	Stored in the body	Cooking destroys some of vitamin	Effects of Deficiency	Toxicity from overdose of Animal or Synthetic sources**
D	Promotes the absorption of calcium from the intestine. Essential for calcium and phosphorus metabolism. For maintaining a stable nervous system, heart action, and blood clotting.	Precursors are found in yeast and plant foods, which must be acted on by sunlight to become active.	yes sunlight activates sterols found in the skin.	yes	no	Rickets, softening of the bones and skull. Poorly developed muscles, nervous irritability.	Deposition of calcium in arteries and soft tissue, anorexia, nausea, abdominal pain, loss of weight, can result in permanent damage to kidneys, heart, and blood vessels.
E	Helps prevent the oxidation of polyunsaturated fatty acids in cell membranes and other body structures. Protects other vitamins from oxidation. Plays a role in the structural integration of muscle.	Green leafy vegetables, whole grains, vegetable oils.	no	yes	yes	Very rare occurrence. Fragility of blood cells. Muscle wasting, anemia of premature infants.	Nontoxic May raise blood pressure.

Vitamins	What it Does	Outstanding Vegetable Sources	Made in the Body	Stored in the body	Cooking destroys some of vitamin	Effects of Deficiency	Toxicity from overdose of Animal or Synthetic sources**
K	Promotes the formation of prothrombin, which is necessary for normal blood clotting.	Kelp, alfalfa, green plants, and green leafy vegetables.	intestinal* synthesis	yes	yes	Hypoprothrombinemia, which may result in hemorrhage. Occurs with malabsorption disorders of the bowel such as sprue, celiac disease, and colitis, (less than 20 mg/ per day).	Anemia, breakdown of blood cells. Flushing, sweating, and chest tightness.

*Intestinal synthesis of vitamins by bacteria present in the bowel occurs in people and contributes substantially to our needs. The major sites of synthesis are the cecum and large intestine; however, there are few sites for active absorption of these vitamins. In more primitive, less hygienic environments, large vitamin intake occurs from the contamination of foods with feces. The oral cavity and the small intestine also harbor vitamin-producing bacteria. Vitamins produced in these sites are absorbed efficiently by the small intestine. Niacin, riboflavin, and thiamine are held within cells and hence are available only after digestion of bacterial cells. Pantothenic acid, folic acid, B_6, biotin, and vitamin K diffuse from the cells and are ready for absorption even while in the large intestine. B_{12} is also synthesized by bacteria present in the small intestine and along with the bacteria ingested, enough B_{12} is supplied to meet the needs of most people, even those who avoid entirely concentrated sources of B_{12} found in animal foods.

**Toxicity from an overdose of vitamins does not occur when vitamins are obtained from a plant source in the natural form. Also, Vitamin D toxicity from excess sunlight does not occur. Pigmentation of the skin regulates the amount of vitamin D found in the skin by regulating the amount of sunlight which penetrates the skin.

MINERALS

Minerals	What it Does	Outstanding Vegetable Sources	Effects of Deficiency	Toxicities
Calcium (Ca)	Principle component of the skeleton and teeth. Roles in blood coagulation, neuromuscular excitability, cellular adhesiveness, transmission of nerve impulses, activation of enzymes and hormones. 99% of the calcium is stored in the skeleton.	Green leafy vegetables.	Not known to occur on natural diets.	Large intakes in ulcer patients taking antacid may result in high blood calcium and deposition of calcium in soft tissues with serious kidney damage (milk-alkali syndrome).
Chloride (Cl)	Found inside and outside body cells with sodium and potassium. Functions in the regulation of the body's acid-base balance; forms hydrochloric acid in the stomach.	All plant foods. (High concentration in salt, NaCl).	Unknown	Unknown
Chromium (Cr)	Activates enzymes for carbohydrate, fat, and cholesterol metabolism. Functions in insulin and protein metabolism.	Yeast, whole grains.	Possibly glucose intolerance in diabetes.	Unknown. Chromium is poorly absorbed through the intestinal tract.

Minerals	What it Does	Outstanding Vegetable Sources	Effects of Deficiency	Toxicities
Cobalt (Co)	Component of vitamin B_{12} and other enzymes. Can replace zinc in a number of enzymes. Stimulates blood cell formation.	Sea vegetables	Resembles B_{12} deficiency. Anemia and degeneration of the nervous system.	Congestive heart failure, thyroid enlargement, polycythemia, neurological abnormalities. "Beer drinkers cardiomyopathy."
Copper (Cu)	Essential for growth and a broad range of metabolic functions. Hemoglobin and melanin synthesis, bone and elastic tissue development, and normal function of the nervous system.	Whole grains, leafy vegetable, dried legumes (high concentrations from copper cookware).	Relatively unknown, possibly anemia in severely malnourished infants and adults.	Nausea, vomiting, abdominal pain, headache, dizziness, and metallic taste. More severe may cause hypertension, coma, jaundice, anemia, kidney failure, and death.
Fluoride (F)	Found as calcium fluoride. Concentrated in teeth. Improves "crystallinity" of calcium, thereby strengthens bones and teeth.	Widespread in nature, whole grains, vegetables, and fruits (high concentration naturally or artifically present in water supply).	Very unusual unless increased dental decay is considered a result of deficiency.	1.0 ppm in drinking water results in lowest tooth decay. 2.5 ppm or greater causes mottled tooth enamel. At 8 ppm almost all individuals have mottled teeth. Higher levels can cause excess calcification of bone (osteosclerosis) and soft tissues.

Minerals	What it Does	Outstanding Vegetable Sources	Effects of Deficiency	Toxicities
Iodine (I)	Essential to the development and function of the thyroid gland, which regulates the body's production of energy, promotes growth, and stimulates metabolism. Mental health and the condition of the teeth, hair, nails, and skin are dependent on the thyroid gland.	Plants grown near the sea where iodine content of soil is high. Sea vegetables, vegetables, whole grains.	Enlargement of the thyroid gland and hypothyroidism (goiter), elevated cholesterol, obesity, heart failure, dry hair, mental slowness, irritability, cretinism, physical and mental retardation. Cabbage, turnips, and rutabagas contain goitrogens, which have antithyroid activity and produce goiters. Formation of a goiter is a complex condition not solely because of iodine deficiency. Cretinism may occur in children born to iodine-deficient mothers.	Not reported from food or water. As a drug can block thyroid activity.
Iron (Fe)	Central role in hemoglobin function. Also takes part in myoglobin, hemic enzymes, and protein metabolism.	Green leafy vegetables, wheat, corn, beans (ascorbic acid increases absorption). Iron cookware provides considerable iron.	Iron-deficiency anemia, which is most commonly accompanied by blood loss or dairy product intake.	Hemosiderosis—abnormal iron storage associated with tissue damage, particularly the liver, with cirrhosis, diabetes, and pigmentation of the skin, and eventually heart failure. Susceptibility to infection.

Minerals	What it Does	Outstanding Vegetable Sources	Effects of Deficiency	Toxicities
Magnesium (Mg)	Involved in enzyme reactions for carbohydrate and protein metabolism. It acts along with and sometimes opposite calcium.	Found in fresh green vegetables, parallels (green color) chlorophyll content of plant. Corn, apples.	Personality change, muscle spasms, tremor (usually seen only in severely ill persons such as alcoholics), malnutrition, and kidney failure.	The balance between calcium and magnesium is important. Toxicities seen with combined kidney failure and magnesium containing antacid drugs. Can cause depression, paralysis, respiratory depression, death.
Manganese (Mn)	Involved in numerous enzymes and acts as a catalyst for synthesis reactions.	Tea, whole grain cereals, green vegetables.	No human diseases have been clearly shown to be caused by manganese deficiency.	Low toxicity. No reports of toxicities from food sources. Seen in metal workers.
Molybdenum (Mo)	Role in an enzyme; xanthine oxidase, and various dependent enzymes.	Legumes, cereals, and dark green vegetables. Widely distributed.	No known deficiency.	Possible role in gout and multiple sclerosis. Otherwise toxicity in animals gives diarrhea, debilitation, and death.
Phosphorous (P)	Component of bone and widely distributed in the body. Plays a role in most body reactions; energy production and metabolism of protein, fat, and carbohydrates. In balance with calcium.	Whole grains, vegetables. Widely distributed in nature.	Drug induced only, not seen in natural diets: malaise, bone pain and demineralization, negative calcium balance.	No known toxicity except in kidney failure. Results in bone demineralization.

Minerals	What it Does	Outstanding Vegetable Sources	Effects of Deficiency	Toxicities
Potassium (K)	Essential mineral found mainly inside cells. In balance with sodium. Major function in nerve condition, water, and fluid balance in the kidney, glucose metabolism, and muscle action.	Vegetables and fruits are very high in potassium. Grains are generally lower in potassium.	Seen commonly with diuretic medications; diarrhea and vomiting, diabetes, and excessive salt intake. Symptoms include weakness, paralysis, cardiac arrest, and death.	Cardiac arrhythmias, death, muscle weakness from high intake.
Selenium (Se)	Works closely with vitamin E. Important for cell growth. Natural antioxidant. Essential component of enzymes, erythrocyte glutathione peroxidase.	Whole grains, broccoli, onions, tomatoes and other vegetables.	Possibly cancer. Deficient states involve vitamin E.	Seen where selenium content of soil is high. Symptoms of chronic dermatitis, fatigue, and dizziness. In animals excessive intake is carcinogenic.
Sodium (Na)	Essential mineral found mainly outside cells. In balance with potassium. Regulates fluid balance, functions in nerve conduction, kidney, and muscle. Widely distributed in body.	Widely distributed in foods. Seaweed, artichokes, beets, celery, chard, dandelion greens, kale, mustard greens, spinach.	Unknown from a purely dietary cause. Occurs with dehydration secondary to vomiting, diarrhea, sweating. Also seen with kidney disease, adrenal insufficiency, and diuretics.	Fluid retention, edema, high blood pressure, possible stomach cancer.
Sulfur (S)	A component of several amino acids, insulin, heparin, and keratin as well as other tissues.	Found with proteins—beans, peas, lentils, mushrooms, cabbage, Brussels sprouts.	No known deficiency.	None from food sources.

Minerals	What it Does	Outstanding Vegetable Sources	Effects of Deficiency	Toxicities
Zinc (Zn)	Constituent of more than 80 enzymes. Functions with many vitamins and many proteins.	Whole grain products, brewers yeast, pumpkin seeds.	Seen with alcoholism, rheumatoid arthritis, chronic kidney disease, inflammatory bowel disease, malabsorption, sickle cell disease. Results in poor growth, poor wound healing, loss of appetite, loss of taste and smell, disorders of the nervous system.	Relatively nontoxic, nausea, vomiting, abdominal cramps, bloating, diarrhea and fever. Lowers level of HDL cholesterol, may promote atherosclerosis. Taken during pregnancy may cause premature birth and fetal death.[24]

*Minerals are stable in nature and are neither synthesized nor destroyed. Plants take in minerals found in the soil and incorporate them into a variety of organic compounds. Animals, including people, obtain these essential substances directly from plants or indirectly from the consumption of animal products. Cooking and storage cause little loss of mineral content of food. Additional intake can result when minerals leach from metal cans and cookware and become incorporated into the diet.

Notes

[1] J. Weisburger, "Nutrition and Cancer—On the Mechanisms Bearing on Causes of Cancer of the Colon, Breast, Prostate, and Stomach," *Bull NY Acad Med* 56 (1980):673.

[2] M. Sporn, "Prevention of Chemical Carcinogenesis by Vitamin A and Its Synthetic Analogs (Retinoids)," *Fed Proc* 35 (1976):1332.

[3] C. Mettlin, "Dietary Risk Factors in Human Bladder Cancer," *Am J Epi* 110 (1979):255.

[4] Editorial, "Vitamin A and Cancer," *Lancet* 1 (1980):575.

[5] J. DiPalma, "The Interaction of Vitamins with Cancer Chemotherapy," *Ca-A Cancer J for Clinicians* 29 (1979):280.

[6] N. Wald, "Low Serum—Vitamin A and Subsequent Risk of Cancer, Preliminary results of a prospective study." *Lancet* 2 (1980):813.

[7] Committees on Diet, Nutrition, and Cancer, Assembly of Life Sciences, National Research Council, *Diet, Nutrition, and Cancer,* Washington, D.C.: National Academy Press, 1982.

[8] R. Shekelle, "Dietary Vitamin A and Risk of Cancer in the Western Electric Study," *Lancet* 2 (1981):1185.

[9] R. Peto, "Can Dietary Beta-Carotene Materially Reduce Human Cancer Rates?" *Nature* 290 (1981):201.

[10] V. Genta, "Vitamin A Deficiency Enhances Binding of Benzo(a)pyrene to Tracheal Epithelial DNA," *Nature* 247 (1974):48.

[11] J. Weisburger, "Inhibition of Carcinogenesis: Vitamin C and the Prevention of Gastric Cancer," *Prev Med* 9 (1980):352.

[12] L. Wattenberg, "Studies of Polycyclic Hydrocarbon Hydroxylases of the Intestine Possibly Related to Cancer," *Cancer* 28 (1971):99.

[13] W. Loub, "Aryl Hydrocarbon Hydroxylase Induction in Rat Tissues by Naturally Occurring Indoles of Cruciferous Plants," *J Nat Ca Inst* 54 (1975):985.

[14] V. Herbert, "Facts and Fiction about Megavitamin Therapy," *Resident and Staff Physician* (Dec. 1978):43.

[15] H. Roberts, *Food Safety,* New York: Wiley Interscience, 1981, pp. 79-92.

[16] J. Dipalma, "Vitamin Toxicity," *Clinical Pharmacology* 18 (1978):106.

[17] V. Herbert, "Destruction of Vitamin B_{12} by Ascorbic Acid," *JAMA* 230 (1974):241.

[18] H. HogenKamp, Editorial, "The Interaction Between Vitamin B_{12} and C," *Am J Clin Nutr* 33 (1980):1.

[19] V. Herbert, "Low Serum Vitamin B_{12} Levels in Patients Receiving Ascorbic Acid in Megadoses: Studies Concerning the Effect of Ascorbate on Radioisotope Vitamin B_{12} Assay," *Am J Clin Nutr* 31 (1978):253.

[20] H. Roberts, *Food Safety,* New York: Wiley Interscience, 1981, p. 113. Mertz, *Physiol Rev* 49 (1969):163.

[21] H. Sandsteal, "Zinc interferes with copper metabolism." *JAMA* 240 (1978):2188

[22] P. Hooper, "Zinc Lowers High-Density Lipoprotein-Cholesterol Levels," *JAMA* 244 (1980):1960.

[23] L. Greentree, "Dangers of Vitamin B_6 in Nursing Mothers," *N Engl J Med* 300 (1979):141.

[24] N. Davies, "Zinc balance during pregnancy and lactation." *Am J Clin Nutr* 30 (1977):300.

CHAPTER

11

Food Additives Including Salt Are Avoided on a Health-Supporting Diet

Additives

Food additives are substances that are put directly into a food to produce an intended effect, or they may become part of the food as a consequence of production, distribution, or processing. Additives may include herbicides and pesticides used in growing food and colorings, nutrients, flavorings, fresheners, preservatives, and stabilizers added during the manufacturing of foods.

Before the major technological advances of the twentieth century, approximately fifty additives, including spices and flavorings, were available for use in preparing a variety of foods. Today there are more than 2,000 additives.[1] Nearly 500 of these ingredients are not required to be identified on labels. This inconsistency in labeling goes so far that an additive may have to be listed on the label of one food but not on that of another. For example, monosodium glutamate (MSG) must be noted on soup labels but not on mayonnaise or salad dressings.[2] Deceptive names also can be used on labels. Simple sugars are often listed as "natural" sweeteners, corn syrups, sucrose, glucose, or maltose. Butylated hydroxyanisole (BHA) and butylated hydroxytoluene (BHT) may be found listed as oil preservers or freshness preservers. So, by reading a label, you may not know what additives are present in the food.

The effects of food additives on our bodies can be immediate or long-term. Common immediate reactions to a certain food additive can be hives (urticaria), swelling (angioneurotic edema), runny nose (rhinitis), headaches, asthma, and bleeding (purpura).[3] Uncommon reactions include hyperactivity, irritability, contact dermatitis, and other skin eruptions. Azo dyes, annatto, benzoates, BHT, BHA, and metabisulfites are frequently the causes of these and other reactions.[3]

Sulfiting agents, which include sulfur dioxide, sodium metabisulfate, and potassium metabisulfite, are commonly used in restaurant salads, dried fruits, uncooked vegetables, avocado dips, wines, beers, and shrimp to prevent discoloration and spoilage. Severe reactions can occur in sensitive individuals when they eat these chemicals. They can result in asthma attacks accompanied by weakness, cyanosis, tightness of the chest, shock, and coma.[4]

Another common and immediate reaction to a food additive is seen with monosodium glutamate (MSG), found in a very large variety of foods and sold in concentrated forms such as Accent, Ajinomoto, and MSG. Chinese restaurants are notorious for their liberal use of this flavor enhancer, and the common reactions to it are dubbed "Chinese restaurant syndrome." MSG provides a large amount of sodium and an amino acid—glutamic acid—that can cause illness. Reactions include severe headache and nausea and occasionally chest tightness, facial pressure, weakness of limbs, a burning sensation, and psychiatric reactions.[5-6] There also may be long-term effects of MSG that result in damage to the brain.[7] Severe asthma attacks have been reported from MSG.[8]

Tartrazine, also known as FD&C Yellow No.5, is a yellow coloring agent that can produce itching, hives, runny nose, and asthma in sensitive people. People who are allergic to aspirin have a greater tendency to be allergic to tartrazine. There also have been occasional reports of rash, fast heartbeat, shortness of breath, and chest pain in people sensitive to this dye.[9] Tartrazine is used to make turquoise, green, and maroon colors in addition to yellow in foods. Common processed foods using this dye include the following:[10]

- Beverages
    Orange drinks (Tang, Daybreak, Awake)
    Other drinks: Gatorade (lime-flavored), imitation lemonade mix (Jewel)
- Ice creams and sherbets
    New York ice cream (Hillfarm)
    Rainbow sherbet (Hillfarm)

- Desserts
  Gelatin (Jell-O, Royal)
  Instant pudding and pie filling (Jell-O)
- Salad Dressings
  Golden Blend Italian dressing (Kraft)
  Zesty Italian (reduced-calorie) dressing (Kraft)
- Bakery products
  Cake mix (some) (Duncan Hines, Pillsbury)
  Cake icing (Cake Mate)
- Confections
  Imitation butter flavoring (McCormick)
  Imitation banana extract (McCormick)
  Imitation pineapple extract (McCormick)
  Seasoning salt (French's)
- Other products
  Macaroni and cheese dinner (Kraft, Golden Grain)
  Egg noodle and cheese dinner (Kraft)
  "Cheez" curls, "Cheez" balls (Planters)
  Fruit chews (Skittles)
  Candies—lemon drops, butterscotch, candy corn (Brach's)

Many over-the-counter and prescription drugs contain tartrazine.[11]

Some additives take a more indirect route into our food supply. The Office of Technology Assessment reported in 1979 that nearly 100 percent of swine and veal calves and 60 percent of cattle receive antibacterial feed supplementation.[12] There is concern that allergic reactions can occur to antibiotic residues in meat and milk products.[13] Low levels of antibiotics in feed also promote the development of bacteria resistant to antibiotics, thus creating a threat to human health from these hardy bacteria.[14]

Long-term effects of food additives can result in damage to organs, birth defects, and cancer.[15] Saccharin and cyclamate, used as artificial sweeteners, have been associated with cancer of the urinary bladder.[16-17] Nitrites and nitrates, used as preservatives in packaged meats and found naturally in a variety of foods, are converted in the body to nitrosamines, which are strongly suspected of causing stomach and other gastrointestinal cancers.[18] Another worrisome food additive is diethylstilbesterol (DES), used to stimulate the growth of cattle. DES is a known carcinogen, which has caused cancer of the vagina in the daughters of some women who took this hormone to prevent miscarriage during pregnancy.[19] Abnormalities of the genitals and urinary tract are also found in sons and daughters of women who took this drug.[20] DES is still used today in the livestock industry, and its residues are detected in beef intended for human consumption.[21]

White rice is produced by a process that removes the outer natural coat, leaving the central core of carbohydrate exposed to molds, bacteria, and insects. To prevent spoilage and loss, some manufacturers coat the rice with an outer layer of talc and glucose. Talc is the amorphous form of the same substance that asbestos consists of, and talc used for coating rice often is contaminated with large numbers of actual asbestos fibers.[22] When eaten, some asbestos passes through the intestine and travels throughout the body, and eventually some fibers are filtered through the kidneys into the urine.[23] Asbestos is known to cause cancer of the lung and the lining of the lung (mesothelium) when inhaled. When ingested, asbestos fibers are suspected of causing stomach cancer and other cancers of the gastrointestinal tract.[24] There is also concern over the possibility that cancer of the ovary may be the result of talc granules.[25-26] Recommendations found on the package to wash rice before using are senseless because even after nine thorough washings some talc still remains.[27] Talc-coated rice is sold mostly in Hawaii, California, and Puerto Rico.

It is not possible to establish reliable, harmless levels of cancer-causing substances in our foods. What may seem to be a safe level by one experimental design may be found to cause cancer by another. Some of this contradiction may be explained in part by the experimental observation that the effects of different cancer-causing agents are interrelated. Exposure to agents in concentrations insufficient to produce tumors increases the susceptibility of the organism to subsequent contact with the same or other carcinogens. Therefore, small doses of cancer-causing additives that do not induce cancer under usual conditions may well sensitize the tissues to subsequent contact with cancer-causing substances.[28]

Numerous additives are found in food, and many of them are presently the subject of heated controversy between industry and health advocates. To avoid being part of the human experiment that in the distant future will settle the actual dangers of these additives, the wisest action for us to take now is to avoid as many of these as possible. These additives are far from being essential nutrients for good health. Most additives, especially those with possible health hazards, are found in processed rich foods. A health-supporting diet of starches, vegetables, and fruits is free of all but unavoidable environmental contaminants and is the simplest and most effective answer to the problem of food additives.

Salt

The most commonly used non-caloric food additive is salt. In the past, salt was a rare and valuable commodity and once was even used as money. Ancient Roman soldiers received part of their pay in salt. This was known as *salarium,* from which our word *salary* is derived. Today, what was once a delicacy is easily and cheaply obtained in most parts of the world.

Salt is a combination of two elements—sodium and chloride—which occur naturally in all foods. Sodium is the component with the strongest effect on our health. We need as little as 50 milligrams of sodium per day from our diet.[29] One teaspoon of salt adds more than 2 grams of extra sodium to the diet. People on a western diet consume on the average 5 grams of sodium (2⅓ teaspoons of salt) per day.[30] Much of this is hidden in packaged and processed foods and in restaurant meals. Only about 2 grams are added consciously at the table or during cooking.[30] Salt is added to preserve and flavor and is one of the most prominent tastes in a rich diet. Because of it, the delicious natural flavors of starches, vegetables and fruits are often covered up and lost.

Potassium is another important mineral found in our bodies and in foods. Potassium and sodium work together in cell functions, and their actions frequently counterbalance each other. We can conserve nearly 100 percent of the sodium we take in, yet our kidneys continuously lose potassium. This observation suggests that our bodies require a plentiful supply of potassium from the diet but can function well on a low sodium intake. Plant products are naturally high in potassium and low in sodium; animal foods and processed foods are generally the opposite.

There are many adverse effects of a high-sodium, low-potassium diet. This mineral imbalance can cause elevation of blood pressure, which can result in a condition called hypertension.[31-33] In affluent societies, hypertension is found in as many as 25 percent of adults and 12 percent of the children.[34-35] In non-westernized societies, blood pressure rises hardly at all with age, and hypertension is almost unknown. Experts have stated that reduction of salt in the diet below 2,000 milligrams (approximately 1,000 mg. of sodium) per day would result in the prevention of essential hypertension and its disappearance as a major health problem.[36] However, sodium is only one of the dietary factors involved in the development of hypertension. Fat, fiber, potassium, meat, caffeine, and alcohol are also involved, and these factors may be the other important reasons why vegetarians have lower blood pressure than meat eaters, regardless of their sodium intake.[37-44] Switching to a high-potassium, low-sodium diet most often lowers high blood pressure to normal in just a few days.[45-53]

Recent studies have shown benefit from another mineral in that the administration of supplemental calcium to subjects has resulted in a lowering of blood pressure. The mechanism for this effect is still being speculated but may involve relaxation of the smooth muscles that constrict blood vessels, or it may be a diuretic effect of calcium that causes loss of sodium from the body.[54] (It should not surprise us to find that some of this research is supported by the dairy industry.[55])

Excess sodium in the diet can cause fluid retention and swelling of body tissues, a condition known as edema. One can easily gain 4 pounds of water weight after eating a meal high in sodium content.

Salt is especially harmful to people with heart trouble because the sodium draws excess fluid into the circulatory system. This places a heavy load on the diseased heart muscle, and the weakened heart eventually fails to provide effective circulation. As a result, fluids back up and fill the lungs. This condition is called congestive heart failure.

The kidneys protect us to a point by excreting extra sodium from the body. When the kidneys fail to do this, sodium and fluids accumulate, causing problems such as those just mentioned—high blood pressure, edema, and heart failure. Low-sodium diets are particularly helpful to people with heart and kidney diseases.[56-57]

Concentrated sources of salt can damage the lining of the stomach. The end result may be stomach cancer.[58-59] Japanese people eat up to 7¼ teaspoons of salt (15.5 grams of sodium) a day in the form of miso, soy sauce, and pickled vegetables. They also have one of the highest rates of stomach cancer in the world. (Other dietary factors that are felt to contribute to the high rates of stomach cancer in the Japanese include talc-coated rice that is often contaminated with asbestos, carcinogens produced in the smoking process used to prepare fish and other meats, and the lack of fresh fruits and vegetables high in vitamins A and C, which have anti-cancer effects, as previously mentioned.)

There are a few rare exceptions to the general recommendation for a low-salt diet. People with adrenal insufficiency, salt-losing kidney disease, colostomies, and chronic postural hypotension often have a need for extra sodium because of an inability to conserve this mineral. Contrary to popular belief, hard work in hot climates by healthy people does not require additional sodium in the diet. Our need for sodium is easily met by the foods in a starch-centered diet, without added salt. Sodium deficiency of a purely dietary origin does not occur in humans.[29]

Some fresh vegetables, listed in Table 11.1, have a relatively high sodium content. These should be used sparingly if you have been advised to be on a very salt-restricted diet.

Table 11.1

	Sodium per 100 grams	Average Serving Portion	Sodium per Average Portion
Artichokes	43 mg	1 whole	86 mg
Beets	110 mg	½ cup	110 mg
Celery	110 mg	2 stalks	55 mg
Chard	200 mg	¼ cup	200 mg
Dandelion greens	76 mg	½ cup	76 mg
Kale	110 mg	½ cup	110 mg
Mustard greens	48 mg	½ cup	48 mg
Spinach	82 mg	½ cup	82 mg

The desire for salt is learned, and our tastes quickly change as we lower our sodium intake.[29,60-61] Often, when people first change to a starch-centered diet without added salt, they miss the flavor of salt more than anything else. Herbs and spices are useful for adding taste without reaching for the salt shaker. Experiment by adding more spices than usual when leaving out salt. Some of the most flavorful seasonings are:

basil	paprika
cumin	sage
dill	tarragon
marjoram	thyme
oregano	onion powder
garlic powder	chili powder (salt-free)

Good combinations of these seasonings are:

basil and paprika
oregano, sage, and thyme
basil, dill, cumin, and tarragon
basil, marjoram, and oregano

Lemon juice, lime juice, and vinegar also add delicious flavors to vegetable dishes.

If you do not have high blood pressure, edema, kidney disease, or heart disease, you may want to use a little bit of added salt when starting your dietary change, if you are used to salty foods. This will make the taste of the new foods more familiar, and it will help you get through the early adjustment period. Do not add more than half a teaspoon of salt (1 gram of sodium) per day. Then gradually lower your intake as you adjust. For maximum flavor, add the salt to the surface of the food at the table, not during cooking. Salt is another of the four primary flavors tasted by the tongue. A small amount can add gustatory pleasure without causing harm to most people.

A number of commercial products are available to provide the flavor of salt in your diet. They are mentioned here in order of decreasing sodium content. Sea salt contains as much sodium as salt from the ground and offers little if any advantage over ordinary salt. Tamari and shoyu products contain approximately 800 milligrams of sodium per tablespoon. Low-sodium tamari and salt-reduced soy sauces contain 500 milligrams of sodium per tablespoon. Spike is a salt and dry vegetable combination. Parkelp and SeaZun contain kelp (seaweed), which is high in sea salt. Vegit vegetable seasoning is low in sodium. It is made from dried high-sodium vegetables and contains about 50 milligrams of sodium per serving. Lush 'n' Lemon is made from low-sodium vegetables.

Salt substitutes are made of potassium chloride (KCl) instead of sodium chloride (NaCl). Light salt is a mixture of KCl and NaCl. Inadvertent ingestion of a large amount of potassium chloride salt substitute over a short period of time can cause a dangerous rise in blood levels of potassium, which in turn can result in cardiac arrhythmias and death. Also, concentrated salt substitutes can irritate the lining of the stomach and intestines. Potassium salts are not normal constituents of the diet, and the effects of their long-term use are unknown. Therefore, they cannot be recommended. Using a salt substitute is the wrong approach to dietary change. You should learn to enjoy your food for its natural flavors.

Notes

[1]National Research Council, Food and Nutrition Board 19755, "Chemicals Used in Food Processing," Publication 1274, Washington, D.C.: National Academy of Sciences, 1965.

[2]J. Verret, *Eating May Be Hazardous to Your Health,* New York: Anchor Press/ Doubleday, 1975.

[3]L. Juhlin, "Incidence of Intolerance to Food Additivies," *Int J Dermatol* 19 (1980): 548.

[4]D. Stevenson, "Sensitivity to Ingested Metabisulfites in Asthmatic Subjects," *J Allergy Clin Immunol* 68 (1981): 26.

[5]H. Schaumburg, "Monosodium L-Glutamatic: Its Pharmacology and Role in the Chinese Restaurant Syndrome," *Science* 163 (1969): 826.

[6]A. Colman, "Possible Psychiatric Reactions to Monosodium Glutamate," *N Engl J Med* 299 (1978): 902.

[7]J. Olney, "Status of Monosodium Glutamate Revisited," *Am J Clin Nutr* 26 (1973): 683.

[8]D. Allen, "Chinese-Restaurant Asthma," *N Engl J Med* 305 (1981):1154.

[9]G. Settipane, "Aspirin Intolerence, Subtypes, Familial Occurrence, and Cross-Reactivity with Tartrazine," *J Allergy Clin Immunol* 56 (1975): 215.

[10]C. Tse, "Food Products Containing Tartrazine," *N Engl J Med* 306 (1982): 681.

[11]M. Lee, "Tartrazine-Containing Drugs," *Drug Intelligence and Clin Pharm* 15 (1981): 782.

[12]Office of Technology Assessment, *Drugs in Livestock Feed,* vol. 1, Washington, D.C.: U.S. Government Printing Office, 1979.

[13]W. Hewitt, "Clinical Implications of the Presence of Drug Residues in Food," *Fed Proc* 34 (1975): 202.

[14]P. Gardner, "Antibiotic in Animal Feeds: The Need for Better Epidemiological Studies," *J Inf Disease* 138 (1978): 101.

[15]S. Miller, "Additives in our Food Supply," *Ann NY Acad Sci* 300 (1977): 397.

[16]G. Howe, "Artificial Sweetener and Human Bladder Cancer," *Lancet* 2 (1977): 578.

[17]R. Egeberg, "Report of the Secretary of HEW from the Medical Advisory Group on Cyclamates," *JAMA* 211 (1970): 1358.

[18]F. Fairweather, "Food Additives and Cancer," *Proc Nutr Soc* 40 (1981): 21.

[19]A. Herbst, "Adenocarcinoma of the Vagina, Association of Maternal Stilbesterol Therapy with Tumor Appearance in Young Women," *N Engl J Med* 284 (1971): 878.

[20]A. Siegler, "Fertility of the Diethylstilbesterol-Exposed Offspring," *Fertility and Sterility* 31 (1979): 601.

[21]P. Gunby, "Battles Continue over DES Use in Fattening Cattle," *JAMA* 244 (1980): 228.

[22]R. Merliss, "Talc-Treated Rice and Japanese Stomach Cancer," *Science* 173 (1971): 1141.

[23]P. Cook, "Ingested Mineral Fibers: Elimination in Human Urine," *Science* 204 (1979): 195.

[24]I. Selikoff, "Asbestos Exposure and Neoplasia," *JAMA* 188 (1964): 142.

[25]D. Longo, "Cosmetic Talc and Ovarian Cancer," *Lancet* 2 (1979): 349.

[26]D. Cramer, "Ovarian Cancer and Talc—A Case-Controlled Study," *Cancer* 50 (1982): 372.

[27]H. Matsudo, "Japanese Gastric Cancer, Potentially Carcinogenic Silicates (Talc) from rice." *Arch Pathol* 97 (1974): 366.

[28]J. Neiman, "The Sensitizing Carcinogenic Effect of Small Doses of Carcinogens," *Europ J Cancer* 4 (1968): 537.

[29]L. Dahl, "Salt Intake and Salt Need," *N Engl J Med* 258 (1958): 1152 & 1205.

[30]A. Altschul, "Food Choices for Lowering Sodium Intake," *Hypertension* 4 (Supp III) (1982): 111–116.

[31]L. Dahl,, "Salt and Hypertension," *Am J Clin Nutr* 25 (1972): 231.

[32]G. Meneely, "High-Sodium, Low-Potassium Environment and Hypertension," *Am J Cardiol* 38 (1976): 768.

[33]F. Skrabal, "Low-Sodium, High-Potassium Diet for Prevention of Hypertension: Probable Mechanism of Action," *Lancet* 2 (1981): 895.

[34]U.S. Department of Health, Education, and Welfare, "Hypertension and Heart Disease in Adults, United States, 1960–1962," National Health Survey, National Center for Health Studies Services 11, no. 13, 1966.

[35]J. Loggie, "Hypertension in the Pediatric Patient: A Reappraisal," *J Pediatr* 94 (1979): 685.

[36]E. Fries, "Salt, Volume, and the Prevention of Hypertension," *Circulation* 53 (1976): 589.

[37]B. Armstrong, "Blood Pressure in Seventh-Day Adventists Vegetarians," *Am J Epidemiol* 105 (1977): 444.

[38]S. Malthotra, "Dietary Factors Causing Hypertension in India," *Am J Clin Nutr* 23 (1970): 1353.

[39]B. Armstrong, "Urinary Sodium and Blood Pressure in Vegetarians," *Am J Clin Nutr* 32 (1979): 2472.

[40]F. Sacks, "Blood Pressure in Vegetarians," *Am J Epidemiol* 100 (1974): 390.

[41]F. Sacks, "Effect of Ingestion of Meat on Plasma Cholesterol of Vegetarians," *JAMA* 246 (1981): 640.

[42]M. Burr, "Plasma Cholesterol and Blood Pressure in Vegetarians," *J Hum Nutr* 35 (1981): 437.

[43]I. Rouse, "Blood-Pressure Lowering Effect of a Vegetarian Diet, Controlled Trial in Normotensive Subjects," *Lancet* 1 (1983): 5.

[44]O. Ophir, "Low Blood Pressure in Vegetarians: The Possible Role of Potassium," *Am J Clin Nutr* 37 (1983): 755.

[45]W. Kempner, "Treatment of Hypertensive Vascular Disease with Rice Diet," *Am J Med* 4 (1948): 545. Also, *Arch Intern Med* 133 (1974): 758.

[46]J. Parijs, "Moderate Sodium Restriction and Diuretics in the Treatment of Hypertension," *Am Heart J* 85 (1973): 22.

[47]J. Stamler, "Prevention and Control of Hypertension by Nutritional–Hygienic Means," *JAMA* 243 (1980): 1819.

[48]G. MacGregor, "Double-Blind Randomized Crossover Trial of Moderate Sodium Restriction in Essential Hypertension," *Lancet* 1 (1982): 351.

[49]T. Morgan, "Hypertension Treated by Salt Restriction," *Lancet* 1 (1978): 227.

[50]T. Beard, "Randomized Controlled Trial of a No-Added-Sodium Diet for Mild Hypertension, *Lancet* 2 (1982): 455.

[51]G. MacGregor, "Moderate Potassium Supplementation in Essential Hypertension," *Lancet* 2 (1982): 567.

[52]K. Khaw, "Randomized Double-Blind Crossover Trial of Potassium on Blood Pressure in Normal Subjects, *Lancet* 2 (1982): 1127.

[53]G. MacGregor, "Dietary Sodium and Potassium Intake and Blood Pressure," *Lancet* 1 (1983): 750.

[54]J. Belizan, "Reduction of Blood Pressure with Calcium in Young Adults," *JAMA* 249 (1983): 1161.

[55]D. McCarron. "Calcium, Magnesium, and Phosphorus Balance in Human and Experimental Hypertension," *Hypertension* 4 (Supp III) (1982):III-27.

[56]W. Kempner, "Compensation of Renal Metabolic Dysfunction," *N Carolina Med J* 6 (1945): 61, 107.

[57]W. Kempner, "Treatment of Cardiac Failure with the Rice Diet," *N Carolina Med J* 8 (1947): 128.

[58]W. MacDonald, "Histological Effect of Certain Pickles on the Human Gastric Mucosa," *Canad Med Ass J* 96 (1967): 1521.

[59]J. Joossens, "Salt Intake and Mortality from Strokes," *N Engl J Med* 300 (1979): 1396.

[60]J. Blair-West, "Sodium Homeostasis, Salt Appetite, and Hypertension," *Circ Res* 26, 27 (Supp II) (1970): 11–251.

[61]M. Bertino, "Long-Term Reduction in Dietary Sodium Alters the Taste of Salt," *Am J Clin Nutr* 36 (1982): 1134.

CHAPTER
12
Resolving Food Allergy Through an Elimination Diet

Expert estimates indicate that as many as 60 percent of the people in our affluent societies suffer from food allergies.[1] There are many symptoms and disease processes caused or aggravated by allergy to food. Some of the common conditions are arthritis, colitis, gastritis, diarrhea, bed-wetting, tension, fatigue, skin rashes, and headaches. Respiratory reactions, such as runny nose, sinusitis, and asthma, can be caused by food allergies.[2-6] (See Chapter 5 for a more complete list.)

The foods most commonly causing allergy are milk, eggs, chocolate, shellfish, fish, wheat, corn, citrus fruits, tomatoes, strawberries, and nuts.[5-8]

Substances that cause allergic reactions are known as allergens. They include the proteins found in many kinds of foods and particles breathed in from the air, such as dust, pollen, mold spores, and insect parts. Chemicals found in natural and manufactured products also can cause allergic reactions in sensitive people upon physical contact. Most allergy-prone people will react to several different types of allergens. The body's immune system has a limited capacity to deal with allergens, and when the system becomes overloaded, allergic symptoms appear. If you can reduce the intake of allergens from one source, such as foods, you will ease the burden on the entire immune system. In this way you can help your body deal with other sources of allergy, such as particles in the air. For example, a person who has seasonal asthma triggered by certain kinds of pollens often can be helped considerably by eliminating milk from his or her diet.

The immune system also can react to foreign substances by forming complexes of the allergen (which may also be referred to as an antigen) with its specific antibody.[9-13] These complexes then can deposit in the tissues of the body, causing inflammation, which manifests as a broad group of afflictions called immune-complex diseases.[13-23] They include rheumatoid arthritis, lupus (erythematosus), periarteritis nodosa, polymyositis, scleraderma, vasculitis, Henoch-Schönlein purpura, arteritis, milk-induced gross intestinal bleeding in infants, occult intestinal bleeding, gastroenteropathy, pulmonary hemosiderosis, orthostatic albuminuria, nephrosis, and glomerulonephritis. Although there are many known and unknown sources of the antigens that provoke these antigen–antibody complexes, foods should be considered early in attempts at diagnosis and treatment of an immune-complex disease. This is because foods are the most easily identified and eliminated of all possible causative agents.

Many tests have been advocated to determine the source of allergic symptoms caused by food. They include cytotoxic food testing (leukocytotoxic test), skin testing (intracutaneous titration), intracutaneous and sublingual provocation testing, sublingual desensitization, the pulse tests, and the leukopenia index. These approaches have been studied thoroughly, and their usefulness has failed to be supported by controlled clinical research for a variety of reasons. Interpretations of these tests have been found to be highly subjective, poor correspondence between examiners has often been found when two people read the same test, and many of the test results cannot be successfully duplicated in repetitive runs.[1,24-26]

If you suspect that you suffer from a food allergy, the most accurate and least expensive way to discover the cause is to follow an elimination diet.[1,2,4,7,8,13] This diet consists of the foods that are least likely to cause an allergic reaction. About one week is needed to completely clear the bowel of foods that were eaten before beginning the diet. By this time, most people will be relieved of the problems caused by their food allergies. The elimination diet should be centered around brown rice, sweet potatoes, winter squash, and/or taro (poi), which are the starches least likely to cause a reaction in most people. Rice flour and puffed rice are also allowed. Cooked peaches, cranberries, apricots, papaya, plums, prunes, and cherries can be used freely. However, no citrus fruits are allowed. Cooked fruits are used because cooking alters the proteins in the fruit, making them less likely to act as allergens. Cooked beets, beet greens, chard, summer squash, carrots, artichokes, celery, string beans, asparagus, spinach, and lettuce are allowed. Salt, if not contraindicated for other reasons, may be used for flavoring. All other spices and condiments are excluded. Water is the only acceptable beverage. Some sensitive individuals may be allergic to one or more of the foods listed for the elimination diet. These persons should keep their diets very simple, such as a single starch and vegetable least suspected of causing trouble for the week of elimination.

After a week, most problems caused by food allergies should have ended. Then you begin adding other foods to the diet, one at a time on an empty stomach, to determine which of them cause your allergic reactions. Each "new" food should be eaten in large amounts three times a day for two days. If the food does not cause a reaction, it is considered to be non-allergenic. Most reactions occur within a few hours, but some do not show up for several days. Each food must be tested individually: do not introduce two new foods at once. When you do have an allergic reaction to a specific food, you must wait four to seven days before testing the next item. This interval gives you time to clear your system of that allergy-causing food.

Assuming that you are not interested in testing animal products, begin the introduction of new foods with either wheat or corn, which are the vegetable foods most commonly causing allergy. Next, try fresh citrus fruits, such as oranges or grapefruits. Then add oats, beans, peas, or lentils. Cooked vegetables, such as white potatoes, onions, or green peppers, can be tested last. They are the least likely to be the cause of an allergy problem.

If the elimination diet seems too drastic for you right now, you can first try a simpler procedure. Just avoid entirely the foods mentioned above as the leading causes of allergy. Doing so will relieve most people of many of their allergy symptoms. For many people just the elimination of dairy products and eggs will result in a dramatic improvement.

Gluten, a protein found in high concentrations in wheat, barley, and rye, has been found to contribute to the cause of several serious diseases. They are schizophrenia (a mental disorder), celiac disease (a bowel disorder), and dermatitis herpetiformis (a skin disorder). The elimination of gluten from the diet causes rapid improvement in the health of most people with celiac disease and dermatitis herpetiformis and a few of those with schizophrenia.[13,27-31] Oats are often found on a list of foods to avoid in gluten-sensitive individuals. However, when fed to patients with celiac disease, they do not cause reactions.[32]

A one-pound loaf of bread contains about 40 grams of gluten. This amount of gluten, if eaten in a single day, can cause problems even for "healthy" people.[33-34] The gluten causes changes in the intestinal lining that retard the absorption of nutrients. For this reason, the intake of wheat, barley, and rye should be somewhat limited in nearly everyone's diet. People with allergy problems or any intestinal trouble should always initially question wheat, barley, and rye as the possible cause.

Food allergies are considered by some experts to be one of the most common sources of illness. This elimination diet will give highly effective results with no serious side effects and little, if any, expense—no fancy tests, no magic shots or pills. This approach also takes the responsibility for your health out of the hands of a physician and gives it back to you, where it belongs.

Jean Jones—It's All In Her Head

I could hardly believe it when the last doctor I saw asked me if my teeth itched. I'm sure that's just a silly question he asked to prove that I'm a hypochondriac. I should have said "yes." Maybe he'd have sat up and taken notice! I can't help it that so many things are wrong with me. I'm not making them up. I have headaches every day. On the weekends, when I'm off work, they get worse. After $1,000 worth of tests, the best the neurologist could tell me was I didn't have a brain tumor and said I should take aspirin when the headaches get unbearable.

Every morning after breakfast, just like clockwork, my nose starts to drip and stays stuffed up or runny all day along. I've tried antihistamines, but they make me so sleepy I can't work. I've been to an allergist and had the skin tests. Well, I'm allergic to almost everything according to these tests. I wouldn't know where to start to keep away from grasses, molds, pollens, and trees, and I've never even seen a house-dust mite.

My intestines from one end to the other are my biggest trouble. Every day the heartburn starts in the morning and gets worse after anything I eat. I'll bet I take a whole package of antacid tablets every day. If that isn't bad enough, my bowels keep me guessing. I never know whether I'll have constipation or diarrhea from one day to the next. The only thing I can count on is the severe cramps. This year I've had X-rays of my upper gastrointestinal tract (UGI), gallbladder, and lower intestines. I've had scopes as long as 12 feet stuck down both ends. My stools have been checked for every possible bacteria and parasite. After all this, they smiled and said nothing was wrong. As a final insult I was referred to a psychiatrist, who has spent hours delving into my toilet training, how I felt about my mother, whether my boyfriend treated me OK, and how I feel about my job. After a couple of visits, he handed me a prescription for tranquilizers, and I said goodbye.

I'm not the only one with problems these doctors can't solve. My girlfriend, Gloria, gets rashes all over her body, and all her doctor gives her are creams that hardly help. Tom's the one I really feel sorry for. His asthma is so bad you can hear him wheezing from across the room. The pills he takes make him gain weight, and his face is all puffy.

I know life is full of stress, but I can't believe that all my problems are because I'm neurotic. I do as well as anyone else at coping with life. There has to be something I'm doing wrong, and I'm going to find out in spite of everybody.

I'm going to set up some rules to help me. After all, if something works, it ought to be obvious and not take half a lifetime. If I can recover from major surgery in four weeks, then a couple of months ought to be long enough to see results here, if there are going to be any. From now on, if anyone comes up with a plan to make you healthy, I'll consider first of all whether it's safe and lastly whether it seems reasonable. But before I try I'm going to be reasonably sure it doesn't cost more in money, effort, and time than it seems to be worth. Maybe I'll try vitamins or herbs. I have a friend who swears by chiropractors; maybe I'll ask her about them. I think I'll skip the colon therapists; $50 seems too much to spend for that form of tender loving care.

Now that I think it over, what I put into my stomach should be important. But where do I go for this kind of help? I once saw a dietitian, and she told me to keep eating the same foods I have always eaten. I tried the few changes she offered and saw no improvement. There are lots of diet books out. I'm not fat, so I should look for one that is supposed to help me feel good, not just lose weight. I've read enough to know that fat, cholesterol, salt, additives, and processed foods are not good for me, and also that fiber and carbohydrates are important for good health. I'm going to look for a book that tells me about that kind of food, because food sure meets my set of rules: it's safe, reasonable, and inexpensive. That settles it. I am going to start looking into my diet to solve my "psychiatric" problems.

Comments On Jean Jones

Jean's case represents the usual rather than the exception. She has problems that do not lend themselves to the diagnostic tools and remedies commonly taught to doctors in medical school. As a result of this failing of the medical profession, she suffers the additional burden of being labeled a neurotic and sent to a psychiatrist. If her doctors would have been lucky enough to have received more than the average three hours provided by medical schools on nutrition, she might have had better results from their advice.[35-36]

Jean's problems actually stem from the foods she has learned to eat. The daily headaches are a result of food allergy. On the weekends her severe headaches are because she drinks only half the coffee and suffers from caffeine withdrawal.

Her stuffy and runny nose is another result of food allergies, but the tests won't show that. Only the elimination of offending foods will give her the information she is looking for. The milk she uses on her cereal in the morning probably starts her nose going.

As obvious as it may seem, food is rarely considered as a source of bowel problems by a practicing physician. This is mostly because a diet of rich foods is thought of as proper, well-balanced eating. Once this misconception is established in the minds of health professionals, they become incapable of helping someone with problems caused by commonplace foods. In this instance Jean suffers from a spastic colon. The foods she chooses are deficient in fiber and high in fat and sources of food allergies that trouble the bowel. Her heartburn is from inflammation of the stomach lining known as gastritis and is the result of irritation from coffee and certain foods. Once inflamed, even the mildest of foods provoke pain.

Jean and her friends are not isolated examples of people who suffer from ailments that are not resolved by a visit to the doctor, and for that matter even a specialist doctor. The frustration of living with these ailments eventually sends people looking for other cures. However, other than the medical and nutritional professions, very few, if any, of the professions involved in health attempt to scientifically document their successes and failures. Therefore, the consumer must ultimately evaluate an approach by his or her own standards. Jean has thoroughly thought out what she expects and what she is willing to try. If she sticks to her set of rules, she should find success in resolving her ailments.

Food is the logical place for her to start in her efforts to solve her problems. She has heard and read so much about food that she has formed some definite notions about what is likely to help. With the type of problems she suffers from, there is little doubt she will be well in only a few days when she finds the dietary program that best supports her health and healing processes. Too frequently we forget the cliché, "You are what you eat."

Notes

[1] J. Breneman, *Basics of Food Allergy,* Springfield: Charles C. Thomas, 1978.

[2] Editorial, "Food Allergy," *Lancet* 1 (1979): 249.

[3] D. Heiner, "Multiple Precipitins to Cow's Milk in Chronic Respiratory Disease," *Am J Dis Child* 103 (1962): 40.

[4] A. Bock, "Food Sensitivity—A Critical Review and Practical Approach," *Am J Dis Child* 134 (1980): 973.

[5] S. Bahna, "Control of Milk Allergy: A Challenge for Physicians, Mothers, and Industry," *Ann Allergy* 41 (1978): 1.

[6] R. Finn, "Food Allergy: Fact or Fiction?" *Lancet* 1 (1978): 426.

[7] K. Ogle, "Children withh Allergic Rhinitis and/or Bronchial Asthma Treated with Elimination Diet: A Five-Year Follow-Up," *Ann Allergy* 44 (1980): 273.

[8] F. Speer, "Multiple Food Allergy," *Ann Allergy* 34 (1975): 71.

[9] Editorial," Antigen Absorption by the Gut," *Lancet* 2 (1978): 715.

[10] W. Hemmings, "Transport of Large Breakdown Products of Dietary Protein through the Gut Wall," *Gut* 19 (1978): 715.

[11] C. Cunningham-Rundles, "Milk Precipitins, Circulating Immune Complexes, and IgA Deficiency," *Proc Nat Acad Sci USA* 75 (1978): 3387.

[12] W. Walker, "Uptake and Transport of Macromolecules by the Intestine—Possible Role in Clinical Disorders," *Gastroenterology* 67 (1974): 531.

[13] A. Denman, "Nature and Diagnosis of Food Allergy," *Proc Nutr Soc* 38 (1979): 391.

[14] W. Rea, "Environmentally Triggered Small Vessel Vasculitis," *Ann Allergy* 38 (1977):245.

[15] H.Stanford, "Immunologic Studies in Cow's Milk-Induced Pulmonary Hemosiderosis," *Pediat Res* 11 (1977): 898.

[16] M. Rubin, "Allergic Intestinal Bleeding in the Newborn: A Clinical Syndrome," *Am J Med Sci* 200 (1940): 385.

[17] J. Wilson, "Milk-Induced Gastrointestinal Bleeding in Infants with Hypochromic Microcytic Anemia," *JAMA* 189 (1964): 568.

[18] T. Waldmann, "Allergic Gastroenteropathy: A Cause of Excessive Gastrointestinal Protein Loss," *N Engl J Med* 276 (1967): 761.

[19] T. Matsumura, "Significance of Food Allergy in Etiology of Orthostatic Albuminuria," *J Asthma Res* 3 (1966): 325.

[20] D. Sandberg, "Severe Steroid-Responsive Nephrosis Associated with Hypersensitivity," *Lancet* 1 (1977): 388.

[21] R. Carr, "Studies on Possibility of Food-Induced Immune-Complex Disease," *Fed Pro* 35 (1976): 574.

[22] E. Penner, "Microsomal Antibody and Circulating Immune Complexes in Allergic Gastroenteropathy," *Lancet* 1 (1978): 669.

[23] J. Gerrard, *Food Allergy—New Perspectives,* Springfield: Charles C. Thomas, 1980.

[24] P. Lieberman, "Controlled Study of the Cytotoxic Food Test," *JAMA* 231 (1975): 728.

[25] T. Golbert, "A Review of Controversial Diagnostic and Therapeutic Techniques Employed in Allergy," *J Allergy Clin Immunol* 56 (1975): 170.

[26] M. Grieco, "Controversial Practices in Allergy," *JAMA* 247 (1982): 3106.

[27] F. Dohan, "Relapsed Schizophrenics: Earlier Discharge from the Hospital after Cereal-Free, Milk-Free Diet," *Am J Psychiatry* 130 (1973): 685.

[28] A. Ashkenazi, "Immunologic Reaction of Psychotic Patients to Fractions of Gluten," *Am J Psychiatry* 136 (1979): 1306.

[29] J. Rice, "Another Look at Gluten in Schizophrenia," *Am J Psychiatry* 135 (1978): 1417.

[30] P. Ross-Smith, "Diet (Gluten) and Schizophrenia," *J Hum Nutr* 34 (1980): 107.

[31] S. Katz, "Dermatitis Herpetiformis: The Skin and the Gut," *Ann Intern Med* 93 (1980): 857.

[32] A. Dissanayake, "Lack of Harmful Effect of Oats on Small-Intestinal Mucosa in Coeliac Disease," *Br Med J* 4 (1974): 189.

[33] M. Doherty, "Gluten-Induced Mucosal Changes in Subjects without Overt Small-Bowel Disease," *Lancet* 1 (1981): 517.

[34] I. Anderson, "Incomplete Absorption of the Carbohydrates in All-Purpose Wheat Flour," *N Engl J Med* 304 (1981): 891.

[35] G. McGovern, "Address to the American Society for Parenteral and Enteral Nutrition for the Third Clinical Congress," *JPEN* 3 (1979): 137.

[36] R. Wright, "Nutritional Assessment," *JAMA* 244 (1980): 559.

CHAPTER
13
A Health-Supporting Diet For Children and Pregnant Women

Children

Before the early 1870s nearly all infants in every part of the world were breast-fed by their mothers or wet nurses, and physicians generally cautioned against the feeding of cow's milk formulas, except during emergencies.[1] By the 1930s the infant food industry and the medical profession had established a mutually advantageous relationship, as the industry discovered that it could sell its products more effectively through the physician rather than directly to the mother. Even though these breast milk substitutes did not require a prescription to purchase, the physician advised the mother to buy them and explained how to prepare them; no directions for doing so appeared on the labels.[1] The physician gained control over the nutrition of the infant by giving out free samples and formula aids, and by making variations in the mixtures that kept the mother coming back to the physician's office frequently. Feeding schedules, prescribed until only recently with the attitude that feeding every four hours would avoid "spoiling" the baby, resulted in a hungry, crying infant and served to further convince a frustrated mother that her breast milk was inadequate and that the bottle was the only answer to her problems.[2]

Today many women in western societies have returned to the breast to nourish their babies and thereby have left the infant food industry looking for new markets in underdeveloped nations. These companies use persuasive advertising techniques to convince women in these nations that the modern thing to do is to bottle-feed their babies. Posters claim powdered milks are "the best start in life" for babies, radio advertisements tell mothers their products should be the "first choice," and free samples are given out to new mothers.[3] Infant formula companies have even gone so far as to recruit the scarce health professionals in underdeveloped nations to become "milk nurses," traveling around the countryside to promote bottle feeding among new mothers.[4] The leading cause of death in these nations, lacking as they are in public health measures, is infectious disease. The substitution of formula milk for breast milk removes an immunological advantage for the young infant, resulting in a shocking increase in infant mortality, especially from gastroenteritis and respiratory infections.[4] In addition, the basic roots for the development in economically depressed countries of starvation conditions in young children, known as Kwashiorkor and marasmus, lie in early weaning and bottle feeding.[5] Bottle feeding of infants in underdeveloped countries, such as India, has been described as a virtual death sentence.[6] Estimates are that in developing countries 1 million deaths per year of children under one year of age are the direct result of contaminated infant formula and the resulting diarrhea and malnutrition.[7]

In May 1981, the annual assembly of the World Health Organization adopted the "International Code of Marketing of Breast Milk Substitutes," which basically asked the infant formula companies to refrain from excessive advertising practices. Of the 118 nations voting on the code, only one nation, the United States, voted no, because of lobbying pressures by industry.[8] This recent course of events should leave no doubt about the goal of some industries when it comes to health. Clearly, in this instance, the protection of corporate profits far outweighs the health and welfare of children worldwide.

Infants should be raised on mother's milk alone until they are at least six months old. In addition to providing the most ideal nutrients for a baby, breast milk contains a wide range of factors active against the bacteria and viruses that cause many diseases, including the diarrhea, dehydration, and death that are so common in underdeveloped nations.[9-11] Even in modern developed countries, breast feeding offers important protection against illness. For example, in one recent study from England, all but one of 339 infants hospitalized with gastroenteritis were bottle-fed.[12] One-third of the children in this group were dehydrated, and five died. The one breast-fed infant was not even dehydrated. Breast feeding also offers infants raised in technologically developed countries protection against respiratory infection, otitis media (middle ear infection), neonatal septicemia, bacterial meningitis, thrush (a yeast infection), and many viral illnesses, including polio and herpes simplex.[11] Overall, breast-fed infants in modern societies suffer only one-third to one-half the incidence of significant illness of bottle-fed infants.[13]

Bottle feeding in the very young infant can cause hypocalcemia (which leads to tetany), dehydration, hypernatremia (high sodium level in the body, associated with permanent brain damage), and necrotising enterocolitis (an inflammatory bowel disease seen almost exclusively in artificially fed young infants and associated with a high mortality).[11] Bottle feeding is suspected of contributing to the development, later in life, of food allergies, obesity, ulcerative colitis, coronary artery disease, and multiple sclerosis.[11]

In preindustrialized societies nursing has been commonly practiced until the child reaches one to two years of age, and up to three years is not unusual.[6] In contrast, in 1971, less than 6 percent of infants in the United States received any breast milk after the age of six months. By 1979 that number had increased to 23 percent.[14] Also, better-educated mothers tend to breast feed their children more than less-educated mothers and even today, in modern societies, the major influence of the infant formula industry's advertising pressures is most evident in the less educated and mothers with first children.[15]

Infant formulas, as well as a too early introduction to solid foods, may result in allergies later in life because the infant's intestine and immune system are too immature to offer adequate protection from these foods.[16-17] For example, the introduction of gluten-containing cereals (wheat, barley, rye) too early into a child's diet may be part of the cause of celiac disease, a chronic intestinal problem, later in life.[18] Solid food introduced into the diet of a breast-feeding infant also interferes with the absorption of iron from mother's breast milk.[19] Infants absorb 50 to 70 percent of the iron in breast milk, only 10 percent of the iron in cow's milk, and a paltry 3 to 5 percent of iron in iron-fortified formulas.[19] Infants exclusively breast-fed for six months maintain normal hemoglobin values and levels of iron in the blood. Infants who are breast-fed have higher hemoglobin levels than those who are formula-fed, but the introduction of solid foods eliminates this advantage of "stronger blood" for the breast-fed infants.[19]

A mother may breast feed her child exclusively until the infant is a year old, or longer if she chooses to do so, without having to worry about the infant's nutrition.[20] The mother should maintain a healthy diet and lifestyle, since the baby can receive components from foods, drugs, and environmental chemicals in her breast milk.[21-26]

At about six to eight months of age, teeth begin to appear, and the child will supplement the natural milk diet by reaching for food in mother's hand or on the dinner table. To ensure that your child receives the best possible diet, you should place only health-supporting foods on the table. Even after exclusive breast feeding stops, breast milk (or the best substitute available) should account for 25 to 50 percent of your child's diet up to about two years of age. If you are unable to breast feed your child, several alternative methods are available. Listed in order of decreasing health benefit to the child, they are: a substitute mother (considering our present social values, this alternative will probably receive little favor), human breast milk from a milk bank, soy-based formulas, commercial infant formulas made from denatured animal proteins, goat's milk, and, finally, cow's milk.[27-28] Feeding unmodified goat's and cow's milk to young infants is often lethal. Furthermore, anything other than human mother's breast milk must be considered potentially hazardous to your baby's health.

Bottle-fed infants raised on cow's milk preparations have shown evidence of deficiencies in essential fatty acids.[29-30] Essential fatty acid deficiency in animal experiments has been associated with an increased susceptibility to infection, diminished competence of the immune system, and a high mortality of the young.[29-31] Additionally, a report from the British Department of Health documented risks associated with bottle feeding infants that included gastroenteritis, loss of dental enamel, obesity, increased risk of infection, allergy to cow's milk, and crib death, also known as cot death and sudden infant death syndrome.[18]

Bottle-fed infants die from unexplained causes, classified as sudden infant death syndrome, twice as often as breast-fed infants.[32-34] Approximately 20 percent of deaths in infants from two weeks to two months old are attributed to this syndrome, and many causes are suspected for these deaths.[35] Cow's milk and infant formula preparations are believed to be one of these causes of sudden death, possibly from an allergic-type of reaction. This reaction kills the infant during sleep, following the regurgitation of stomach contents containing milk or formula, and subsequent inhalation of some of this material into the lungs. The lung tissues then rapidly absorb the milk or formula proteins into the bloodstream, and these proteins cause shock and death.[11,36-37]

In support of this hypothesis for the cause of crib death is the finding of milk in the lungs of 40 percent of the cases.[36] Experimental studies demonstrate that guinea pigs that are fed cow's milk over a period of days develop a sensitivity to the milk. Then, when they are lightly anesthetized to simulate sleep and the milk is dripped into their lungs, they stop breathing either immediately or over a thirty-minute period. This course of events is similar to that seen with sudden death in infants. Microscopic examination of the tissues of the dead guinea pigs reveal cellular changes that are remarkably similar to those found in infants who die of crib death.[37]

One of the most important reasons to focus on cow's milk and infant formulas as a cause of sudden infant death syndrome is that these deaths can be prevented or reduced in frequency by simply encouraging breast feeding. Even if other theories for the cause of this syndrome were proved in the future to be correct (such as the genetic-developmental or viral theories), prevention would be much more difficult than simply changing to the naturally intended food for infants.

Heating denatures cow's milk proteins and makes them less reactive. However, these denatured proteins still produce allergic reactions. Soybean-based infant formulas also have the potential for causing sudden death, but the frequency of allergy may be less with them than with cow's milk formulas. As mentioned, food protein, and especially cow's milk proteins when present in mother's breast milk (as a result of mother's food choices), also can cause allergic reactions in infants.[24-26] Therefore, even mother's breast milk, under these circumstances, could have the potential to cause sudden death.

Bottle feeding causes a rampant form of tooth decay, characterized by rapid onset and extensive destruction to most of the anterior deciduous teeth of the infant.[38] Direct contact of the teeth with milk, juice, or sweetened water as the child sleeps provides a perfect environment for the bacteria that destroy teeth.

Added to the many problems of physical health caused by bottle feeding must be the loss of emotional, mental, and physical comfort for the infant who seeks to find warmth and love in the rubber and glass of a bottle.[39]

As the breast-feeding period of an infant's life ends, the child begins to eat solid foods in order to provide calories for his or her active life. With the consumption of large amounts of food to meet children's high caloric needs come large quantities of carbohydrates, proteins, essential fat, vitamins, and minerals to provide the building blocks for growth. A diet composed of only starches, vegetables, and fruits easily satisfies a child's nutritional requirements. However, the addition of high-fat plant foods and dried fruits to a child's diet is a convenient and safe way to provide a source of highly concentrated calories. These rich plant foods are well tolerated by most healthy, active children.

Special occasions may warrant feast foods in a child's diet. You could be laying the foundation for rebellion if your child is always refused the foods that his or her friends eat. Your responsibility is to teach the correct nutritional value and use of foods. Starches, vegetables, and fruits are the child's basic diet. Chocolate candy, ice cream, cheese, milk, and meat are delicacies that should be reserved for birthdays, festive holidays, or an occasional night out. These treats should be distinguished clearly from the foods that best satisfy nutritional needs and support health. An important role for the homemaker is to keep rich foods out of the house and make every effort to ensure that a wide variety of nutritious foods are available for the family. Reserving delicacies for only those occasions when you go out will make it easier for you and your family to avoid the temptation associated with these treats.

Children also require clean air, pure water, moderate exercise, and sunshine for good health. The need for sunshine is apparent even in the newborn infant who frequently develops yellow skin and eyes soon after birth, a condition known as jaundice.[40] This condition quickly clears up with short exposures to the ultraviolet rays of sunlight. Visible light is also important in controlling sexual development, circadian rhythm, and numerous neuroendocrine functions, and it affects a variety of hormones, including vitamin D.

Pregnancy

When discussing proper nutrition, the next most highly emotional issue after children is pregnancy. Experts in the fields of nutrition and pediatrics have failed to reach agreement on the proper food for the mother-to-be.[41] But what is clear is that most children in the history of the world have been born to mothers nourished by a variety of starch-centered diets. As the pregnant woman increases her food intake on such a diet, she increases the intake of calories, carbohydrates, proteins, essential fat, vitamins, and minerals to provide the raw material for the growing fetus. Common complications of pregnancy, such as constipation and body swelling, can be prevented when rich foods are avoided and a health-supporting diet is eaten. A starch-centered meal plan provides the lowest level of environmental contaminants that can cause injury to the developing fetus and possible birth defects. Furthermore, the chances of developing high blood pressure and a life-threatening complication of pregnancy known as toxemia or eclampsia are drastically reduced.[42]

You will need to call upon all of your intellectual strengths when dealing with the emotional issues of the pregnant woman and her young offspring. The food industry and associated allies are spending billions of dollars a year to teach us incorrect, profit-oriented concepts of nutrition that have caused illness and suffering for parents and their children worldwide for the past several generations. Be strong!

Notes

[1] R. Apple, " 'To Be Used Under the Direction of a Physician:' Commercial Infant Feeding and Medical Practice, 1870–1940," *Bull Hist Med* 54 (1980): 402.

[2] S. Slaven, "Unlimited Suckling Time Improves Breast Feeding," *Lancet* 1 (1981): 392.

[3] A. Chetley, "Marketing Breast Milk Substitutes," *Lancet* 2 (1980): 258.

[4] R. Brown, "Breast Feeding in Modern Times," *Am J Clin Nutr* 26 (1973): 556.

[5] D. McLaren," A Fresh Look at Protein–Calorie Malnutrition," *Lancet* 2 (1966): 485.

[6] J. Gordon, "Weanling Diarrhea," *Am J Med Sci* 245 (1963): 129.

[7] S. Joseph, "The Anatomy of the Infant Formula Controversy," *Am J Dis Child* 135 (1981): 889.

[8] Editorial, "The Infant Formula Controversy: An International Health Policy Paradigm," *Ann Intern Med* 95 (1981): 383.

[9] J. Welsh, "Anti-Infective Properties of Breast Milk," *J Pediatr* 94 (1979): 1.

[10] W. Pittard, "Breast Milk Immunology—A Frontier in Infant Nutrition," *Am J Dis Child* 133 (1979): 83.

[11] D. Addy, "Infant Feeding: A Current View," *Br Med J* 1 (1976): 1268.

[12] A. Ironside, "A Survey of Infantile Gastroenteritis," *Br Med J* 3 (1970): 20.

[13] A. Cunningham, "Morbidity in Breast-Fed and Artificially Fed Infants," *J Pediatr* 90 (1977): 726.

[14] G. Martinez, "1980 Update: The Recent Trend in Breast Feeding," *Pediatr* 67 (1981): 260.

[15] Y. Bergevin, "Do Infant Formula Samples Shorten the Duration of Breast Feeding?" *Lancet* 1 (1983): 1148.

[16] U. Saarinen, "Prolonged Breast Feeding as Prophylaxis for Atopic Disease, *Lancet* 2 (1979): 163.

[17] U. Sarrinen, "Does Dietary Elimination in Infancy Prevent or Only Postpone a Food Allergy?" *Lancet* 1 (1980): 166.

[18] Department of Health and Social Security, "Present-Day Infant Feeding Practice Reports," no. 9, 1974.

[19] F. Oski, "Inhibition of Iron Absorption from Human Milk by Baby Food," *Am J Dis Child* 134 (1980): 459.

[20] C. Ahn, "Growth of the Exclusively Breast-Fed Infant," *Am J Clin Nutr* 33 (1980): 183.

[21] S. Harris, "Statement of Stephanie G. Harris before the Subcommittee on Health and Scientific Research of the Senate Committee on Human Resources." June 8, 1977.

[22] C. Catz, "Drugs and Breast Milk," *Ped Clin N Am* 19 (1972): 151.

[23] A. Binkiewicz, "Pseudo-Cushing Syndrome Caused by Alcohol in Breast Milk," *J Pediatr* 93 (1978): 965.

[24] I. Jakobsson, "Cow's Milk as a Cause of Infantile Colic in Breast-Fed Infants," *Lancet* 2 (1978): 437.

[25] J. Gerrard, "Milk Allergy: Clinical Picture and Familial Incidence," *Canad Med Ass J* 97 (1967): 780.

[26] H. Donnally, "The Question of elimination of Foreign Protein (Egg White) in Woman's Milk," *Immunololology* 19 (1930): 15.

[27] D. Johnstone, "Dietary Prophylaxis of Allergic Disease in Children," *N Engl J Med* 274 (1966): 715.

[28] P. McLaughlan, "Effect of Heat on the Anaphylactic Sensitizing Capacity of Cow's Milk, Goat's Milk, and Various Infant Formulas Fed to Guinea Pigs," *Arch Dis Child* 56 (1981): 165.

[29] M. Crawford, "Essential Fatty Acid Requirements in Infancy," *Am J Clin Nutr* 31 (1978): 2181.

[30] A. Hansen, "Role of Linoleic Acid in Infant Nutrition," *J Pediatr* 31 (1963): 171.

[31] J. Clausen, "Allergic Encephalomeylitis Induced by Brain Antigen after Deficiency in Polyunsaturated Fatty Acids during Myelination," *Acta Neurol Scandinav* 43 (1967): 375.

[32] C. Protestos, "Obstetric and Perinatal Histories of Children Who Died Unexpectedly (Cot Death)," *Arch Dis Child* 48 (1973): 835.

[33] R. Steele, "The Relationship of Antenatal and Postnatal Factors to Sudden Unexpected Death in Infancy," *Can Med Ass J* 94 (1966): 1165.

[34] J. Mason, "Cot Deaths in Edinburgh: Infant Feeding and Socioeconomic Factors, *"J Epidemiology and Community Health* 34 (1980): 35.

[35] S. Kendeel, "Sudden Infant Death Syndrome—A Review of the Literature," *J Forens Sci Soc* 17 (1977): 223.

[36] R. Coombs, "The Enigma of Cot Death: Is the Modified-Anaphylaxis Hypothesis an Explanation for Some Cases?" *Lancet* 1 (1982): 1388.

[37] W. Parish," Hypersensitivity to Milk and Sudden Death in Infancy," *Lancet* 2 (1960): 1106.

[38]G. Winter, "Role of the Comforter as an Etiologic Factor in Rampant Caries of the Deciduous Dentition," *Arch Dis Child* 41 (1966): 207.

[39]N. Newton, "Psychologic Differences between Breast and Bottle Feeding," *Am J Clin Nutr* 24 (1971): 993.

[40]R. Behrman, "Preliminary Report of the Committee on Phototherapy in the Newborn Infant," *J Pediatr* 84 (1974): 135.

[41]Editorial, "Nutrition in Pregnancy," *Lancet* 1 (1983): 1142.

[42]R. Chung, "Diet-Related Toxemia in Pregnancy—Fat, Fatty Acids, and Cholesterol," *Am J Clin Nutr* 32 (1979): 1902.

CHAPTER
14

Taking Care of Yourself Is The Key to a Health-Supporting Lifestyle

Drugs

Many dangers are associated with taking recreational, prescription, and nonprescription drugs.[1-3] Significant side effects are seen in more than 40 percent of people from prescribed medicines outside a hospital setting. As many as 20 percent of admissions to some hospitals happen because of adverse effects of physician-prescribed and over-the-counter drugs. Once he or she is hospitalized, a patient's risk of suffering a serious adverse drug reaction is as great as 30 percent, and of the deaths that occur in hospitals the chance of dying from such a reaction is about 6.5 percent.[4-6]

One infrequently considered but most important consequence of taking medication is the relief of symptoms that are important for us to be aware of. Pain is a signal that something is wrong and must be attended to. The person suffering from chest pain from disease of the arteries that supply the heart may be lulled into a false sense of security by taking medication such as long-acting nitroglycerine preparations, which only relieve the chest pains and do nothing to improve the actual disease process. This drug-induced sense of well-being removes a strong motivator—the chest pain—which could keep the person very interested in a health-supporting diet and lifestyle.

In consultation with your physician, you should decide whether the medications you are taking are absolutely necessary or could be discontinued. A diet and lifestyle change can help most people to discontinue and stay off most drugs.

Vitamin and mineral supplements should be categorized as medicines just as penicillin and digitalis are. They are all produced by concentrating and refining certain natural substances, which then are consumed for a desired effect. The primary difference between vitamins and the medicines prescribed by physicians is the potency of the effects and side effects. Many people spend hundreds of dollars a year on vitamin pills and yet obtain little or no objective beneficial result from them. Fortunately the adverse effects from vitamins are few. People who claim that vitamins make them feel better probably are describing a placébo effect—that is, the imagined benefit that might come from taking an inactive preparation. Except for a rare occurrence of vitamin deficiency caused by a very unbalanced diet, there are few substantiated benefits to be gained from taking vitamin pills.[7]

Medical science has long been aware of the hazards associated with the use of alcohol, tobacco, caffeine, and illegal drugs such as cocaine and marijuana. Even though chronic users and distributors of these substances may make claims for their safety and benefits, these drugs are damaging to health. However, like rich foods, the sparing use of these "recreational" drugs is tolerated without serious adverse effects by most people. *Sparing,* of course, is the key word. The chronic abuser of drugs emphasizes the body's remarkable ability to survive. Two of these drugs—alcohol and caffeine—are ingested like food and therefore deserve further discussion.

Alcohol

Several studies have demonstrated increased longevity and decreased risk of heart disease in people who consume alcohol moderately.[8] Those who consume alcohol may try to justify their habit with these studies. However, alcohol cannot be generally recommended, primarily because so many people become addicted to this drug. More than 7 percent of the adult population suffers from alcoholism, which results in decreased productivity, accidents, crime, mental and physical disease, and disruption of family life. Furthermore, any benefit of alcohol related to the risk of heart disease is offset by a rise in total deaths from other causes.[9] Alcohol also provides 7 "empty calories" per gram, which can lead to obesity. Other adverse effects of excess alcohol include high triglycerides (blood fat), liver disease, cancer, birth defects (fetal alcohol syndrome), and multiple vitamin deficiency diseases, such as scurvy from lack of vitamin C, night blindness from lack of vitamin A, pellagra from lack of niacin (B_3), and nervous system diseases, such as Wernicke-Korsakoff Syndrome, from deficiency of thiamin (B_1).

Caffeine

Some of the most popular drugs consumed by people of affluent western nations are found in coffee beans, tea leaves, cocoa beans (chocolate), kolanuts, and matté, all of which contain a group of natural substances known as methylxanthines. These chemicals include caffeine, theophylline, and theobromine. Many prescription and nonprescription drugs also contain methylxanthines.

One of the most important of the methylxanthines is the popular drug caffeine. Desirable effects of caffeine include mental stimulation, relief of fatigue and drowsiness, keener perception and clearer thinking. However, in some sensitive people the opposite effects occur.

Definite undesirable effects from the stimulating properties of caffeine include elevated heart rate, irregular heartbeat, increased blood pressure, frequent urination, increased gastric acid secretion (which contributes to indigestion, gastritis, and ulcers), nervousness, irritability, insomnia, loss of appetite, nausea, and diarrhea. Obviously, discontinuing caffeine will relieve the problems caused by this drug. It is particularly important for someone with hypertension who is trying to lower his or her blood pressure to stop drinking caffeinated beverages.[10]

Caffeine has been shown to cause birth defects in animals and is suspected of causing the same defects in humans.[11-13] It would follow that you should completely avoid coffee, tea, colas, and chocolate in all forms during pregnancy.

All three of the methylxanthines can stimulate growth of breast cells, causing painful enlargement of breast tissue and benign lumps.[14-15] This condition is known as fibrocystic disease. Your physician could well recommend something as simple as a biopsy or even an operation as mutilating as a bilateral mastectomy for this problem. Fortunately, merely avoiding these stimulating chemicals can be an effective and much less drastic alternative. In as many as 90 percent of women with fibrocystic disease, these benign breast lumps significantly improve or completely disappear in two to six months when methylxanthines are eliminated from the diet.[15,16] There is also concern from investigators that the chronic stimulation of the breast tissue by methylxanthines may eventually progress to cancer of the breast in some women.[15,17]

Excessive intake of caffeine may cause a rise in blood fats, a condition known as hypertriglyceridemia, which may contribute to illness.[18] Cancer of the urinary bladder also has been related to caffeine use.[19-20] One more undesirable effect of caffeine is that this drug has been shown to cause loss of calcium from the body.[21] Therefore, another dietary maneuver you can use to prevent and possibly correct thin, calcium-deficient bones, or osteoporosis, would be to discontinue use of caffeine.

The body actually becomes physically addicted to caffeine. When you quit taking this drug, expect withdrawal symptoms such as headaches, anxiety, irritability, drowsiness, tension, and depression. Withdrawal symptoms can last as long as a week.

All over the world caffeinated beverages are popular for the mental and physical stimulation they provide. They are commonly used in an attempt to counteract the depression of bodily functions caused by eating rich foods and drinking alcohol. On a starch-centered diet, people are alert and active without the use of stimulants.

Exercise

Exercise has many beneficial effects on your health. When you exercise regularly your body burns more calories than it does when you are sedentary. This tends to promote weight loss in overweight people, and it allows slender people to eat more without gaining weight. People who exercise regularly have an appetite that is more appropriate for their energy needs. Furthermore, the mechanism that controls appetite seems to be in better balance, and the amount of food consumed more closely meets the daily energy expenditure. In sedentary people this mechanism does not work as well, and obesity is often the long-term consequence.[22-24] Ideally, when obese people start a program of regular exercise they will burn more calories than they eat and thereby lose weight.

Regular exercise develops muscles and keeps them in shape. Good muscle tone improves the appearance of your body and gives you more strength and endurance for daily tasks. During periods of exercise the muscles need more oxygen because they are working harder. To supply this oxygen, the heart beats faster and pumps more blood throughout the body. Since the heart itself is a muscle, exercise that causes it to beat faster also strengthens it. A strong heart muscle can pump more blood with each beat, which means that it can do its job more efficiently. As a result, the pulse rate usually becomes slower in people who exercise, and their circulation improves.[25] Exercise lowers the total serum cholesterol levels only slightly, if at all; however, it does increase the proportion of high-density lipoprotein (HDL) cholesterol in the blood.[26-28] Exercise also lowers blood pressure and serum triglyceride and insulin levels and improves blood sugar control in diabetics.[28-33] The cumulative effect is a decreased risk of heart and blood vessel disease.[34] Most of these benefits are accomplished even with exercise as easy to perform as regular brisk walking.[35]

Exercise also affects the hormones controlling reproductive and sexual functions. Women who are very athletic have a greater incidence of irregular menstrual periods and later onset of sexual maturity.[36] This may bring some concern to those who exercise competitively; however, later onset of first menses (sixteen years versus twelve years) is associated with a lower risk of certain health problems, including cancer. Strenuous exercise programs have not been associated with infertility problems unless also accompanied by an inadequate calorie intake.

Exercise requires motion at the joints, and this motion causes circulation of fluids within the joints. The joints have no blood vessels that supply nutrients directly, so these fluids must nourish the joint surfaces and keep them healthy.

Sedentary people gradually lose minerals, especially calcium, from their bones. Inactivity eventually leads to a condition of thin, fragile bones known as osteoporosis. Exercise has actually been shown to increase the mineral content of bones.[37] This mineral loss is also affected by dietary factors and hormones.

Daily exercise is an excellent way to alleviate psychological stress. It provides an outlet for excess nervous energy and can relieve minor mental disturbances such as anxiety and depression.[38] Moderate, sustained exercise increases the level of morphine-like chemicals in the brain, called beta-endorphins, which produce a feeling of mental well-being.[39] This is also known as the "runner's high." Two additional advantages seen in runners are that they lose weight and quit smoking more often than nonrunners.

A matter of some debate is how much exercise is enough to maintain good health. A sedentary lifestyle certainly has been associated with less than ideal health and should be avoided. The benefits obtained from the daily activities performed by the young parent who follows a two-year-old around the house, or by the salesperson who is on his or her feet most of the day, are usually enough to prevent illness and premature death. This may be all you want to accomplish. However, if you are interested in an improved physical being that will be mirrored by the appearance of your body, the way you feel, your mental outlook, and the way you perform various activities, then you will have to condition your body with an extra measure of regular daily exercise.

Ideal exercises are those that involve moderate exertion and can be sustained over a period of time. If you are just beginning an exercise program, you might want to start with walking, slow jogging, bicycling, swimming, or aerobic dancing. Choose something you enjoy doing; otherwise, you are unlikely to stick with it. You should begin at a comfortable level and duration of activity and then build up gradually. For most people, one-half to one hour of exercise per day will provide the physical condition most of us would be happy with. When your body has adapted to moderate daily exercise, you may want to progress to more strenuous activities. Endurance bicycling, long-distance running, cross-country skiing, and prolonged rope jumping will all provide excellent physical conditioning. However, a few words of caution must be given to those who wish to take up jogging or similar strenuous activities. A sevenfold increase in sudden death from heart disease has been observed with jogging when compared to less vigorous activities.[40] However, the absolute risk is actually very small (one death per 7,200 joggers per year), so it appears that routine testing of healthy people before exercise training is really not justified. There is also a high risk of suffering a serious injury to the muscles and bones when running. In one study, one-third of the runners experienced significant injuries, and one in seven had to have medical attention.[41]

When you are recovering from an illness, such as a heart attack or surgery, the best way to gauge your limit of activity is not to get overtired. After you have finished exercising you should recover from the exertion and feel fine in a couple of minutes. If you are sore, fatigued, short of breath, or just not feeling as well as you did before your activity, then you overdid it.

Exercise is one very important part of a health-supporting lifestyle. When added to a health-supporting diet, exercise will quickly help you to reach and maintain your full potential.

Stress

When people are exposed to difficult or challenging situations that they cannot immediately resolve or escape from, they will often experience mental–emotional stress. The history of the human race is marked by stressful daily experiences forced upon us from so many sources that one must conclude that stress is a natural and expected condition we must learn to live with. Stress is functional and necessary in that it creates an environment that motivates us to get the job done and the situation resolved. When satisfactory progress is not being made in resolving the stress-producing situation, health problems may be the consequence. Unfortunately, stress has become the scapegoat for an infinite number of physical and mental health problems. The scientific evidence to support the theory of stress as the immediate cause of disease is insufficient in most cases.

Although stress in itself is only a small factor in the processes that lead directly to disease, it can have significant indirect effects. Stress frequently brings on self-destructive behavior that is characterized by the abuse of food, tobacco, alcohol, and drugs. When people placed under stress abandon a health-supporting diet and lifestyle, they become physically ill. Stressful situations also can bring on an interesting form of behavior where one rewards or comforts one's self by indulging in harmful habits to help compensate for all the suffering one is going through.

When progress in resolving a situation is not satisfactory, there are many constructive means of dealing with the unpleasant situations at hand to help prevent them from becoming overwhelming and destructive. Some activities that can help us better handle stress in our lives are exercise, games, hobbies, religion, meditation, psychotherapy, and biofeedback. Often, a change in occupation, family, or other unsolvable situation is the only available means to alleviate the stress. One final point is that everything is easier to deal with when we are in good health, so one of the fundamental principles in handling stress is to maintain a health-supporting diet and lifestyle.

Adequate Rest

Most adults function best on between five and eight hours of sleep a night. People who complain of insomnia or difficulty in sleeping often falsely perceive a need to sleep for eight to twelve hours. This may be more sleep than they actually require and is not conducive to good health. In most cases, when they're closely observed, insomniacs get almost as much sleep as those who believe their sleep pattern is normal.

People who are ill, pregnant women, and growing children do require more rest than the average healthy person. When people change to a health-supporting diet, they often report less hours spent sleeping, more restful sleep, and increased dream activity. Studies actually have confirmed this observation by demonstrating an increase in rapid eye movement (REM) sleep by electroencephalogram when subjects were switched to a high-carbohydrate, low-fat diet.[42] REM sleep is associated with increased body activity and dreaming. Adjustment to new patterns of sleep occurs in just a few days.

Personal Hygiene

Personal hygiene goes far beyond personal appearance and is an essential part of health and its preservation.

Pure soaps should be used to cleanse skin and hair. Antibacterial soaps should be avoided because they contain chemicals that can irritate the skin and may cause severe itching after exposure to sunlight.[43-44] Many people are sensitive to a wide variety of perfumes, body lotions, and deodorants. These should be avoided when possible, and only products with simple natural ingredients should be used. Roll-ons and lotions are preferred because sprays and aerosols often are inhaled into the lungs and aggravate respiratory illnesses, such as asthma.

At most, occasional tapwater douches are recommended for feminine hygiene. Sprays, creams, and other unnatural substances introduced into the vagina can cause irritation, itching, and discharge.

Teeth should be cleaned with a soft toothbrush and flossed daily to remove food particles and reduce plaque formation. Bleeding gums can be caused by toothbrushes with firm bristles. Bad breath is often the result of food decaying in spaces between the teeth. Toothpastes should contain as few chemical additives as possible. The need for fluoride is superfluous if you follow the recommended diet, since tooth decay is virtually unknown in societies whose members have eaten according to a starch-centered meal plan.[45] However, fluroide is an effective aid in preventive dentistry with few established side effects. You may choose this extra protection for the children in your family especially if they indulge in sweets.[46]

Most natural food stores carry a variety of soaps, toothpastes, lotions, and doedorants free of potentially harmful additives. However, this is not the time to abandon your skills in reading labels, because more often than not manufacturers of "natural" products are still more interested in promoting their business than in protecting your health.

Preventive Medicine

During the past century most of the increase in lifespan has been the result of achievements in the fields of public health and preventive medicine. The effects are most apparent in decreased infant mortality.[47] (See Figure 14.1.)

Deaths from infectious diseases have been reduced by the development of sterile techniques used in surgical and obstetrical procedures, advancements in public sanitation, and the widespread use of immunizations. Childbirth fever, whooping cough, cholera, smallpox, tetanus, and diphtheria are now only memories for most members of our older generation and are unknown to their descendants. The crippling effects of polio still can be seen among individuals in the present adult population and continue to remind us of the remarkable benefits immunizations have given us. Unfortunately, many people now are neglecting to have their children immunized. Too frequently, this is because they believe that a good diet and healthful lifestyle are the complete answer to all health problems. This belief is not correct. Even though good nutrition is a very important part of the ability to resist disease, diet alone fails to protect us from many virulent bacteria, viruses, and parasites.

Early detection of disease is the primary preventive measure advocated by cancer societies. Common forms of skin cancer and cancer of the cervix of the uterus are treated easily and effectively when caught in their early stages. The American Cancer Society has recommended that women routinely obtain a Pap smear every three years after two yearly negative tests.[48] This allows enough time for early detection of cervical cancer before it becomes invasive and beyond control by simple surgical means.

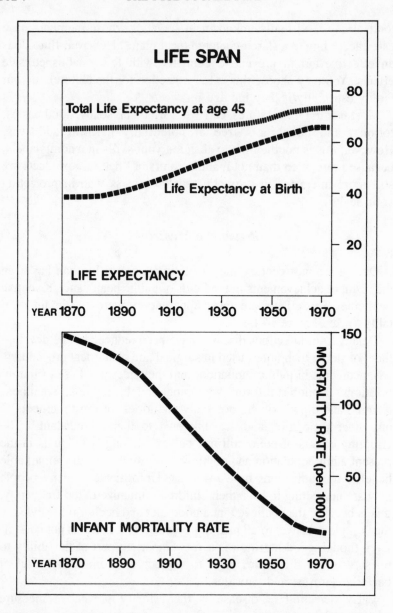

Figure 14.1. Total life expectancy for people is increasing, but if you are 45 or older, your life expectation today is not much different than a hundred years ago. An actual increase of only 6 years. The major increase in life expectancy has benefited the young with a remarkable decrease in infant mortality. Babies born today have an expected lifespan 23 years longer than a hundred years ago.[47]

Self-examination to detect breast cancer and examination of stools for minute quantities of blood to detect colon cancer are also widely recommended. However, such detection methods and the subsequent therapies are having little, if any, effect on the ultimate time of death from these common diseases.[49-62] It appears that even with our modern methods of detection we cannot catch these cancers in time before they have spread. Cancer begins as a single cell that goes awry and becomes malignant. This malignant cancer cell divides into two cells in about 100 days in many types of cancer. In turn, these two cells become four in another 100 days, and so on. At this rate of doubling it takes many years before a cancerous lump becomes detectable and therefore treatable.[63,64] This may surprise you, but in the case of breast cancer, researchers estimate that the malignant cells have been present in a woman's breast for an average of ten years before the smallest lump (about one-half inch) can be detected by self-examination.[63-64] (See Figure 14.2.) Even sophisticated X-ray exams called mammograms can only detect tumors six months to two years earlier than self-examination. Spreading to other tissues takes place much earlier and is proved by the poor results obtained with surgical procedures, such as mastectomies.[57-62] Approximately 90 percent of women diagnosed as having breast cancer will die of breast cancer.[65] Similar disappointing results are obtained with the treatment

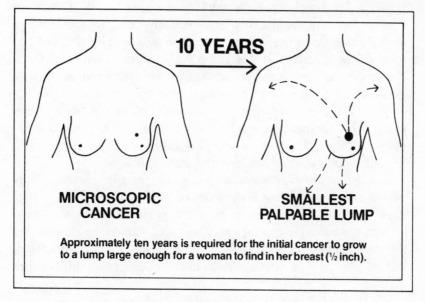

10 YEARS

MICROSCOPIC CANCER

SMALLEST PALPABLE LUMP

Approximately ten years is required for the initial cancer to grow to a lump large enough for a woman to find in her breast (½ inch).

Figure 14.2

of colon cancer and with most other tumors that are found as a solid mass at the time of diagnosis (esophagus, stomach, gallbladder, liver, pancreas, prostate, ovary, kidney, and lung).[52,53,66]

For cancer and many other diseases, money and efforts in public education are best spent not on early detection, but rather on programs that help people avoid the factors that cause the problems: cigarette smoking, alcohol consumption, rich foods, radiation, and chemical contaminants. To be quite realistic, in most cases the only real beneficiaries from early detection are the health professionals. Early detection gets the patient going to the doctor earlier and, thereby, a longer total time period is available for more expensive doctor visits, hospitalizations, and tests.[67] And the patient lives no longer or better from all of this well-meaning effort.

A study group for the National Academy of Science recently reviewed a large body of evidence that supported the claim made by investigators worldwide that 60 percent of female cancers and 40 percent of cancers found in men are related to diet.[68] However, this body of scientists would not go so far as to recommend that we discontinue all those tasty foods that they suspected caused cancer, partially because some members may have misunderstood our actual protein and calcium needs. Possibly, the greatest barrier to more sensible recommendations was that of their own dietary habits. Because diet is such a personal part of everyone's life, their ability to think objectively could easily have been hindered. As the message about health-supporting foods becomes more generally received and some of the members of this and other scientific committees make changes in their own diets, you can bet we will find recommendations for starch-centered meal plans forthcoming. With no more supporting evidence, cigarette smoking was condemned more than twenty years ago by the Surgeon General, but this action also required a long-overdue shift in the thinking and personal habits of the general and scientific population of the United States.

Enough information is available so that experts in scientific fields now attribute more than 90 percent of cancers to elements in our environment.[69-71] Because we have the potential to control these elements, we can prevent their consequences and change the unfortunate fact that one out of every three people living in a modern affluent society develops a major life-threatening cancer in his or her lifetime.[72]

Safe Living

Attention to safety is a very broad and important approach to guarding our health. Volumes have been written to convey this message. Rules designed to prevent accidents around the home and place of employment have been taught to most of us for years. The area of greatest concern for safety today involves automobiles. The use of safety belts and car seats for small children and the avoidance of intoxication while driving cannot be overemphasized.[73-75] Estimates are available that 16,000 to 18,000 lives could be saved each year in the United States if safety belts were used properly. One persuasive study revealed that no fatalities occurred in cars that were involved in collisions happening at rates up to sixty miles per hour when shoulder and seat belt combinations were worn.[76] Accidents are the fourth leading cause of death overall and the leading cause of death among children and young adults. In retrospect, almost all accidents are preventable. Now is the time to think ahead.

Low-Level Radiation

Recent, highly publicized reports of accidents at nuclear power plants have focused public atttention on the dangers of low-level radiation.[77] Increased rates of cancer have been seen following exposure to levels of radiation once thought to be safe. Soldiers involved in atomic bomb tests in 1957, nuclear power plant workers, naval shipyard workers, and individuals with a history of therapeutic radiation to the head and neck area in infancy and childhood are victims of the cancer-causing effects of low-level radiation. The risk of developing cancer is directly related to the amount of exposure, and the damage is cumulative with repeated exposures. Furthermore, there is no safe threshold below which an increased risk of developing cancer does not occur. Cancers of the thyroid, female breast, bones, liver, and lung and leukemia are the forms most commonly found following exposure to radiation. About 2.5 percent of all cancers in the general population are attributed to radiation.[78]

Diagnostic X-rays from medical and dental services represent the most common sources of exposure, above the natural background radiation, for most of us. Here, the risk versus benefit of a test must be weighed carefully. Routine dental X-rays, chest X-rays (even in smokers), and barium enema X-rays are not justifiable in most circumstances.[79-81] If the X-ray is warranted, then every effort should be made to keep the exposure as low as possible.

Harmful effects of radiation also result in genetic disorders and damage to a developing fetus. Whenever possible, lead shields should be placed over the testicles or ovaries of adults and children during X-ray procedures. Usually, a lead apron can be worn over body areas outside the field of X-ray to minimize exposure to other body areas. Women who are pregnant or who suspect possible pregnancy should make every effort to avoid X-rays. Frequently, less dangerous diagnostic methods, such as ultrasound, can obtain the same information with less risk. Ask your doctor.

X-ray treatment performed in the past for acne, enlarged tonsils and adenoids, or an enlarged thymus gland has resulted in a 600 percent increase in the risk of developing cancer of the thyroid.[82] Because of these findings, X-ray treatment to the head and neck has generally been abandoned. However, X-ray as a form of treatment continues not only in cancer therapy but also in the treatment of benign conditions. A September 1977 HEW report notes that 40 to 55 percent of dermatologists surveyed were still using superficial X-rays to treat keloid scars, acne, and plantar warts.[83] In high voltage X-ray therapies for the treatment of cancerous conditions, such as Hodgkin's disease, long-term follow-up shows a very high rate of leukemia and other cancers caused by the therapy, hence the benefits of various treatments must be weighed against the carcinogenic potential.[84,85]

An entirely different type of radiation—microwave—causes most of its damage by the heat it generates. Current research has found that relatively low levels of microwave radiation over a prolonged period of time have a variety of adverse effects on animals, which include cataract formation, increased numbers of birth defects, and impairment of the immune system. Whether or not humans will show similar effects is unknown, but likely. One of the most common sources of exposure to this type of radiation is microwave ovens. Does the convenience and efficiency of the applicance outweigh the possible danger? If you choose a microwave oven, have it checked periodically for leakage.[86]

Sunlight is a form of radiation that is essential for good health, yet overexposure can cause serious skin damage. Sunburn is the short-term effect. Long-term overexposure, particularly in fair-skinned people, can cause damage to the skin with consequences of premature aging and skin cancers.[87] There is also evidence that a more serious form of cancer, called melanoma, is caused in some people by an excess of radiation from the sun. Protective clothing and sunscreen preparations that contain PABA (para-amino-benzoic acid) are very helpful in preventing such skin damage.

Considering our present technological and political situation, illness from radiation may soon lead the list in causes of death and disability. It would be just our luck to solve the health problems of people in modern societies that are caused by eating rich foods only to find ourselves confronted with this whole new challenge.

Notes

[1]C. Martys, "Adverse Reactions to Drugs in General Practice," *Br Med J* 2 (1979): 1194.

[2]L. Cluff, "Is Drug Toxicity a Problem of Great Magnitude? Yes!" *Controversies in Therapeutics*. Lasagna, Philadelphia 1980, p. 44.

[3]E. Martin, *Hazards of Medication*, 2nd ed., Lippincott, Philadelphia and London p. 1.

[4]D. Slone, "Computer Analysis of Epidemiologic Data on Effect of Drugs on Hospital Patients," *Public Health Report*, 84 (1969): 39.

[5]J. Porter, "Drug-Related Deaths among Medical Inpatients," *JAMA* 237 (1977): 879.

[6]G. Caranosas, "Drug-Associated Deaths of Medical Inpatients," *Arch Intern Med* 136 (1976): 872.

[7]V. Herbert, "Facts and Fiction about Megavitamin Therapy," *Resident and Staff Physician* (Dec. 1978): 43.

[8]K. Yano, "Coffee, Alcohol, and Risk of Coronary Heart Disease among Japanese Men Living in Hawaii," *N Engl J Med* 297 (1977): 405.

[9]W. Blackwelder, "Alcohol and Mortality: The Honolulu Heart Study," *Am J Med* 68 (1980): 164.

[10]S. Freestone, "Effect of Coffee and Cigarette Smoking on Blood Pressure of Untreated and Diuretic-Treated Hypertensive Patients," *Am J Med* 73 (1982): 348.

[11]T. Collins, "Review of Reproduction and Teratology Studies of Caffeine," *FDA By-Lines* 9 (1979): 352.

[12]Citizen Petition, Center for Science in the Public Interest, Washington, D.C., FDA Hearing Clerk no. 79P-0443/Cp, Nov. 15, 1979.

[13]J. Goyan, Statement by the Commissioner of Foods and Drugs, FDA Press Release, Washington, D.C., Sept. 4, 1980, p 3.

[14]J. Milton, "Caffeine, Cyclic Nucleotides, and Breast-Disease," *Surgery* 86 (1979): 105.

[15]J. Milton, "Response of Fibrocystic Disease to Caffeine Withdrawal and Correlation of Cyclic Nucleotides with Breast Disease," *Am J Obstet Gynecol* 135 (1979): 157.

[16]P. Brooks, "Measuring the effect of Caffeine Restriction on Fibrocystic Breast Disease," *J of Rep Med* 26 (1981): 279.

[17]J. Elliot, "Cyclic Nucleotides as Predictors of Benign to Malignant Progression of Breast Cancer," *Breast* 7 (1981): 6.

[18]J. Little, "Coffee and Serum-Lipids in Coronary Heart Disease," *Lancet* 1 (1966): 732.

[19]P. Cole, "Coffee Drinking and Cancer of the Lower Urinary Tract," *Lancet* 2 (1971): 1335.

[20]L. Marrett, "Coffee Drinking and Bladder Cancer in Connecticut," *Am J Epidimol* 117 (1983): 113.

[21]R. Heaney, "Effects of Nitrogen, Phosphorus, and Caffeine on Calcium Balance in Women," *J Lab Clin Med* 99 (1982): 46.

[22]B. Franklin, "Losing Weight through Exercise," *JAMA* 244 (1980): 377.

[23]R. Woo, "Effect of Exercise on Spontaneous Calorie Intake in Obesity," *Am J Clin Nutr* 36 (1982): 470.

[24]R. Woo, "Voluntary Food Intake During Prolonged Exercise in Obese Women," *Am J Clin Nutr* 36 (1982): 478.

[25]J. Morganroth, "The Athletes' Heart Syndrome," *Ann NY Acad Sci* 301 (1977): 931.

[26]M. Adner, "Elevated High-Density Lipoprotein Levels in Marathon Runners," *JAMA* 243 (1980): 534.

[27]G. Hartung, "The Relation of Diet to High-Density Lipoprotein Cholesterol in Middle-Aged Marathon Runners, Joggers, and Inactive Men," *N Engl J Med* 302 (1980): 357.

[28]P. Wood, "The Distribution of Plasma Lipoproteins in Middle-Aged Male Runners," *Metabolism* 25 (1976): 1249.

[29]J. Boyer, "Exercise Therapy in Hypertensive Men," *JAMA* 211 (1970): 1668.

[30]P. Bjorntorp, "Hypertension and Exercise," *Hypertension* 4 (1982): 111-56.

[31]R. Lapman, "Effectiveness of Unsupervised and Supervised High-Intensity Physical Training in Normalizing Serum Lipids in Men with Type IV Hyperlipoproteinemia," *Circulation* 57 (1978): 172.

[32]F. Gyntelberg, "Plasma Triglyceride Lowering by Exercise Despite Increased Food Intake in Patients withType IV Hyperlipoproteinemia," *Am J Clin Nutr* 30 (1977): 716.

[33]V. Soman, "Increased Insulin Sensitivity and Insulin Binding to Monocytes after Physical Training," *N Engl J Med* 301 (1979): 1200.

[34]J. Morris, "Vigorous Exercise in Leisure-Time: Protection against Coronary Heart Disease," *Lancet* 2 (1980): 1207.

[35]R. Lampman, "Comparative Effects of Physical Training and Diet in Normalizing Serum Lipids in Men with Type IV Hyperlipoproteinemia," *Circulation* 55 (1977): 652.

[36]R. Frisch, "Delayed Menarche and Amenorrhea of College Athletes in Relation to Age of Onset of Training," *JAMA* 246 (1981): 1559.

[37]J. Aloia, "Prevention of Involutional Bone Loss by Exercise," *Ann Intern Med* 89 (1978): 356.

[38]J. Greist, "Running Through Your Mind," *J Psycho-Somatic Res* 22 (1978): 259.

[39]D. Carr, "Physical Conditioning Facilitates the Exercise-Induced Secretion of Beta-Endorphin and Beta-Lipotropin in Women," *N Engl J Med* 305 (1981): 560.

[40]P. Thompson, "Incidence of Death During Jogging in Rhode Island from 1975 through 1980," *JAMA* 247 (1982): 2535.

[41]J. Koplan, "An Epidemiologic Study of the Benefits and Risks of Running," *JAMA* 248 (1982): 3118.

[42]F. Phillips, "Isocaloric Diet Changes and Electroencephalographic Sleep," *Lancet* 2 (1975): 723.

[43]P. Osmundsen, "Contact Photoallergy to Tribromsalicylanilide," *Br J Derm* 81 (1969): 429.

[44]E. Cronin, *Contact Dermatitis,* Churchill Livingston, Edinburgh London and New York 1980, pp. 432–37.

[45]W. Price, *Nutrition and Physical Degeneration,* Santa Monica: Price-Pottenger Nutrition Foundation, 1977.

[46]"Lords Debate on Fluoridation," *Br Dent J* 147 (1979): 309.

[47]J. S. Siegel, U.S. Public Health Service, National Center for Health Status and Current Population Reports, Special Studies Section P-23, no. 59, May 1976.

[48]American Cancer Society, "ACS Report on the Cancer-Related Health Check-up," Ca-A *Cancer J for Clinicians* 30 (1980): 215.

[49]Editorial, "Screening for Colon–Rectal Cancer," *Lancet* 2 (1979): 1222.

[50]A. Ribet, "Occult Blood Tests and Colon–Rectal Tumors, *Lancet* 1 (1980): 417.

[51]B. Jancin, "Mass Screening for Colon, Breast, Lung Cancer Criticized," *Intern Med News* (Feb. 1, 1981): 1.

[52]H. Polk, "Surgical Mortality and Survival from Colonic Cancer," *Arch Surg* 89 (1964): 16.

[53]F. Ederer, "Survival of Patients with Cancer of the Large Intestine and Rectum, Connecticut 1935–1954," *J Nat Ca Inst* 26 (1961): 489.

[54]H. Holliday, "Delay in Diagnosis and Treatment of Symptomatic Colon–Rectal Cancer," *Lancet* 1 (1979): 309.

[55]J. Bailar, "Screening for Early Breast Cancer: Pros and Cons," *Cancer* 39 (1977): 2783.

[56]Editorial, "Screening for Breast Cancer," *Lancet* 1 (1982): 1103.

[57]A. Langlands, "Long-Term Survival of Patients with Breast Cancer: A Study of Curability," *Br Med J* 2 (1979): 1247.

[58]J. Stehlin, "Treatment of Carcinoma of the Breast," *Surg Gynecol Obstet* 149 (1979): 911.

[59]C. Mueller, "Breast Cancer in 3,558 Women—Age as a Significant Determinant in the Rate of Dying and Causes of Death," *Surgery* 83 (1978): 123.

[60]D. Greenberg, " 'Progress' in Cancer Research—Don't Say It Isn't So," *N Engl J Med* 292 (1975): 707.

[61]M. Baum, "The Curability of Breast Cancer," *Br Med J* 1 (1976): 439.

[62]D. Brinkley, "The Curability of Breast Cancer," *Lancet* 2 (1975): 95.

[63]P. Gullino, "Natural History of Breast Cancer—Progression from Hyperplasia to Neoplasia as Predicted by Angiogenesis," *Cancer* 39 (1977): 2697.

[64]I. MacDonald, "The Natural History of Mammary Carcinoma," *Am J Surg* 111 (1966): 435.

[65]C. Mueller, "Bilateral Carcinoma of the Breast: Frequency and Mortality," *Can J Surg* 21 (1978): 459.

[66]Cancer Surveillance, Epidemiology, and End Results (SEER) Program, Cancer Patient Survival—report no. 5, DHEW Publ no. (NIH) 77-992, 1976.

[67]T. Brewin, "The Cancer Patient—Too Many Scans and X-Rays?" *Lancet* 2 (1981): 1098.

[68]Committee on Diet, Nutrition, and Cancer, Assembly of Life Sciences, National Research Council, *Diet, Nutrition, and Cancer.* Washington, D.C.: National Academy Press, 1982.

[69]J. Higgison, "Present Trends in Cancer Epidemiology," *Proc Can Cancer Conf* 8 (1969): 40.

[70]E. Wynder, "Contribution of the Environment to Cancer Incidence: An Epidemiologic Exercise," *J Nat Ca Inst* 58 (1977): 825.

[71]Report to Congress from the Office of Technology Assessment, Assessment of technologies for determining cancer risks from the environment. June 1981.

[72]Cancer Facts and Figures—1983. American Cancer Society New York. Based on rates from NCI-SEER Program (1973-1979).

[73]"Road Accidents—Seat Belts and the Safe Car," *Br Med J* 2 (1978): 1695.

[74]J. Karwacki, "Children in Motor Vehicles—Never Too Young to Die," *JAMA* 242 (1979): 2848.

[75]H. Mackillop, "Effect of Seat Belt Legislation and Reduction of Highway Speed Limits in Ontario," *CMA J* 119 (1978): 1154.

[76]H. Pyle, "Safety Belts—The Real Preventive Medicine in Automotive Safety," *Prev Med* 2 (1973): 3.

[77]A. Upton, "Low-Level Radiation—Interview," *Ca–A Cancer J for Clinicians* 29 (1979): 306.

[78]A. Upton, "Low-Dose Radiation—Risk vs. Benefits," *Postgrad Med* 70 (1981): 35.

[79]S. Sagel, "Efficacy of Routine Screening and Lateral Chest Radiographs in a Hospital-Based Population," *N Eng J Med* 291 (1974): 1001.

[80]A. Feingold, "Routine Chest Roentgenograms on Hospital Admission Do Not Discover Tuberculosis," *S. Med J* 70 (1977): 579.

[81]Guidelines for the Cancer-Related Checkup—Recommendations and Rationale, *CA–A Cancer J for Clinicians* 30 (1980): 194.

[82]B. Modan, "Thyroid Cancer Following Scalp Irradiation," *Radiology* 123 (1977): 741.

[83]A review of the use of ionizing radiation for the treatment of benign diseases. A report of the committee to review the use of ionizing radiation for the treatment of benign diseases. Assembly of Life Sciences. National Research Council, National Academy of Sciences, Washington D.C. HEW Publ (FDA) 78-8043. Sept. 1977.

[84]P. Valagussa, "Second Malignancies in Hodgkin's Disease: A Complication of Certain Forms of Treatment," *Br Med J* 1 (1980): 216.

[85]M. Baccarani, "Second Malignancies in Patients Treated for Hodgkin's Disease," *Cancer* 46 (1980): 1735.

[86]"Microwave Ovens," Consumer Reports 41 (1976): 314.

[87]H. Blum, "On the Mechanism of Cancer Induction by Ultraviolet Radiation," *J Nat Ca Inst* 11 (1950): 463.

CHAPTER
15

Getting Started on Your Health-Supporting Diet

Advantages Besides Health

You Save Money

Health-supporting foods are less expensive than the rich foods consumed by most westerners. A 40 percent reduction in food costs is not uncommon with a change to a starch-centered diet. (Initially, you may not achieve this saving when you are in the process of restocking your kitchen.)

The benefits for your health that occur because of the diet change result in a dramatic reduction in the need for prescription and nonprescription medications. Medications are expensive. The money saved by not buying them can be spent on better things.

Improvement in your health also results in fewer visits to doctors and dentists and less use of hospital services. Furthermore, when you feel and function better you are more productive and have the potential for greater earnings and further growth in your life's work. You're able to enjoy life more fully when in good health.

Kitchen Cleanup Is Easier and Faster

Health-supporting foods will keep your kitchen as clean as your body. Cleaning pots, pans, dishes, and utensils is much easier with low-fat foods. Water, and at most a little soap, is all you should need for most of your kitchenware. Avoiding fats, oils, and high-fat foods in cooking will eliminate that slick covering of grease on the stove, kitchen walls, floor and ceiling.

Storage Is Easier and There Is Less Spoilage

Starches, vegetables and fruits keep much better than animal products. Refrigeration is required for only a few perishable vegetables. Otherwise, storage in airtight jars or in a cool, dry place is sufficient. However, refrigeration will greatly increase the shelf life of most vegetable foods. Leftovers and cooked beans freeze well and maintain excellent flavors for months.

Your Social Consciousness Is Raised

Rich foods, such as meat, poultry, milk, and cheese, are ecologically wasteful. In order to provide you with a certain amount of calories and protein, the cow or chicken must eat a very large amount of grain. The conversion ratio is high: 7 plant calories are required in order to produce 1 calorie of animal food.[1] In our world today, food of any kind is becoming scarce, and millions of unfortunate people are starving. A change to a starch-centered diet would make more food available for more people everywhere. The solution to the world's hunger problem must include a change in our own food preferences. Considering the present trends in our economy, it is likely that in ten to fifteen years most of us will be unable to afford rich foods. A change now may be good preparation for our own future and that of our neighbors.

Most western and eastern religions encourage a starch-centered diet for their followers.[2] The harmful influence of rich foods and the benefits of wholesome vegetable foods on health have been observed for thousands of years. Consider this passage from the Bible:

> Daniel (talking to his overseer about 600 B.C.): "Give us nothing but vegetables to eat and water to drink. Then compare our appearance with that of the young men who eat the royal food and treat your servants in accordance with what you see." So, he agreed to this and tested them for ten days.
> At the end of ten days, they looked healthier and better nourished than any of the young men who ate the royal food. Daniel 1:12–15. (The Holy Bible—New International Version)

If You Are Sincere about Making the Change, Do So with 100 Percent Of Your Effort

Many people feel that it would be easier for them to slide into this diet plan gradually. Unfortunately, we seldom manage to discard old ways and old established tastes unless 100 percent of our effort is devoted to the change and unless, from the beginning, we make a clear break from our old behavior. For example, a smoker who cuts down to four cigarettes per day only goes through slow torture and rarely quits. Alcoholics don't stand a chance until they take their last drink. The same thing seems to happen with eating. Consider this advice on changing habits from William James, the father of American psychology:[3] "In the acquisition of a new habit or the leaving off of an old one, we must take care to launch ourselves with as strong and decided an initiative as possible." To this first step he added a second: "Never suffer an exception to occur until the new habit is securely rooted in your life."

When you make a complete dietary change, you are placed in a position to:

1. Learn to like new foods. No others are available.
2. Lose the taste for rich foods. "Just a little" butter, cheese, chicken, or fish will be an invitation to slow torture.
3. Find the new foods in stores and restaurants.
4. Learn to function sensibly in social and work situations.

Most people take from one to four months to become fully accustomed to the diet plan. A commitment of four months will help you stick to the diet and learn it thoroughly. It is very important to be strict with yourself during this learning period.

This four-month commitment also serves as an adequate test of the advice given in this book. Most people searching for health have heard many unwarranted claims for the benefits of vitamins, herbal remedies, special diets, and dozens of other hopeful approaches.

Why should this advice be any different? After four months of following this diet, you can answer the following questions and judge for yourself:

1. How much better do I look, feel, and function?
2. Am I taking less medication?

3. How inconvenient is it to eat this way at work and with friends?
4. Are the meals difficult to prepare?
5. Have I saved money on my health and food bills?
6. How well do I enjoy the taste of the meals?

Only after you have learned this diet and earned its rewards can you honestly answer these questions and fully understand the value of the recommended changes in diet and lifestyle.

You owe it to yourself to see just how much of your lost health you can regain. Don't compromise; if you do, you'll only be cheating yourself. Within four months most of the healing has occurred, except in people who are very obese.

After you have completed the four-month learning and healing period and you are in good health (cholesterol less than 160 mg%, weight ideal, no medication), you can begin to add a few richer foods back to your diet, if you choose. Rich foods, such as high-fat plant foods (nuts, seeds, avocados), and simple sugars (juice, honey, brown sugar) cause little adverse effects for most people even when eaten daily in small amounts. Foods like ice cream, meats, poultry, fish, cheeses, and chocolate candy should be considered delicacies and ought to be reserved for special feast occasions. Only in modern societies as wealthy as ours does "special" become "everyday," and as a result people end up eating and looking like fat kings and queens.

How often such feasts occur will depend on you. Some people will find the rich foods too disturbing to their bodies for any occasion. Others neither mind nor detect the discomforts associated with these foods. Certainly the very rich feast foods should not be included on a daily basis or in large amounts by anyone.

Eating in this manner gives you control over your health. When you eat properly every day, the unpleasant reactions from an occasional indulgence in rich foods will be very apparent to you. The reasons for constipation, stomach cramps, stuffy nose, and fatigue are no longer a mystery. The long periods of health you enjoy between these unpleasant reactions will reinforce the fact that you do have a good body as long as you treat it well by feeding it well.

It may be comforting to know that your favorite rich food is still available to you once your health has returned, on an anniversary, a birthday, or an occasional night out. But never again consider them a part of your basic health-supporting diet.

Rules for Selecting Foods

1. No foods from animal sources.
2. No processed or refined foods.
3. No added oil or fat.
4. No spoiled foods.
5. No additives (colorings, flavorings, preservatives, sugar, or salt, etc.)
6. No high-fat plant foods (vegetable oils, nuts, seeds, avocados, olives, etc.)
7. No concentrated simple sugars (honey, sugar, maple syrup, fruit juice, etc.)
8. High-protein starches (which include beans, peas, and lentils) limited to one cooked cupful per day. All high-protein plant foods (legumes, mushrooms, edible yeast, etc.) removed from the diet of people with osteoporosis, gout, kidney stones, and liver or kidney failure.
9. Fresh fruits limited for people with obesity, elevated triglycerides, and hypoglycemia.
10. Offending foods removed from the diet for people who have adverse reactions, including allergies, to certain plant foods.

Otherwise, you are allowed to choose freely from the many edible plants. A word of caution should be given to those people who choose wheat and especially wheat flour products. Wheat is the most common plant food to cause food allergy, and, like barley and rye, it contains large amounts of gluten. Gluten causes intestinal and other problems for some people. Even whole wheat flour is a refined product with some of the fiber extracted from the whole grain. The result is a product with four to seven times as many calories per gram as are present in the natural grain.

Relative Hazards of Foods

Since it may not always be possible for you to choose the foods that support your health, it will be helpful for you to know the relative hazards of different rich foods. Progression from Categories I through IV below leads from harmful to health-supporting foods. For those who usually follow the diet closely, these categories will identify foods least damaging to you when you do indulge on those special occasions. Anyone who is not yet ready for a complete change to a health-supporting diet as set forth in Category IV may want to improve his or her diet by beginning with the elimination of foods in Category I and progressing at his or her chosen rate.

Category I—Dangerous Foods

You should never eat these foods. Government, medical, and scientific authorities have considered these foods dangerous enough to hold committee hearings, to issue warnings about them, or even to ban these products from use. All of these foods are suspected causes of cancer. You have no reason to eat these, because there are safer alternatives.

1. Nitrite-containing meats: ham, hot dogs, sausages, cold cuts, bacon.[4]
2. Supermarket quality meat: pork, beef, organ meats, poultry (14 percent of these are contaminated with illegal levels of substances that are known to cause or suspected of causing birth defects and cancers).[5]
3. Hydrogenated and partially hydrogenated vegetable oils: margarines, vegetable shortenings, imitation milk; (found in most packaged foods from cookies to breath mints).[6]
4. Canned, bottled, or packaged foods containing artificial preservatives, flavorings, and colorings, especially saccharin, and cyclamates.[7-8]
5. Highly salted vegetables (brine pickled) or any highly salted foods.[9]
6. Talc-coated rice (contaminated with asbestos).[10-11]
7. Charcoal-broiled and smoked foods.[12]

Category II—Feast Foods

IIA. These foods should be eaten rarely, if ever. Never eat them if you are trying to regain your health and appearance. These are very rich foods. They should be reserved for that special occasion, the feast. For most healthy people, these feasts should occur less than once a month. Anyone still trying to regain the best possible level of health should always avoid feasts.

1. Range-fed beef without hormones or chemicals.
2. Organically grown poultry.

3. Shellfish.
4. Fresh fish.
5. Cream.
6. Whole milk.
7. Cheese.
8. Creamed cottage cheese.
9. Sour cream.
10. Ice Cream.
11. Yogurt.
12. Butter.
13. Eggs.
14. Mayonnaise.
15. Coconut oil.
16. Coconut meat.
17. Chocolate.
18. Soda pop.

Fresh fish is included here because it is high in protein and often high in fat. Fish has no carbohydrates and no fiber. It is high in cholesterol, high in environmental contaminants, and a common cause of food allergy. In its favor, it is the least harmful of all the flesh foods and has the important asset of containing a polyunsaturated fat with properties that thin the blood (prevent platelet aggregation). The low incidence of heart disease among fish-eating populations may be in part the result of this quality of fish.[13] However, fish is still a delicacy intended for sparing use or an occasional feast.

IIB. These modified feast foods should be eaten no more than once a week, and then only in small amounts. They should never be eaten by someone looking for improvement in health. These dairy and egg foods have been modified to lower the fat and cholesterol content. Removal of the fat reduces the level of fat-soluble chemical contaminants. However, they are still too high in protein, as well as being fiber-free. Dairy products are the leading cause of food allergies, and eggs are often listed as the second most common cause.

1. Low-fat yogurt.
2. Low-fat milk (skim milk).
3. Buttermilk.
4. Low-fat (dry curd) cottage cheese.
5. Low-fat cheese (mozzarella).
6. Kefir.

7. Sherbet (contains water, sugar, fruit juice, and often egg whites or low-fat dairy products).
8. Egg whites.

Category III—Rich Plant Foods

The rich plant foods may account for a small portion of your daily food (less than 10 percent of your calories per day) but only after you have attained the level of health you are striving for. In general, these foods are more harmful than health-supporting. Never eat these foods if you have problems with your health that remain unsolved. If you begin using this group of foods and find that you are also gaining weight or getting back some of your old ailments, then stop eating these foods immediately.

IIIA. *High-fat plant foods* contain excessive fat, and most are high in calories.

1. Vegetable oils (safflower, sesame, olive, peanut, and other unprocessed oils).
2. Olives.
3. Avocados.
4. Nuts
5. Nut butters (like peanut butter).
6. Seeds.
7. Seed spreads (like tahini).
8. Tofu (fiber also has been removed).
9. Tempeh.
10. Soybeans.
11. Textured vegetable protein (TVP) (check for hydrogenated oils).
12. Wheat germ (frequently rancid).
13. Miso.

IIIB. *Simple sugar foods* provide concentrated calories and often little else.

1. White sugar (worst).
2. Brown sugar.
3. Corn syrup.
4. Honey.
5. Maple syrup.
6. Molasses.
7. Malt syrup.
8. Jams and jellies.

9. Fruit puree (like applesauce—significant content of fiber, vitamins and minerals).
10. Dried fruit (best) (significant content of fiber, vitamins and minerals).

IIIC. *Refined grains and flours* have had much of their fiber content, vitamins, and minerals removed. Some products have had a few vitamins and minerals added and are therefore called enriched.

1. White rice (cereal-coated).
2. Refined flours (white flour, used in white bread and white noodle products).
3. Cornstarch.
4. Potato starch.

Category IV—Health-Supporting Foods

These foods are health-supporting. They allow your body to attain and maintain its naturally intended state of good health. They should account for the greatest share (at least 90 percent) of your calories if you are healthy and for all of them if you are still working to regain your health.

1. Whole grains, such as wheat, rice, barley, millet, rye, oats, corn, popcorn.
2. Milled grains, such as whole wheat flour, corn meal, rice flour, rye flour, oatmeal, bulgur.
3. Vegetables, such as white potatoes, sweet potatoes, yams, taro (including poi), spinach, zucchini, broccoli, onions.
4. Sprouted seeds and beans, such as alfalfa, radish, wheat, mung bean, lentil.
5. Beans, peas, lentils, such as split peas, kidney beans, white beans, garbanzo beans, pinto beans, defatted soybean flour, garbanzo bean flour. (These are also high-protein foods—restricted use.)
6. Fresh fruits. (All edible varieties of these are suitable; however, they should be limited by most people to about three per day. They contain simple sugars that are largely protected by fiber.)

Trouble-Shooting Your Diet

Many adjustments take place when you change your diet. These can result in unfamiliar feelings and a change in the functions of your body. Within two weeks you should be well adjusted and comfortable with how your body responds to a starch-centered diet. Keep in mind that not everything that happens to you is the result of the dietary change. You are still subject to nondietary ailments, such as the common cold, flu, airborne allergies, and injuries. The following are the more common problems seen following a diet change.

Allergies may develop when you change your diet and add completely new foods or larger amounts of familiar foods. Allergic symptoms are highly variable. If you suspect they are coming from the recommended foods, begin by eliminating wheat, corn, and citrus fruits. (See Chapter 12 for further help.)

Bowel gas is common during the first two weeks. This decreases as the bacteria in your colon change in kind and number, as they adapt to the large amount of carbohydrates and fiber.[14] Beans, peas, lentils, and cabbage cause gas in most people. The legumes can be sprouted to reduce the amount of gas produced. (Soak for twelve hours in water to cover, pour off water, let them stand for twelve hours to sprout, and then add more water and cook as directed in the recipe.) The process of sprouting utilizes some of the sugars that we cannot digest and that are usually left for the intestinal bacteria to ferment into methane, carbon dioxide, and hydrogen gas. These gases are odorless. The malodors of the intestine probably come from traces of volatile substances produced by putrefaction, the microbial breakdown of protein.[15] These volatile substances also are absorbed through the intestinal wall into the body, where they are eliminated through the lungs and skin and produce bad breath and body odor. Fortunately, the bowel gas produced from vegetable food is less malodorous than that from animal food, most likely because they are lower in certain types of protein. Even after your best attempts to keep gas to a minimum, legumes and other foods that contain carbohydrates that you can't digest well may have to be avoided for social reasons. The addition of bran to your diet will frequently cause stomach cramps and gas.

Cramps are occasionally seen as a result of the sudden introduction of a large amount of fiber into an intestine unaccustomed to so much vegetable food. Adjustment occurs quickly. If you are still eating lactose from whole or skim milk, yogurt, or other dairy products, these may cause stomach cramps. People who have had previous surgery or radiation to their abdomens may develop severe stomach cramps and even bowel obstruction when suddenly introducing high-fiber foods, because of adhesions (scar tissues) that constrict the bowel. Someone with a history of adhesions caused by surgery or radiation or a history of bowel obstruction from any cause should begin the diet with a doctor's supervision. Start the diet by pureeing some or all of the foods, especially those with long, stringy fibers such as oranges, celery, and string beans.

Constipation is contrary to what is expected on a high-fiber diet. However, if any dairy product, even a small amount of skim milk, is retained in your diet, bowel movements may not pass easily or regularly. However, occasionally someone will have slow or hard bowel movements during the first week of the new diet for no apparent reason. This can be helped by drinking eight to ten glasses of water each day. Flaxseed is a natural and well-tolerated laxative. Add two to four tablespoons to one cup of rice or other grain before cooking. Some cold cereals sold in the natural foods stores and some supermarkets contain flaxseed. Many fresh and dried fruits will increase bowel function. Prunes are the old standby. In any case, the normal pattern for bowel movements is highly variable. Most people on a starch-centered diet have one to three soft, large movements each day. However, movements may occur every two to three days and are not a sign of poor bowel function as long as they are soft and easy to pass. Frequency of bowel movement is highly dependent on the amount of food and water consumed each day.

Diarrhea or large, loose stools may be a temporary reaction from the sudden introduction of high-carbohydrate, high fiber foods, but adjustment occurs quickly. In some people this condition may result from excessive amounts of wheat, barley, or rye in the diet. Even small amounts of these grains can produce problems in a few people because of their sensitivity to gluten, a protein found in high concentration in these foods. The sensitivity, if serious, is known as celiac disease. If you have stayed on a health-supporting diet for a considerable time and then eat a rich food to which you are not accustomed, such as beef or cheese, you may experience a very unpleasant reaction marked by foul gases, stomach cramps, and diarrhea. Diarrhea from any cause will aggravate hemorrhoids and cause bleeding, pain, and itching. The best immediate treatment is to stop the diarrhea and soak the hemorrhoids in warm water at least twice a day. A health-supporting diet can bring almost overnight relief to people who suffer from diarrhea caused by the irritation of the colon by excess amounts of bile acids that reach the colon. This is a distressing and common problem in persons who have undergone a resection of the last part of their small intestine, the ileum, or have had a disease of the ileum, such as Crohn's disease.[16] Bile normally reabsorbed by the ileum passes into the colon, where it causes irritation and diarrhea.

Dizziness occurs frequently when people on blood pressure pills or other medication change their diet. You should see your physician often if you take such medicine and change your diet. You also may become dizzy when you stand quickly, because the blood runs from your head to your feet and legs. This is common and troublesome for people with diseased blood vessels that have lost the ability to constrict and prevent the blood from pooling in the legs. Be careful when standing up.

Dry skin occasionally occurs because this diet is very low in oils and fats. This can be a healthy condition, especially for those with acne. If the skin becomes too dry, you can use a lotion to moisturize it. Do not oil your skin from the inside!

Fatigue and weakness are reported by some people during the first week on the diet. In western societies meat has been associated incorrectly with strength. On a meat-free diet you may feel initially like you're missing something. You should be reassured by the experimental evidence that shows endurance can be as much as tripled when you have succeeded in changing from a meat- and cheese-centered diet to a starch-centered one. In one of the most optimistic studies done, bicyclists were able to increase their stamina by 300 percent when they switched their fuel from fat to carbohydrate.[17] Their "maximum work time" on an exercise bike went from 57 minutes to 167 minutes on the average. Actual weakness can be expected if you take in too few calories. This is easy to do if you're still eating the same size portions as before. A starch-centered diet is very low in calories. Eating more should quickly relieve weakness from this cause. Weakness is also common in people on medications such as blood pressure pills (especially with a group of medicines called beta blockers), diabetic medicines, and tranquilizers. Adjustment of the amounts of medicines to be taken is necessary under the direction of a physician.

Gout attacks can occur in a few people when they change their diet. Anyone with a history of gout, uric acid kidney stones, or high uric acid levels in the blood (hyperuricemia) runs the risk of developing a painful joint during the first two weeks of dietary change. This will not occur in people who do not have previous problems with uric acid. When a health-supporting diet low in uric acid precursors, called purines, is started, uric acid stored in body tissues begins to mobilize and can settle in the joints, causing an attack of arthritis. This same occurrence is seen with weight loss alone from any type of diet and when a drug for reducing elevated levels of uric acid, called allopurinol, is started. To prevent this painful condition, anyone suspected of having problems with uric acid may choose to take, under a doctor's supervision, 0.5 milligrams a day of colchicine for the first three to six months after beginning the new diet.

Headaches are often a symptom of withdrawal from a chemical or food in the diet. Withdrawal from caffeine will almost always result in a headache for several days. After one week most symptoms of withdrawal are over. The headaches are rarely severe enough to require more than a mild analgesic. Migraine headaches may be a result of such common food allergens as oranges or wheat.[18-19]

Hunger is a common complaint during the first few days. You should respond appropriately and eat some more. Starches are low in calories, so you can eat a lot and still maintain a trim weight. The quick return of hunger is well known on high-vegetable diets. Certainly you have heard the famous complaint about Chinese food: "I'm hungry an hour after I leave the table." The sensation of fullness you get from a starch-centered meal is different from that obtained from the great lump of muscle and fat that is served on the rich western diet. Soon you will adjust and find that starches, vegetables, and fruits are very satisfying without the indigestion so common after a high-fat meal.

Indigestion is common when raw onions, green peppers, cucumbers, and radishes are eaten. Cooking usually makes these foods more tolerable. Cabbage, both raw and cooked, bothers some people. Juices made from citrus fruits, tomatoes, pineapples, and apples are acidic and result in a burning sensation in the esophagus and stomach in many people.[20] Paradoxically, whole fruit and citrus fruit will relieve indigestion from various causes in many people. There are many other individual sensitivities to food. If you discover any, you should eliminate the offending foods from your diet. Hot peppers, ground peppers (chili, cayenne, white and black) and products prepared with these spices, such as kim chi, and Mexican chili salsa, can burn your intestinal tract from one end to the other. Be careful with them. On the western diet, fats, alcohol, and caffeine are the most frequent causes of indigestion. However, some foods on a health-supporting diet can cause unpleasant reactions in sensitive people. If you are a good observer and respond to your observations, you can quickly design the best diet for you from information no one else can appreciate—the way *you* feel after eating.

Rapid weight loss can be disturbing for some people. As much as ten pounds can be lost in the first week on a starch-centered diet. Much of this initial loss is water, because you are no longer eating as much salt and oil and therefore are retaining less fluid. Body fat is lost at the rate of two to five pounds per week in most overweight people. Weight loss stops once a trim body weight is attained. As you develop a taste for the new foods, you will be eating more and therefore losing less rapidly. Bread, and beans, are the higher-calorie starches and can slow down weight loss. If you are otherwise in good health, you can add rich plant foods to your diet for extra calories. Simple sugars such as dried fruits are better tolerated than high-fat plant foods.

Slow weight loss may be your problem. Are you following the diet strictly? If you are, you should use squash, potatoes, true yams, and corn as the starch center for your meals. Stay away from bread of all types, and possibly limit beans. Fruits should be limited to three per day. Green and yellow vegetables, such as celery, onions, carrots, lettuce, wax beans, green beans, and zucchini, are ideal for weight loss because of their very low calorie concentration. An active daily life and exercise will increase caloric expenditure and thereby hasten weight loss.

Triglycerides are fats found circulating in the blood. If a test tube of blood is allowed to sit overnight on the counter, a layer of fat will accumulate at the top by next morning, as with chicken soup left overnight in the refrigerator. Elevation of triglyceride levels have been associated with an increased risk of heart disease. However, this association may not be a direct involvement of triglycerides in the cause of this disease.[21] High levels of triglycerides will sludge the blood, increase coagulation of the blood, and cause insulin resistance. These factors result in health problems. Diets high in carbohydrates will raise triglycerides in some sensitive individuals. However, complex carbohydrate foods protected with generous amounts of fiber will prevent this elevation in most people and actually cause a drop in those who had elevated triglycerides before they began their new diet.[22] Populations in underdeveloped countries, who are living naturally on high-complex-carbohydrate diets, have low triglyceride levels.[23] Only after living for years on the wrong fuel—rich food—does the body lose its ability to regulate the metabolism of carbohydrates and triglycerides. The maximum elevation of triglycerides after a dietary change occurs in three to five weeks in sensitive individuals. Following this elevation almost all people by the end of eight months have returned to their initial levels. Simple sugars (even those found in fruits), alcohol, polyunsaturated fats and saturated fats, caffeine, and fiber-deficient refined foods will cause triglycerides to rise. Therefore, someone with elevated triglycerides should avoid these "foods" even to the point of completely avoiding fruits.

Frequent urination is common, especially during the first week, because of the low salt content of this diet. Also, fruits and vegetables are high in water content, which will yield more urine.

As you complete your dietary change and learn what it is like to feel really good every day, you will stop wondering how such a simple, obvious factor as diet could cause so much illness. Instead, you will find yourself appreciating the strength the human body has to call upon in order to survive and function as well as it does on the rich western diet.

You May Be One of Those Very Sensitive People

You may be one of those people who work very hard at maintaining a good diet most of the time but occasionally cheat a little, with disastrous results. Your cholesterol level goes up, you gain five pounds, or your bowels are not quite functioning right. You can't understand why this small amount of cheating has such a great effect; after all, you are eating so much better than you were before you changed your diet.

Some people actually do more cheating than they recognize or care to admit. Then there are those who really do only have an occasional harmful meal, and the results are worse than expected.

You may be one of those very sensitive people who can tolerate only health-supporting foods. The reason for this begins with the fact that you started out sick before you went on the diet. At that time you had exceeded the capacity of your body to compensate for the harmful foods you ate, and illness resulted. Because of all the years you spent overburdening your system with cholesterol, salt, fat, proteins, refined foods, and harmful chemicals, you have exhausted your reserves. Therefore, any little indiscretion will show up in a big penalty.

After months or years of proper eating and moderate exercise, your body should recover to where it can withstand a small insult of rich food without expressing signs of protest and symptoms of illness. If you make the change when you are ill , do it all the way, and don't be surprised if your cheating shows. Actually, we should consider ourselves fortunate that our bodies have put up with the abuses we've dealt them for as long as they have.

Adjustments in Medications

Among the main tools of the medical profession are drugs to treat almost every symptom and ailment. Medications often provide for a dependent relationship that keeps the patient returning to the doctor at regular intervals.

Most people will be able to discontinue altogether, or at least decrease, the use of prescription and nonprescription medications after a change in diet and lifestyle. However, adjustment and elimination of medication should be done *only* under the supervision of your physician. Furthermore, all people on medication who choose to change their diet and lifestyle should proceed only under the direction of a physician who is familiar with the interaction of foods and medication and with the body's responses to dietary change. Unfortunately, most physicians, unless they have taken a special interest in this approach to health care, do not have this ability. But things are rapidly changing.

Many people will still be taking medications during the early days of change and even after a complete dietary and lifestyle change medication may be needed by some people. As an extra precaution, in addition to your doctor's awareness, it is important for you to know the effect of food on the medications you take to avoid serious complications.

When foods are consumed along with medications, most often the rate of absorption into the body is decreased but not the amount of drug absorbed. This is commonly seen with antibiotics such as erythromycin, lincomycin, and penicillin, and with sulfadiazine and aspirin. Dairy products result in very poor absorption of the class of antibiotics called tetracyclines.

Some drugs are better absorbed when taken with food. These include lithium, riboflavin, tegretol, hydralazine, nitrofurantoin, Inderal, aldactone, and methoxsalen.

Dairy products, all types of vegetables, almonds, chestnuts, coconuts, and citrus fruits cause the urine to become alkaline (pH greater than 7.0). This causes acidic drugs (like aminoglycosides and nitrofurantoin, both antibiotics) to be excreted faster and alkaline drugs (such as imipramine and amitriptyline, both antidepressants) to remain in the body longer.

Beans, peas, lentils, meats, fish, and poultry are generally high in protein and, therefore, produce an acidic urine with effects on excretion of the medications opposite to those named above.

Certain medications are affected significantly by a change to a high-complex-carbohydrate, low-fat, low-protein, low-sodium diet such as the one recommended in this book. If you are taking any of these medicines, they probably will require adjustment.

Symptomatic medications are drugs used to control the symptoms of a disease process. Common symptoms for which medications are consumed include pain, fatigue, chronic diarrhea, constipation, and indigestion. Once the symptoms are relieved you will no longer need the medications, and they should be discontinued.

Antihypertensive (high blood pressure) medication will have to be lowered in dosage as your pressure corrects because you stop consuming salt, meats, saturated fat, and caffeine. Often, if the blood pressure problem is mild and only a single medication such as a diuretic is being used for treatment, the medication can be discontinued by the physician as soon as the diet is started. With more serious blood pressure problems the medications are reduced more slowly. Weekly blood pressure checks are usually adequate to assess the need to reduce the dosage. Fainting and dizziness associated with your change in diet will indicate a need for more frequent followup visits to your physician. In four to six weeks most blood pressure disorders have been corrected, and all blood pressure pills are stopped; then, less frequent followup is indicated. An ideal blood pressure is $110/70$ or less, taken at rest. Although it is not an ideal pressure, no medication is used when the pressure is below $160/104$ in most individuals.[24-26] Too aggressive reduction of blood pressure in severely hypertensive patients toward normal levels with medications has been associated with a five-fold increased risk of heart attack over those treated less vigorously.[27] Care must be taken whenever medication is used to treat a blood pressure problem. A considerable amount of judgment must be exercised by a physician when determining the need for each individual. Blood pressure medications are associated with serious side effects ranging from impotency, to growth of facial hair, to death. The benefit of medication has come under serious question because of recent findings that people with abnormalities on their EKG who take medication to control their blood pressure have a greater death rate from heart disease than those with the same pretreatment blood pressures who do not take medication.[28] One possible reason for this observation is that the diuretics used to treat hypertension cause an elevation of cholesterol, blood sugar, uric acid and triglyceride levels, which are factors associated with an increased risk of heart attacks.[29] The purchase of an inexpensive blood pressure cuff (sphygmomanometer) and stethoscope will allow you to follow your own pressure more closely and could save you a few visits to your doctor's office. The blood pressure you obtain at home when you are relaxed is often more indicative of your true state of health than one that is obtained under stressful conditions in a doctor's office. One additional point is that licorice in large amounts can also raise your blood pressure.

Insulin and oral hypoglycemic agents (diabetic pills) may need daily adjustment when you decrease the fat and increase the carbohydrate and fiber content of your diet. Hypoglycemia caused by the medicine may be a dangerous side effect of not lowering the dosage of insulin and diabetic pills rapidly enough. Childhood-type diabetics will not be able to stop their insulin. However, with this type of diabetes a change to a high-complex-carbohydrate diet can result in a reduction in insulin dosage of about 30 percent, and daily insulin requirements will become more stable (less brittle). Every effort should be made to discontinue diabetic pills because of the associated side effects, which include a doubling of the chance of suffering a fatal heart attack.[30] If one is not able to discontinue all medication for diabetes through a change in diet and lifestyle, then insulin would be a far safer choice for most people than diabetic pills. In most cases of the adult type of diabetes the indication for insulin therapy would be symptoms directly caused by the disease, such as frequent urination, excessive thirst, and uncontrollable weight loss. Theoretically, better control of blood sugar levels should forestall complications of diabetes. The best chance for a long, healthy life for an insulin-dependent diabetic would be with a health-supporting diet and multiple daily doses of regular insulin (instead of or in addition to long- or intermediate-acting insulin) to obtain best control of blood sugar.[31] A health-supporting diet contains the fewest of the disease-causing components that are commonly found in rich foods, including cholesterol, salt, fats, simple sugars, contaminants, and lack of fiber, and also offers the best nutrients for a diabetic.

Anticoagulants (Coumadin, Dicumarol, Panwarfin) interfere with the blood-clotting action of vitamin K.[32] These drugs often are used with the hope of preventing blood clots, heart attacks, and strokes by thinning the blood. Foods high in vitamin K, such as green tea, asparagus, broccoli, cabbage, kale, lettuce, spinach, turnip greens, and watercress, may inhibit the action of these drugs. The dosage must be adjusted by your physician, guided by appropriate blood tests.

Antifungal agent (griseofulvin) is better absorbed with high-fat foods. Your low-fat diet will decrease absorption.[32]

Bronchodilators (theophylline) will stay in your body longer and at a higher level on your new low-protein, high-carbohydrate diet. Your physician may need to lower your dosage to prevent side effects of nausea, tremor, and loss of appetite.

Cardiovascular drugs (quinidine) will be kept in the body longer on a diet that produces alkaline urine.[32] Higher levels may result and cause serious toxicity, including heart arrhythmias and death.

Antidepressants (lithium) are excreted less from the body on a low-salt diet. Therefore, lithium can become toxic when you lower your salt intake. Toxic effects include fatigue, weakness, slurred speech, and nausea. Appropriate lab tests will guide your physician to recommending the correct dosage on your new salt intake.

Antidepressants (monoamino oxidase inhibitors), when consumed with tyramine-containing foods such as brie, camembert, cheddar, and gruyere cheeses, yogurt, avocados, bananas, chocolate, canned figs, caviar, chicken liver, fava beans, pickled herring, sour cream, soy sauce, and beer and wine, can result in a dangerous elevation of your blood pressure.[32]

Cholesterol-lowering drugs can be discontinued shortly after the dietary change. The diet alone will cause in most people a marked reduction in levels of cholesterol and blood fats (triglycerides). Evaluation of blood cholesterol and triglycerides is recommended initially every three weeks for about three months, then every three to six months or less often.

Gout medication should be continued in persons on medication for about six months before discontinuing it, in order to avoid the slight possibility of precipitating a gouty arthritic attack. A diet change results in mobilization of uric acid stores found in the body and allows this uric acid to settle in a joint and to cause severe pain. To avoid a gout attack, some physicians may choose to place patients with elevated uric acid levels or a history of gout on a medicine called colchicine during the first six months of the diet change. This recommendation for colchicine should apply only to an occasional person with strong tendency to gout.

Blood tests and blood pressure measurements are often used to determine the new dosage of medication you require. This should be done under supervision of a qualified physician familiar with the effects of foods on your health. There are few, if any, adverse or damaging effects from making the change to a health-supporting diet. Concurrent use of medication is the primary exception to this general statement of safety.

Notes

[1] A. Kurtha, "The Nutritional, Clinical, and Economic Aspects of Vegan Diets," *Pl Fds Hum Nutr* 2 (1970): 13.

[2] M. Hardinge, "Nonflesh Diets—Historical Background," *J Am Diet Assoc* 43 (1963): 545.

[3] W. James, *Psychology: The Briefer Course*. New York: Harper Torch Books, 1961, pp. 1–17.

[4] P. Isenberg, "Nitrites, nitrosamines and cancer." *Fed Proc* 35 (1976): 1322.

[5] Comptroller General on the United States, Report to the Congress, "Problems in Preventing the Marketing of Raw Meat and Poultry Containing Potentially Harmful Residues," GA 1.13, HRD 79-10, April 17, 1979.

[6] M. Enig, "Dietary Fat and Cancer Trends—A Critique," *Fed Proc* 37 (1978): 2215.

[7] R.Egeberg, "Report to the Secretary of HEW from the Medical Advisory Group on Cyclamates," *JAMA* 211 (1970): 1358.

[8] "Saccharin and Its Salts Proposed Rule Making," *Fed Reg* 42 (April 15, 1977): 19996–20010.

[9] W. MacDonald, "Histological Effect of Certain Pickles on the Human Gastric Mucosa: A Preliminary Report," *Can Med Ass J* 96 (1967): 1521.

[10] Department of Health, Education, and Welfare, FDA 21CF Report 133, *Fed Reg* 38 (1973): 27074.

[11] R. Merliss, "Talc-Treated Rice and Japanese Stomach Cancer," *Science* 173 (1971): 1141.

[12] W. Lijinsky, "Benzo(o)pyrene and Other Polynuclear Hydrocarbons in Charcoal-Broiled Meat," *Science* 145 (1974): 53.

[13] W. Siess, "Platelet–Membrane Fatty Acids, Platelet Aggregation, and Thromboxane Formation during Mackerel Diet," *Lancet* 1 (1980): 441.

[14] D. Marthinsen, "Excretion of Breath and Flatus Gases by Humans Consuming High-Fiber Diets," *J Nutr* 112 (1982): 1133.

[15] J. Cummings, "Fermentation in the Human Large Intestine: Evidence and Implications for Health," *Lancet* 1 (1983): 1206.

[16] H. Andersson, "Fat-Reduced Diet in the Symptomatic Treatment of Small Bowel Disease," *Gut* 15 (1974): 351.

[17]P. Astrand, "Something Old and Something New . . . Very New," *Nutrition Today* (June 1968): 9.

[18]E. Grant, "Food Allergies and Migraines," *Lancet* 1 (1979): 966.

[19]E. Hanington, "Diet and Migraine," *J Hum Nutr* 34 (1980): 175.

[20]S. Price, "Food Sensitivity in Reflux Esophagitis," *Gastroenterology* 75 (1978): 240.

[21]S. Hulley, "Epidemiology as a Guide to Clinical Decisions, the Association between Triglyceride and Coronary Heart Disease," *N Engl J Med* 302 (1980): 1383.

[22]J. Anderson, "Plant Fiber, Carbohydrate, and Lipid Metabolism," *Am J Clin Nutr* 32 (1979): 346.

[23]A. Antonis, "The Influence of Diet on Serum Triglycerides in South African White and Bantu Prisoners," *Lancet* 1 (1961): 3.

[24]N. McAlister, "Should We Treat Mild Hypertension?" *JAMA* 249 (1983): 379.

[25]"Therapy of Mild Hypertension—Toward a Balanced View," *JAMA* 249 (1983): 365.

[26]Editorial, "Treatment of Mild Hypertension and the Reduction of Cardiovascular Mortality: The "Of or By" Dilemma," *JAMA* 249 (1983): 399.

[27]I. Stewart, "Relation of Reduction in Blood Pressure to First Myocardial Infarction in Patients Receiving Treatment for Severe Hypertension," *Lancet* 1 (1979): 861.

[28]"Multiple Risk Factor Intervention Trial," *JAMA* 248 (1982): 1465.

[29]R. Grimm, "Effects of Thiazide Diuretics on Plasma Lipids and Lipoproteins in Mildly Hypertensive Patients," *Ann Intern Med* 94 (1981): 7.

[30]M. Goldner, Effects of hypoglycemic agents on vascular complications in patients with adult-onset diabetes. III. Clinical implications of the UGDP results. *JAMA* 218:1400, 1971.

[31]R. Holman, "Prevention of Deterioration of Renal and Sensory-Nerve Function by More Intensive Management of Insulin-Dependent Diabetic Patients, a two-year randomized prospective study" *Lancet* 1 (1983): 204.

[32]P. Lamy, "How your patients' diet can affect drug response." *Drug Therapy* (August 1980): 82.

CHAPTER

16

Getting The Kitchen Set Up

How to Begin

1. Sit down with members of your household who are beginning the diet. Talk about recipes you would like to try. Incorporate these into your weekly menu plan.
2. Plan your menu for the week. Choose recipes that sound familiar and contain some ingredients that you or your family are accustomed to. Keep your meal plan simple.
3. Make a shopping list from this menu plan. Many of the ingredients can be purchased in supermarkets, although for some things you will need to go to a natural food store. If you are not familiar with a good natural food store, read over the section on such stores later in this chapter, and be prepared to spend some extra time looking for the right place.
4. Make a large pot of soup if you have the time and ingredients. Soups are familiar to most people and may be helpful in beginning the diet plan. They may be used to supplement meals, as between-meal snacks, as fillings for pita bread, served over rice or potatoes, or even as substitutes for the more conventional kind of breakfast. If you pack your lunches, it is easy to take soup along in a thermos container.

5. Prepare an assortment of fresh raw vegetables such as carrots, celery, radishes, cucumber, zucchini, broccoli, and daikon. Store these "munchies" in water in the refrigerator.

6. Use plain frozen vegetables found in the supermarket to supplement your daily meal plan. They are easy to prepare and usually are well liked by everyone. This will leave you more time to prepare your main dish.

7. Bake or boil ten potatoes—white, sweet, or yams—for each person beginning the diet. Store them in the refrigerator. These are good for snacks between meals or as added vegetables at mealtimes. They are easy to carry along for a meal or a snack away from the home. A large potato and a fruit can serve as a complete meal. They may be eaten plain, seasoned with pure vegetable seasonings (Vegit, Lush 'n' Lemon, Hidden Valley), chili salsa, oil-free dressing, or leftover soups or sauces.

8. Cook a pot of brown rice every day or two. This easily prepared starch may be added to meals or eaten between meals. Serve plain or seasoned with pure vegetable seasonings or low-sodium tamari. Leftover soups, sauces, and vegetable dishes make delicious toppings for rice.

9. Serving frequent meals offering a wide variety of foods often helps during the early period of adjustment.

10. Don't get discouraged. It takes time to change lifelong tastes and habits. Your rewards will be the most interesting and tasty meals you've ever eaten—along with a dramatic improvement in your health. Within three to six weeks most individuals and families are well accustomed to a starch-centered diet and are enjoying it too!

Your Stock List

Suggested amounts are given below. Buy in small amounts at first until you know what you like. Options are indicated by asterisks.

Cookware: Glass, porcelain, stainless steel, ceramic, cast iron, Silverstone, silicone-coated bakeware.

Grains and flours

Barley (1 lb.)
Brown rice (5–10 lbs), long and short grains

*Arrowroot (1 lb.)
*Millet (1 lb.)
 Whole wheat flour (5 lbs.)
 Whole wheat pastry flour (2 lbs.)
*Brown rice flour (1 lb.)
*Barley flour (1 lb.)
*Garbanzo flour (1 lb.)
*Bulgur wheat (1 lb.)
 Cornmeal (2 lbs.)
*Wheat berries (1 lb.)
*Buckwheat flour (1 lb.)

Whole grain cereal products

*Cold cereals (no sweeteners, no oils, many contain salt, some contain BHA and BHT in the packaging material): Grape Nuts, Shredded Wheat, Nutri-Grain, Uncle Sam, puffed cereals, (rice, wheat, millet, corn), Crispy Brown Rice, oil-free granola
Hot cereals (no sweeteners, no oils); oatmeal, Zoom, Roman Meal, 4-Grain Cereal Mates, Hot Apple Granola, Bearmush, Wheatena, cracked wheat
*Flakes   oats, wheat, rye, barley, triticale

Whole grain pasta

 Spaghetti (whole wheat, spinach)
 Macaroni (whole wheat, spinach, vegetable, corn)
*Buckwheat noodles (soba, made with buckwheat and wheat flour)
*Corn pasta (no wheat)
*Lasagna (whole wheat, spinach)

Crackers, breads (no oil, no sweeteners)

*Sprouted wheat bread (Essene or Wayfarer's)
 Whole wheat pita bread
*Corn tortillas (not fried), found in frozen or chilled foods section, made with cornmeal, water, and lime
 Chapati (whole wheat, frozen)
 Whole wheat bread (no oil, no sugar)
*Rice cakes (plain, puffed brown rice)
*Whole wheat flatbread (Palaoa)

*Ryekrisp (natural, unseasoned)
*Wasa bröd

Beans, peas, and lentils (legumes)

*Black beans (1 lb.)
*Garbanzos (1 lb.)
 Kidney beans (2 lbs.)
 Lentils (1 lb.)
*Lima Beans (1 lb.)
*Pink beans (1 lb.)
 Pinto beans (2 lbs.)
 Split green peas (1 lb.)
*Split mung beans (1 lb.)
*Split yellow peas (1 lb.)
 White beans (2 lbs.)

Seeds and beans for sprouting

*Alfalfa (½ lb.)
*Mung (½ lb.)
*Specials: radish, mustard, wheat berries, sunflower, lentils,
 whole green peas, adzuki beans, red clover, etc.

Root Vegetables

 Carrots (2 lbs.)
*Daikon (2 lbs.)
 Onions (3 lbs.)
 Potatoes (5 lbs.)
*Garlic (1 head)
*Sweet potatoes (3 lbs.)
*Yams (3 lbs.)
*Turnips (2 lbs.)

Seasonings: bottled and packaged products

*Active dry yeast (8 ozs.)
*Nutritional yeast (contains B vitamins rich in B_{12} when fortified),
 to be added at end of cooking (8 ozs.)
 Tamari, natural soy sauce (16 ozs.), salt-reduced type (Kikkoman
 Milder Soy Sauce, Soken Shoyu)
 Pure vegetable seasoning, no salt (Vegit, Hidden Valley, or
 Lush 'n' Lemon)

*Vanilla extract
*Carob powder (unsweetened)
*Tabasco sauce
*Bragg's Liquid Aminos (no wheat, high salt)
*Egg replacer (Ener G), not an egg substitute but a blend of refined
    flours used for binding and leavening only
*Dried shiitake mushrooms
*Seaweed (kombu, salty)
  Vinegar (apple cider)
*Agar-agar (for gelling)
*Tapioca
*Baking powder
*Baking soda
*Cornstarch (for thickening)

*Spices

Allspice	Italian seasoning blend
Basil leaves	Marjoram leaves
Bay leaves	Mustard (ground)
Cayenne pepper	Nutmeg
Celery seed	Onion powder
Chervil	Oregano (ground)
Chili powder (no salt)	Oregano leaves
Cinnamon	Paprika
Cloves (ground)	Parsley flakes
Coriander (ground)	Rosemary
Cumin (ground)	Sage
Curry powder	Tarragon leaves
Dill weed	Thyme
Garlic powder	Turmeric
Ginger (ground)	

Some spices are irritating to the intestinal tract when used in large
amounts, especially in sensitive people. These include allspice,
cinnamon, curry powder, cayenne pepper, black and white pepper,
chili powder, ginger and nutmeg. Cinnamon is also a common cause
of food allergy. Use these spices with caution.

Canned Foods

These should be avoided as much as possible. They usually contain
additives to preserve color and flavor. All but a very few contain at

least salt. Because they are not fresh, canned foods preserved by the heating process lose many vitamins. Canned fruits are often peeled, which removes a lot of the fiber. The cans, which usually are made of steel or tin, leach out dangerous metals, especially lead found in the seams, into the food.[1-3]

In their favor, canned foods are convenient and often a lot cheaper than fresh; this is especially true of tomatoes and other fruits out of season. You can find canned products without sugar or oil easily. If you are not on a severely salt-restricted diet, the small amount of salt in most products will be acceptable. As a general rule, canned products in your diet should be limited to less than one canned product per day.

Be sure to read the labels carefully. You will find that the following brand-name canned products contain the least additives, (no sugar, dextrose, sweeteners, oil).

Tomatoes, whole, not stewed (Contadina, Hunt's, Del Monte, Town House)
Tomato paste (Contadina, Hunt's, Del Monte, Town House)
Tomato puree (Contadina, 6 in 1)
Tomato sauce (Contadina, Town House)
*Mexican-type chili sauce, hot or mild, no additives (Ortega, Pure & Simple, Pace)
*Beans (Ashley's)
*Ketchup (Hain, Johnson's)
*Pasta sauce (Westbrae, Johnson's)
*Green Chilis (Ortega, Ashley's)
Tomato juice
*V-8 juice
*Oil-free salad dressings (Hain, El Molino)

Perishables

All types of vegetables
All kinds of sprouts
All types of fruits

Frozen Foods

Vegetables (plain, with no salt, sweetener, or sauces)
Fruits (unsweetened)
Pure lemon juice (Minute Maid)

*Bottled water (less than 10 mg sodium per 8-oz. glass)

Canada Dry Seltzer Pure Sparkling
Poland Spring Sparkling Pure Natural Mineral
Perrier Naturally Sparkling Mineral
Vittelloise Natural Spring
Bartlett Mineral Spring Sparkling
Sheffield's O₂ Sparking Spring
Deer Park Sparkling 100% Spring
Safeway Bel-Air Sparkling Mineral

Read labels carefully so you don't get a high-sodium water from the same company; for example, Canada Dry Club Soda has 44 mg sodium per serving, but Canada Dry Seltzer Pure Sparkling has 1 mg sodium per serving.

*Herb Teas

Celestial Seasonings
Mandarin Orange Spice
Cinnamon Rose
Country Apple
Grandma's Tummy Mint
Iced Delight
Mint Iced Delight
Orange Iced Delight
Mellow Mint
MO's 24
Pelican Punch
Peppermint
Red Zinger
Roastaroma
Sleepytime
Spearmint
Lemon Mist
Almond Sunset
Lemon Iced Delight

Lipton
Quietly Chamomile
Almond Pleasure
Gentle Orange
Toasty Spice

Magic Mountain
Sweet Apple Spice
Sweet Cinnamon Spice
Sweet Almond
Morning Sun
Sweet Orange Spice
Peppermint Spice

*Optional Rich Food (Category III)

Tofu (1 tub)
Malt syrup
Pure honey (1 lb.)

Maple syrup
Cold-pressed vegetable oil (safflower, used for lightly oiling pans if
   necessary)
Unsulphured molasses
Unsweetened applesauce
Raw cashews or almonds (1 lb.)
Fruit juices (unsweetened)
Fruit purees (Whole Earth unsweetened spread, Westbrae un-
   sweetened spread)
Raisins
Currants
Mustard
Miso (salty)

Utensils

1 large mixing bowl
2 medium mixing bowls
muffin tin
large baking dish (9" x 13")
8" square baking dish
9" deep pie plate
2 large bread pans (9" x 5" x 3")
colander/strainer
large soup pot
blender
medium fry pan (Silverstone)
griddle (Silverstone)
2 medium saucepans
large saucepan with lid
2 medium saucepans with lids
steamer basket

medium casserole dish with lid
large casserole dish with lid
sprouting jars and lids
grater
potato–bean masher
garlic press
wire whisk
several wooden spoons
bread knife
vegetable knife
vegetable brush
rubber spatula
1 or 2 pizza pans
2 large baking sheets
storage containers for leftovers

**Optional utensils*

food mill/grinder
pressure cooker
crock pot/slow cooker
wok
double boiler
hot-air popcorn popper
silicone-coated baking pans
   (Baker's Secret)

rice cooker
toaster
electric mixer
food processor
large canning pot with steamer
ginger grater

Herbs

Herbs are plants or parts of plants used for the purpose of medicinal treatment, nutritional value, food seasoning, coloring, or dying of other substances. Teas made from herbs contain pharmacologically active substances that can have both beneficial and adverse effects on your health. Herbal medicine can be an effective form of therapy when used in the right circumstances. Usually only the use of large amounts of herbs in the form of herbal teas will lead to problems. This section is intended only to point out some of the ingredients the shopper should be aware of when choosing a tea. Some of the more important ingredients that might be harmful include the following:[4-11]

Aloe: Causes diarrhea.

Bracken fern: Contains high levels of tannin, which causes cancer in rats. Tannin is present in many teas, sorghum, grapes, wine, and betel nuts.

Buckthorn: Causes diarrhea.

Burdock: Has anticholinergic effects, which include dry mouth, dilated pupils, and a slowed heart rate.

Catnip: Has anticholinergic effects, which include dry mouth, dilated pupils, and a slowed heart rate.

Chamomile teas: May cause severe allergic reaction (anaphylactic reactions have been reported) in a few individuals who are also allergic to ragweed, asters, or chrysanthemums.

Coffee: Contains methylxanthines, which include caffeine, theophylline, and theobromine, and which have many effects including elevating blood pressure and fibrocystic breast disease.

Comfrey tea: Contains pyrolizidine alkaloids, which are toxic to the liver. Some of these alkaloids have caused liver cancer in rat studies.

Dandelion tea: Is a mild and probably harmless diuretic.

Dock: Causes diarrhea.

Foxglove tea: Contains digitalis, which can have toxic effects on the heart and gastrointestinal tract.

Ginseng: Is a mild stimulant and gives a feeling of well-being. Long-term overuse can cause high blood pressure and have steroid-like effects and a strong estrogen effect.

Golden rod: Causes allergic reactions in sensitive people.

Horsetail plants: Has poisonous effects on the nervous system.

Hydrangeas: Has anticholinergic effects. (See *Burdock* above.)

Jimson weed: Has anticholinergic effects. (See *Burdock* above.)
Juniper: Has anticholinergic effects. (See *Burdock* above.)
Juniper berries: Have diuretic effects and can cause irritation of the intestines.
Licorice: In large amounts can cause irritation of the intestine, and high blood pressure.
Marigold: Causes allergic reactions in sensitive people.
Mistletoe: May cause liver disease and hepatitis.
Quack grass: Is a mild and probably harmless diuretic.
Sassafras tea: Is a mild stimulant. There is serious concern because it contains a very strong carcinogen called safrole. Safrole also can inhibit certain liver enzyme systems, which can lead to secondary toxicity from other drugs usually metabolized by these enzymes.
Senna: Causes diarrhea.
Shave grass: Has a poisonous effect on the nervous system.
"Teas": Most green and black teas contain methylxanthines, which include caffeine, theophylline, and theobromines. They also contain tannin, which has been linked to cancer.
Yarrow: Causes allergic reactions in sensitive people.

Tamari or Soy Sauce?

Tamari and soy sauce are similar products usually made from wheat, soy, salt, and water. They do contain sodium and therefore should not be used indiscriminately. One tablespoon of tamari or soy sauce contains approximately 800 milligrams of sodium. It is possible to buy both tamari and soy sauce in a salt-reduced variety, and this is recommended. The salt-reduced version contains approximately 500 milligrams of sodium per tablespoon.

Tamari is usually found in natural food stores. Many brands are available. Soy sauce is usually found in supermarkets. Most commercial soy sauces are made with added chemicals, preservatives, and artificial colors. Monosodium glutamate (MSG) is almost always found in commercial soy sauces. Kikkoman makes the most acceptable product, which is a salt-reduced variety of soy sauce and contains no MSG.

Tamari: Made from wheat, whole soybeans, sea salt, and water. The wheat is washed, parched, and ground, then steamed and mixed with cooked soy beans. It is innoculated with a preferred fungus and allowed to incubate for three days. Then it is mixed with salt brine and put into wooden vats, where it ages for at least fifteen months. It is pressed, and then the fluid is pasteurized for the minimum required time and put into bottles to be sold. No preservatives are added.

Kikkoman soy sauce: Made from wheat, defatted soy grits, salt and water. The wheat is washed, parched, and ground, and then steamed and mixed with cooked soy grits. It is innoculated with a preferred fungus and allowed to incubate for three days. Then it is mixed with salt brine and put into stainless steel holding tanks, where it is aged for six months. It is pressed, the fluid is pasteurized, and it is put into bottles to be sold. Sodium benzoate is added to the regular soy sauce as a preservative. It is not added to the low-salt soy sauce.

Wheat-free soy sauce: Available and helpful for anyone who has an allergy to wheat and must be on a wheat-free diet. Bragg's Liquid Aminos is one brand; another is Wheat-Free Tamari.

Reading Labels for a Starch-Centered Diet

An essential skill for shopping in grocery and natural food stores is the ability to read labels. Food labels are inadequate, confusing, and often deceptive. To stand a chance, you need to develop skills at label reading so you can shop successfully for health-supporting foods.

Food labels all contain the following:

1. Name of the product
2. Net contents or weight
3. Name and address of the producer.

Most foods by law also must contain a list of ingredients. However, many foods have a "recipe formula" established by the FDA that describes specific ingredients in a standardized food, such as canned fruit, canned vegetables, bread, flours, ice cream, and cheese, to name only a few. These standardized ingredients do not have to be listed, or a manufacturer can selectively list ingredients to make the product appear free of chemicals.

Labels on foods that do not have a standard identity must list ingredients. The major ingredient by weight is listed first, followed by other ingredients in descending order.

A very tricky practice of food manufacturers is the use of the terms "pure," "natural," or "wholesome" to describe their products.

These deceptions have little, if any, value for identifying a food as health-supporting. Or they may add such phrases as "no cholesterol," "no added sugar," or "no preservatives." Such labels tell you what is not contained but do not tell you what harmful ingredients are contained.

Simple sugars found in the ingredients are listed as sugar, brown sugar, dextrose, sucrose, fructose, maltose, corn syrup, malt, honey, molasses, and natural sweeteners. Dextrinization is a prolonged, low-heat cooking process that breaks down complex carbohydrates into simpler sugars. This is why sprouted wheat breads taste sweet.

Fats and oils are described as fat, animal fat, lard, oil, vegetable oils, vegetable shortenings (which are hydrogenated), hydrogenated oils, and partially hydrogenated oils. Specific oils may be listed, such as olive oil, safflower oil, or corn oil. This phrase may appear in the ingredients: "May contain soybean oil, cottonseed oil, or palm oil." This gives the manufacturer the opportunity to use whichever oil is least expensive to buy when the product is made.

Many preservatives are used in all kinds of foods. Their names are difficult to remember, much less to pronounce. When you have a choice, it is best to avoid them. Nature has provided whole foods with protective coverings, vitamins, and enzymes, which preserve their freshness.

Flavorings can be listed individually or may be found only as "artificial flavorings" or "natural flavorings." Adding them is really unnecessary, since foods naturally have a wonderful range of enjoyable tastes. Cyclamates, and saccharin should be strictly avoided. They are suspected as being causes of cancer.

You should periodically check the labels of foods you regularly buy, since the ingredients may be changed from time to time.

As a general rule, you should keep your foods as nature made them and avoid multiple ingredients that may be difficult for the body to digest and defend itself against. Health-supporting meal plans should be kept simple. Natural foods are well designed for our nutritional requirements and enjoyment.

Select Your Natural Food Store Carefully

After you have taken maximum advantage of the low prices and convenience of your local supermarket, then you need to find a genuine natural food store. Distinguish this from the "health food store," which specializes in selling vitamins, "healthy" candy bars, and protein powders, instead of whole food and recommended condiments.

When you are looking for a natural food store, your initial concerns may be the price of the merchandise and the convenience of the location. However, these should be lesser considerations, since you probably will buy only a small number of products every two to three weeks.

The store should be neat, clean, well stocked, and busy. Products will not be fresh if the turnover is slow. Spoiled food loses vitamins, has rancid oils, and contains molds, some of which produce poisons called aflatoxins. Aflatoxins are potent carcinogens causing liver cancer in experimental animals and probably also in humans. These powerful liver-damaging compounds are produced by a fungus called *Aspergillus flavus*. Infection of crops, such as peanuts and grains, can occur during improper harvesting and storage conditions and is more common in tropical and subtropical areas.[12] A flour mill in the store is important so that your grains can be ground at the time of purchase to ensure freshness.

Your store will be a source of education on health and foods. Determine early where the management's interests lie. There is no lack of free advice to be obtained from the salespersons. Most of these people are sincere and very enthusiastic. Salespeople should be helpful and willing to answer your questions. A store with a large variety of foods and accessories for preparing them will give you an opportunity to learn about many new items.

The store you choose should carry a selection of books that generally reflect attitudes toward whole foods, moderate exercise, sunshine, and relief of mental stress. Emphasis on vitamin pills, protein powders, and enemas should tell you that you're in the wrong place.

Your natural food store can serve as a referral center to doctors, dentists, and other health professionals and nonprofessionals. You may want to ask about their community interest in issues that directly affect you and your family, such as school lunches, local use of pesticides in agriculture, and preventive medicine.

Your selection of a natural food store could be one of the most important decisions you make. Try several before deciding upon one.

Cookware

Pots and pans should be made of a material that does not come off in the food. Porcelain and glass are excellent. Metals such as aluminum, copper, iron, and stainless steel leach out into the foods being cooked. The levels of these metals can become high enough to cause illness. Aluminum is the most toxic and least desirable material for cookware. Iron and copper are actually essential trace elements necessary for good health. Therefore, small amounts of these leached into the foods during cooking may be beneficial. However, excessive amounts of these metals also can be very harmful. Rarely will copper, iron, and steel cookware become a problem, even with everyday use.

Therefore, we recommend for general purposes cookware made of glass, porcelain, copper, iron, and stainless steel.

Foods frequently stick to pots and pans. Because of this problem, small compromises are made in our general health principles. A very light coating of safflower oil or other pure "cold-pressed" vegetable oil can be used on bakeware to prevent sticking. Place a small amount of oil on a paper towel and wipe baking dishes before using. Cast iron pans and woks should be coated with oil before their first use and then "seasoned" by heating. When cleaning up, do not wash with soap; scrub stubborn areas with a stiff brush and hot water, then simply wipe the surfaces with a paper towel. The seasoned cooking surface lasts when soap and detergent are avoided, so repeated coats of oil are needed only rarely.

A second compromise is to use synthetic coatings, such as Teflon, Silverstone, and silicone-coated bakeware like Baker's Secret. If you purchase a quality utensil or appliance, then the surface should stay attached to the base and not end up in your food. A light oiling when you first get a Teflon or Silverstone griddle or waffle iron will help further to prevent sticking. Clean with a brush and water; do not use soap.

Food Storage

Starches, vegetables, and fruits keep much better than animal products. Dried beans, peas, and lentils keep well in airtight jars without refrigeration. They rarely are attacked by bugs because their outer skin is so tough. Brown rice and other whole grains will keep well with only a little more care. They also should be stored in airtight jars and put in a cool, dry place. The best place to keep them would be in the refrigerator, if you have the space. Milled grains, such as wheat flour, rolled oats, and cornmeal, should be stored in the refrigerator if you plan to keep them longer than two weeks.

Root vegetables, such as potatoes, sweet potatoes, carrots, and onions, last for months in cool, dry places. If you do not have a cool, dry place to store your root vegetables, buy them in small amounts to last about two weeks. Store carrots in the refrigerator. Potatoes and onions should not need refrigeration; however, do not store potatoes and onions together, because a chemical reaction occurs that hastens spoilage. Winter squashes also keep well without refrigeration. Most other vegetables, such as lettuce, green onions, celery, zucchini, mushrooms, and sprouts, must be stored in the refrigerator and used within a short time.

Fruits can be allowed to ripen without refrigeration. After ripening, they should be eaten as soon as possible to prevent spoilage. Buy only enough for about seven to ten days at one time. Refrigeration slows ripening and does prevent spoilage.

Refrigeration greatly increases the shelf life of all of your vegetable foods. A cool, dry basement can be a good place to store beans, grains, and root vegetables for long periods.

Proper storage of leftovers, cooked beans, and grains can save you time in preparation of future meals. Most leftovers freeze well. When freezing, plan ahead and leave arrowroot or cornstarch out of the recipe. Add these later when you reheat. This will prevent lumps from forming in the reheated foods. You can plan ahead and make extra servings, then freeze these in smaller amounts to use for another meal, as a topping for potatoes, or as a sandwich spread.

Cooked beans and grains also freeze well in two to three cups or larger amounts. Plan ahead and save cooking time later.

After cooking beans or potatoes you can save the leftover water in a large container in the freezer. Add more liquid whenever you have leftover vegetable cooking water. Then use this liquid for vegetable stock when needed.

For short-term storage of certain products, airtight containers are recommended. Here are some suggested uses:

1. Cereal products (oatmeal, Hot Apple Granola, cracked wheat, puffed cereals)
2. Pasta products
3. Crisp corn tortillas, pita, or crackers
4. Bags of different herb teas
5. Dried fruit

Good airtight storage containers are:

1. Canning jars with attached lids
2. Large glass jars with screw-on lids
3. Glass jars with cork tops
4. Glass or plastic cannister sets with tight-fitting tops
5. Plastic storage containers like Tupperware

Notes

[1] Food and Drug Administration, "Lead in food," *Federal Reg* 44 (1979): 51233.

[2] D. Settle, "Lead in Albacore: Guide to Lead Pollution in Americans," *Science* 207 (1980): 1167.

[3] M. Johnson, "Effects of Dietary Tin on Tin and Calcium Metabolism of Adult Males," *Am J Clin Nutr* 35 (1982): 655.

[4] "Toxid Reactions to Plant Products Sold in Health Food Stores," *Medical Letter* 21 (1979): 29.

[5] A. Pamukcu, "Carcinogenicity of Tannin and Tannin-Free Extracts of the Bracken Fern *(Pteridium Aquilinum)* in Rats," *JNCI* 65 (1980): 131.

[6] J. Morton, "Is There a Safer Tea?" *Morris Arboretum Bulletin* 26 (1975): 24.

[7] A. Mattocks, "Toxic Pyrrolizidine Alkaloids in Comfrey," *Lancet* 2 (1980): 1136.

[8] E. Dickstein, "Foxglove Tea Poisoning," *Am J Med* 69 (1980): 167.

[9] R. Siegel, "Ginseng Abuse Syndrome—Problems with the Panacea," *JAMA* 241 (1979): 1614.

[10] J. Harvey, "Mistletoe Hepatitis," *Br Med J* 282 (1981): 186.

[11] A. Segelman, "Sassafras and Herb Tea—Potential Health Hazards," *JAMA* 236 (1976): 477.

[12] J. Miller, "Carcinogens Occurring Naturally in Foods," *Fed Proc* 35 (1976): 1316.

CHAPTER

17

Making Your Health-Supporting Diet Successful

Introducing New Foods to the Family

Learning to like new foods takes time. If you're trying to change the eating habits of all of the members of your family, don't rush them. Introduce your family to a new, healthy recipe at least once a week. Soon they will enjoy the variety.

When others are not eating the same dishes as you are, persuade them to try your new recipe as a side dish. In this way they'll develop new tastes. If you're eating spaghetti, serve their meatballs separately. A chicken breast for them, added to the fried rice you've prepared for yourself, will make your fried rice dinner seem almost complete to those who are not ready to change. Later you can decrease the size of the meat portion being served or "accidentally" forget it altogether.

Encourage everyone at the table at least to try every new dish that's been prepared.

Choose recipes with familiar ingredients, ones you know your family enjoys, such as oatmeal for breakfast, soups for lunch, and spaghetti for dinner. Later you can add dishes made with unfamiliar ingredients.

Have at least one food at the table that everyone will eat, perhaps rice, potatoes, or bread. Be assured that, with a fruit and a vegetable added, these simple starch foods are nutritionally adequate even for the young. Proper balancing for good nutrition occurred with the creation and growth of the foods long before they arrived on your table.

If at first the members of your family won't eat a variety of new foods, don't worry. Let them choose the things they like, as often as they like, as long as they follow the principles of the diet.

For young children, you may find it helpful to blend certain foods into palatable mixtures, such as soups, stews, or spaghetti sauce. Vegetables are less frightening in this form. But, because blending disrupts some of the natural fibers, it's best nutritionally to eat unblended foods.

Be sure to provide the family with nutritious snack foods, such as fresh fruits, fresh vegetables, dried fruits, frozen juice popsicles, whole grain crackers, and breadsticks.

Hunger is an excellent persuader for developing new tastes. If family members aren't eating what you serve for dinner, could they have been filling themselves on snacks all afternoon? You can't imagine how good the new foods will taste after they've skipped a meal or two—or the snacks.

This may seem obvious, but be sure to have only health-supporting foods available in the house.

Going out to eat in restaurants is an expensive habit that you need to break except for very special occasions.

If every member of your family understands the importance of proper nutrition, success in making the change will be assured. Education is imperative.

Children especially need to be educated, not forced into dietary change. When they are younger than six years, you can quietly replace the junk food without much objection from them. They already will have favorites that are healthy for them, such as fruits, whole grain cereals, whole wheat bread, potatoes, rice, soups, and spaghetti. All you need to do is emphasize these. They may complain a little when they don't find the junk in your cupboards or refrigerator, but they adjust quickly. In effect, you are educating them by promoting the development of their taste for wholesome foods and thereby allowing them to lose the taste for rich foods.

Food preferences are established more strongly in older children. They will need more help in making the change. You will need to teach them by giving more scientific information concerning the harmful effects of rich foods. In addition, politely point out the effects of the rich foods that you have observed in their young bodies, such as pimples, oily skin, plumpness, tiredness, lack of endurance, and constipation.

If you have assumed the role of leader in your family, you will find that providing a proper diet is one of the most important of your many responsibilities to your children.

Seasoning Foods

Our usual reaction to foods that are unfamiliar is instant dislike or, at the least, a sniffing wariness. The foods recommended in this diet plan are different from the typical meals most westerners have grown up on. It is expected that, initially, few people will find all of these recommended recipes enjoyable. However, as you become familiar with the recipes suggested in this meal plan, you will learn to like most of them. Keep this clearly in mind as you are making the change to health-supporting foods.

As you begin to change, choose foods that you already enjoy. For example, mashed or baked potatoes are favorites for many people. Most often they are presented as side dishes. The change places them at the heart and center of your meal, displacing the health-damaging rich foods. By using a starch as the center, you will easily be able to organize a satisfying and healthy meal around brown rice, corn, sweet potatoes, pasta, or whole wheat bread.

Hot cereals, such as oatmeal or cracked wheat, are familiar breakfast foods. Adding a little extra water and some fruit and spices for extra flavor makes them very tasty.

Soups are made mostly of vegetables, even in a rich diet. By leaving out the meat and the fats and adjusting the flavoring, you can produce a soup that is not much different in taste or appearance from "the kind that Mother used to make."

The amounts and types of spices people enjoy are highly variable. You already may have your favorites, which you should identify and use in your new diet. These spices can make a world of difference in your acceptance of the new and unfamiliar dishes. Experiment a little. The nutritional value of the food is affected very little by the spices you use.

More than anything else, people miss the taste of salt when they change to a starch-centered diet. This is because, since infancy, salt has played an important role in our enjoyment of food. Salt is one of the tongue's basic tastes. However, the amount of salt we like is a learned response and therefore can be changed in a process of re-education. Foods taste bland when their salt content is decreased. The adaptation to low-salt foods occurs in about three weeks, and after that they will taste just as salty as before. The recipes presented in this book are designed for people who need to be on somewhat of a salt-restricted diet. If you are in good health, with no heart or kidney disease, high blood pressure, or water retention, you may start this diet plan with a small amount of added salt. This familiar flavor may make a big difference in the ease with which you accept the new dishes.

You should add no more than half a teaspoon of salt (1,000 milligrams of sodium) daily. This will bring the total sodium intake to about 2,000 milligrams per day, at most, which is considerably less than the 5,000 milligrams or more consumed by many westerners. Add extra salt to the food at the table, not during cooking. Salt applied to the surface of the food will give the most flavor. Later, as you adapt to the new foods, lower your salt intake to the amount present in the original recipes, which is less than 1,000 milligrams of sodium added per day.

People with severe high blood pressure, heart failure, kidney failure, or edema should make adjustments in the menu plans by leaving out the tamari and high-sodium vegetables.

Those people who eat only the rich diet of affluent societies are cheating their senses. For them the flavors of salt and cooked fat are dominant. Our ability to adapt to almost anything is so great that we have actually learned to enjoy chemical, synthetic flavoring agents. Changing to a health-supporting, starch-centered diet will acquaint you with an exciting world of natural aromas and tastes you may never have known before.

Meal Planning

1. Become familiar with most of the recipes in this book and with the details for each one you propose to serve. When starting the change, read and reread this book.
2. Once a week, make a menu plan and shopping list. Shop when you are not rushed. Take time to read all labels.
3. Plan ahead. Take a few minutes early in the day to think about your evening meal and what needs to be prepared. For

example, beans need to be started early; they take hours to cook. Some complete meals may be prepared ahead of time, then reheated before dinner. Soups are good for this. Some recipes are easy to prepare in a slow cooker, needing no watching during the day.

4. A meal should be centered around a starch, such as rice, white potatoes, sweet potatoes, beans, corn, wheat, or other grains. Then add vegetables and fruits.

5. Keep your meal plan simple. Do not try to prepare several hearty dishes for each meal. One basic dish should be enough at each meal. Then add simple foods to round out your meal, such as steamed vegetables, tossed salad, bread, or rolls.

6. On the day you order or bake bread, prepare soup for dinner. Hot soup and fresh bread make a delightful meal.

7. Soups can be converted to vegetable toppings to serve over potatoes, brown rice, and other whole grains. Omit one or two cups of water from the original soup recipe—bean soups are especially good for this—or use leftover bean or grain soups as a topping, since they thicken as they cool.

8. Keep baked potatoes, rice, cut-up vegetables, leftovers, and fruits in the refrigerator for a quick meal or snack.

9. Eat simple meals when you have less time to spend on food preparation—for example, plain baked potatoes with one or two steamed vegtables, pancakes served with applesauce and cinnamon, or easy sauces or gravies served over pasta.

10. Vegetable foods keep well. Prepare a large portion and refrigerate or freeze half of it. Get two to four meals for the work of one.

11. When you have the time, cook beans and grains to be frozen and used later in recipes calling for those ingredients. This is a great time saver. Freeze in two- or three-cup portions.

12. Vegetables can be cut up ahead of time and kept in the refrigerator in plastic bags until you're ready to prepare your meal. If you grate or chop potatoes ahead of time, keep them covered with water until you use them or they will turn brown.

13. Some dishes can be half-cooked (soups, stews, casseroles) and then finished just before dinner.

14. Most of the dishes described in this book reheat well. Microwave ovens are convenient for this purpose. The questionable safety of microwave cooking must be weighed against its efficiency.

15. Add spices and vegetables to please your taste preference. If you or your family like more or less onion, green peppers, or mushrooms, feel free to change the recipes. The amounts of herbs and spices used also should be varied according to your preferences. Some people like to add more spices; some prefer none at all. These recipes are only guidelines. Use them for ideas, varying acceptable ingredients as you choose. By changing the kinds of beans, grains, vegetables, or spices put into a dish, you can invent your own favorite recipes.

Breakfast, Lunch, and Dinner Suggestions

Breakfast

1. Porridge: cooked cereals (oatmeal, cornmeal, millet, cracked wheat, rice, rolled rye, rolled wheat) served or cooked with a fruit.
2. Dry cereals, such as Nutri-grain or puffed cereals served with water, fruit juice, or one of the acceptable "milks" described in this book.
3. Fruit sauces or purees (banana, applesauce, peaches, pears, melons) served with toast or pancakes.
4. Bean mixtures with griddle cakes, waffles, toast, or whole grains.
5. Oil-free granola.
6. Baked potatoes (white, sweet, or yams).
7. Sweet potato and banana salad, or yam and apple casserole.
8. Rice and vegetables or rice and fruit.
9. Fruits alone.
10. "Smoothies."
11. Leftovers.

Lunch

1. Leftovers.
2. Soup and bread.
3. Reheated bean soups or chili served over pasta, toast, rice, or other whole grain products.
4. Cold bean or grain soups and other leftovers used warm or cold as a sandwich spread or stuffed in pita bread. Bean and grain soups thicken as they cool, and they spread well.
5. Cold vegetable sandwiches. Use any combination of tomatoes, sprouts, cucumbers, onions, green peppers, grated carrots, and

lettuce. Sprinkle with chili salsa, ketchup, or spread a little mustard (use sparingly, it's high in fat) on bread.

6. Griddle cakes with beans or fruit sauces.
7. Waffles with gravy, vegetable, or fruit sauces.
8. Raw vegetables and eggplant dip or other vegetable or bean dips.
9. Large green salad with oil-free dressing or lemon juice, vinegar, chili salsa, or other no-oil dressing. Cooked rice or beans can serve as a good base over which to put green salads.
10. Fruit salad.
11. Raw fruits and vegetables.
12. Stuffed pita bread with warm or cold leftovers (spicy Mexican toppings, layered dinner, bean soups, ratatouille) and vegetables (tomatoes, sprouts, onions). Sprinkle with chili salsa.
13. Baked potatoes (white, sweet, or yam). Use leftover pasta sauce, gravies, and soups for toppings. Or simply sprinkle with various seasonings.
14. Rice with vegetables or fruit.
15. If you're in a hurry and must eat away from home, just pack a baked potato, pita bread, or cold rice with some fruit and raw vegetables.
16. Don't forget about packing your own dressings and ordering baked potatoes and salads at restaurants.

Sandwiches

Appetizing sandwiches can be made with whole grain bread, in pockets of whole wheat pita bread, on crisp corn tortillas, on rice cakes, or on whole wheat chapati bread. Add sliced tomatoes, onions, cucumbers, grated carrots, lettuce, alfalfa sprouts, mung bean sprouts, watercress, and so on.

Flavor with mustard (but remember, it's high in fat), chili salsa, ketchup, or tofu spreads (high fat), if desired.

Different kinds of beans may be ground or mashed for use as sandwich spreads:

garbanzo puree	black bean soup
refried beans	dals
taco beans	curried beans
chili beans	barbequed beans
split pea soups	sloppy lentils

lentil soups   Brazilian black beans
white bean soup   spicy Mexican toppings.

Ideas for vegetable sandwiches:

Layered dinner in pita bread.
Spicy Mexican topping, using rice instead of beans.
Eggplant dip as a sandwich spread.
Tabouli stuffed in pita bread.
Potato bhaji in pita or chapati.
Ratatouille in pita bread.
Szechuan eggplant in pita bread.
Vegetable curry rolled in chapati or stuffed in pita.

Ideas for fruit sandwiches:

Mashed banana or sliced papaya.
Mashed mango with sliced bananas.
Fruit jams or fruit butters, such as apple butter.

Ideas for richer sandwiches (these are high-fat plant foods; do not use if ill):

Ground-nut-seed mixture, as a spread.
Nut butters, such as peanut butter.
Seed spreads, such as tahini.
Tofu spreads.

Soups

1. Make soups with vegetable stock instead of plain water. Vegetable stock can be as simple as a bit of pure vegetable seasoning and tamari in water, or you can make your own from fresh vegetables with your favorite herbs and spices.
2. Use water left over from steamed vegetables for the stock. Liquid from cooking beans makes a good soup base.
3. Adding tomatoes, tomato juice, or V-8 juice (low sodium) to a soup will change the flavor to a tomato-based soup.
4. Soup recipes can be varied by adding different kinds of grains. Use more water than the recipe calls for, and add some rice or barley thirty minutes before serving. Use about a third cup of grain to two cups of water. This will thicken the soup because the grain absorbs some of the liquids.

5. Different types of pasta, too, can be added to soup recipes. Add these fifteen minutes before serving. Additional water is not necessary. The soup will be thicker because the pasta absorbs some of the liquid.
6. For a thick, creamy soup, puree half of it in a blender; then return this portion to the pot and mix well. This method works especially well with bean soups.
7. Add long-cooking vegetables about one hour before the soup is to be served. Add medium-cooking vegetables about thirty minutes ahead and the fast-cooking ones about ten minutes before serving. This will bring out the best flavor of the vegetables without allowing them to get soggy.
8. To adapt other recipes, use water for sauteing, rather than oil, or use water or vegetable stock instead of chicken or meat broth. Most recipes can be adapted very nicely to this style of cooking.
9. Soups usually can be made early in the day and reheated later. They are good for busy days when you're not sure just when the family will be home for dinner. Soup served with bread or rolls and a salad provides a satisfying meal.
10. Soups freeze well.
11. Most bean soups make great sandwich spreads when cold.

Dinner Suggestions for Sixty Days

Day 1
Brown rice
Vegetable stew
Broiled zucchini

Day 2
Baked potatoes
Mushroom gravy
Mixed peas and carrots

Day 3
Spaghetti noodles
Marinara tomato sauce
Tossed salad
French tomato dressing

Day 4
White bean soup
Whole wheat bread
Raw vegetables

Day 5
Brown rice
Vegetable chop suey

Day 6
Baked sweet potatoes
Cooked broccoli
Mixed sprout salad

Day 7
Stuffed pita bread
Garbanzo puree
Vegetables for stuffing

Day 8
Potato bhaji
Cauliflower with nutty
white sauce

Day 9
Chinese noodles with
vegetables
Whole wheat muffins

Day 10
Stuffed green peppers
Cooked carrots

Day 11
Middle East vegetable stew
Bulgur wheat

Day 12
Mashed potatoes
Brown gravy
Herbed green beans

Day 13
Baked winter squash
Tossed salad

Day 14
French onion soup
Whole wheat bread

Day 15
Peasant's pie
Tossed green salad
Oil-free dressing

Day 16
Brown rice
Chili beans
Corn on the cob

Day 17
Tabouli
Gazpacho

Day 18
Chinese vegetable soup
Rice
Steamed vegetables

Day 19
Potato scramble
Szechuan eggplant

Day 20
Griddle cakes
Split peas (on toast)
Raw vegetables

Day 21
Fried rice
A steamed vegetable

Day 22
Pizza

Day 23
Vegetable soup
Soft corn tortillas

Day 24
Brown rice
Black beans *with*
Marinated tomatoes and onions

Day 25
Whole wheat noodles
Ratatouille
Tossed green salad

Day 26
Mild mixed vegetable curry
Muffins

Day 27
Assorted raw vegetables
Tomato–onion soup
Eggplant dip

Day 28
Chapatis
Refried beans
Vegetable toppings
Chili salsa sauce

Day 29
Tossed green rice
Steamed sweet corn

Day 30
Lasagna
Italian green beans

Day 31
Stove-top stew
Five-grain rice
Cucumber–onion–tomato salad

Day 32
Potato pancakes
Ketchup sauce
Steamed peas

Day 33
Spanish rice
Steamed Brussels sprouts

Day 34
Sloppy lentils
Whole wheat buns or bread
Yellow beans

Day 35
Whole wheat macaroni
Chinese vegetable sauce

Day 36
Latin black bean soup
Pita bread

Day 37
Rice medley
Muffins

Day 38
Tamale pie
Tossed salad

Day 39
Brown rice
Heather's mushroom delight
Chinese peas and mushrooms

Day 40
Golden potatoes
Ketchup sauce
Steamed vegetables

Day 41
Spicy Mexican topping
Corn tortillas

Day 42
Stuffed cabbage rolls
Muffins

Day 43
Layered dinner
Tossed green salad
French Tomato Dressing

Day 44
Paella
Tossed salad

Day 45
Enchiladas
Raw vegetables
Chili Salsa Sauce

Day 46
Hearty brown stew
Pita bread
Salad

Day 47
Hot German potato salad
Muffins

Day 48
Indian rice
Steamed vegetables
Salad

Day 49
Barbecued beans
Pita bread
Cucumber–onion–tomato salad

Day 50
Chapati–vegetable rolls
Mixed sprout salad

Day 51
Pea soup
Muffins

Day 52
Shish Kebabs
Bulgur wheat

Day 53
Barley and beans
Tossed salad
French tomato dressing

Day 54
Baked eggplant casserole
Brown rice
Steamed vegetables

Day 55
Dal
Pita bread
Assorted vegetable toppings

Day 56
Spicy vegetable stew
Five-grain rice

Day 57
Vegetable-stuffed peppers
with spicy tomato sauce
Tossed green salad
Herbed vinegar dressing

Day 58
Lentil–rice surprise
Steamed vegetables

Day 59
Sherried rice
Tossed salad

Day 60
Tomato scalloped potatoes
Steamed vegetables

Quick-and-Easy, Prepare-Ahead, and Slow-Cooker Recipes

Quick and Easy

Some recipes take less time to prepare than others and are good for days when you have less time to spend in the kitchen on preparing meals.

Simple Tomato Pasta Sauce
Split Peas on Toast
Onion Soup
Potato Scramble
Pancakes
Waffles
Chickenless à la King
Lentil Soup
Barley Mushroom Soup
Easy Curried Lentil or Pea Soup

Sloppy Lentils
Marinara Sauce
Potato Pancakes
Chinese Vegetable Soup
Mushroom Delight
Easy Ratatouille
Most simple sauces and gravies
to serve over rice or other whole
grains

Some recipes are prepared quickly if you have cooked rice or cooked beans in your refrigerator or freezer. On the days when you prepare rice or beans, make some extra and refrigerate or freeze them in two- or three-cup containers.

Fried Rice
Tossed Green Rice
Spicy Mexican Topping
Spanish Rice
Sherried Rice
Spanish Bulgur
Indian Rice
Hot German Potato Salad

Taco Beans
Barbecued Beans
Simple Refried Beans
Chapatis and Beans
Garbanzo Puree
Stuffed Pita Bread
Rice Salad

Prepared Ahead

Some recipes may be prepared completely ahead of time. The final baking or reheating is done just before dinner. This is particularly helpful when you entertain guests for dinner.

Soups
Spaghetti Sauce
Stuffed Peppers
Peasant's Pie
Lasagna
Refried Beans
Chili
Ratatouille
Barbecued Beans
Rice Salad

Baked Stuffed Squash
Stews
Layered Dinner
Stuffed Cabbage Rolls
Bean Enchiladas
Baked Eggplant Casserole
Chapati Vegetable Rolls
Shish Kebabs
Mild Mixed Vegetable Curry
Tamale Pie

Slow Cookers

Some recipes are easy to prepare in a slow cooker. Add all ingredients at once. The amount of water used may have to be reduced by one or two cups because slow cookers usually do not lose much water while cooking. It is not necessary to saute any of the vegetables first. Times given may vary, depending on which brand of slow cooker you have. You may need to halve some recipes if your slow cooker is small.

The following may be cooked for four hours on the high temperature setting or eight hours on low:

Marinara Sauce
Stove-Top Stew
Easy Ratatouille
Dal
Sloppy Lentils

The following may be cooked for six hours on the high temperature setting or ten hours on low:

Hearty Brown Stew
Sweet and Sour Lentil Stew

The following may be cooked for six hours on high or twelve hours on low:

Vegetable Stew and Spicy Vegetable Stew
Butch's Chili
Brazilian Black Beans
Barley and Beans
Middle East Vegetable Stew
Layered Dinner

The following soups may be cooked for four hours on high or eight hours on low:

Onion
Vegetable
Lentil
Tomato–Onion

The following soups may be cooked for six hours on high or twelve to fourteen hours on low:

Black Bean
Pea
White Bean
Vegetable Bean

Sample Seven-Day Menu Plan and Stock List

These are only suggestions. You can design a much more enjoyable menu plan by choosing recipes with familiar ingredients that you have always liked.

Day 1

Breakfast
Oatmeal (follow directions for porridge).
Herbal tea.
Midmorning snack
orange or apple and/or rice (leftover).
Lunch
1 piece whole wheat pita bread cut in half and stuffed with lettuce, tomatoes, other vegetables such as cucumbers, grated carrots, radishes, onions, sprouts.
Spoon some Ortega green chili salsa over the top if desired.
1 fruit such as apple, banana, orange, or ½ papaya or grapefruit
Herbal tea or water.
Midafternoon snack
Raw vegetables such as carrots, celery, or zucchini.
Dinner
Fried rice (use rice you prepared earlier in the day).
Tossed green salad (use lettuce with various chopped vegetables and sprouts if desired).
French tomato dressing for salad (make in the afternoon before dinner; refrigerate before serving).
Corn on the cob—either fresh or frozen (follow directions on bag, no salt in water).
Evening snack
1 apple.
Raw vegetables as desired.
Herbal tea.

Day 2

Breakfast

Cracked wheat or 4-grain cereal.

Herbal tea

Midmorning snack

1 orange or apple and/or potato or rice (leftover).

Lunch

1 piece whole wheat pita bread or leftover brown rice covered with split peas on toast. Takes about 1 hour. May be prepared early in morning and reheated.

1 fruit—apple, banana, or orange.

Water.

Midafternoon snack

Raw vegetables.

Dinner

Marinara tomato sauce.

Whole wheat spaghetti noodles or buckwheat soba noodles.

Whole wheat bread.

Salad—lettuce, sprouts, onions, cucumber.

French tomato dressing.

Water

Evening snack

1 orange or ½ grapefruit.

Raw vegetables.

Herbal tea.

Day 3

Breakfast

Oatmeal.

Herbal tea.

Midmorning snack

1 banana.

Potato or leftover rice.

Lunch

1 whole wheat pita bread, cut in half, spread with cold leftover split pea recipe and stuffed with tomatoes, lettuce, or sprouts.

Raw vegetables as desired.

1 fruit—apple, orange, papaya, banana, pear.
Herbal tea or water.

Midafternoon snack
Raw vegetables.

Dinner
Vegetable soup
1 piece whole wheat pita bread or 1 cup leftover brown rice.
Lettuce salad—lettuce, assorted chopped vegetables.
French tomato dressing.
Water.

Evening snack
Raw vegetables.
1 fruit.
Herbal tea.

Day 4

Breakfast
Roman Meal or Zoom hot cereal.
Herbal tea.

Midmorning snack
1 fruit and/or potato or leftover rice.

Lunch
Leftover vegetable soup.
Special whole wheat bread or whole wheat pita bread.
Raw vegetables as desired.
Water

Midafternoon snack
Raw vegetables.

Dinner
Vegetable curry with brown rice.
Whole wheat chapati.
Vegetable salad—lettuce and assorted raw vegetables.
French tomato dressing or lemon and/or vinegar.
Water.

Evening snack
1 fruit.
Raw vegetables.
Herbal tea.

Day 5

Breakfast
  Zoom or Roman Meal hot cereal.
  Herbal tea.
Midmorning snack
  1 fruit and/or potato or leftover rice.
Lunch
  Leftover vegetable curry over baked potato, brown rice, or whole
  wheat pita bread. Garnish with sprouts.
  1 fruit.
  Water.
Midafternoon snack
  Raw vegetables.
Dinner
  Tamale pie.
  Assorted raw vegetable platter.
  Chili salsa for dip.
  Water.
Evening snack
  1 fruit.
  Raw vegetables.
  Herbal tea.

Day 6

Breakfast
  Oatmeal.
  Herbal tea.
Midmorning snack
  1 fruit and/or potato or leftover rice.
Lunch
  Leftover fried rice.
  Assorted raw vegetables with chili salsa for dip.
  1 fruit.
  Herbal tea or water.
Midafternoon snack
  Raw vegetables.

Dinner
Buckwheat soba noodles.
Vegetable chop suey.
Frozen Oriental-style mixed vegetables (follow directions on bag, no salt or butter).
Water.

Evening snack
Assorted raw vegetables.
1 fruit.
Herbal tea.

Day 7

Breakfast
Oatmeal.
Herbal tea.

Midmorning snack
1 fruit and/or potato or leftover rice.

Lunch
Tomato–onion soup.
Whole wheat bread.
Assorted raw vegetables.
Water.

Midafternoon snack.
Raw vegetables.

Dinner
Vegetable stew.
Brown rice.
Green salad—lettuce with assorted raw vegetables.
Water.

Evening snack
Raw vegetables.
1 fruit.
Herbal tea.

This is the kitchen stock list for one-week menu plan. This shopping list is estimated for two adults. All stock can be found in most supermarkets except where noted.

Grains and Flours

10 lbs. brown rice
2 lbs. whole wheat flour

8 ozs. arrowroot (health food store) (optional)
1 lb. corn meal

Cereal Products

3 lbs. oatmeal (for example, "Quaker Oats")
1 box Roman Meal cereal
1 box Zoom cereal
2 lbs. Cracked Wheat or 4-Grain cereal

Pasta

1 lb. whole wheat spaghetti (health food store)
1 lb. buckwheat soba noodles (Oriental section of grocery store or health food store)

Breads

6 pkgs. whole wheat pita bread
2 pkgs. whole wheat chapati or corn tortillas

Beans and Peas

3 lbs. pinto beans
2 lbs. green or yellow split peas

Frozen vegetables (may be purchased fresh if you choose)

1 bag frozen corn
1 bag frozen corn on cob
1 bag frozen peas
1 bag frozen peas and carrots
1 bag frozen mixed vegetables (Oriental style)

Canned goods

2 cans Ortega green chili salsa
6 8-oz. cans tomato sauce (all brands have salt or sugar, except those found in some natural food stores)
2 28-oz. cans tomatoes (almost always contain salt; do not buy if it contains sugar or dextrose)
1 46-oz. can tomato juice (contains salt except low sodium varieties)
1 can Ortega green chilis

Seasonings

8 ozs. lemon juice (frozen pure "Minute Maid")
8 ozs. apple cider vinegar
12 ozs. tamari (low-sodium, health food store)
1 jar Vegit (or other pure vegetable seasoning)

Spices (1 jar of each)

Italian herb seasoning	basil
onion powder	celery seed
ground cumin	dill weed
oregano	dry mustard
sage	ground ginger
thyme	chili powder
marjoram	cinnamon
tarragon	mace
bay leaves	parsley flakes
nutmeg	curry powder

To save money, we recommend that you purchase spices in bulk from a natural food store, where you can buy only what you need, about ½ oz. of each to start.

Perishables

You may wish to purchase more if you like extra raw vegetable snacks.

4 lbs. carrots	1 lb. tomatoes
1 bunch celery	10 oranges
6 lbs. onions	10 apples
15 lbs. potatoes	10 bananas
1 head garlic	1 lb. cauliflower
8 zucchini	1 lb. broccoli
1 lb. green beans	1 lb. green peppers
2 lbs. mushrooms	2–4 leeks
lettuce as desired for salads	parsley

Herbal teas as desired, no caffeine, no green or black tea. We suggest red zinger, sleepytime, sweet orange spice, sweet cinnamon spice, roastaroma, peppermint, lemon mist. (Herbs are often potent "medicines." Herb books list desirable and undesirable effects.)

Optional

cucumbers	papaya
radishes	grapefruit
alfalfa sprouts	pears
green onions	Chinese peas

18

Eating Out and Other Special Occasions On A Health-Supporting Diet

Eating Out

Try a vegetarian restaurant or a snack bar in a health food store. Some places offer meals, others only sandwiches. An acceptable menu should offer dishes that contain no dairy products, no meats, low salt and low oil content, and no foods that have been refined.

Some restaurants are starting to serve what they call a vegetarian entree. But be sure to inquire if dairy products, eggs, salt, and oil have been used in preparing such an entree. If no vegetarian plate is available, double helpings of potatoes, vegetables, and whole grains, such as brown rice, whole wheat bread, and cereals, can be ordered. Often, appetizers are vegetarian and will go nicely with a vegetable salad. For salad dressing use plain vinegar or lemon juice, or bring your own from home. Old spice jars are perfect containers for carrying low-fat dressings from home. Each holds enough for a single serving and can easily fit into pocket or purse. Restaurants serve hot and cold cereals. Pass up the cream jug and the milk pitcher. Use water or fruit juice.

Major airlines now offer pure vegetarian meals. You must specify that you want no oil or salt. Often, you can order specific foods, such as potatoes, rice, or fruit. You must call ahead to order any special meal. Try ordering "pure vegetarian, no oil."

To be safe, prepare your lunch at home, and take it with you, even to business meetings.

For an occasional quick lunch, buy fresh fruits or vegetables at a nearby grocery or supermarket.

Before going to a party or dinner where you know only rich food will be served, eat a good meal at home. This will help you to avoid temptation, and with that, subsequent disaster to your body. This is good advice to parents for their children also.

Avoid fast-food restaurants and other establishments that soak foods in oils and salt.

If all else fails, and you're trapped by circumstances, don't eat. Missing a meal or two rarely hurts anyone.

Being a Proper Guest

Being a proper guest can be a very challenging task. When old friends or new acquaintances discover that you eat foods that differ from theirs, you may find a hint of discomfort creeping into your relationship. They may feel that they are doing something wrong, or that you think you are a little better than they are. Such defensive feelings must be avoided, especially if part of your intention is to share your new lifestyle and eating habits with them.

It is important from the beginning to be clear and consistent with your message about food preferences. When you are invited for dinner there are several ways to break the news to your host or hostess. You might try the following approaches to direct the conversation toward healthier meals:

- "Have you been reading about all the unhealthy things that can happen to you when you eat meat and dairy foods? I've been making a lot of changes in my diet. Right now I'm trying to eat as healthy a diet as possible, mostly vegetables with no oil."
- "I'm under doctor's orders to eat only foods that are good for me and to stay away from fats, salt, cholesterol, and sugar."
- "I've really enjoyed the meals you have fixed for me in the past. You're such a great cook. But I've discovered a sensible way to keep my weight down and still eat all I want. Did you know that starches make you slim?"

Then, explain to your host or hostess exactly what your diet is and that simple things such as baked potatoes, rice, salads without dressing, steamed vegetables, and fruits are more than enough for you. After all, the real reason you're going to dinner at their house is to be with them and to enjoy their company. The food should be secondary.

If these are new acquaintances, you might decline dinner altogether and suggest that after-dinner refreshments might be better. Explain that you are on a diet that might be unfamiliar to them and that you don't want to put them through all the trouble of accommodating their menu to you. This suggestion may be viewed by your new hosts as a challenge and could end up by presenting everyone with a very pleasant meal, as well as a healthy one.

An easy way to introduce new foods to your host or hostess is to offer to bring something along or to arrive early and help with preparing the meal. This is a comfortable way to introduce the subject of a healthier way of eating. Choose a dish that you know everyone will enjoy, and make a lot of it so that at least you will have enough to eat when dinnertime comes.

If you are a guest at a large dinner party, you should eat before you go and then confine yourself to sampling the few dishes that are acceptable to your dietary principles.

If you are a house guest for any period of time, get involved with the shopping and cooking. You might even be willing to take over these responsibilities altogether. This could be a simple solution to your eating problems and a genuine education for your host or hostess.

More often than not, you will find that both old friends and new acquaintances will be very interested in what you are doing. Avoiding rich meats and dairy foods and eating more "vegetarian" meals is becoming a national movement. When they find that you have already gone a little further in this direction, your diet is likely to be the main subject of conversation during the evening. Most of us true believers are very happy to share this information with our friends.

How to Use Rich Foods

It is possible to use some of your old favorite recipes by adapting them to your new style of cooking. These modifications will substitute healthier ingredients to make your recipes less rich.

Whole Wheat Flour

Use whole wheat flour in sauces and breads. Use whole wheat pastry flour for a lighter, more cakelike texture in pancakes and desserts.

As a general guideline, use whole wheat flour in recipes calling for yeast; use whole wheat pastry flour in recipes calling for baking powder.

Sweeteners

In general, the amount of sweetening called for in a recipe can easily be cut down. Start by cutting the amount in half. Use honey, malt syrup, or rice syrup as sweetners instead of white or brown sugar. For a different flavor, use unsweetened apple juice concentrate as a sweetener, or ground-up dates or raisins.

Oils

Butter, shortening, or oil can be simply omitted in most recipes.

In baking, substitute applesauce or water for the oil used. Usually, add no more than a quarter cup of applesauce per recipe. If more moisture is needed, replace the rest with water.

In cooking, the oils called for usually can be omitted, and an equal amount of vegetable stock or water is used instead. For pie crusts, cookies, and some desserts, nuts ground with a small amount of water help to hold ingredients together. Cashews or almonds work best for this.

Eggs

"Ener G" makes an acceptable product called Egg Replacer. It is a mixture of refined flours. It is good for use in baking. It does not make scrambled eggs or anything resembling them. One teaspoon of Egg Replacer mixed with two tablespoons of water is equal to one egg in baking.

You can also use your own mixtures. For binding, add one of the following:

1. 1 tablespoon defatted soy or garbanzo flour
2. 3 tablespoons potato flour or tapioca
3. ½ cup cooked oatmeal

For leavening, use one teaspoon of baking yeast dissolved in a quarter cup of warm water to which a half teaspoon of honey has been added. This works well in muffin recipes.

Tofu, Nuts, and Seeds

Tofu can be made into many delicious, creamy dips for cooked and raw vegetables, dressings for salads, and spreads for breads. It goes well with either sweet or spicy dressings for salads and with spreads for breads. Tofu is rather bland and picks up the taste of other foods and spices mixed with it.

Nut milk can be used in place of dairy milk in all recipes. It makes a good base for white sauces. Nuts can be ground up and used as a base for spreads or to hold crusts and cookies together. Nuts are high in fat, and it is not recommended that you eat them as a snack food. To make acceptable "nuts" for snack foods, use garbanzo beans that have been cooked until tender. Drain beans well, and place them on a non-stick baking sheet. Sprinkle with onion powder, garlic powder, or chili powder. Bake at 350 degrees until dried, about forty-five minutes. (These are in category IV—health-supporting.)

Seeds are also high in fats. They can be ground into spreads, made into seed milk, or used as bases for sauces such as tahini sauce.

Planning a Party Meal

When planning a meal for a party, it is often helpful to have a theme, such as Mexican, Italian, or Indian. This makes it easier to choose the foods you wish to serve.

Obviously, the amount of food to make will depend on the number of people you plan to serve. Try to cook as many things beforehand as possible, to avoid being too busy when the guests arrive.

Before you plan the menu, decide whether you want to serve buffet-style or have a sit-down dinner. The type of menu you want may depend on what kind of arrangements you choose. Some dishes adapt well to either type of arrangement, while others are best for either one kind or another. For example, spaghetti is easier to serve at a sit-down dinner. However, Mexican food and Indian food can be served buffet-style quite easily.

If you plan to serve a late dinner, arrange to have a tray of assorted raw vegetables with several dips for your guests to munch on while waiting.

CHAPTER

19

Cooking For A Health-Supporting Diet

Vegetables

Most vegetables can be placed in one of three groups depending on the time it takes to cook them. Cooking times can be shortened by cutting the vegetables into smaller pieces. The times given here are based on large chunks or whole vegetables. When cooking a soup or stew, add the vegetables according to their cooking times. However, plan on an additional ten to fifteen minutes for each group. Getting the vegetables just the way you like them every meal may take some practice.

Vegetable Cooking Times

Long-Cooking Vegetables, 20–30 minutes
  Brussels sprouts
  Carrots
  Green beans
  Celery
  Onions
  Potatoes
  Winter squash
  Turnips
  Artichokes

Medium-Cooking Vegetables, 10–15 minutes
  Broccoli
  Cauliflower
  Cabbage
  Corn
  Eggplant
  Green pepper
  Leeks
  Snow peas
  Summer squash
  Asparagus

Fast-Cooking Vegetables, 5–10 minutes
  Bean sprouts
  Chinese cabbage
  Green onions
  Green peas
  Mushrooms
  Spinach
  Tomatoes
  Greens

Steaming Vegetables

Steaming is a delicious way to prepare fresh vegetables. You will need a saucepot with a tight-fitting lid and a collapsible steamer basket. Stainless steel steamer baskets are available and very inexpensive. They are found in most supermarkets, drug stores, and department stores. This steaming method preserves the fresh flavors of the vegetables and allows minimum loss of vitamins and minerals into the cooking water.

To steam vegetables, bring an inch of water to boil in a saucepot. Place the steamer basket in the pot, then place the vegetables in the basket, put the cover on the pot, and reduce heat to medium. Cook until just tender enough for your taste, using the cooking times suggested above as a guide. Times for steaming can be varied and will result in changes in the firmness of the vegetables. Steaming times will also vary depending on the size of the vegetables, how old they are, what type of pan you are using, and whether you are cooking with a gas or electric stove.

Sauteing Vegetables

Another way to prepare vegetables is to saute them. Usually, when cookbooks talk about sauteing vegetables, they are using oil. When we talk about sauteing, we do not use oil. Instead, we saute in a small amount of water or vegetable stock. Various seasonings can be added to the water to create a wide range of flavors. Some suggested seasonings are:

1. 2 tbsp. red or white wine
2. 1 tbsp. low-sodium tamari
3. 1 clove garlic, crushed, and 1 tsp. grated ginger root
4. 1 tsp. low-sodium tamari, ½ tsp. dry mustard, ½ tsp. powdered ginger
5. 2 tbsp. tomato juice, ½ tsp. chili powder
6. ½ tsp. vinegar and 1 tbsp. pineapple juice
7. 1 tbsp. lemon juice and ⅛ tsp. garlic powder
8. 2 tbsp. sherry and ¼ tsp. nutmeg
9. ½ tsp. curry powder
10. ¼ tsp. dill weed and 1 tsp. parsley flakes
11. ⅛ tsp. garlic powder, ¼ tsp. oregano, ½ tsp. paprika
12. ¼ tsp. onion powder, ½ tsp. oregano, ½ tsp. basil

To saute vegetables, heat a quarter cup water or stock in a wok, frying pan, or saucepan. Add seasonings as desired. When liquid is boiling, reduce heat to medium and then add the chopped vegetables. Cook and stir until they are tender.

When sauteing, it is best to cut the vegetables into bite-sized pieces. Long-cooking vegetables may be cut even smaller. The vegetables should cook as quickly as possible this way, preserving their flavor and preventing nutrient loss. Most vegetables will be tender in five to fifteen minutes when sauteed by this method.

When cooking vegetables, such as boiled potatoes, save the water; it contains flavors and nutrients from the vegetables. Then, use it later for soup stock or as a base for gravies or sauces.

Root Vegetables

Beets should be red in color and sweet in flavor. Beet tops (or greens) are edible and mild-tasting. Beets are usually cooked separately, then added later to other vegetables because they turn everything they are cooked with pink. They are usually not eaten raw. Use beets in salads, soups, casseroles. To prepare: Cut off all but 2 inches of beet tops; save the rest of the tops for use in vegetable stock or soups. Wash beets and leave whole. 1. Heat 6 cups water to boiling. Add 5 medium beets. Cover and cook 35–45 minutes, until tender. Drain. Run cold water over beets, slip off skins, and remove roots. Slice, grate, or cut into pieces, as desired. Or 2. Bake at 350 degrees for 30–60 minutes. Remove skins and serve.

Carrots should be firm and bright orange in color. They are eaten raw or cooked and are a good vegetable for dipping. Carrots add sweetness to many dishes. To prepare: Scrub carrots with vegetable brush; cut off ends. Leave whole, cut lengthwise, slice into ¼-inch slices, or grate. Place in steamer basket and steam in covered pot, over 1 inch of boiling water, until tender—30 minutes for whole carrots, 15 minutes for slices. Or bake with other vegetables; use in soups, casseroles, salads, or baked goods.

Potatoes should be white, well-shaped, and smooth, with firm unblemished skins and free from discolorations. Spoiled, green, or budded potatoes should be discarded and not eaten because of a toxic substance called solanine that is formed under the skin with aging and spoilage. They usually are not eaten raw. Use in salads, soups, casseroles, or mashed. To prepare: Scrub with vegetable brush. Leave skins on whenever possible, or pare thinly. Leave whole or cut into large chunks. Heat 1 inch water to boiling, add potatoes, cover, cook until tender—35–45 minutes for whole potatoes, 20–25 minutes for chunks. Or prick potatoes in several places with a fork to allow steam to escape and bake in 375-degree oven for 1–1½ hours, depending on size of potato.

Sweet potatoes and yams should have smooth skins and be firm and bright-colored. Sweet potatoes have light yellowish skins and are relatively dry and mealy. What we commonly call yams have reddish-orange skins and moist, deep-orange insides. They are eaten cooked and used in salads, casseroles, and soups. They may be baked whole or mashed. True yams are rarely found in supermarkets in the United States. They are grown in the tropics. The deep-orange, sweet-tasting root vegetable that we and most produce markets call yams are actually a variety of sweet potatoes. To prepare: Prick with fork, bake at 325 degrees about 45–60 minutes until tender. Or cook in boiling water to cover potatoes until tender—30–40 minutes. Save the water for soup stock.

Turnips and Rutabagas should be firm, heavy, well-shaped, with fresh tops if possible. They are used in casseroles, soups, and stews, and eaten cooked. Turnips are white in color, rutabagas are yellow. To prepare: Scrub with vegetable brush; pare thinly. cut into cubes or slices. Cook covered, in 1 inch of boiling water, until tender—20–30 minutes.

Grains

Rinse grain in cool water and drain. Bring water to a boil and slowly add grain. Stir. Let the water come to a boil again, then reduce the temperature to low. Cook, covered, until water is absorbed. Do not stir more than necessary, or your grains will be gummy.

Grain (1 cup)	Water (cups)	Time (minutes)	Yield (cups)
Brown rice	2	60	3
Barley	3	60	3½
Buckwheat (kasha)	2	15	2½
Bulgur	2	15	2½
Cornmeal	4	30	3
Five-grain rice	2½	60	3
Millet	3	45	3½
Rye	2	60	2½
Whole wheat berries	3	120	3

Bulgur also may be prepared by pouring boiling water over it in a bowl. Cover the bowl with a towel. Wait one hour. Pour the bulgur and water into a mesh strainer; press out excess water with your hands.

For a fluffier grain, allow cooked grains to "rest" in the covered pot for fifteen minutes before serving.

Mix two or more grains together while cooking for a varied flavor. Rice and rye are good together. A product available at some natural food stores is called five-grain rice. It consists of brown rice, barley, millet, wheat berries, and rye. Cook the same as plain brown rice.

Cook grains in vegetable stock instead of water for a different flavor.

Pasta

Many kinds of whole grain pasta are available in natural food stores and some supermarkets.

Some of the ones most commonly found are:

Spaghetti—long thin noodles.
Elbows—short curved tubes.
Flat noodles—two- to three-inch flat noodles.
Ribbons—short flat noodles, twisted in center.
Shells—large or small, shaped like seashells.
Alphabet—letters and numbers.
Spirals—twisted many times.
Lasagna—wide flat noodles.

Usually all of these are made from the following ingredients:

Whole wheat pasta—made from whole wheat flour.
Spinach pasta—made from dehydrated spinach and wheat flour.
Soy pasta—made from soy flour and wheat flour.
Vegetable pasta—made from wheat flour and dehydrated
            vegetables.
Corn pasta—made from ground corn (no wheat).
Buckwheat soba—made from buckwheat flour and wheat flour.

The wheat flour used in most of these pastas, except for the whole wheat variety, is highly refined. None of them use eggs or oils.

To cook whole grain pasta, you need about four quarts of water per pound. Do not add oil or salt to the water. One pound of pasta will serve four people.

1. Bring water to a rolling boil.
2. Drop noodles into water. It is not necessary to break long strands; as they soften they'll sink into the water.
3. Keep the water boiling. Stir noodles occasionally. Test for doneness after about five minutes. Take out one noodle and bite into it. Noodles should be firm, never soggy. They should take no longer than ten minutes to cook.
4. When noodles are done, drain them in a colander, rinse with tap water, and put them in a bowl. Serve immediately with a sauce, or mix with sauce before serving.

Beans

Sort through beans and rinse well. Remove stones and wrinkled or discolored beans. To reduce cooking time by about thirty minutes, presoak beans overnight or bring to a boil for two minutes, remove from heat, cover, and let set for one hour. Then bring to a boil again, lower the heat, cover, and let simmer until tender. Add more water if necessary.

For a suggestion on how to reduce bowel gas that many people complain of when consuming beans, see the section on bowel gas under Trouble-Shooting Your Diet (Chapter 15).

Cooking times given here may vary slightly according to the age of the beans. Older beans take longer to cook. For use in salads, they should be cooked just to the tender stage. For soups and stews, they may be cooked much longer, until they are very soft.

Beans (1 cup)	Water (cups)	Time (hours)	Yield (cups)
Lentils and split peas (do not need presoaking)	3	1	2
Pinto beans	3	2½	2
Kidney beans	3	2	2
White beans	3	2	2
Lima beans	3	1½	2
Garbanzos	4	3	2
Black-eyed peas	3	1	2
Black beans	4	1½	2

Turn a bean soup into a stew by adding chunks of other vegetables during the last thirty minutes of cooking. Use lemon juice or vinegar for seasoning. Experiment with different herbs and spices. Try a combination of dill weed, celery seed, and bay leaves, or one of chili powder, cumin, and garlic. Serve with various sauces or gravies. Save the water the beans were cooked in for use in gravy, sauces, or soups.

Thickening Soups, Stews, and Sauces

Using Arrowroot or Cornstarch

Make a thin paste with arrowroot or cornstarch in a small amount of water, usually a quarter to a half cup. One to three tablespoons of arrowroot will thicken one cup of liquid, depending on the thickness desired. Cornstarch has more thickening ability, so a little less will be needed for the same amount of liquid. For arrowroot, bring to a boil the liquid to be thickened, remove from heat, and slowly add the arrowroot mixture, stirring as you do so. Return to heat, and stir until mixture boils and thickens. Serve at once.

For cornstarch, bring to a boil the liquid to be thickened. Slowly add the cornstarch mixture, stirring as you do so. Stir until liquid thickens and clears. Boil one minute. Serve hot.

Using Whole Wheat flour

To make a smooth sauce using whole wheat flour, combine the liquid with flour in a blender. Then transfer the mixture to a saucepan, heat, and stir until thickened. About two tablespoons of flour will thicken one cup of liquid.

Reduction Method

Some sauces and stews can be thickened by removing the cover of the pan and cooking over low heat until enough water is evaporated and the remaining sauce is thickened and richer in flavor. This method is good for preparing spaghetti sauces, stews, vegetable toppings, and apple butter.

Blending

Some soups and stews can be thickened by blending a portion of the soup in an electric blender. Return this portion to the pot and mix in well. This method is most effective with bean soups and stews.

Adding Grains or Noodles

Thin vegetable soups can be thickened by adding some uncooked rice, barley, or pasta to the broth. One cup of these starches will nicely thicken a large pot of soup (eight to ten cups).

Growing Your Own Sprouts

Sprouts of almost all seeds, whole grains, and legumes can be grown at home. You will need a large jar and a sprouting lid (or a piece of fine netting or cheesecloth secured with a rubber band or mason jar ring). The basic method for sprouting is as follows:

1. Place chosen seeds, grains, or legumes in a jar (see the sprouting chart for the amount to use). Cover with sprouting lid

or cloth secured with rubber band. Run warm water through the top to cover the seeds.

2. Soak seeds overnight in water (use three or four times as much water as seed).

3. Next morning, pour off all water, rinse under running water, and invert the jar over a bowl (tip it sideways a little to let some air circulate). The jar needs room to drain or the seeds will rot. Keep the jar out of direct sunlight. Cover with a towel or place in a cabinet if necessary.

4. Rinse and drain seeds about two or three times every day. Run some water into the jar through the screening, slosh it around a bit, and pour it off. Invert jar over bowl, and let excess water run into bowl.

5. In three to six days you will have a jar full of sprouts. Put them in the light at this point to develop the chlorophyll and fresh green color.

6. Your sprouts are ready to eat. Remove from jar and place in plastic bag. You can also keep them in the same growing jar by simply replacing the screen top with a jar cover. Sprouts will keep in the refrigerator five to seven days. Sprouts develop a very unpleasant odor when spoiled.

When buying seeds for sprouting, be sure to only buy sprouting seeds. Planting seeds have been treated with chemicals. Legumes that are used for cooking will sprout very well.

Sprouting Chart

Seeds or Legumes	Dry Measure	Yield (qt.)	Growing Time (Days)	Harvest Length (ins.)
Alfalfa	2 tbsp.	1	4	1–2
Radish	3 tbsp.	1	3–4	½–1
Mustard	3 tbsp.	1	3–4	½–1
Chinese cabbage	¼ cup	1	4–6	¾–1½
Mung beans	½ cup	1	3–5	1–2
Lentils	¾ cup	1	3–4	¼–½
Adzuki beans	¾ cup	1	3–4	¼–½
Garbanzo beans	¾ cup	1	3–4	½–1
Soybeans	¾ cup	1	4–6	1–2
Sunflower seeds	2 cups	1	2–3	¼–½
Wheat berries	1 cup	1	2–3	¼–½

Recipes

Recipes with this symbol contain high-fat plant foods:

Recipes with this symbol contain foods with simple sugars:

Recipes with this symbol contain added salt (tamari–soyu):

Recipes with this symbol contain high-protein foods
(legumes):

In many recipes the simple sugars, salt, and high protein ingredients can be reduced or completely eliminated for people requiring more restricted diets.

Because of space limitations only a few recipes could be printed in this book. When you exhaust these ideas you can send for additional recipes (including gluten-free, desserts, special occasion suggestions, "rich foods," and many more recipes that fit the basic diet plan for health-supporting foods). Mail requests to:

RECIPES
c/o John McDougall M.D.
P.O. Box 14039
Santa Rosa, CA 95402

Enclose no money. Cost and information on additional recipes and meal-planning suggestions will be mailed to you.

How to Read a Recipe

1. When you first find a recipe, read it all the way through to familiarize yourself with the contents, directions, and hints. This will help you decide whether you want to try the recipe, save it for another time, or eliminate it altogether.
2. If you plan to make it, read the recipe ingredients again, and make a list of things you will need to buy.
3. When the time comes to prepare your meal, read the entire recipe again. Pay attention to the helpful hints, preparation time, and cooking time.
4. Assemble the needed ingredients in the place of preparation.
5. Follow the directions step by step, as given in the recipe.

We suggest that you read a new recipe three times before preparing it. This will help you become familiar with the ingredients used and the way the recipe is prepared, and it will give you hints for easier preparation or suggestions for serving.

BREAKFASTS

Porridge

SERVINGS: 4

PREPARATION TIME: 5 mins.   COOKING TIME: 15–30 mins.

3½ to 4½ cups water (start with 3½, add more if porridge gets too thick while cooking)

1 cup cereal (cracked wheat, corn meal; oatmeal or mixed
    grains—1½ cups)
½ cup dried fruit (raisins, apples, apricots, etc.)

Bring water and fruit to a boil. Slowly add cereal to boiling water while stirring. Reduce heat to low, cook, stirring frequently, 15 to 30 minutes. The longer the ingredients cook, the softer they will be.

The porridge should be like a thick soup. Do not add milk at the table.

HELPFUL HINTS: Most health food stores sell many kinds of whole grain cereals. Follow directions on package, but increase the amount of water by ½ cup for every two servings.

For added flavor, add a sprinkle of nutmeg, mace, cinnamon, or any combination of these.

Slow Porridge
(made in slow cooker overnight)

SERVINGS: 4

PREPARATION TIME: 5 mins.   COOKING TIME: 8–10 hrs.

5 cups water
1 cup cereal (oatmeal, cracked wheat, brown rice, corn meal,
    etc.)
½ cup dried fruit (raisins, chopped apples, apricots, etc.)

Place water, cereal, and dried fruit in slow cooker. Stir. Cook on low for 8–10 hours. The mixture should be like a thick soup, so do not add milk at the table.

HELPFUL HINTS: Each slow cooker is a little different from the others, so you may have to adjust the amount of water needed.

For added flavor sprinkle a bit of nutmeg, mace, or cinnamon, in any combination. Try brown rice, barley, rye berries, whole oats, or wheat berries. Cracked grains, such as oatmeal or cracked wheat, may get too mushy for some tastes.

Griddle Cakes

SERVINGS: 12 cakes

PREPARATION TIME: 10 mins. (6–8 hrs. fermentation) COOKING
TIME: 20 mins.

1
3 cups brown rice flour
3 cups water

2
2 cups brown rice flour
1 cup garbanzo flour
3 cups water

3
2 cups cornmeal
1 cup whole wheat flour
3 cups water

Using any one of the three variations, mix all ingredients. Let rest for 6–8
hours to ferment. (Cover bowl and leave on counter.) Using a small non-stick
frying pan, ladle about ¼ cup of batter into the pan, and thinly spread.
Bubbles will form immediately. Do not turn until the cake has dried out a
little. Loosen gently and turn to cook on other side. The first side takes about
1½ minutes, the other side about 1 minute at medium temperature. Serve
with a bean mixture spooned over them, or use like a crepe.

HELPFUL HINTS: May be made without allowing to ferment. Follow the
above directions, omitting the time for fermentation. Stir batter often while
ladling; it tends to separate. Griddle cakes freeze well. Cook these, then
stack, wrap, and freeze. May be made several at a time on a griddle, like
pancakes. Griddle cakes are very difficult for beginners to make. With a
little practice they will turn out.

Pancakes or Waffles

SERVINGS: 14 pancakes

PREPARATION TIME: 10 mins.   COOKING TIME: 10 mins.

2 cups whole wheat flour
2 tsp. baking powder
1 tbsp. honey
2 tbsp. applesauce

2 cups water, apple juice, nut
　milk, or rice milk
2 tsp. egg replacer mixed with 4
　tbsp. water

Stir dry ingredients together. Mix egg replacer with water. Add honey, applesauce, and remaining liquid. Mix well. Add to dry ingredients. Stir. Pour batter onto hot nonstick griddle. Cook over medium heat, turning once when bubbles come to the surface and the edges are beginning to dry.

FOR WAFFLES: Use same recipe as above. Let stand 5 minutes to thicken slightly. Pour batter onto preheated waffle iron. Cook until lightly browned, about 5 minutes. (Time will vary slightly, depending on your waffle iron.) Keep warm in 200-degree oven on bare oven racks until ready to serve. Waffle iron may need to be lightly oiled before using, to prevent sticking.

Nut Milk

SERVINGS: 1 quart

PREPARATION TIME: 5 mins.   COOKING TIME: none

4 cups water
¾ cup raw cashews or blanched almonds

Place water in blender jar, add nuts, and blend at high speed about 60 seconds. Keep milk refrigerated.

HELPFUL HINTS: May be strained before pouring into refrigerator jar. This is a good milk substitute. Use in recipes in place of milk. Children like it on cereal. It spoils just as milk does, so it must be refrigerated. Shake well before using.

Rice Milk

SERVINGS: 1 quart

PREPARATION TIME: 5 mins.   COOKING TIME: none

4 cups water
1 cup cooked brown rice
1 tsp. vanilla (optional)

Place all ingredients in blender jar and process until smooth. Refrigerate. Shake before using.

HELPFUL HINTS: This is a sweet tasting milk, especially when the vanilla is used. May be used in almost any recipe calling for milk. For a smoother milk, let set for 30 minutes; then, without shaking, pour the milk into another container leaving the sediment in the original container. The sediment may be added to soups or stews, if desired.

BREADS

Whole Wheat Bread

SERVINGS: 2 loaves

PREPARATION TIME: 1 hr.   RISING TIME: 4 hrs.
  COOKING TIME: 50 mins. at 325 degrees

2½ cups warm water   6–8 cups whole wheat flour
2 tbsp. active dry yeast

Pour warm water into large bowl. Sprinkle yeast on top of the water. After about 3 minutes the yeast will begin to react and produce bubbles. Stir in half of the flour and beat well until dough becomes smooth (100 strokes). Cover; let rise about 1½ hours. Add the remaining flour, one cup at a time, mixing well after each cup. Knead in the bowl until dough does not stick to sides, then turn out onto a floured board. Flour your hands. Knead, push, and fold, adding flour as necessary to prevent the dough from sticking to the board. Continue kneading until dough is soft and springy and does not stick to hands or board. Return to bowl. Cover with a damp towel and set in warm place. Allow to rise until double in bulk. Divide dough in half, shape into oblongs and place in loaf pans, non-stick. (Sprinkle pans with cornmeal to make removing easier.) Cover and let rise until double. Place in preheated oven and bake for 50 minutes at 325 degrees.

HELPFUL HINTS: Don't put flour on top of the dough while kneading. Put it on the board, then knead the dough on top of it. Dough may rise in bowl either once or twice. A lighter loaf is the result of two risings. After first rising, just punch down with fist, cover, and let rise again. Each rising takes about 45 minutes. After shaping into loaves, let rise about 20 minutes. When bread is done, it should be a golden brown and will sound hollow when tapped. Remove from pans immediately.

No-Knead Bread

SERVINGS: 2 loaves

PREPARATION TIME: 30 mins.   COOKING TIME: 60 mins.

7½ cups whole wheat flour   1 tbsp. unsulphured molasses or
2 tbsp. active dry yeast   malt syrup
                                         4 cups warm water

Put flour in a large bowl. Place in a warm oven for 30 minutes to warm flour and bowl to 110 degrees (1½ minutes in microwave). Dissolve yeast in 1 cup warm water (110 degrees). Add molasses and mix well. Let rest about 3 minutes. Then, add the yeast mixture and the remaining water (3 cups, warm). Mix well by stirring or use one hand to mix in bowl. Do not Knead. Dough will be sticky. Use non-stick pans or lightly oil two large loaf pans (9" x 5" x 3"). Sprinkle with cornmeal. Spoon dough mixture into pans. Smooth top with hand dampened with water to prevent sticking. Cover with towel. Place in a warm spot. Let rise about 1 hour or until dough reaches top of pans. Preheat oven to 400 degrees. Bake for 20 minutes. Reduce heat to 350 degrees. Bake 30–40 minutes longer. Remove pans from oven, tip pans on sides, and let cool on racks for 15 minutes. Remove loaves from pans and continue to cool before storing. Bread is moist, so keeps best in refrigerator.

HELPFUL HINTS: Recipe may be doubled to make four loaves. Refrigerate or freeze extra loaves until ready to use. Other flours may be used in place of 1½ cups of whole wheat, such as brown rice flour, garbanzo flour, or barley flour. Use of nonstick pans is recommended.

Whole Wheat Muffins

SERVINGS: 12 muffins

PREPARATION TIME: 15 mins.   COOKING TIME: 30 mins.

2 cups whole wheat flour
2 tsp. baking powder
¼ cup honey
1½ cups nut milk, rice milk, or
    water

2 tbsp. applesauce
1 tsp. egg replacer mixed with 2
    tbsp. water

Combine dry ingredients. Combine wet ingredients. Fold dry and wet ingredients together, until just moistened. Spoon into lightly oiled or non-stick muffin tins. Bake at 350 degrees for 30 minutes.

HELPFUL HINTS: 1. For variety, try adding ½ cup raisins, currants, dates, or chopped apricots. 2. Substitute 1 cup corn meal for the whole wheat flour, add a dash of chili powder, oregano, or marjoram. 3. Substitute 1 cup bran for 1 cup whole wheat flour. Use molasses instead of honey. 4. Try spicing them up with ½ tsp. cinnamon, ½ tsp. mace, ¼ tsp. nutmeg, ¼ tsp. allspice, ¼ tsp. ginger, ¼ tsp. cloves.

Quick Corn Bread

SERVINGS: 8–10

PREPARATION TIME: 5 mins.   COOKING TIME: 20 mins.

1 cup corn meal
1 cup whole wheat flour
3 tsp. baking powder
1 tbsp. honey
1½ cups warm water

Mix dry ingredients together in a medium bowl. Add optional spices, if desired. Mix honey and warm water together, then add to dry ingredients, stirring just until mixed. Pour into lightly oiled or non-stick 8-inch square baking dish. Bake at 375 degrees for 20 minutes.

HELPFUL HINTS: Various spices may be added for different flavors. Some suggestions are:
1. 1 tsp. cinnamon, ¼ tsp. nutmeg
2. ½ tsp. chili powder, ¼ tsp. oregano
3. ¼ tsp. onion powder, ¼ tsp. cumin, ¼ tsp. marjoram.

Pieces of finely chopped or grated vegetables also may be added. Try finely chopped onion, finely chopped green pepper, chopped green chilis, chopped pimiento, grated carrots, grated zucchini. Used alone or in various combinations, they add special appeal to this simple, tasty corn bread. If you have a nonstick baking pan, it is not necessary to oil it first. This recipe also may be used for muffins. Increase baking powder to 4 tsp. Fill oiled or papered muffin tins two-thirds full. Bake at 375 degrees for 15–20 mins.

Pizza Crust

SERVINGS: 1 large crust

PREPARATION TIME: 15 mins.   COOKING TIME: 5 mins.
 (1 hr. to rise)   (prebake)

1 tbsp. active dry yeast   2½ cups whole wheat flour
1 cup warm water

Mix the yeast in the warm water (110 degrees). Let rest 5 minutes. Stir in the flour, 1 cup at a time. Mix well. Knead dough in bowl about 50 times.

Dough will be sticky. Cover bowl and let rise for 1 hour. Use non-stick or lightly oil a pizza pan or flat baking sheet. Sprinkle with cornmeal. Remove dough from bowl (it will be sticky) and place on prepared pan. Spread and pat it out with fingers and heels of hands. Spread it out to the edge of the pan. Be sure to make a slight edge to keep the sauce in. Bake at 400 degrees for 5 minutes. This keeps the crust from being soggy.

HELPFUL HINTS: Flour will be easier to work with and will rise faster if it is warmed before adding to yeast mixture—110 degrees is about right. This takes about ½ hour in a regular oven, about 1½ minutes in a microwave oven. Use this crust for a traditional pizza with tomato sauce and toppings, or with refried beans instead of tomato sauce, plus toppings of your choice.

Tortilla Chips

SERVINGS: 48 chips

PREPARATION TIME: 5 mins.   COOKING TIME: 20–30 mins.

    12 soft corn tortillas, thawed in bag (These can be purchased
       frozen in most food stores.)

Preheat oven to 275 degrees. Cut tortillas into four quarters. Lay pieces on a dry baking sheet in a single layer. Bake at 275 degrees about 20–30 minutes, until crisp. May also be served soft. Let thaw in bag, remove from bag, wrap in foil or place in covered baking dish, and heat in a warm oven for a few minutes. Serve warm.

HELPFUL HINTS: Before baking, sprinkle tortillas with some onion powder, garlic powder, or chili powder. This may also be done with pita bread. Cut into triangles and separate one side from the other. Lay on a baking sheet and bake as above. Makes delicious whole wheat crackers for dipping.

SALADS

Tabouli

SERVINGS: 3–4

PREPARATION TIME: COOKING TIME: none
60 mins. to soak bulgur, 15 mins. to put together, 2 hrs. to chill

½ cup dry bulgur wheat   1 tomato, chopped
1 cup boiling water   ½ cup fresh parsley, chopped

2 tbsp. lemon juice
⅛ tsp. garlic powder
¼ cup chopped green onions
    (about 3)

¼ cup fresh mint, chopped
½ cup cooked garbanzo beans

Put the bulgur in a small mixing bowl. Pour the boiling water over the bulgur. Mix. Cover with a towel and let stand for 1 hour. After 1 hour the excess water should be removed. The easiest way to do this is to pour the bulgur and water into a fine mesh strainer. Let the water drain off, pressing the bulgur with your hands to remove as much of the excess water as possible. Place the drained bulgur in a bowl. Add the remaining ingredients. Toss well to mix. Cover and refrigerate at least 2 hours to blend flavors.

HELPFUL HINTS: This is a great make-ahead dish, easy to take to a pot-luck dinner or picnic. Try it stuffed in pita bread for a different sandwich idea. This recipe can be doubled or quadrupled easily for larger amounts. Keeps well in refrigerator.

Rice Summer Salad

SERVINGS: 6–8

PREPARATION TIME: 30 mins.
  2 hrs to chill

COOKING TIME: none

4 cups cooked, long-grain brown
    rice
½ cup cider or wine vinegar
¼ tsp. dry mustard
1 tsp. tarragon
6 green onions, finely chopped
2 stalks celery, chopped

1 large green pepper, chopped
1 large tomato, chopped
1 cup cooked green peas
4–5 tbsp. diced pimiento
¼ cup chopped parsley
1 cucumber, chopped (optional)

Mix vinegar, mustard, and tarragon. Pour over the cooked rice. Mix well. If rice is warm, let cool to room temperature before adding remaining ingredients. When rice is cool, add remaining ingredients. Toss gently. Cover and refrigerate at least 2 hours before serving.

HELPFUL HINTS: For a variation, substitute basil or dill weed for the tarragon. Short-grain brown rice also may be used. Serve as a cool main dish for a hot summer's evening, either plain or piled on lettuce leaves and garnished with tomatoes and watercress.

Mixed Sprout Salad

SERVINGS: 8

PREPARATION TIME: 15 mins.   COOKING TIME: none
  1 hr. to chill

4 cups mixed bean sprouts (such
    as lentils, mung, adzuki,
    green peas)
1 cup alfalfa sprouts
1 bunch green onions, chopped
2 stalks celery, sliced

1 green pepper, chopped
¼ cup chopped pimiento
2 tbsp. cider vinegar
2 tbsp. salt-reduced tamari
1 tbsp. lemon juice

In a large bowl, combine the sprouts and the chopped vegetables. Toss to mix well. Combine the vinegar, tamari and lemon juice in a small bowl. Pour over the sprouts and vegetables. Toss to coat with sauce. Cover and refrigerate at least 1 hour before serving.

HELPFUL HINTS: Some health food stores will have sprouted mixed beans for sale in packages. Or you can sprout your own. Other sprouts may be used as desired. This salad is also good with the Lemon-Garlic Dressing. Omit the vinegar, tamari, and lemon juice and use about ½ cup of dressing.

Hot German Potato Salad

SERVINGS: 6

PREPARATION TIME: 15 mins.   COOKING TIME: 30 mins.

10 medium potatoes, cooked and
    sliced
1 onion, chopped
¼ cup water
2 tbsp. whole wheat flour
1 tbsp. honey

1 tsp. low-sodium tamari
½ tsp. celery seed
dash pepper (optional)
¾ cup water
½ cup vinegar

In a large pot, saute the onion in ¼ cup water over medium heat until tender and beginning to brown. Stir in flour, honey, tamari, and celery seed. Mix well until smooth. Stir in water and vinegar. Heat to boiling, stirring constantly. Add potatoes, stirring carefully. Heat through. Serve hot.

HELPFUL HINTS: To cook potatoes, wash, remove skins if desired. Cut into large chunks. Cook in small amount of boiling water until tender, about 30 minutes. Drain. Cool slightly and slice thinly.

DRESSINGS AND SPREADS

Ketchup Sauce

SERVINGS: about 2 cups

PREPARATION TIME: 5 mins.   COOKING TIME: none

1 cup tomato sauce
6 ozs. tomato paste
1½ tbsp. cider vinegar

2 tsp. low-sodium tamari
¼ tsp. onion powder
⅛ tsp. ground oregano

Mix all ingredients in a jar. Store covered in the refrigerator. Will keep for several weeks.

Thick French Tomato Dressing

SERVINGS: about 2½ cups

PREPARATION TIME: 5 mins.   COOKING TIME: none

1 cup tomato juice
1 cup tomato sauce
⅓ cup vinegar
¾ tsp. lemon juice

1 tsp. Italian herb seasoning
1 tsp. low-sodium tamari
   (optional)

Combine all ingredients in a quart jar. Cover. Shake well. Refrigerate before serving to blend flavors.

HELPFUL HINTS: Italian herb seasoning is a mixture of oregano, marjoram, thyme, savory, basil, rosemary, and sage. Usually found made by Schilling or Spice Islands. Use dressing on tossed salads or vegetable salads. Keeps in refrigerator for several weeks.

Lemon Garlic Dressing

SERVINGS: 2½ cups

PREPARATION TIME: 15 mins.   COOKING TIME: none

1 cup cider or wine vinegar
1 cup water
2 tbsp. lemon juice

2 garlic cloves
¼ tsp. pepper (optional)
½ tsp. celery seed

½ cucumber, cut in chunks   ½ tsp. dill weed
1 small onion, cut in chunks   1 tbsp. parsley flakes

Put all ingredients into blender jar. Blend until smooth. Refrigerate. Keeps well in refrigerator.

Hot Mexican Salsa

SERVINGS: 1¼ cups

PREPARATION TIME: 10 mins.
   1 hr. to chill

1 can tomatoes, drained   3–4 tbsp. chopped fresh coriander
   (14–15 ozs.)   1 clove garlic
½ small onion   ½ tbsp. vinegar
¼ cup chopped green chilis   ¼ tsp. Tabasco sauce
   (canned)   ⅛ tsp. ground cayenne pepper

Place all ingredients in blender jar. Process briefly until blended but not smooth. Cover and refrigerate.

HELPFUL HINTS: If you prefer a chunkier sauce, blend only half the onion, chilis, and coriander with the tomatoes. Finely chop the remaining onion, chilis, and coriander and add them to the blended sauce. Keeps well in refrigerator. This is a very hot salsa. Use less cayenne pepper, if desired. The amount of coriander may also be varied to suit your taste.

Garbanzo Puree

SERVINGS: 2 cups

PREPARATION TIME: 15 mins.   COOKING TIME: 3 hrs.

3 cups cooked garbanzo beans   1 tsp. onion powder
1 tbsp. lemon juice   ½ tsp. ground cumin
¼ tsp. basil   1 tbsp. parsley flakes
¼ tsp. garlic powder

Puree the beans and mix all of the ingredients together. (This may be done in a blender.) Also, some water or bean-cooking liquid may be added to make a creamy consistency.

HELPFUL HINTS: Let stand an hour at room temperature to blend flavors. Use as sandwich spread, to fill "pocket bread" (pita), or as a dip for crackers or pita.

Eggplant Dip

SERVINGS: 2–3 cups

PREPARATION TIME: 15 mins.   COOKING TIME: 1 hr.

1 large eggplant
2 cloves garlic, crushed
1 green onion, chopped

¼ cup chopped parsley
1 tbsp. lemon juice
½ tsp. dill weed

Cut the stem off the eggplant and prick it all over with a fork. Place directly on the oven rack in a 350 degree oven. Bake about 1 hour or until eggplant is soft and has wrinkled skin. Remove from oven and cool. When it is cool enough to handle, peel and chop. Place in blender with remaining ingredients and blend until smooth. Chill before serving.

HELPFUL HINTS: Use as a dip for raw vegetables, such as broccoli, cauliflower, carrots, zucchini. Or use as a dip for whole wheat pita bread. If you add more water when blending, this makes an interesting salad dressing. Also good as a sandwich spread.

Apple Butter

SERVINGS: 1 qt.

PREPARATION TIME: 5 mins.   COOKING TIME: 1 hr.

1 jar applesauce (about 32 ozs.
    or more)
1½ tsp. cinnamon

½ tsp. ground cloves
½ tsp. allspice

Combine all ingredients. Place in saucepan. Cook uncovered over low heat at least 1 hour to thicken and blend flavors. Pour into covered container and refrigerate. Use as a spread on toast, muffins, crackers.

HELPFUL HINTS: Also makes a delicious fruit syrup for waffles and pancakes. Just thin to desired consistency with a small amount of water. Serve hot or cold.

Soups

Vegetable–Bean Soup

SERVINGS: 8–10

PREPARATION TIME: 45 mins.   COOKING TIME: 3 hrs.

1 cup dried kidney beans
2 cloves garlic, pressed
1 onion, chopped
2 potatoes
1 carrot
2 zucchini
¼ lb. green beans
2 leeks
¼ lb. cabbage (Savoy is best)

⅓ cup long-grain brown rice or ½
    cup broken whole wheat
    spaghetti
2–3 tomatoes, cut in wedges
¼ cup chopped parsley
¼ tsp. celery seed
¼ tsp. marjoram
1 tsp. basil
1 tsp. oregano

Place beans in pot with 2 quarts of water. Bring to boil, remove from heat and let rest 1 hour. Then add chopped onion, garlic, and simmer for 1½ hours.

Chop potatoes in large chunks; do not peel. Slice carrots ½ inch and zucchini 1 inch thick, scrub them, do not peel. Slice leeks and cut beans into 1 inch pieces. Add to soup pot along with seasonings. Simmer for 1 hour longer.

Thinly slice cabbage and add to soup along with rice or spaghetti. Simmer another 20 minutes. Add more water if too thick. Add tomato wedges for the last 10 minutes, just before serving.

HELPFUL HINTS: Kidney beans make a good rich broth, but any kind of bean also may be used. Soup freezes well, so make a large batch when you have time and freeze half for use on a busy day. Try using some chopped spinach, instead of the cabbage. By changing the vegetables and beans used, the soup can be different each time you make it. It is a meal in itself.

Vegetable Soup

SERVINGS: 8–10

PREPARATION TIME: 30 mins.   COOKING TIME: 45 mins.

10 cups water
2 potatoes, cut in medium-sized
    chunks

¼ cup tamari, salt-reduced
1 tsp. basil
1 tsp. thyme

2 carrots, sliced
2 onions, sliced
2 zucchini, chopped medium-sized
2–3 tomatoes, chopped
2 cloves garlic, crushed
½ tsp. onion powder

1 cup string beans, cut in 1-in.
    pieces
1 tsp. oregano
½ tsp. cumin
½ tsp. dill weed
1 tbsp. parsley flakes

Place 10 cups water in a large pot. Add chopped vegetables. Bring to boil. Add seasonings. Simmer over medium-low heat about 45 minutes. Variations: use 2 cups tomato juice in place of 2 cups water. About 15 minutes before end of cooking time, add cooked grains or spaghetti noodles to pot, such as: cooked brown rice, 1 cup; barley, 1 cup; or 1 cup broken whole wheat spaghetti.

HELPFUL HINTS: Other vegetables also may be used in addition to or in place of the ones listed above. Try ½ cup fresh or frozen peas; ½ cup fresh or frozen corn; 1 green pepper, chopped; sliced leeks; sliced mushrooms; or some chopped spinach added for the last 5 minutes of cooking time.

Tomato–Onion Soup

SERVINGS: about 6 cups

PREPARATION TIME: 30 mins.   COOKING TIME: 1½ hours

2 onions, diced
2 leeks, thinly sliced (if leeks are
    unavailable, use one more
    onion)
1 garlic clove, pressed
4 cups water

8 large tomatoes, chopped
2 tbsp. chopped parsley
1 tsp. thyme
1 bay leaf
1 tsp basil
1 tbsp. tamari, salt-reduced

Saute onions, leeks, and garlic in ½ cup water until transparent (about 15 minutes). Add the remaining 3½ cups of water, the tomatoes, parsley, thyme, basil, and the bay leaf. Simmer, covered, over low heat for 60 minutes. Remove cover; simmer for 30 minutes longer. Add tamari just before serving.

HELPFUL HINTS: This soup is great with fresh, homemade bread. Add a green salad for an interesting meal. A large can of tomatoes (28 ozs.) may be substituted for the fresh tomatoes.

Chinese Vegetable Soup

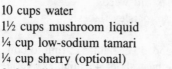

SERVINGS: 4–8

PREPARATION TIME: 30 mins.   COOKING TIME: 30 mins.

10 cups water
1½ cups mushroom liquid
¼ cup low-sodium tamari
¼ cup sherry (optional)
2–3 garlic cloves, crushed
1 tbsp. grated fresh ginger
2 pkgs. dried shiitake mushrooms

1 onion, cut in wedges
1 bunch green onions, cut in 1-
    inch pieces
3 stalks celery, sliced
½ lb. Chinese cabbage, sliced
½ lb. buckwheat soba noodles.

Pour 2 cups hot water over the mushrooms in a bowl; soak for 15 minutes. Meanwhile, put 10 cups water in a large soup pot. Add tamari, sherry, ginger, and garlic. Bring to a boil. Add onion wedges. Reduce heat. Squeeze excess water from the mushrooms, reserving the liquid. Add 1½ cups of this liquid to the hot broth. Chop mushrooms, discarding tough stems, and add to broth. Add remaining ingredients, except the noodles. Simmer over low heat 15 minutes, add noodles, and cook an additional 10 minutes. Serve hot.

HELPFUL HINTS: This will make a meal for four people, or a first course, with other Chinese food, for eight people.

Onion Soup

SERVINGS: 4

PREPARATION TIME: 15 mins.   COOKING TIME: 60 mins.

4 cups water or vegetable stock
3 onions, chopped or sliced
¼ cup water
2 tbsp. salt-reduced tamari

Optional
½ tsp. dry mustard
dash of thyme
¼ tsp. garlic powder

Saute onions in ¼ cup water. Cook about 15 minutes until soft and tender. Add 4 cups water (or vegetable stock) and bring to a boil. Reduce heat to low. Add tamari. Simmer covered for at least 30 minutes before serving. The longer it cooks the more flavor it will have.

HELPFUL HINTS: Double the recipe and freeze some for another day.

Pea Soup

SERVINGS: 8–10

PREPARATION TIME: 45 mins.   COOKING TIME: 2 hrs.

1 cup split green peas	1 tsp. basil
¼ cup barley	1 tsp. thyme
½ cup dried lima beans	2 carrots, chopped
8–10 cups water	1 potato, chopped
2 onions, chopped	2 celery stalks, chopped
2 bay leaves	½ cup parsley, chopped
1 tsp. celery seed (optional)	

Begin by placing peas, barley, and lima beans in large soup pot with 8 cups of water, onion, bay leaves, and celery seed. Cook over low heat, covered, about 1½ hours. Then add the remaining vegetables and seasonings and cook about 45 minutes longer. Add more water if necessary.

HELPFUL HINTS: Also can be made without lima beans; in this case, increase split peas to 2 cups. Freezes well. Makes a good sandwich spread; also good on baked potatoes.

White Bean Soup

SERVINGS: 6

PREPARATION TIME: 15 mins.   COOKING TIME: 3–4 hrs

2 cups navy beans or	2 bay leaves
Great Northern beans	½ tsp. sage
8 cups water	½ tsp. oregano
2 onions, chopped	1 tbsp. low-sodium tamari
2 stalks celery, chopped	

Put beans and water in large pot. Soak overnight or bring to a boil, remove from heat, and let rest 1 hour. Add onions, celery, and seasonings. Simmer over low heat, covered, about 3 hours.

HELPFUL HINTS: Can be made in slow cooker, about 8 hours on high or 10–12 hours on low. For a thicker, creamier version, place about 2–3 cups of the soup in a blender jar. Blend until smooth. Return to soup pot and mix in well. This soup makes a good sandwich spread when cold.

Latin Black Bean Soup

SERVINGS: 6

PREPARATION TIME: 15 mins.   COOKING TIME: 3 hrs.

1 cup black beans
8 cups water
1 onion, chopped
1 green pepper, chopped
2 cloves garlic, crushed
1 tsp. oregano
1 tsp. ground cumin
1 (6 ozs.) can tomato paste

3 tbsp. red wine vinegar
1 tbsp. low-sodium tamari
2 cups cooked brown rice
¼ cup chopped green chilis
⅛–¼ tsp. Tabasco Sauce
1 to 2 tbsp. chopped fresh
  coriander

Place beans and water in a large soup pot. Bring to boil; cook for 2 minutes. Remove from heat, cover, and let rest for about 45 minutes. Return to heat. Add onion, garlic, green pepper, oregano, and cumin. Cover and let cook over low heat for 1½ hours. Add tomato paste, vinegar, and tamari. Cook an additional 30 minutes. Add chilis, rice, Tabasco, and coriander. Cook 10 minutes. Serve hot.

HELPFUL HINTS: This is a very spicy soup. Use less Tabasco and less coriander if you prefer your foods less spicy.

Lentil Soup

SERVINGS: 8–10

PREPARATION TIME: 30 mins.   COOKING TIME: 60 mins.

2 cups uncooked lentils
10 cups water
2 carrots, sliced
1 celery stalk, chopped
2 onions, chopped

2 small potatoes, chopped
⅓ cup barley
2 tbsp. parsley flakes
2 bay leaves
2 tsp. cumin

Combine all ingredients in soup pot and cook until the lentils are soft, about 1 hour. Remove bay leaves before serving.

HELPFUL HINTS: Brown rice may be substituted for the barley. This soup freezes well; save some for a busy day.

Sweet and Sour Lentil Soup

SERVINGS: 8–10

PREPARATION TIME: 30 mins. COOKING TIME: 1½ hrs.

2 cups lentils
10 cups water
2 onions, chopped
2 celery stalks, chopped
3 carrots, chopped
3 potatoes, chopped
28 ozs. canned tomatoes,
  broken up

1 green pepper, chopped
¼ cup red wine (or apple juice)
2 tbsp. lemon juice
3 tbsp. molasses
2 tbsp. wine vinegar
2 tbsp. low-sodium tamari
1 tsp. basil

Combine all ingredients in a large pot. Bring to a boil. Cover and cook over low heat for 1½ hours.

Easy Curried Lentil or Pea Soup

SERVINGS: 8

PREPARATION TIME: 5 mins. COOKING TIME: 1 hr.

10 cups water
2 cups lentils or green split peas
1 chopped onion

2 tsp. curry powder
2 cups cooked rice

Start by cooking the lentils and onion or split peas and onion in the water over low heat for about 30 minutes. Add the curry powder and the rice and cook 30 minutes longer.

HELPFUL HINTS: Makes a great cold sandwich spread.

Barley–Mushroom Soup

SERVINGS: 6–8

PREPARATION TIME: 15 mins. COOKING TIME: 1¼ hrs.

8 cups water
½ cup barley
1 chopped onion
2 cloves garlic, pressed

3 tbsp. low-sodium tamari
3 tbsp. sherry (optional)
1 lb. fresh mushrooms, sliced

Place 8 cups water in large soup pot. Add barley, onion, garlic, and tamari. Cook over low heat for 1 hour until barley is tender. Add sliced musrhooms (and optional sherry). Cook 15 minutes longer. Serve hot.

Mild Gazpacho

SERVINGS: 6–8

PREPARATION TIME: 20 mins.   COOKING TIME: none
2 hrs. to chill

4 cups tomato juice
2 tomatoes
1 green pepper
1 cucumber
2 green onions

2 celery stalks
½ cup fresh parsley
juice of ½ lemon
1 tbsp. low-sodium tamari
1 tsp. basil

Put 2 cups tomato juice in blender along with half of the vegtables. Cut the vegetables in large chunks to make blending easier. Blend well. Pour into large jar. Repeat with remaining ingredients, parsley, basil, lemon juice, and tamari. Blend. Add to the first batch. Mix well. Cover and chill at least 2 hours to blend flavors. Serve cold.

HELPFUL HINTS: Makes a good salad dressing or a delicious cold drink. Serve gazpacho and a salad on those summer nights when its too hot to cook.

Sauces

Simple Tomato Pasta Sauce

SERVINGS: 1 qt.

PREPARATION TIME: 10 mins.   COOKING TIME: 15 mins.

2 cups tomato puree
2 cups canned tomatoes
1 tsp. onion powder
½ tsp. garlic powder
½ tsp. basil

½ tsp. oregano
1 tbsp. parsley flakes
1 tbsp. low-sodium tamari
dash Tabasco sauce (optional)

Combine all ingredients in a saucepan, breaking up the tomatoes with a fork. Bring to a boil, reduce heat, and cook over low heat about 15 minutes. Stir occasionally. Serve over whole grain pasta.

HELPFUL HINTS: This is a quick and easy tomato sauce for those days when you are pressed for time. It will not be as thick or as richly flavored as sauces that have cooked all day. Use as a sauce for pasta, grains, or on baked potatoes.

Pizza Sauce

SERVINGS: 3½ cups

PREPARATION TIME: 10 mins.   COOKING TIME: 15 mins.

2 cups tomato sauce   ½ tsp. oregano
1½ cups tomato paste   ½ tsp. garlic powder
½ tsp. basil   1 tsp. onion powder

Combine all ingredients in a saucepan and simmer over low heat about 15 minutes to blend flavors.

HELPFUL HINTS: Use as a pizza sauce, as a sandwich spread, or as a substitute for ketchup. Will keep in refrigerator for several weeks.

Mexican Chili Sauce

SERVINGS: about 4 cups

PREPARATION TIME: 10 mins.   COOKING TIME: 10 mins.

2 cups tomato sauce   ¼ tsp. garlic powder
2 cups water   4 tbsp. chili powder blend
6 tbsp. whole wheat flour

Mix ⅔ cup water with the garlic powder and whole wheat flour in a saucepan. Cook over low heat about 1–2 minutes, stirring constantly. Remove from heat. Mix the chili powder in ⅓ cup hot water. Stir to dissolve. Add to the flour mixture. Stir to mix. Add the tomato sauce and 1 cup water. Mix well. Return to heat. Heat to boiling, stirring frequently, about 10 minutes.

HELPFUL HINTS: Serve over burritos or enchiladas. Keeps well in refrigerator. Quite spicy; reduce the amount of chili powder for a milder sauce.

Spicy Gravy

SERVINGS: 4 cups

PREPARATION TIME: 5 mins.   COOKING TIME: 15 mins.

3 cups tomato sauce   ¾ tsp. basil
½ cup red wine (or apple juice) ½ tsp. dry mustard

2 tsp. chili powder	¼ tsp. oregano
2 tbsp. low-sodium tamari	¼ tsp. cumin
2 tbsp. parsley flakes	2 tbsp. cornstarch or arrowroot
½ tsp. thyme	mixed in ½ cup water

Place all ingredients, except cornstarch or arrowroot and water, in a saucepan. Heat over medium heat, Gradually add the cornstarch mixture to the pan, stirring until thickened. Serve over grains, mashed potatoes, or steamed vegetables.

HELPFUL HINTS: A little more or less cornstarch may be used as desired, depending on how thick you want the sauce to be.

Brown Gravy

SERVINGS: 1½ qts.

PREPARATION TIME: 10 mins.   COOKING TIME: 30 mins.

¼ cup water	5½ cups water
1 onion, finely chopped	½ cup salt-reduced tamari
1 cup whole wheat pastry flour	

Heat water in large saucepan over medium heat and saute onion for 5 minutes,until transluscent. Blend in the flour and stir well. Cook for 3–4 minutes, until lightly browned. Add water and tamari. Cook over medium heat, stirring often, until sauce thickens. Add more water if too thick.

HELPFUL HINTS: Some chopped mushrooms could be sauteed with the onions. Use as a sauce for steamed vegetables, grains, potatoes, or a vegetable pie. Try steaming your favorite vegetables, serve with brown rice, and top with brown gravy. Freezes well. If you prefer a smooth gravy (no onion or mushroom pieces), blend at high speed in blender about halfway through the cooking time. Then return to pan and continue to cook and stir until thickened.

This makes a large amount of gravy. Freeze some for later use or cut the recipe in half if you don't want so much.

Mushroom Gravy

SERVINGS: about 2½ cups

PREPARATION TIME: 15 mins.   COOKING TIME: 30 mins.

½ lb. mushrooms, chopped	1 tsp. thyme
2 leeks, sliced	1 tbsp. salt-reduced tamari

2¼ cups, water   4 tbsp. arrowroot or cornstarch
1 tsp. oregano

Saute the mushrooms and leeks in ¼ cup water with the oregano and thyme for 10 minutes. Mix the cornstarch or arrowroot and tamari with 2 cups of cold water. Add to mushroom–leek mixture. Cook over low heat, stirring frequently, until it thickens (about 20 minutes).

HELPFUL HINTS: Use 1 chopped onion if no leeks are available. Serve over rice or other grains, potatoes, griddle cakes, waffles, bean or grain loaves or burgers, or vegetables.

Whole Wheat Sauce

SERVINGS: 2 cups

PREPARATION TIME: 5 mins.   COOKING TIME: 15 mins.
   Basic Sauce: ½ cup whole wheat flour
               2 cups water

Seasonings:

1. ½ tsp. basil   2. ½ tsp. basil
   ½ tsp. dill   ¼ tsp. marjoram
   ½ tsp. cumin   ½ tsp. tarragon

3. ½ tsp. thyme   4. ½ tbsp. tamari
   ¼ tsp. oregano   1 tsp. onion powder
   ½ tsp. sage   ⅛ tsp. turmeric

Place flour in a dry saucepan over medium heat. Stir for 5 minutes. Remove from heat. Gradually add the water, stirring with a wire whisk to blend well. Return to heat, cook over low heat, stirring occasionally until thickened. Add seasonings as desired.

HELPFUL HINTS: This makes a good substitute for white sauce. By varying the seasonings used, the sauce takes on a different flavor for different uses.

Nutty White Sauce

SERVINGS: about 2 cups

PREPARATION TIME: 5 mins.   COOKING TIME: 15 mins.

   2 cups nut milk or rice milk (recipes elsewhere in book)
   2 tbsp. arrowroot or cornstarch
   ¼ cup water

Place the nut milk or rice milk in a saucepan. Mix arrowroot or cornstarch with water to form a smooth liquid. Add to the milk. Cook over medium heat, stirring frequently, until it thickens. Season as desired.

HELPFUL HINTS: If you cook this over low heat, it may take 30 minutes to thicken, but you won't have to stir as often.

Seasoning suggestions:

1. 1 tbsp. tamari
   1 tsp. onion powder

2. ½ tsp. basil
   ½ tsp. dill
   ½ tsp. cumin

3. ½ tsp. tarragon
   ½ tsp. basil
   ¼ tsp. marjoram

4. ½ tsp. thyme
   ¼ tsp. oregano
   ½ tsp. sage

5. ½ tbsp. tamari
   ½ tsp. onion powder
   ½ tsp. ground ginger
   ¼ tsp. garlic powder

Main Dishes—
Vegetable Stews and Sauces

Marinara Spaghetti Sauce

SERVINGS: 4

PREPARATION TIME: 20 mins. COOKING TIME: 60 mins.

2 onions, chopped
4 cloves garlic, crushed
½ lb. mushrooms, chopped
4 cups tomato sauce

2 cups canned tomatoes
2 tsp. oregano
1 tsp. basil
1½ tbsp. parsley flakes

Saute onions, garlic, and mushrooms in ¼ cup water until slightly tender, about 10 minutes. Stir in tomato sauce, tomatoes, and spices, breaking up tomatoes with a fork. Simmer over low heat about 1 hour, stirring occasionally. Do not cover. Serve over whole wheat spaghetti or vegetable spaghetti.

HELPFUL HINTS: May be made ahead and reheated. Freezes well. May be cooked longer than 1 hour if you like sauces thicker. Also try over whole grains, whole wheat macaroni, or whole wheat shells. This recipe may be doubled easily for guests or to have leftovers to freeze. Makes a good topping for baked potatoes.

Enchilada Sauce

SERVINGS: about 6 cups

PREPARATION TIME: 30 mins.   COOKING TIME: 35–40 mins.

¼ cup water
1 onion, chopped
3 cloves garlic, crushed
¼ cup chopped green chilis
1 can tomatoes (28 ozs.)
½ tsp. basil

½ tsp. ground cumin
¼ tsp. ground oregano
1 cup water
1 tbsp. low-sodium tamari
3 tbsp. arrowroot or cornstarch
¼ cup water

Place ¼ cup water, onion, and garlic in large saucepan. Saute about 10 minutes. Chop the tomatoes well, add them and the juice to the pan, along with the green chilis and the spices. Simmer for 15 minutes. Mix the tamari in 1 cup water. Add to the tomato mixture. Dissolve the arrowroot in ¼ cup water. Add to the tomato mixture, stirring well. Simmer about 10 minutes longer over very low heat, stirring occasionally. Serve with vegetable or bean enchiladas, polenta, whole grains, or pasta.

Chickenless à La King

SERVINGS: 4

PREPARATION TIME: 15 mins.   COOKING TIME: 30 mins.

1 onion, chopped
2 green peppers, chopped
½ lb. mushrooms, chopped
¾ cup water
¾ cup whole wheat flour

3 cups nut milk or rice milk
1 cup water
2 tbsp. low sodium tamari
1 jar (4 ozs.) pimiento, chopped

In a large pan, cook onions, green pepper, and mushrooms in ¾ cup water for 10 minutes. Remove from heat. Blend in flour. Then slowly stir in 3 cups nut (high-fat) or rice (low-fat) milk, 1 cup water, and the tamari. Cook over medium heat, stirring almost constantly until mixture boils and thickens. Stir in pimiento. Cook and stir about 2 minutes longer to heat pimiento. Serve hot over rice, whole grains, whole wheat toasted bread, or baked potatoes.

Vegetable Curry

SERVINGS: 4–6

PREPARATION TIME: 30 mins.   COOKING TIME: 30 mins.

2 carrots, sliced ¼ inch thick
2 stalks celery, sliced ¼ inch thick
2 zucchini, cut in half lengthwise,
   then sliced ½ inch thick
1 bunch broccoli, cut into stems
   and flowers
1 cup fresh or frozen peas

½ head cauliflower, broken into
   flowerettes
1 onion, cut in half and thinly
   sliced
1½ tbsp. curry powder
4 tbsp. whole wheat flour
3 cups water

Saute the sliced onion in ¼ cup water until tender. Add the curry powder and whole wheat flour, Mix well and continue to stir for about 1 minute. Gradually add the 3 cups water while stirring. Cook over low heat, stirring occasionally, until sauce thickens. Steam the carrots and celery for 5 minutes, add the broccoli and cauliflower, and steam for 5 minutes longer. Finally, add the zucchini and peas and continue to steam for 10 more minutes. Place steamed vegetables in a serving bowl, pour the curry sauce over them, and stir to make sure the vegetables are coated with the sauce. Serve over brown rice or bulgur wheat. Makes a good meal with dal and whole wheat chapatis.

Vegetable Chop Suey

SERVINGS: 6–8

PREPARATION TIME: 45 mins.   COOKING TIME: 30 mins.

¼ cup water
2 cloves garlic, crushed
2 onions, sliced
8–10 leaves Chinese cabbage,
   sliced
1 stalk celery, sliced
¼ lb. broccoli, sliced
¼ lb. mushrooms, sliced

1 cup snow peas (optional)
½ cup green onions, sliced in 1-
   inch pieces
1 cup mung bean sprouts
3 tbsp. low-sodium tamari
2 tbsp. sherry (optional)
3 cups water
5–6 tbsp. arrowroot or cornstarch

Put ¼ cup water into a large pot or wok. Add the crushed garlic and heat water to boiling. Add onions, celery, cabbage, and broccoli. Saute about 10 minutes. Add the mushrooms. Saute 5 more minutes. Add the water, tamari, sherry, green onions, snow peas, and bean sprouts. Bring to a boil and cook about 10 minutes. Dissolve the arrowroot or cornstarch in a small amount of cold water. Remove pot from heat. Gradually add arrowroot or cornstarch mixture, stirring well. Return to heat. Stir until thickened. Serve over brown rice, whole wheat spaghetti, or buckwheat soba noodles.

HELPFUL HINTS: Prepare rice before starting to cook vegetables. Keep warm until serving. If you prefer noodles, have the water boiling while vegetables are cooking. About 15 minutes before serving, drop the noodles into the boiling water, return to boil, reduce heat, and simmer about 10 minutes.

Heather's Mushroom Delight

SERVINGS: about 4 cups

PREPARATION TIME: 20 mins.   COOKING TIME: 15 mins.

3 pkgs. dried mushrooms
   (shiitake)
1 round onion, chopped
1 bunch green onions, chopped
2 cloves garlic, crushed
1½ tbsp. grated fresh ginger root

¼ cup sherry (or apple juice)
⅓ cup low-sodium tamari
1 cup mushroom stock
2 cups water
⅓ cup cornstarch or arrowroot

Place mushrooms in bowl. Pour 2 cups boiling water over them. Soak for 15 minutes. Squeeze to remove excess water. Cut off tough stems and discard. Chop mushrooms into bite-sized pieces. Set aside. Strain and reserve 1 cup mushroom stock.

Place chopped round onion in saucepan with ¼ cup water. Saute for 5 minutes. Add chopped green onion and chopped mushrooms, garlic, ginger, sherry, and tamari. Mix well. Add the mushroom stock and water. Heat to boiling, stirring frequently.

In a separate bowl, mix the cornstarch or arrowroot in ½ cup water. Add to sauce. Continue to cook and stir until thickened. Serve over whole grains.

Vegetable Stew

SERVINGS: 6–8

PREPARATION TIME: 45 mins.   COOKING TIME: 2 hrs.

5 medium potatoes, cut in large cubes (unpeeled)
1 lb. boiling onions, or 2 round onions cut in wedges
2–3 carrots, cut in ½-inch rounds
½ lb. mushrooms, cut in half
2 medium zucchini, cut in half, then sliced 1 inch thick

½ lb. green beans, cut in 1-inch pieces
2½ cups tomato juice mixed with ¼ cup tamari (salt-reduced)

Place potatoes, onions, carrots, and beans in a large casserole dish. Pour about ⅔ of the tomato juice mixture over the vegetables. Sprinkle with a little paprika and basil. Put covered casserole in oven at 350 degrees for 1¼ hours. Remove from oven and add mushrooms, zucchini, and the rest of the tomato juice mixture. Sprinkle a little more paprika and basil on the top. Return to oven for 30 minutes longer.

HELPFUL HINTS: Serve with fresh bread or brown rice. Vegetables may be stirred from time to time during cooking to make sure they are all coated with juice mixture. To make a thicker sauce before serving, remove vegetables to serving bowl. Put liquid in a pan, heat to boiling, and add a small amount of arrowroot and water mixture until desired thickness is obtained (try 3 tbsp. arrowroot or cornstarch in ½ cup cold water). Pour over vegetables.

Hearty Brown Stew

SERVINGS: 6–8

PREPARATION TIME: 20 mins.   COOKING TIME: 1½ hrs.

2 onions, sliced
2 celery stalks, sliced
2 carrots, sliced
3 potatoes, chunked
½ lb. mushrooms, quartered
2–3 large cloves garlic, crushed
2 cups water

¼ cup low-sodium tamari
¼ cup red wine (or apple juice)
½ tbsp. grated fresh ginger
½ tsp. marjoram
½ tsp. thyme
3–4 tbsp. cornstarch or arrowroot

Combine all ingredients, except the cornstarch or arrowroot, in a large pot. Bring to a boil, lower heat, cover, and simmer about 1½ hours until vegetables are tender. Mix the cornstarch or arrowroot in ½ cup water. Slowly add to the stew. Stir until thickened.

HELPFUL HINTS: This also can be made in a slow cooker. Follow above directions. Cook on high for 6 hours or on low for 12 hours. Add the cornstarch or arrowroot mixture just before serving and stir until thickened.

Chinese Vegetable Sauce

SERVINGS: 6–8

PREPARATION TIME: 30 mins.   COOKING TIME: 20 mins.

6 cups assorted chopped
   vegetables
1 pkg. dried mushrooms
1 cup mung bean sprouts
2 cloves garlic, crushed
1 cup mushroom stock
2 cups water

¼ cup low sodium tamari
1 tbsp. grated ginger root
1 tsp. dry mustard
2 tbsp. chopped fresh coriander
few dashes Tabasco sauce
   (optional)
4 tbsp. cornstarch or arrowroot

Place dried mushrooms in a bowl. Pour 2 cups hot water over them. Let rest for 15 minutes to soften. Squeeze out excess liquid, reserving 1 cup of stock for later use. Cut off stems and discard. Chop mushrooms and set aside. Place ½ cup water in a large wok or saucepan. Add crushed garlic, grated ginger, and dry mustard. Add the chopped vegetables and mushrooms and saute 5 minutes. Add remaining ingredients, except cornstarch or arrowroot. Cover and simmer over low heat 10 minutes. Mix cornstarch or arrowroot in ½ cup cold water. Add to sauce and stir until thickened.

HELPFUL HINTS: Serve over rice or buckwheat soba noodles. The smaller you chop the vegetables, the faster they will cook. Some good ones to use are green onions, celery, carrots, broccoli, green pepper, round onions, Chinese cabbage, and snow peas. Use several kinds in various combinations. Try some asparagus when it is in season.

Easy Ratatouille

SERVINGS: 8–10

PREPARATION TIME: 20 mins.   COOKING TIME: 60 mins.

2 large onions, chopped
2 green peppers, chunked
6 zucchini, sliced
2 large eggplant, chunked
2 cloves garlic, crushed

4 cups chopped tomatoes (use
   fresh or canned with their
   juice)
1 tbsp. basil
1 tbsp. oregano
2 tbsp. chopped parsley

Place all ingredients in a large pot. Cover. Cook over medium-low heat about 60 minutes. Stir occasionally. Serve hot or cold.

HELPFUL HINTS: Serve over noodles, grains, potatoes, or stuffed in pita bread. Makes a large amount. Freezes well, reheats well. May be made in a slow cooker. Add all ingredients at once. Cook on low about 6–8 hours.

Stove-Top Stew

SERVINGS: 8

PREPARATION TIME: 45 mins.   COOKING TIME: 60 mins.

3 onions, sliced
4 cloves garlic, pressed
4 potatoes, chunked
4 stalks celery, sliced
4 carrots, sliced
2 zucchini, chunked (optional)
½ lb. mushrooms, sliced
   (optional)

1 stalk broccoli, sliced (optional)
1 can tomatoes (28 ozs.) chopped
2 tbsp. molasses
1 tbsp. parsley flakes
2 tsp. dill weed
¾ cup burgundy wine (or apple
   juice)
3 tbsp. arrowroot or cornstarch

Put ½ cup water in a large pot, add onions, garlic, potatoes, celery, and carrots. Saute about 15 minutes. Add optional broccoli if desired, along with burgundy wine. Cover and steam vegetables about 10 minutes. Add tomatoes, molasses, parsley, dill, and optional zucchini and mushrooms if desired. Cover and simmer over low heat about 30 minutes longer. Mix arrowroot or cornstarch in ⅓ cup water. Gradually add to stew, stirring constantly until thickened.

HELPFUL HINTS: This may be made ahead and reheated just before serving. Other vegetables may be used in place of optional ones, or they may be omitted.

Spicy Vegetable Stew

SERVINGS: 6–8

PREPARATION TIME: 30 mins.   COOKING TIME: 1½ hrs.

2 sliced onions
2 cloves garlic, crushed
2 potatoes, chunked
2 stalks celery, sliced
2 carrots, sliced
2 zucchini, chunked

2 tsp. chili powder
2 tbsp. low-sodium tamari
2 tbsp. parsley flakes
½ tsp. thyme
¾ tsp. basil
½ tsp. dry mustard

½ lb. mushrooms
½ cup red wine (or apple juice)
15 ozs. canned tomatoes,
  broken up

1 cup tomato sauce
¼ tsp. oregano
¼ tsp. cumin

Saute onions, garlic, potatoes, celery, and carrots in ½ cup water for 10 minutes. Add wine. Cover and steam for 15 minutes. Add remaining ingredients. Stir to mix well. Cover and cook over low heat about 1 hour. Stir occasionally. Just before serving, mix 2 tbsp. cornstarch or arrowroot with ¼ cup water. Stir into stew and continue stirring until thickened. Serve over rice or other whole grains.

HELPFUL HINTS: Other vegetables may be added. A stalk of broccoli is a nice addition.

Main Dishes—
Rice and Grains

Brown Rice

SERVINGS: 3 cups

PREPARATION TIME: none   COOKING TIME: 1 hr.

Long-grain brown rice—firm, separate grains
Medium-grain brown rice—soft, sticks together
Short-grain brown rice (sweet rice)—very soft and sticky grains

1 cup raw brown rice
2 cups water

Put rice and water into a pan with a tight-fitting lid. Bring to boil, reduce heat to low, cover, and cook for 45 minutes. Do not stir or it will become gummy. Try to restrain yourself from checking it while cooking—the rice will be fluffier for this. After 45 minutes the water should be absorbed (if it is not, continue cooking about 15 minutes longer). Remove pan from heat, leave cover on, and let rest 15 minutes before serving.

HELPFUL HINTS: Brown rice will be fluffier if it is allowed to rest at least 15 minutes after cooking. Longer is preferred. Do not stir while cooking.

Brown rice can be cooked in a rice cooker. Add the water first, then the brown rice. Add more water if you find you would like your rice softer. Use less water for crunchier brown rice.

Tossed Green Rice

SERVINGS: 4

PREPARATION TIME: 10 mins.   COOKING TIME: 10 mins. (plus 1 hr. for rice)

4 cups hot, cooked brown rice
1½ cups green onions, chopped (2 bunches)
2 stalks celery, sliced
1 green pepper, chopped
1 clove garlic, crushed

2 tbsp. water
½ cup parsley, finely chopped
½ tsp. basil
½ tsp. dill weed
¼ tsp. paprika
2 tomatoes, chopped

Begin cooking the rice about 45 minutes before you start to cook the vegetables. Rice should be hot. Saute the green onions, celery, green pepper, and garlic in 2 tbsp. water for 5 minutes. Add the parsley, basil, dill, and paprika. Cook about 5 minutes longer. Put the hot brown rice in a large serving bowl. Add the sauteed vegetables. Toss to mix well. Then add the chopped tomatoes. Toss lightly and serve at once.

HELPFUL HINTS: This is like a hot rice salad. It can be a simple complete meal or a side dish for a more elaborate dinner.

Fried Rice

SERVINGS: 4

PREPARATION TIME: 15 mins.   COOKING TIME: 20 mins.

3 cups mixed vegetables, chopped
(Examples: carrots, onions,
    broccoli: 1 cup each
green pepper, carrots,
    bean sprouts: 1 cup each
carrots, bean sprouts,
    green onions: 1 cup each)

¼ cup water
2 cups cooked brown rice
1 tbsp. salt-reduced tamari
½ tsp. dry mustard
½ tsp. ground ginger

Mix mustard and ginger with ¼ cup water in a large soup pot. Heat to boiling. Add vegetables and cook over medium heat until tender (about 10–15 minutes). Use a wok if you have one. If the vegetables are cut in small strips they will cook faster. Add the cooked rice; stir until heated. Add the tamari. Mix well. Continue cooking until heated through (1–2 minutes).

HELPFUL HINTS: This will serve two hungry people for a fast, complete meal. Any combination of vegetables may be used. Just keep the pieces small so they cook quickly.

Spanish Rice

SERVINGS: 4–6

PREPARATION TIME: 20 mins.   COOKING TIME: 30 mins.

3 cups cooked brown rice
1 onion, chopped
1 green pepper, chopped
1 stalk celery, chopped (optional)
½ cup chopped mushrooms

1 green chili pepper, chopped
2 cloves garlic, crushed
1 cup tomato sauce
1 tbsp. salt-reduced tamari

Saute the onion, green pepper, celery, mushrooms, and garlic in ½ cup water for about 15 minutes. Use a large pot. Add the tomato sauce, tamari, and the green chili pepper. Mix well. Add the cooked rice. Heat about 15 minutes. Serve hot.

HELPFUL HINTS: Use 2 green chili peppers if you like spicy foods. Try adding ½ tsp. basil and ½ tsp. oregano.

Vegetables and Rice

SERVINGS: 4–6

PREPARATION TIME: 45 mins.   COOKING TIME: 45 mins.

3 cups cooked brown rice
1 onion, chopped
1 carrot, sliced
1 cup broccoli, sliced
1 cup cauliflower, sliced
1 cup mushrooms, sliced
2 zucchini, sliced or cubed
1 cup mung bean sprouts

1 cup alfalfa sprouts
¼ tsp. paprika
¼ tsp. basil
¼ tsp. sage
¼ tsp. marjoram

Begin with onion, carrot, broccoli, and cauliflower. Saute in a small amount of water (½ cup) until crisp-tender, or steam in steamer basket until crisp-tender (15–20 minutes). Then add mushrooms, zucchini, and mung bean sprouts for another 10 minutes. Then add the cooked rice and alfalfa sprouts and spices. Heat for about 5 minutes and serve.

HELPFUL HINTS: Cook rice early in the day and refrigerate, or cook a large amount on one day to use in several different recipes. Rice also can be frozen. Vegetables can be changed as desired. Begin with longer-cooking ones; then add short-cooking ones.

Sherried Rice

SERVINGS: 4–6

PREPARATION TIME: 30 mins.   COOKING TIME: 20 mins.

2 onions, cut in half and sliced
½ lb. mushrooms, sliced
2 cloves garlic, crushed
1 stalk broccoli, coarsely chopped
½ head cauliflower, coarsely
    chopped
1 zucchini, cut in half and sliced
½ cup snow peas

¼ cup sauterne wine (optional)
¼ cup sherry (optional)
¼ tsp. curry powder
¼ tsp. allspice
¼ tsp. nutmeg
¼ tsp. herb seasoning mix
3 cups cooked brown rice

Saute onions, mushrooms, and garlic in ¼ cup water and ¼ cup sauterne wine for 5 minutes. Add broccoli, snow peas, cauliflower, zucchini, ¼ cup sherry, plus the seasonings. Cook and stir over medium heat until vegetables are tender, about 10 minutes. Add cooked rice. Heat through and serve.

HELPFUL HINTS: Apple juice may be substituted for the wine and sherry, if desired.

Indian Rice

SERVINGS: 4–6

PREPARATION TIME: 15 mins.   COOKING TIME: 30 mins.

1 onion, chopped
1 green pepper, chopped
3 stalks celery, chopped
1 large green apple, chopped
½ cup currants or raisins

1 cup water
4 cups cooked brown rice
2 tsp. curry powder
1 tbsp. low-sodium tamari

Cook onion, green pepper, celery, and apple in ½ cup of water for 10 minutes. Add raisins and remaining water. Cook 10 minutes longer. Add rice, curry powder, and tamari. Stir to mix well. Continue to cook until heated through, about 10 minutes. Stir occasionally. Serve hot or cold.

Paella

SERVINGS: 6–8

PREPARATION TIME: 20 mins.   COOKING TIME: 60 mins.

2 onions, sliced
4 tomatoes, cut in large chunks

2 tbsp. low-sodium tamari
⅛ tsp. saffron

1 green pepper, sliced or chunked
2 cups uncooked brown rice
4 cups water
2 tbsp. paprika
¼ tsp. pepper (optional)

½ lb. mushrooms, sliced
2 cups frozen green peas, thawed
1 jar pimiento (4 ozs.) sliced or
chopped

In a large pan, cook the onion and tomatoes in ½ cup water for 5 minutes. Add the green pepper, rice, the remaining water, and the spices and seasonings. Bring to boil, reduce heat to low, cover, and cook for 30 minutes without stirring.

Then add the mushrooms and peas, stir once lightly, cover, and continue to cook an additional 20 minutes. Remove from heat. Stir in the pimiento, cover, and let rest for 10–15 minutes before serving, in order to absorb any excess moisture.

Rice Medley

SERVINGS: 6–8

PREPARATION TIME: 20 mins.   COOKING TIME: 1¼ hrs.

1 cup chopped celery
1 cup chopped onions
1 cup chopped green peppers
1 cup sliced carrots
2 cloves garlic, crushed
½ tsp. paprika

½ tsp. sage
½ tsp. marjoram
½ tsp. rosemary
2 cups uncooked brown rice
3 cups water
¼ cup low-sodium tamari

Saute vegetables in ¼ cup water for 15 minutes. Stir in herbs, rice, water, and tamari. Bring to a boil. Lower heat, cover, and simmer on low heat until liquid is absorbed, about 45 minutes. Do not stir while cooking. Turn off heat. Leave cover on and let rest for 15 minutes before serving.

Lentil–Rice Surprise

SERVINGS: 6

PREPARATION TIME: 1 hr. for lentils to cook; 30 mins. to prepare casserole.   COOKING TIME: 45 mins.

1 cup dried lentils
¼ cup water
1 onion, chopped
1 clove garlic, pressed
3 celery stalks, chopped

1 can tomatoes (28 ozs.)
1 tsp. dill weed
3 cups cooked brown rice
1 cup whole wheat bread crumbs

Cover lentils with water, bring to a boil, cover, and simmer over low heat, about 1–1½ hours, until tender. Drain off liquid, reserving ½ cup liquid.

Heat ¼ cup water in a large pot; add onion, garlic, and celery. Cook over medium-low heat until tender, about 15 minutes. Add tomatoes, drained lentils, ½ cup lentil water, cooked rice, and dill weed. Mix well.

Using a 3-qt. casserole, sprinkle a few bread crumbs over the bottom. Pour lentil–rice mixture into casserole. Sprinkle the rest of the bread crumbs over the top. Bake at 350 degrees for 45 minutes.

HELPFUL HINTS: This dish may be made ahead of time and refrigerated until ready to put in oven. Add 15 minutes to baking time.

Spanish Bulgur

SERVINGS: 4

PREPARATION TIME: 10 mins.   COOKING TIME: 30 mins.

1 cup bulgur wheat	1 cup cooked beans, any kind
1 bunch chopped green onions	1 clove garlic, crushed
1 green pepper, chopped	1 tsp. paprika
2 cups canned tomatoes and juice	1 tsp. low-sodium tamari

Combine all ingredients in a large pot. Cover, bring to boil, reduce heat, and simmer over low heat about 20 minutes, until liquid is absorbed.

Main Dishes—
Beans

Patrick's Simple Refried Beans

SERVINGS: 8–12

PREPARATION TIME: 5 mins.   COOKING TIME: 20 mins.

6 cups cooked pinto beans	½–1 cup bean cooking water (or
½ tsp. onion powder	water)
¼ tsp. garlic powder	

Mash cooked beans with a small amount of bean water until desired consistency is reached. Add onion and garlic powder. Mix well. Cook over low heat about 15 minutes. Serve on chapatis, on tortillas, in pita bread, or as a sandwich spread.

HELPFUL HINTS: Cook pintos in a slow cooker, either overnight or all day. Refried beans freeze well, so make a large batch and save some. Freeze the bean cooking water also, and use it for soup stock. Try adding ¼–½ tsp. of chili powder for variety.

Taco Beans

SERVINGS: 6

PREPARATION TIME: 5 mins.   COOKING TIME: 15 mins.

¼ cup chopped onion
3 cups cooked and mashed pinto
  or kidney beans
½ cup tomato sauce
½ cup water

¼ cup chopped green chilis
  (canned)
¼ cup raisins (optional)
½ tsp. oregano
¼ tsp. ground cumin

Saute onion in ¼ cup water, until translucent. Add remaining ingredients. Stir to mix. Cook over low heat about 10–15 minutes until thickened and heated through. Serve in pita bread, on chapatis, or on corn tortillas. Top with chopped tomatoes, shredded lettuce, and salsa.

Barbequed Beans

SERVINGS: 6

PREPARATION TIME: 15 mins.   COOKING TIME: 20 mins.

1 onion, chopped
1 green pepper, chopped
1 clove garlic, crushed
1½ tsp. dry mustard
1½ tsp. chili powder
½ tsp. ground cumin
½ tsp. turmeric

1 cup tomato sauce
1½ tbsp. unsulphured molasses (or
  malt syrup)
½ tbsp. apple cider vinegar
dash (or two) Tabasco sauce
4 cups cooked beans (pink,
  kidney, red, or pinto)

Saute onion, green pepper, and garlic in ¼ cup water for 5 minutes. Add mustard, chili powder, cumin, and turmeric. Stir to mix well. Add remaining ingredients. Mix well. Cook over low heat until heated through, about 15 minutes.

HELPFUL HINTS: This is great on a whole wheat bun, like a Sloppy Joe mix, with some acceptable ketchup and mustard. Good take-along for picnics. Use either hot or cold. Also good over whole grains or as a sandwich spread.

Barley and Beans

SERVINGS: 6–8

PREPARATION TIME: 20 mins.   COOKING TIME: 3 hrs.

1 cup pinto, kidney, or pink beans
1 cup barley
8 cups water
1 onion, chopped
½ lb. mushrooms, chopped

2 cups chopped spinach
1 tbsp. lemon juice
1 tbsp. low-sodium tamari
¼ tsp. rosemary

Place beans and water in a large pot. Bring to boil. Boil for 1 minute, remove from heat, cover, and let rest 1 hour (or soak overnight and eliminate 1 hour resting time). Then bring to boil, cover, and simmer over low heat about 1 hour. Add barley, onions, and mushrooms. Continue to cook 45 minutes longer. Add spinach and remaining ingredients 15 minutes before serving. Stir to mix well. Cook 15 minutes. Serve hot.

HELPFUL HINTS: Test beans for tenderness before adding spinach. You may want to cook the beans and barley a little longer. This dish also can be made in a slow cooker. Add beans, 6 cups water, barley, onions, and mushrooms. Cook on high 6–8 hours or on low 10–12 hours. Add spinach and remaining ingredients 30 minutes before serving. Cook on high after adding spinach.

Chili

SERVINGS: 8

PREPARATION TIME: 30 mins.   COOKING TIME: 2½ hrs.

¾ cup brown rice
2 cups dried kidney beans
6½ cups water
2 onions, chopped
2 green peppers, chopped
6 cloves garlic, crushed

1 large can tomatoes (28 ozs.)
   or 2 cups chopped fresh
   tomatoes
   plus ½ cup water
1 tsp. ground cumin (optional)
3 tsp. chili powder

Place beans, rice, and water in a large pot. Cover and cook over low heat, about 1 hour. (While this is cooking, prepare the vegetables.) After beans and rice have cooked about 1 hour, add the remaining ingredients to the pot, breaking up the canned tomatoes with a fork. Continue to cook about 1½ hours longer, 60 minutes covered, then 30 minutes uncovered.

HELPFUL HINTS: Instead of cooking the rice with the beans, cook the beans in 5 cups of water, use the same remaining ingredients, and serve the chili over rice or other grains such as bulgur wheat, barley, millet, or cornmeal. Leftover cooked grains also may be added about 30 minutes before serving. Try adding 1 cup of corn kernels to the chili for the last 30 minutes of cooking time. This is also good stuffed in pita bread and topped with alfalfa sprouts.

Butch's Chili

SERVINGS: 8

PREPARATION TIME: 30 mins.   COOKING TIME: 3 hrs.

2 cups dried red kidney beans
5 cups water
2 onions, chopped
2 green peppers, chopped
½ lb. mushrooms, sliced
    (optional)

6 cloves garlic, crushed
15 ozs. canned tomatoes, broken
    up
2 cups tomato sauce
1 tbsp. chili powder
1 tbsp. low-sodium tamari

Place beans and water in a large pot. Bring to a boil, cover, and simmer over low heat for 1 hour. Add remaining ingredients. continue to cook over low heat an additional 2 hours.

HELPFUL HINTS: Add 1 cup frozen corn kernels to chili during last hour of cooking. Chili is good made ahead and reheated. May be cooked longer than 3 hours if desired. This makes the .beans softer and allows flavors to blend more. Bean cooking time may be reduced by soaking beans overnight. This chili also may be made in a slow cooker. Add all ingredients at once. Cook on high 6–8 hours, on low 12–14 hours.

Spicy Mexican Topping

SERVINGS: 6–8

PREPARATION TIME: 30 mins.   COOKING TIME: 30 mins.

1 lg. onion, chopped
2 lg. carrots, thinly sliced
1 clove garlic, pressed
2½ tsp. chili powder
¾ tsp. cumin
¾ tsp. oregano

4 zucchini, cut into ½-inch cubes
1 green pepper, chopped
1 cup frozen corn
2 cups cooked kidney beans
1 tbsp. arrowroot or cornstarch

Place onion, carrots, and garlic in a large pot with ¼ cup water. Cook over low heat. Add chili powder, cumin, and oregano. Cook about 10 minutes. Add zucchini, green pepper, corn, and beans. Mix well. Cover and cook over low heat about 20 minutes. Stir often. Mix arrowroot in small amount of cold water. Remove pan from heat. Add arrowroot mixture. Mix in well. Return to heat; stir until thickened.

HELPFUL HINTS: This can be used for many different dishes. It's good over brown rice or stuffed into pita bread. It's also good as a filling for chapatis, tostadas, or tacos. Use chopped green onions, tomatoes, cucumbers, or alfalfa sprouts as toppings. Spoon some green chili salsa over the top if desired.

Sloppy Lentils

SERVINGS: 6

PREPARATION TIME: 15 mins.   COOKING TIME: 60 mins.

2 cups dried lentils
1 large chopped onion
1 carrot, chopped
1 green pepper, chopped
4 cups water
4 cups tomato sauce

1 tbsp. parsley flakes
1 bay leaf
½ tsp. basil
¼ tsp. garlic powder
1 tbsp. salt-reduced tamari

Place lentils, onions, carrots, and green pepper in a large pot with 4 cups of water. Cover and simmer for 30 minutes. Add tomato sauce and seasonings to the pot and simmer for 30 minutes longer. Serve over whole grain bread, muffins, or whole grains.

HELPFUL HINTS: May be made ahead and reheated. Also freezes well.

Sweet and Sour Lentil Stew

SERVINGS: 6

PREPARATION TIME: 30 mins.   COOKING TIME: 90 mins.

⅓ cup raw brown rice
1 cup uncooked lentils
4 cups water
1 onion, chopped or sliced
1 carrot, chopped or sliced
2 potatoes, chopped
1 green pepper, chopped
1 cup fresh tomatoes, chopped

1 clove garlic, crushed
1 bay leaf
½ tsp. basil
1 tbsp. low-sodium tamari
1 tbsp. lemon juice
1 tbsp. molasses
1 tbsp. cider vinegar

Put lentils, rice, and water in a large pot. Bring to a boil. Reduce heat, cover, and simmer for 30 minutes. Add onions, carrots, potatoes, and green pepper. Simmer for 30 minutes more. Add tomatoes and seasonings. Cook an additional 30 minutes. Serve hot.

HELPFUL HINTS: One 16-oz. can of tomatoes may be used instead of the fresh tomatoes. Other vegetables may be added as desired. Longer-cooking ones should be added with the onions. Shorter-cooking ones may be added with the tomatoes.

Brazilian Black Beans With Marinated Tomatoes

SERVINGS: 6–8

PREPARATION TIME: 30 mins.   COOKING TIME: 3 hrs.

Beans
2 cups dried black beans
6 cups water
2 large garlic cloves
1 onion, studded with 8 cloves
2 onions, chopped
1 large green pepper, chopped

Marinated Tomatoes
6 tomatoes, chopped
1 bunch green onions, chopped
½ onion, chopped
1 clove garlic, crushed
3 tbsp. wine vinegar
4–5 dashes Tabasco sauce

BEANS: Place beans and water in large pot. Add 2 whole garlic cloves and 1 whole onion, studded with 8 whole cloves. (Make a small hole for each clove in the side of the onion with a toothpick; then push the stem end into the hole.) Cook over low heat about 2 hours. Remove the garlic and the whole onion. Add chopped onions and green pepper. Cook an additional hour until beans are tender.

MARINATED TOMATOES: Combine all ingredients. Refrigerate until ready to serve, at least 1 hour. Serve the beans over brown rice, with some of the marinated tomatoes on top.

Limas 'N' Noodles

SERVINGS: 6

PREPARATION TIME: 10 mins.   COOKING TIME: 2 hrs.

2 cups uncooked lima beans
6 cups water
2 onions, sliced or chopped
2 stalks celery, sliced or chopped
2 cloves garlic, crushed
1 tbsp. low-sodium tamari

1 tsp. tarragon
1 tsp. basil
½ tsp. thyme
¼ cup chopped pimiento
2 cups uncooked whole wheat
  spirals or elbows

Place limas and water in large pot. Bring to a boil, reduce heat, cover, and simmer over low heat for 1 hour. Add remaining ingredients, except pimiento and noodles. Continue to cook 45 minutes longer. Add pimientos and noodles. Cook until noodles are tender, about 15 minutes.

HELPFUL HINTS: Use either large or small limas in this recipe. If you soak the limas overnight, 45 minutes of the first lima cooking time can be eliminated. Total cooking time will be about 1¼ hours.

Dal

SERVINGS: 6

PREPARATION TIME: 15 mins.   COOKING TIME: 60 mins.

1½ cups moong dal (or yellow
    split peas or lentils)
4 cups water
1 tsp. cumin seeds (or ½ tsp.
    ground cumin)
1 tsp. ground turmeric

½ tsp. ground cinnamon
¼ tsp. ground ginger
¼ tsp. ground coriander
½ tsp. mustard seeds
⅛ tsp. ground cloves

Place the dal (or split peas) in a large pot with 4 cups water. Bring to a boil, cover, and simmer about 30 minutes. Heat ¼ cup water in a small saucepan. Add all the spices and stir them until well heated (2–3 minutes). Add the spice mixture to the dal after it has been cooking for 30 minutes. Mix well. Continue to cook about 30 minutes longer, until the dal is thick. Serve hot.

HELPFUL HINTS: Moong dal is mung beans split and with skins removed. Sometimes they are hard to find. Yellow split peas or lentils may be used in place of the mung beans. An easier way to prepare this is to omit all the spices listed above. Add 1 tbsp. curry powder after the beans have cooked for 30 minutes.

Bean Enchiladas

SERVINGS: 6–8

PREPARATION TIME: 30 mins.   COOKING TIME: 30 mins.

6 cups enchilada sauce or Mexican
    chili sauce (recipes in this
    book)
12 soft corn tortillas
3 cups refried beans (recipe in this
    book)

1 bunch green onions, chopped
½ lb. mushrooms, chopped
    (optional)
2 tomatoes, chopped (optional)
1 cup fresh or frozen corn kernels
    (optional)

Heat the enchilada sauce or Mexican chili sauce until it is just warm. Thaw the corn tortillas until soft. Prepare remaining ingredients of your choice. Choose a large area to work in and place all ingredients there.

Take 1 cup of the sauce and spread over the bottom of a 9″ x 12″ baking dish. Place to one side. Take one tortilla at a time and place it on top of the remaining heated sauce, one side only (This makes it easier to roll the tortilla.) Remove carefully. On the sauced side, spread some refried beans down the middle of the tortilla; sprinkle on some green onions, and any of the options you choose. Roll up the tortilla (or fold over if it's too fat) and place in baking dish, seam side down. Repeat until all tortillas are used; overlap as necessary in baking dish to keep them folded over. Pour the remaining enchilada sauce over them. Bake at 350 degrees for 30 minutes.

HELPFUL HINTS: This dish is easy to prepare ahead. Cover and refrigerate until ready to put into the oven. Add 15 minutes to baking time.

Chapatis and Beans

SERVINGS: 12

PREPARATION TIME: 15 mins.   COOKING TIME: 15 mins.

2 pkgs. whole wheat chapatis (12)
3 cups refried beans (recipe in
    this book)
2 chopped tomatoes
1 bunch chopped green onions

1 cup alfalfa sprouts
2 cups shredded lettuce
1–2 chopped green chilis
    (optional)
1 cup Mexican-style chili salsa

Heat bean mixture over low heat until warm, about 15 minutes. Place in serving bowl. Place assorted vegetables in individual serving bowls. Let everyone assemble their own chapatis.

HELPFUL HINTS: Spread a line of beans down the center of the chapati. Add assorted vegetables as desired. Spoon a little hot sauce down the center. Fold up chapati and eat with fingers, or, if it's too full, use a fork.

Stuffed Pita Bread

SERVINGS: 10–12

PREPARATION TIME: 15 mins.   COOKING TIME: 15 mins.

1 pkg. whole wheat pita bread
3 cups refried beans or garbanzo
    puree (recipes in this book)

1 chopped green pepper (optional)
1 chopped cucumber (optional)
1 grated carrot (optional)

2 chopped tomatoes
1–2 cups alfalfa sprouts or
   shredded lettuce

1 cup Mexican-style chili salsa
1 bunch chopped green onions

Heat the bean mixture over low heat until warmed through. Place in serving bowl. Place chopped vegetables on table in individual bowls. Let everyone assemble their own pita.

HELPFUL HINTS: Cut pita in half with scissors. Spread apart. Fill with some bean mixture. Then add garnishes as desired. Spoon a little hot sauce over the garnishes and enjoy.

Curried Beans

SERVINGS: 8–10

PREPARATION TIME: 20 mins. COOKING TIME: 1 hr.

3 cups cooked small white beans
1 cup celery, diced
1 onion, finely chopped
½ cup carrots, diced
1 clove garlic, crushed
1 green pepper, diced

1½ cups water or bean cooking
   liquid
2½ tsp. curry powder
½ tsp. ground cumin (optional)
1 tbsp. low-sodium tamari

In a large pan, saute the celery, onion, carrots, green pepper, and garlic in ½ cup water, about 10 minutes. Add beans, cooking liquid or water, and spices. Mix well. Pour into a baking dish and bake at 350 degrees until liquid is absorbed, about 1 hour.

HELPFUL HINTS: Makes a delicious cold sandwich spread. Mash beans with a potato masher or put through a food grinder for the best consistency.

Split Peas on Toast

SERVINGS: 6

PREPARATION TIME: 20 mins. COOKING TIME: 1 hr.

4 cups water
1 onion, chopped
1 potato, scrubbed (not peeled)
   and chopped

1 cup dry yellow split peas
1 carrot, grated
1 tsp. basil
¼ tsp. dill (optional)

Bring water to boil in large saucepan. Add the onion, potato, and split peas. Simmer for 45 minutes. Add grated carrot and basil. Simmer for 15 minutes. Serve over toasted whole grain bread.

HELPFUL HINTS: Also may be made with green split peas. Good over waffles or cooked whole grains.

Main Dishes— General

Peasant's Pie

SERVINGS: 6–8

PREPARATION TIME: 1 hr.   COOKING TIME: 30–45 mins.

Topping: 4 medium potatoes, cooked and mashed (mash with about ¼ cup water, not with milk or butter) to yield 3 cups mashed
Sauce: 2 cups brown gravy, mushroom gravy, or other sauces (try tomato)
Filling: 1 onion, coarsely chopped
3 carrots, sliced thinly
1 green pepper, diced
½ lb. broccoli, cut into stems and flowers
¼ lb. green beans, cut into 1-inch pieces
1 bunch spinach, torn into bite-sized pieces.

Steam vegetables (except spinach) about 15 minutes, until crisp-tender. Remove from heat. Stir in spinach and 2 cups gravy. Spoon this filling into a 9″ x 12″ baking dish. Spread mashed potatoes over the top. Sprinkle with a small amount of paprika. Bake 30 minutes at 350 degrees.

HELPFUL HINTS: Add ½ pound Brussels sprouts when they are available. Use favorite vegetables for filling, cut into bite-sized pieces. Use about 8 cups of chopped vegetables. If prepared ahead, add 15 minutes to baking time. Use leftover vegetables, added to others after they have been steamed. Frozen vegetables also may be used. Peas and corn are good additions.

Layered Dinner

SERVINGS: 8

PREPARATION TIME: 30 mins.   COOKING TIME: 1½ hrs.

6 potatoes, sliced
1 lg. onion, sliced
2 carrots, sliced
1 green pepper, sliced

1 zucchini, sliced
1 cup corn (frozen or fresh)
1 cup green peas (frozen or fresh)

Optional vegetables: mushrooms, broccoli, green beans, etc.

Sauce:

3 cups tomato sauce	2 tsp. chili powder blend
¼ cup low-sodium tamari	½ tsp. cinnamon
1 tsp. ground thyme	⅛ tsp. oregano
1 tsp. dry mustard	⅛ tsp. sage
1 tsp. basil	2 tbsp. parsley flakes

Layer vegetables in large casserole in order given. Use optional vegetables as desired. Mix ingredients of sauce together. Pour over vegetables. Bake, covered, in a 350 degree oven for about 1½ hours.

HELPFUL HINTS: Other vegetables may be used, according to your preference. This dish is easy to prepare ahead and hold in oven for a company dinner. Serve with whole grains or bread and a green salad.

Stuffed Peppers

SERVINGS: 8

PREPARATION TIME: 45 mins.   COOKING TIME: 1¼ hrs.

8 lg. green peppers, stemmed and cored	3 cups cooked brown rice
1 onion, diced	1 tsp. thyme
½ cup celery, chopped	1 tsp. sage
½ lb. mushrooms, chopped	½ tsp. basil
¼ cup water	¼ tsp. garlic powder
2 cups tomato sauce (1 cup for topping)	

Cook onions, celery, and mushrooms in the water for about 15 minutes, until tender. Mix in 1 cup tomato sauce, rice, and seasonings. Pack the mixture into raw green peppers that have been stemmed and cored. Place in baking dish. Pour the remaining 1 cup tomato sauce over the peppers, a little on each. Add about 1½ cups water to the bottom of the baking dish to prevent peppers from drying out. Cover and bake at 375 degrees for 45 minutes, uncover and bake for 15 minutes longer.

HELPFUL HINTS: May be prepared ahead of time. Keep in refrigerator until ready to bake. Add 15 minutes to baking time. As a variation, use 1 cup of corn, fresh or frozen, in place of 1 cup of rice. The green peppers may be steamed before stuffing, if desired. Place stemmed and cored peppers in a steaming basket. Steam over 1 inch of boiling water for 5 minutes. Stuff and bake as above.

Middle East Vegetable Stew

SERVINGS: 8

PREPARATION TIME: 1 hr.   COOKING TIME: 1½ hrs.

6 potatoes, sliced
1 cauliflower, cut into flowerettes
1 broccoli, cut in pieces
2 onions, halved and sliced
4 carrots, sliced
2 zucchini, thickly sliced
4 cloves garlic, pressed
2 cups water
1 tbsp. paprika
½ tsp. cumin
½ tsp. oregano
1 bay leaf

¼ tsp. dill
¼ tsp marjoram
¼ tsp. thyme
Pinch of each:
    turmeric
    nutmeg
    cinnamon
    allspice
    cloves
    ginger
    coriander
    cardamon

Layer the vegetables in a large casserole dish in this order: potatoes, carrots, cauliflower, broccoli, onions, and zucchini. Mix the water, the garlic, and all of the herbs and spices. Pour over the vegetables. Cover the casserole, place in a 350 degree oven for 1½ hours. When finished baking, remove from oven, drain juices into saucepan, and heat. Make a paste of 2 tbsp. cornstarch or arrowroot and ⅓ cup water. Add slowly to juice mixture; stir until thickened. Pour sauce over cooked vegetables and serve.

HELPFUL HINTS: Serve with brown rice or other whole grains.

Lasagna

SERVINGS: 8–10

PREPARATION TIME: 2 hrs.   COOKING TIME: 1 hr.

8–12 ozs. whole wheat lasagna
    noodles, uncooked
1 recipe of marinara tomato sauce
    (recipe in this book)
4 cups chopped spinach, steamed
    (about 1 lb.)

2 cups whole wheat sauce, basic
    (recipe in this book)
3 large zucchini, sliced and
    steamed.

Begin by making the marinara tomato sauce and whole wheat sauce. While sauces are simmering, wash and trim spinach. Chop coarsely. Steam until barely tender. Combine the spinach with the whole wheat sauce. Steam the zucchini about 10 minutes, until tender but not mushy. To assemble lasagna, place a thin layer of sauce on the bottom of a 9″ x 12″ baking dish (or larger), then a layer of the uncooked noodles over the sauce. Spread a third of the tomato sauce over the noodles. Then use half of the zucchini and lay them over the tomato sauce. Next spoon half of the spinach mixture over the zucchini. Repeat the layer of noodles, a third more of tomato sauce, the remaining zucchini and spinach mixture. Then add another layer of noodles and spread the remaining tomato sauce over the top. Cover and bake in a 350 degree oven for 30 minutes, uncover, and bake for 30 minutes longer. Let rest about 10 minutes after removing from oven before cutting.

HELPFUL HINTS: This dish may be prepared ahead of time and refrigerated until ready to bake. Add about 20 minutes to baking time.

Tamale Pie

SERVINGS: 8

PREPARATION TIME: 45 mins.   COOKING TIME: 45 mins.

3 cups cooked pinto beans,
    mashed
1 onion, chopped
1½ tsp. chili powder
¼ cup tomato sauce
1 cup frozen corn

1 green pepper, chopped
1–2 chopped green chilis
1½ cups cornmeal
2½ cups water
½ tsp. chili powder

Place onion in a large pot with ¼ cup water. Saute about 10 minutes, add green pepper, corn, green chilis, tomato sauce, and chili powder. Cook 5 minutes. Add mashed beans and cook about 10 minutes over low heat. Remove from heat.

Combine cornmeal, water, and chili powder in a suacepan. Cook over medium heat until mixture thickens, stirring constantly with a wire whisk or the cornmeal will lump.

Using a non-stick 8″ x 8″ pan, spread half of the cornmeal mixture over the bottom. Pour the bean mixture over this and spread it out. Then spread the remaining cornmeal mixture over the top.

Bake at 350 degrees for 45 minutes, or until it bubbles.

Pizza

SERVINGS: 1 large pizza

PREPARATION TIME: 30 mins.   COOKING TIME: 20 mins.

1½ cups pizza sauce
1 large prebaked pizza crust
Toppings: chopped green onions
         chopped round onions
         chopped green peppers
         sliced mushrooms
         sliced tomatoes (add last 10 mins. of baking)
         alfalfa sprouts (add last 5 mins. of baking)

Spread the sauce on the prebaked crust. Add any or all of the toppings that you prefer. Bake at 400 degrees for 20 minutes. Remove from oven and let rest for 5 minutes before cutting, to make it easier to remove from the pan.

HELPFUL HINTS: Recipes for pizza sauce and the crust are in this book.

Chapati Vegetable Rolls

SERVINGS: 6–8

PREPARATION TIME: 60 mins.   COOKING TIME: 45 mins.

2 carrots, grated
1 zucchini, grated
1 onion, grated
1 potato, grated
2 bunches green onions, chopped
½ lb. mushrooms, chopped

1 tbsp. low-sodium tamari
4 cups whole wheat sauce flavored
    as desired, or 4 cups brown
    gravy
10–12 chapatis

Make the whole wheat sauce first; season as desired. Spread 1 cup of sauce in 9″ x 12″ baking dish. Place ¼ cup water in a large pot. Add the grated raw vegetables. Simmer until crisp-tender, about 10 minutes. Season with tamari. Remove from heat. Using about ⅓ cup of the vegetable mixture, spread it down the center of each chapati. Roll up the chapati and place seam down in the 9″ x 12″ baking dish. Repeat until all chapatis are filled and rolled up. Pour the remaining 3 cups of sauce over the rolls. Cover and bake at 350 degrees for 45 minutes.

HELPFUL HINTS: May be prepared ahead. Whole wheat sauce and brown gravy recipes found in this book. Chapatis may be purchased at most natural food stores in the frozen food department. Also carried in some supermarkets. Thaw before using. For a variation, omit the zucchini and potato and use fresh steamed spinach (1 pound) instead. Mix with other vegetables just before filling the chapatis.

Stuffed Cabbage Rolls

SERVINGS: 6–8 (14 rolls)

PREPARATION TIME: 45 mins.   COOKING TIME: 45 mins.

1 head cabbage	⅛ tsp. garlic powder
1 onion, chopped	dash pepper (optional)
½ lb. mushrooms, chopped	3 cups cooked brown rice
¼ cup currants (optional)	4 cups tomato sauce
¼ tsp. nutmeg	

Remove core from cabbage. Steam over boiling water for 5 minutes. Let cool slightly. Peel off leaves carefully and set aside. Saute onions, mushrooms, and currants in ½ cup water for 10 minutes. Stir in nutmeg, garlic powder, and pepper. Stir in brown rice and 1 cup of the tomato sauce. Remove from heat. Pour 1 cup tomato sauce over the bottom of a 9″ x 12″ baking dish. Spoon about ⅓–½ cup rice mixture into the center of each cabbage leaf. Roll up and place seam side down in baking dish. Pour remaining tomato sauce over the rolls in the baking dish. Cover and bake at 350 degrees for 45 minutes.

HELPFUL HINTS: May be prepared ahead. Keeps well in the refrigerator. Bake just before serving and add 15 minutes to baking time.

Vegetable-Stuffed Peppers with Spicy Tomato Sauce

SERVINGS: 6

PREPARATION TIME: 40 mins.   COOKING TIME: 45 mins.

6 large green peppers	2 stalks celery, chopped
½ cup water	3 green onions, sliced
1 onion, chopped	2 cups fresh or frozen corn kernels
1 clove garlic, crushed	2½ cups cooked brown rice
1 tsp. ginger root, minced	1 tbsp. low-sodium tamari
1 tomato, chopped	½ tsp. chili powder blend

Sauce:

2 cups tomato sauce	2–3 drops Tabasco sauce
1 small onion, quartered	¼ tsp. basil
½ green pepper (use 3–4 tops of	¼ tsp. oregano
peppers)	1 tbsp. parsley flakes

Begin by preparing peppers. Cut off tops (reserve for later use), clean out insides, and steam over 1 inch of boiling water for 5 minutes (steaming is an optional step). In a large pan, saute onion, garlic, and ginger for 5 minutes. Add tomato, celery, green onions, and corn. Cook for 5 minutes longer. Add rice and seasonings. Stir to mix well. Remove from heat. Pack the mixture into green pepper shells. Combine all ingredients for the tomato sauce in a blender. Blend until smooth. Pour over the peppers in a baking dish. Cover, bake at 350 degrees for 30 minutes, uncover, and bake an additional 15 minutes.

HELPFUL HINTS: May be prepared ahead and baked just before eating.

Baked Stuffed Squash

SERVINGS: 4

PREPARATION TIME: 30 mins.   COOKING TIME: 1¼ hrs.

2 acorn squash	¼ tsp. thyme
1 onion, chopped	¼ tsp. marjoram
¼ lb. mushrooms, chopped	3 cups cooked rice or 3 cups
1 tbsp. salt-reduced tamari	whole wheat bread crumbs
¼ tsp. sage	

Cut squash in half lengthwise. Scoop out seeds and stringy portion. Place in a baking dish with ½ inch of water in bottom. Bake for about 1 hour at 350 degrees. While squash is baking, prepare the stuffing mix. Cook onions and mushrooms in ¼ cup water for 5 minutes. Add tamari and spices. Cook over low heat for 5 more minutes. Remove from heat. Add the rice or the bread crumbs and mix together well. When the squash has baked about 1 hour and is almost tender, remove from oven. Fill each with stuffing mix. Return to oven and bake an additional 15 minutes.

HELPFUL HINTS: May be served as is or with a gravy. To prepare ahead, bake the squash for 1 hour and remove from oven. Let cool. Prepare stuffing. When ready to prepare dinner, fill with stuffing mix and bake at 350 degrees for 30 minutes.

Baked Eggplant Casserole

SERVINGS: 6–8

PREPARATION TIME:　30 mins.　　COOKING TIME:　10 mins. (prebake)

　　　　　　　　　　　　　　　　　　　　　　　　　　　45 mins. (casserole)

2 medium or 3 smallish round
　　eggplants
½ cup cornmeal
¼ tsp. garlic powder
1 large onion, sliced in rings
1 large green pepper, sliced in
　　rings

1 jar pimiento, chopped
4 cups tomato sauce
1 tsp. basil
½ tsp. oregano

Slice eggplant ½ inch thick. Mix cornmeal and garlic powder, and dip the eggplant slices in this mixture until both sides are well coated. Place these slices on a dry baking sheet. Bake at 400 degrees for 10 minutes. Meanwhile prepare onion, pepper, and pimiento. Combine the tomato sauce, basil, and oregano. Arrange baked eggplant slices in the bottom of a 9″ x 12″ baking dish. Lay the onion and pepper rings on top of the eggplant; scatter the chopped pimiento over all of this. Pour the tomato sauce mixture over the vegetables. Bake, uncovered, in a 375 degree oven for 45 minutes.

HELPFUL HINTS: May also be made in a smaller casserole dish. Arrange it in two layers: eggplant, onions, peppers, and sauce, then repeat.

Chinese Noodles with Vegetables

SERVINGS: 4

PREPARATION TIME:　45 mins.　　COOKING TIME:　20 mins.

1 lb. whole wheat spaghetti or
　　buckwheat soba noodles
4–6 dried mushrooms (shiitake)
6 green onions, chopped
1 tsp. grated fresh ginger

2 cups thinly sliced vegetables
2 tbsp. low-sodium tamari
1 tbsp. sherry or rice vinegar
1 cup mushroom stock

Place about 6 cups water in large pan. Heat to boiling. Add the noodles. Reduce heat to medium low. Stir to separate noodles. Cover. Simmer 10 minutes. Drain, rinse well, and chill. Place mushrooms in a bowl. Pour 1 cup boiling water over them. Soak for 15 minutes. Squeeze to remove excess water. Reserve stock. Cut the stems off and discard. Cut mushrooms into strips. Set aside. In a wok or large pan, heat ¼ cup water. Add green onions and grated ginger. Saute for 1 minute. Add mushrooms and vegetables. Cook and stir for 5 minutes. Add the cooked noodles. Cook and stir 2 minutes longer. Add the reserved mushroom stock, the tamari, and the sherry or vinegar. Mix well. Bring to boil. Reduce heat, cover and cook over medium heat 5 to 10 minutes, until liquid is absorbed. May be served either hot or cold.

HELPFUL HINTS: Some good vegetables to use: celery, carrots, green beans, asparagus, snow peas, Chinese cabbage, broccoli. Use all one vegetable or combinations such as celery and carrots; asparagus and snow peas; snow peas and Chinese cabbage.

Shish-Kebabs

SERVINGS: 6–8

PREPARATION TIME: 60 mins.   COOKING TIME: 15 mins.

Marinade:	Vegetables:
¾ cup vinegar	1 lb. mushrooms
1¼ cups tomato juice	4 long eggplants
¼ cup red wine (or apple juice)	2 green peppers
¼ cup salt-reduced tamari	1 lb. boiling onions
¼ tsp. garlic powder	6 tomatoes
1 tsp. basil	
1 tsp. oregano	

Begin by mixing the marinade and set it aside in a large bowl. Cut the eggplant into 1-inch slices, place them on a dry baking sheet, and broil them 8 inches from broiler about 5 minutes (watch them). Add them to the marinade. Clean the mushrooms and leave whole unless they are very large. Add the mushrooms to the marinade. Stir well to make sure the mushrooms and eggplant are well coated with marinade. Let stand at room temperature at least 3 hours. Clean the onions and cut in half. Cut the peppers into 1-inch chunks. Cut the tomatoes into wedges. Skewer the vegetables in any order you choose. I find the long bamboo skewers work best. Place the skewers on a broiling tray (or on a rack in a baking dish). Broil at least 8 inches from heat for 10–15 minutes. Watch them carefully. You may baste them with extra marinade as they broil, if desired. Serve at once.

HELPFUL HINTS: Serve with brown rice or bulgur wheat. A good dish for guests or a special occasion. A delicious sauce for this meal can be made by adding 3 tablespoons arrowroot or cornstarch to the marinade, place mixture in a saucepan over medium heat, cook, and stir until thickened.

Mild Mixed Vegetable Curry

SERVINGS: 6–8

PREPARATION TIME: 30 mins.   COOKING TIME: 45 mins.

1 onion, sliced
1 apple, peeled and chopped
1 clove garlic, crushed
1 tsp. grated ginger root
1 tsp. mustard seeds
½ tsp. turmeric
½ tsp. ground cumin
½ tsp. ground coriander
⅛ tsp. chili powder
1½ cups water

1 tsp. lemon juice
2 potatoes, peeled and chopped
1 carrot, sliced
1 tomato, chopped
½ head cauliflower, cut into
    flowerettes
1 eggplant, chopped
1 cup peas
½ cup raisins

In a large pot, saute onion, apple, garlic, and ginger in ½ cup water for 5 minutes. Stir in the spices, cook, and stir for 2 minutes. Add 1 cup water, bring to a boil, stirring constantly until sauce thickens slightly. Mix in lemon juice. Add potatoes, carrots, and tomatoes. Cover and cook for 10 minutes, stirring occasionally. Add cauliflower and eggplant. Continue to cook 10 more minutes. Add peas and raisins; cook 10 more minutes. Serve hot over rice.

HELPFUL HINTS: This is a mild, rather sweet curry. It's also good cold as a salad.

Potato Pancakes

SERVINGS: 6

PREPARATION TIME: 30 mins.   COOKING TIME: 15 mins.

½ raw onion, grated
2 large potatoes, grated (not
    necessary to peel, but scrub
    well)

4 tbsp. whole wheat flour
2 tbsp. water
2 tbsp. parsley, chopped

Mix all ingredients in a bowl. Lightly oil a griddle and heat to 325 degrees or medium heat. Ladle potato mixture on griddle, flattening slightly. Cook about 8–10 minutes on first side; turn and cook an additional 5–8 minutes.

HELPFUL HINTS: Serve with applesauce, ketchup, or gravy. If you have a Silverstone non-stick griddle or frying pan, you will not need to oil it before using.

Golden Potatoes

SERVINGS: 4

PREPARATION TIME: 10 mins.   COOKING TIME: 50–55 mins.

   6 medium potatoes, scrubbed
        (use salad potatoes, white or red rose; do not use russet or
        baking potatoes, which will get too mushy and stick to
        pan)

Preheat oven to 375 degrees. Slice potatoes into ½-inch slices. Lay them on a large baking sheet (do not grease it). Bake at 375 degrees for 40 minutes, remove baking sheet from oven, turn the potatoes over, and return to oven for an additional 10–15 minutes. They will be golden brown when done.

HELPFUL HINTS: Let potatoes stand on tray a few minutes before turning them the first time. They will be easier to loosen from pan. Then return to oven for the last 10–15 minutes. Good for potato lovers in your family. Serve with homemade ketchup, gravy, or plain. Try cutting them like thick French fries for variety. They may also be cut in ¼-inch thick slices. Bake at 400 degrees for 30 minutes, 15 minutes on each side.

Potato Scramble

SERVINGS: 4

PREPARATION TIME: 15 mins.   COOKING TIME: 30 mins.

2 medium onions, sliced
1 carrot, thinly sliced
4 salad potatoes, thinly sliced

½ lb. mushrooms, sliced
1 tbsp. low-sodium tamari
½ cup water

Saute the onions and carrots in ¼ cup water for 5 minutes. Add the sliced potatoes and more water if necessary. Mix well. Cover the pan at this point so vegetables can steam. Remove cover to stir occasionally. Steam about 15 minutes, then remove cover, and add the mushrooms and tamari. Continue to cook and stir about 10 minutes longer. Serve hot.

HELPFUL HINTS: A simple green vegetable or a tossed salad goes well with this.

Tomato Scalloped Potatoes

SERVINGS: 6

PREPARATION TIME: 20 mins.   COOKING TIME: 1½ hrs.

5 cups peeled and sliced potatoes (about 8)
1 onion, chopped
1 cup corn kernels or sliced carrots

1 cup tomato sauce
1 cup water
2 tbsp. whole wheat flour
1 tbsp. low-sodium tamari

Layer potatoes, onions, and chosen vegetables in a large casserole dish. Combine the remaining ingredients, stirring well to mix flour. Pour over potatoes and vegetables. Cover and bake at 375 degrees for 1½ hours. Uncover and bake for 15 minutes longer to form a crust on top if desired.

HELPFUL HINTS: This also may be made in a microwave oven. It will take about 20 mintutes on high power.

Potato Bhaji

SERVINGS: 4–6

PREPARATION TIME: 45 mins.   COOKING TIME: 30–45 mins. for potatoes
30 mins. for bhaji

4–5 medium potatoes
¼ cup water
½ tsp. mustard seed
1 onion, chopped

1 green pepper, chopped
1 tsp. turmeric powder
¼ tsp. ground coriander
1 tbsp. lemon juice

Boil the potatoes in a covered pot, using only a small amount of water. Cook until tender but not too soft. Remove from water and allow to cool. Remove skins and cut into large chunks. Set aside. Put ¼ cup water in a large saucepan. Add the mustard seed. Cook over medium heat for 5 minutes. Add the onion and green pepper. Cook until soft, about 10 minutes. Add the turmeric and coriander. Stir to mix well. Add the potato chunks and 2 tablespoons water. Mix well and cook over low heat about 10 minutes, stirring frequently. Remove from heat; stir in lemon juice. Serve.

HELPFUL HINTS: This dish can be served hot, warm, or cool, depending on your preference. It is an Indian dish and therefore goes best with other Indian food, such as dal, rice, vegetable curry, chapatis.

Szechuan Eggplant

SERVINGS: 4–6

PREPARATION TIME: 20 mins.   COOKING TIME: 30 mins.

2 medium round eggplant	1 tbsp. fresh ginger root, minced
1¾ cups water	1 green onion, finely chopped
2 tbsp. low-sodium tamari	½ tsp. Tabasco sauce
1 tbsp. cornstarch or arrowroot	

Slice eggplant into ½-inch thick pieces. Place on baking sheet. Bake at 400 degrees about 10 minutes. Remove from oven and set aside. Meanwhile, mix remaining ingredients in a saucepan. Cook and stir over medium heat until mixture boils, about 10 minutes. Remove from heat. Place prebaked eggplant in 9″ x 12″ baking dish (overlap slices if necessary). Pour sauce over eggplant. Bake at 350 degrees for 20 minutes.

HELPFUL HINTS: This may also be made by cutting the eggplant into chunks instead of slices. Mix with the sauce and bake in a casserole dish. Serve with brown rice.

APPENDIX I

Protein, fat and carbohydrate (CHO) content expressed as percent (%) of total calories and the calorie concentration expressed as calories per gram (cal/gm) of selected foods. Reported as cooked food unless otherwise stated. Percentages do not always equal 100% because of the base line data used. Data obtained from *Nutritive Value of American Foods in Common Units*, Agriculture Handbook No. 456. *means less than 1%.

	% CALORIES FROM			
				Calories concentration
Food	**Protein**	**Fat**	**CHO**	**calories/gm**
Almonds	12	82	13	5.98
Apples	1	9	100	0.58
Apricots	8	4	100	0.48
Artichokes	22	3	75	0.21
Asparagus	38	7	77	0.26
Avocado	5	88	15	1.67
Bacon, cured, raw, sliced	5	94	*	6.64
Bamboo shoots	39	10	77	0.27
Banana	5	3	104	0.85
Barley (raw)	9	3	90	3.49
Bass, black sea	25	55	18	2.59

% CALORIES FROM

Food	Protein	Fat	CHO	Calories concentration calories/gm
Beans, broad (raw):				
Immature seeds	32	3	68	1.05
Beans, kidney (red)	26	4	72	1.18
Beans, lima (flour)	25	4	73	3.43
Beans, lima (raw)	27	4	72	1.11
Beans, mung (raw)	28	3	71	3.40
Beans, mung sprouts	43	5	75	0.35
Beans, white, (navy)	26	4	72	1.18
Beans, snap, green	26	6	88	0.25
Beef (boneless chuck, lean with				
fat cooked)	32	68	0	3.77
Beef, ground (hamburger)	34	65	0	2.90
Beef, T-bone steak, cooked				
(broiled)	16	82	0	4.73
Beef, corned, boneless	25	74	0	3.72
Beets (red)	15	2	92	0.43
Beets (greens)	37	12	76	0.24
Blackberries	8	14	89	0.58
Blueberries, raw	5	7	99	0.62
Breads:				
Cracked wheat bread, fresh	13	8	79	2.63
American (⅔ wheat + ⅓ rye				
flour)	15	4	86	2.43
Broccoli	45	9	74	0.32
Brussels sprouts	44	8	74	0.45
Buckwheat flour				
dark, sifted	14	7	87	3.33
light, sifted	7	3	92	3.47
Bulgur (parboiled wheat)				
club wheat	10	4	89	3.59
hard red winter	13	4	86	3.54
Burbot, raw, whole	84	10	0	0.12
Butter	0.3	101	0.2	7.16
Buttermilk	40	3	57	0.36
Butternuts, shelled	15	88	5	6.28
Cabbage	22	7	90	0.24
Cabbage, chinese	34	7	85	0.14
Carambola, raw				
(refuse; skin & seeds, 19%)	8	14	90	0.29

% CALORIES FROM

Food	Protein	Fat	CHO	Calories concentration calories/gm
Carissa (refuse 14%), raw, whole	3	19	91	0.61
Carrots	10	4	92	0.42
Cashew nuts	12	73	21	5.61
Cauliflower	40	7	73	0.27
Caviar, sturgeon, granular	41	52	5	2.64
Celery	21	6	92	0.15
Cheese:				
Natural Blue or Roquefort type:	23	75	2	3.68
Brick	24	74	2	3.70
Camembert (domestic type)	23	74	2	2.99
Cheddar (domestic type)	25	73	2	3.98
Cottage cheese	51	36	11	1.06
Cottage cheese, (low-fat)	79	3	13	0.85
Cream cheese, regular	9	91	2	3.74
Limburger	24	73	3	3.45
Parmesan	37	60	3	3.93
Swiss (domestic)	30	68	2	3.70
Pasteurized processed cheese:				
American	25	73	2	3.70
Pimiento (American)	25	73	2	3.71
Swiss	30	68	2	3.55
Cherimoya	5	4	102	0.55
Cherries	8	4	99	0.63
Chestnuts	6	7	87	1.94
Chicken: cooked (all classes) light meat without skin (roasted)	76	18	0	1.66
dark meat, without skin (roasted)	64	32	0	1.76
Fryers, fried: flesh giblets	49	43	5	2.49
Chick peas or garbanzos	23	12	68	3.60
Chives	40	trace	80	0.33
Chocolate candy (milk)	6	56	44	5.25
Clams, raw meat only	68	21	6	0.82
Coconut meat	4	92	11	3.46
Coconut milk	5	89	8	2.52

% CALORIES FROM

Food	Protein	Fat	CHO	Calories concentration calories/gm
Coconut water	5	8	85	0.22
Codfish	89	5	0	1.30
Collards, raw leaves without stems	43	16	67	0.45
Corn flour	8	6	83	3.68
Corn starch	*	trace	97	3.62
Corn, sweet	12	8	94	0.84
Cowpeas	28	6	69	1.27
Crab, bleu, dungeness, rock, king, steamed	74	18	2	0.93
Cranberries	3	14	94	0.44
Cress, garden, raw	33	20	69	0.32
Cucumbers	24	7	91	0.15
Custard-apple, raw	7	5	99	0.59
Dandelion greens, raw	24	14	82	0.45
Dates	3	*(2)	106	2.74
Eggs:				
Chicken, raw, whole fresh	33	65	2	1.63
Chicken, whites fresh	85	7	8	0.51
Chicken, yolks fresh	19	80	1	3.48
Duck, whole fresh, raw	28	68	1	1.91
Goose, whole, fresh, raw	30	65	3	1.85
Turkey, whole, fresh, raw	31	62	4	1.70
Eggplant	21	9	87	0.19
Endive, raw	34	5	82	0.20
Figs (medium)	6	5	102	0.80
Filberts (hazel nuts), shelled	8	89	11	6.33
Flounder, baked with butter or margarine	59	37	0	2.02
Garlic clove, raw	20	*trace	90	1.33
Ginger	11	18	77	0.46
Gooseberries	8	5	99	0.39
Granadilla purple (passion fruit) raw	10	6	97	0.46
Grapefruit	5	2	104	0.20
Grapes	8	13	91	0.46
Honey	*	0	108	3.08
Horseradish, raw	15	3	124	0.63
Kale, leaves without stems, raw	45	14	68	0.53
Kumquats	28	4	88	0.24

% CALORIES FROM

Food	Protein	Fat	CHO	Calories concentration calories/gm
Lamb, retail cuts:				
leg, raw, lean with fat	32	66	0	1.86
loin chops, raw	22	76	0	2.52
Lemons (medium)	16	9	120	0.18
Lentils	29	3	71	1.06
Lettuce	34	13	71	0.14
Lobster northern, cooked	79	14	1	0.95
Loganberries, raw	6	9	96	0.62
Loquats	3	3	103	0.37
Lychees	6	5	102	0.39
Mackerel, Atlantic	37	60	0	2.36
Mangos	4	5	102	0.66
Margarine, regular	*	101	*	7.19
Milk, goat, fluid	19	54	27	0.67
Milk, human	5	45	48	0.78
Milk (whole-3.5%)	21	49	30	0.65
Milk (low-fat-2%)	28	31	41	0.59
Milk (skim)	41	2	57	0.36
Mushrooms	38	9	62	0.28
Muskmelons:				
Cantaloupe	9	3	100	0.30
Honeydew	10	8	93	0.33
Mustard greens	39	15	72	0.31
Mustard, spinach, raw	47	13	71	0.22
Nectarines	4	trace	107	0.59
New Zealand Spinach, raw	47	15	66	0.19
Oatmeal	15	16	71	0.55
Ocean perch, Atlantic (redfish), fried	33	53	12	2.27
Okra	27	8	85	0.36
Olives	5	98	4	1.16
Onions	16	3	92	0.37
Onions, young green, raw	17	5	91	0.36
Oranges	8	4	100	0.35
Oysters, raw	51	25	21	0.66
Papayas	6	2	102	0.26
Parsley	34	14	78	0.43
Parsnips, raw	9	6	92	0.65
Peaches	6	2	102	0.33

% CALORIES FROM

Food	Protein	Fat	CHO	Calories concentration calories/gm
Peanuts	18	75	14	5.82
Peanut butter (fat + sweetener added)	17	77	13	5.89
Pears	5	6	100	0.61
Peas (green)	30	4	68	0.84
Peas (split)	28	3	72	1.15
Peppers, hot, chili* immature, green	14	4	100	0.20
mature, red, canned chili sauce	17	26	75	0.21
Peppers, sweet, immature, green, raw	22	8	87	0.22
Persimmons, raw (native)	3	3	105	1.03
Pineapple	3	3	105	0.52
Pinenuts, pinon, shelled	8	86	13	6.43
Pistachio nuts, shelled	13	81	14	5.93
Plums	3	trace	108	0.60
Pomegranate, raw	3	5	104	0.35
Pork, fresh, retail cuts:				
Ham, raw	21	78	0	2.62
Loin chops, raw, with bone	23	75	0	2.35
Spareribs, raw	16	83	0	2.15
Potatoes	11	1	90	0.57
Prunes (dehydrated)	4	1	106	3.44
Pumpkin (canned)	12	8	95	0.33
Pumpkin and squash seed kernels, dry, hulled	21	76	11	5.52
Radishes, common, raw	9	1	85	0.17
Raisins	3	*	107	2.89
Raspberries	8	17	86	0.73
Rice (brown)	8	5	86	1.19
Rice (polished)	7	1	89	1.09
Rutabagas, raw	9	1	96	0.46
Rye flour:				
Light, unsifted	11	2	87	3.57
Dark	20	7	83	2.27
Scallops, steamed	83	11	-	1.12
Sesame, dry, hulled	13	83	12	5.82
Shallot, bulbs, raw	17	trace	97	0.70

% CALORIES FROM

Food	Protein	Fat	CHO	Calories concentration calories/gm
Shrimp, cooked (fried)	84	8	*	1.15
Soybean:				
Soybean curd (tofu)	43	53	13	0.72
Soybean, flour (full fat)	35	43	29	1.30
Soybeans, (dry seeds)	34	40	33	1.30
Soybeans, sprouts	54	28	46	0.46
Soy sauce	33	17	56	0.68
Spaghetti (white)	14	3	81	1.13
Spinach	49	11	66	0.26
Squash, summer	23	5	89	0.19
Strawberries, raw	8	12	91	0.37
Sturgeon, cooked, steamed	63	32	0	1.60
Sunflower seed, kernels, dry,				
hulled	17	76	14	5.59
Sweet potatoes	6	3	92	1.02
Tangerines, raw	7	4	101	0.34
Tapioca, dry (raw)	1	1	98	3.52
Tomatoes	18	8	85	0.20
Tuna:				
Canned, in oil solids and				
liquids	34	64	0	2.88
canned, in water and liquids	88	56	0	1.27
Turkey, all classes, roasted	41	56	0	2.63
Turnips (raw)	13	7	88	0.30
Turnip greens	43	10	71	0.28
Veal, rib roast, raw with bone	36	61	0	1.59
Walnuts, black, shelled	13	85	9	6.28
Watercress	46	13	63	0.20
Watermelon	8	7	98	0.26
Wheat flour, white, enriched	12	3	84	3.64
Wheat flour (whole)	16	5	85	3.33
Wheat germ	31	27	52	3.80
Wild rice, raw	16	2	85	3.53
Yam, raw	8	2	92	0.87
Yeast, bakers	57	4	52	0.86
Yogurt, made from:				
partially skim milk	27	31	41	0.50
whole milk	19	49	32	0.62
Zucchini	28	6	85	0.17

* Less than one percent

APPENDIX II

Sodium Content in Some Common Prepared Foods

Canned Goods	Milligrams of Sodium
Whole tomatoes–solids & liquids–1 cup	
Del Monte	318
Contadina	450
Hunts	736
Tomato sauce–1 cup	
Del Monte	1,252
Contadina	1,296
Hunts	1,662
Tomato puree–1 cup	
Contadina	24
Hunts	497
Tomato paste–6 oz. can	
Contadina	25
Del Monte	26
Hunts	600
Tomato juice–6 oz.	
Del Monte	300
Heinz	537
Hunts	566
Campbell	618
V-8	555
Low sodium V-8	60

Cereals–packaged–1 oz.

Oatmeal (Quaker)	1
Wheatena (Standard Milling)	2
Shredded Wheat (Nabisco)	10
Nutri-grain, Wheat (Kellogg's)	190
Grape Nuts (Post)	195
Instant Oatmeal (Quaker)	281

Miscellaneous

Baking powder–1 tsp. (Calumet)	135
Milder soy sauce (Kikkoman)–1 tsp.	182
Regular soy sauce–1 tsp.	325
Lite salt (Morton)–1 tsp.	1,100
Baking soda–1 tsp.	1,360
Salt–1 tsp.	2,132

Frozen Vegetables–3.3 oz.

Green beans (Birds Eye)	4
Broccoli (Birds Eye)	20
Cauliflower (Birds Eye)	38
Corn (Birds Eye)	33
Corn on the cob (Birds Eye), 1 ear	1
Peas (Birds Eye)	152
Peas (Green Giant)	80
Summer squash (Birds Eye)	3
Winter squash (Birds Eye)	1
Peas and carrots (Birds Eye)	86
Peas and onions (Birds Eye)	428
Corn, peas and tomatoes (Birds Eye)	447

Sources: *The Dictionary of Sodium, Fats, and Cholesterol,* by Barbara Kraus (New York: Grosset & Dunlap, 1974) and the Center for Science in the Public Interest, 1982.

GENERAL INDEX

331

RECIPE INDEX

Apple Butter, 277

Baked Eggplant Casserole, 316
Baked Stuffed Squash, 315
Barbequed Beans, 301
Barley and Beans, 302
Barley-Mushroom Soup, 283
Bean Enchiladas, 306–307
Beans, 300–309
   Barbequed, 301
   Barley and, 302
   Brazilian Black, with Marinated Tomatoes,
      305
   Chapatis and, 307
   Curried, 308
   Enchiladas, 306–307
   Limas 'N' Noodles, 305–306
   Patrick's Simple Refried, 300–301
   Taco, 301
Brazilian Black Beans with Marinated
     Tomatoes, 305
Breads, 269–272
   No-Knead, 269–270
   Quick Corn, 271
   Stuffed Pita, 307–308
   Whole Wheat, 269
Breakfast, recipes for, 265–268
Brown Gravy, 286
Brown Rice, 295
Butch's Chili, 303

Cabbage Rolls, Stuffed, 314
Chapati Vegetable Rolls, 313–314
Chapatis and Beans, 307
Chickenless à La King, 289
Chili, 302
   Butch's, 303
Chinese Noodles with Vegetables, 316–317
Chinese Vegetable Sauce, 293
Chinese Vegetable Soup, 280
Chop Suey, Vegetable, 290–291
Corn Bread, Quick, 271
Curried Beans, 308

Dal, 306
Dip, Eggplant, 277

Dressings, 275–277
   Lemon Garlic, 275–276
   Thick French Tomato, 275

Easy Curried Lentil or Pea Soup, 283
Easy Ratatouille, 293–294
Eggplant, Szechuan, 321
Eggplant Casserole, Baked, 316
Eggplant Dip, 277
Enchilada Sauce, 289

Fried Rice, 296

Garbanzo Puree, 276–277
Golden Potatoes, 319
Grains and rice, 295–300
Gravy
   Brown, 286
   Mushroom, 286–287
   Spicy, 285–286
Griddle Cakes, 267

Hearty Brown Stew, 292
Heather's Mushroom Delight, 291
Hot German Potato Salad, 274
Hot Mexican Salad, 276

Indian Rice, 298

Ketchup Sauce, 275

Lasagna, 311–312
Latin Black Bean Soup, 282
Layered Dinner, 309–310
Lemon Garlic Dressing, 275–276
Lentil-Rice Surprise, 299–300
Lentil Soup, 282
Limas 'N' Noodles, 305–306

Main dishes
   beans, 300–309

The McDougall Books

THE MCDOUGALL PLAN—Learn how to successfully live by a health-supporting diet and lifestyle, shop, meal plan, and eat out, with 108 recipes.

MCDOUGALL'S MEDICINE—A CHALLENGING SECOND OPINION—Here are the reasons why present therapies are not improving or prolonging lives for most people. There is a way for prevention and help for the victims of cancer, osteoporosis, atherosclerosis, heart disease (bypass surgery), hypertension, diabetes, arthritis, and kidney disease.

THE MCDOUGALL HEALTH-SUPPORTING COOKBOOKS, VOLUMES I & II—Each volume contains 250 original recipes from health-supporting (category IV) to many with richer ingredients (category III). Includes desserts, gluten-free recipes, party plans and suggestions for children.

These books can be purchased in better book stores throughout the country. However, further information and assistance in finding books can be obtained by writing John McDougall, M.D., P.O. Box 14039, Santa Rosa, CA 95402.

The McDougall Live-In Health Program

Dr. McDougall is the medical director of the live-in lifestyle/nutrition program at St. Helena Hospital & Health Center, Deer Park, CA 94576. Health facilities in other areas of the country are planned to open in the future. This program is designed to help people discontinue medications, avoid surgeries when possible, regain lost health and appearance through sensible changes in diet and personal habits, and maintain good health. More information can be obtained by writing John McDougall, M.D. at P.O. Box 14039, Santa Rosa, CA 95402.

Newsletter and Tapes

Information on subscribing to a newsletter to keep you up to date on timely medical information, important health events throughout the country, and new recipes produced by the McDougalls can be obtained by writing them at P.O. Box 14039, Santa Rosa, CA 95402.

A professionally produced album of eight audio tapes by Dr. McDougall and his staff is also available that will inform and inspire you change your diet and your life, forever.